THE WAR HOTEL

To ~~John~~ ~~~~

from

~~~~

april, 2005

Cover images

First row Exhumation, South Africa (photo by Jillian Edelstein); Sera Monastery (photo by Nancy Jo Johnson); '1984' (painting by Arpana Caur); Synagogue after 'Kristallnacht' (Bildarchive Abraham Pisarek, Berlin); *New York Times* after Versailles Treaty (*New York Times*)

Second row Signs to Osijek, Croatia (Osservatorio sui Balcani, Rovereto Italy); PSYOPS comics from the Vietnam War's Phoenix Programme (de-classified US government document); Day of the Dead, Mexico (by Bryant Holman); Gaki-zoshi, Scroll of the Hungry Ghosts (Courtesy of Kyoto National Museum); Amnesty Hearing, South Africa (photo by Jillian Edelstein)

THE WAR HOTEL

PSYCHOLOGICAL DYNAMICS
IN VIOLENT CONFLICT

ARLENE AUDERGON PhD

WHURR PUBLISHERS
LONDON AND PHILADELPHIA

© 2005 WHURR PUBLISHERS LTD

First published 2005
by Whurr Publishers Ltd
19b Compton Terrace
London N1 2UN England and
325 Chestnut Street, Philadelphia PA 19106 USA

British Library Cataloguing in Publication Data

A catalogue record for this book
is available from the British Library.

ISBN 1 86156 451 1

Typeset by Adrian McLaughlin, a@microguides.net
Printed and bound in the UK by Athenæum Press Ltd, Gateshead, Tyne & Wear.

CONTENTS

INTRODUCTION

PART 1: JUSTICE AND THE WHEELS OF HISTORY

PART 2: TERROR AND THE SPIRIT THAT SURVIVES

Part 3: Trauma – the nightmare of history

Part 4: The warrior's call – altered states of war

PART 5: AWARENESS AT THE HOT SPOT

PREFACE

The War Hotel is about how our psychology is used as fuel for violent conflict. We are active and complicit. We get outraged and we go silent. Throughout history there have been 'experts' who know how to use human nature to divide communities and carry out atrocities. The manipulation of our psychology to create violent conflict is deeply disturbing. Yet there's something profoundly hopeful here. If we are the players in violent conflict, our awareness can make a difference.

I've been working on this book for about 7 years. Political events and the changing spirit of the times have created a dramatic increase in public discussion about such issues. The film-maker Jean-Luc Godard once said, 'In a book, the primordial space is the margin, because it joins with that of the preceding page. And you can write in the margin, and take notes, which is as important as the "main text"'.[1] I hope you will take a pencil along – not only to help keep the book current, but to bring it meaning from the contexts where you live, work and dream.

I work as a psychologist and conflict resolution facilitator, and also in theatre. My approach and most of the ideas in this book arise out my training and practice working with individuals, organizations and community groups, using the orientation and methods of Process Oriented Psychology. I've had the fortune to work with and study for many years with Dr Arnold Mindell who originated this approach, also known as 'Process Work' and, together with his partner Amy Mindell and colleagues, developed its theory and application in the areas of dreaming and illness, relationship and family work, extreme states and mental health, and organizational development and conflict resolution. Originally a Jungian analyst and physicist, Mindell developed far-reaching methods of working with field dynamics and the deepest creativity in us, whether the innermost tensions of an individual, an organization or communities dealing with political and social conflict.[2]

Throughout this book, I look at how dynamics of justice, terror and trauma, and such experiences as sacrifice and love can be turned into violent conflict and how our awareness of these dynamics, personally and collectively, can influence its prevention. There are examples from many conflict zones, past and present, around the world. I particularly focus on the Balkans, because of my work there over several years. As I grew up and lived for many years in the USA, I also refer to violent conflicts of my country, including the oppression of Native Americans and African Americans in its history and still present, the war in Vietnam, and the current 'war on terror'. I also call on examples from

Hitler's Third Reich, the Israeli–Palestinian conflict, South Africa and its Truth and Reconciliation process after Apartheid, Rwanda, communism and its collapse in Europe, and more. From 1996 to 2002, I went to Croatia many times with my colleague Lane Arye, to facilitate forums in a project of post-war reconciliation and community building. The project was supported by the United Nations High Commission for Refugees and other sources, and was organized by a non-governmental organization in Croatia, Udruga Mi. Several stories from our project in Croatia are woven throughout the book and the idea for the book originated there.

I hope that some of the ideas in this book add to dialogue that rouses heart and understanding along with heat between people, as well as hope in the possibility of transforming serious conflict. Reading about violent conflict, traumatic, unresolved issues and points of serious contention can set off outrage, grief, anxiety and hopelessness – even jadedness. It can be important to find people to talk to about these experiences. I apologize for any hurt that may be triggered by the limits of my views and formulation. I've written this book based on the belief and experience that communities are in need and are capable of reckoning with and transforming the tragedies and atrocities that influence our lives together. Collectively, we may be able to face the dynamics of community trauma and accountability, and our deepest feelings for life, to find our way into a different future.

Charlie Rose interviewed Desmond Tutu and spoke about the 10-year anniversary of the end of Apartheid in South Africa. With a beaming smile, Tutu said that, whenever things look their bleakest, he stops to remember that we are in the process of creation.[3]

ARLENE AUDERGON
London, October 2004

The author would be glad to receive correspondence
on the following email address: *warhotel@cfor.info*

ABOUT THE AUTHOR

Arlene Audergon PhD is a psychotherapist and conflict resolution facilitator. She teaches Process Oriented Psychology in the UK and internationally, and her work has brought her to Croatia, Kosovo, Slovakia, Poland, Germany, South Africa, India, the UK, and the USA. In a long-term post-war project in Croatia, she co-facilitated forums on reconciliation and community building. Arlene is co-founder of CFOR, an organization for community forums on preventive and post-conflict issues, diversity and democracy building. She lives in London, where she also works in theatre.

Acknowledgements

Many people have been very important to me in creating this book. My parents met in Chicago, after escaping the Holocaust in Germany. Their warmth and support always encouraged me to feel involved in the world. My interest in violence and conflict resolution in part stems from my need to grapple with and warm up the frozen states around our response to traumatic events as individuals and societies.

I thank Arny and Amy Mindell for their development of Process Oriented Psychology and worldwork, which have impacted on me so profoundly and personally, giving me the opportunity to experience with people again and again that our most terrible personal and collective problems can transform. Thanks to Arny and Amy for their friendship over many years and to Arny for his personal care as well as professional guidance and constant inspiration when he dives underneath the most difficult situations to find the seeds of something creative. I'm grateful for his constant support to follow my dreams, even when they lead me into trouble! When I told him a dream I had while I was in Croatia, he encouraged me to write this book.

My partner Jean-Claude Audergon has helped me with every single stage of this work over several years. We've worked together in countless situations of high tension from forums with gangs, to community conflicts on racism, and mental health forums, not to mention our own relationship issues at the kitchen sink. Not only has he been insanely patient, from brainstorming and working with me deeply on ideas, dreams, feelings, details and many drafts, he has given me dynamic supervision, while I was in the midst of conflict resolution work on the other end of a phone. He's been my constant friend and mentor, as well as the love of my life, supporting me to explore my innermost dreams and blocks, and their relation to my outer work. He never fails to inspire me in the way he has the heart to turn himself inside out for the sake of living and engaging fully and wholly.

Thank-you from my heart to Lane Arye for our work together in Croatia – not only for being a wonderful co-facilitator in the work we did together, which has been so meaningful for both of us, but also for his constant friendship. Over six years, we shared all of the work of this project in Croatia, along with the joy and tremendous learning from our experiences. Special thanks to Tanja Radocaj and Mirela Miharija for following their dreams to create the project in Croatia, and to Tanja and Nives Ivelja for consistently carrying it close in their hearts and on their shoulders, for the enormous and extraordinary work they do and for their friendship. Also to their families. Special thanks to Edi and Bobo and everyone at Udruga Mi. Thanks to each participant of those forums who I can't name individually. Special thanks go to Misko Mimica for his belief in the project, the UNHCR (United Nations High Commission for Refugees) for their support to make it happen as well as the IRC (International Rescue Committee), OSI (Open Society Institute), OTI (Office of Transition Initiatives), USAID, OSCE (Organization for Security and Cooperation in Europe) and the Threshold Foundation. Thanks to the participants from Sarajevo at our first conference in 1996. Their experiences and teaching spurred us to soul search and to essential learning about issues of community trauma. Special thanks to Faruk.

I'd also like to thank the participants of the many organizations, forums and training seminars where I have facilitated and co-facilitated in the UK, Germany, Slovakia, Poland, South Africa, Kosovo, the United States, Greece and India, learning and exploring dynamics of conflict, trauma and accountability.

Several people have given their time, care and expertise, reading and commenting on portions of this manuscript or its entirety. Thanks to Lane Arye, Jean-Claude Audergon, David Clark, Tanja Radocaj, Nives Ivelja, Arny Mindell, Amy Mindell, Nick Totton, John L. Johnson, Richard Williams, Michael Graham, Harvey Motulsky, Gretel and Arno Motulsky, Sara Halprin, David Lisbona and Charles Hanley. Thanks to Phelim McDermott, Julian Crouch and Lee Simpson of London's Improbable Theatre and Guy Dartnell (as well the Royal Court Theatre) for our work together devising SPIRIT, where we explored some of these ideas in very personal, creative and theatrical ways. A big thanks to Judy Walker and Dan Bonow for their hospitality in Kauai, while I was completing a draft of the manuscript at their place. Thanks to Jane Sugarman for her lively interest and attention in editing and Carol Saumarez for her engagement and corrections. Thanks to Stanya Studentova for her endless practical support and friendship, in working side by side with me with such good heart and humour in the gathering of illustrations for the project.

Thanks to Arpana Caur for her generous permission to include several images of her beautiful paintings in the chapters on trauma. Arpana was born into a Sikh family who had to leave Lahore during the partition of India and Pakistan in 1947, settling in Delhi. She also witnessed the riots and killing of Sikhs in 1984. Her work with themes of violence, trauma and life-giving spirit has been exhibited internationally. (The colour paintings are reproduced here in black and white.) I am delighted to include three of Nancy Jo Johnson's photographs from Tibet. Nancy Jo has photographed throughout South

Asia. She is a member of the board of directors of the US Tibet Committee and raises awareness about Tibetans through her photography. I'm also grateful to be able to use some of Jillian Edelstein's powerful photographs documenting the Truth and Reconciliation process in South Africa, from her project and book *Truth and Lies* (Granta, London). Many individuals, archives, museums and organizations helped me not only in giving permissions and reproductions, but also by way of giving guidance and support along an exciting and winding path. Thanks to: the Metropolitan Museum of Art, NY, the Southern Alleghenies Museum of Art, PA, the Huntington Archive, Ohio State University, Ullstein-Cinetext Berlin, Warner Brothers Entertainment Co., Dave Neal Multimedia, Osservatorio sui Balcani, Rovereto, Italy, Maren at the Photo Archives of the US Holocaust museum, Randall Bytwerk of German Propaganda Archive, *The New York Times*, Laurenz Bobke, Wiesbaden, Germany, Summerhill School, Leiston, UK, Laura M. Anderson, Diogenes Verlag AG Zurich, The Fitzwilliam Museum, University of Cambridge, Maria Warner's (2000) *No Go the Bogeyman*, London: Vintage, Robert V Schmidt of Peace Party and Blue Corn Comics, Alan Howard of University of Virginia, George Cohenour, Museum of the City of New York, The Library of Congress, Wn.DC, Hoover Institute, Stanford University, CA, Pauline Ismail for her help with translation from Chinese, the Metropolitan Police, London, Ferne Clements and the Committee of 500 Years of Dignity and Resistance, The Jim Crow Museum at Ferris State University, Big Rapids, MI, Associated Press London, Charles Hanley, co-author of *The Bridge at No Gun Ri,* Paul Wolf of www.cointel.org, South End Press, Douglas Valentine, author of *The Phoenix Program*, Bildarchive Abraham Pisarek, Berlin, Denis Gouey, British Film Institute, Association Chaplin and Roy Export Co. Establishment, Alex Johnson, The State Hermitage Museum, St Petersburg, The British Library, Bryant Holman, Stanislav Slavik of the Department of Contemporary History, National Museum, Prague, Mark Schumacher of Onmark Productions, Maya M Hara and the Kyoto National Museum, and Dan and Kristen Ciprari.

Introduction

Welcome to 'The War Hotel'

Whether we are up close in the clutches of violent conflict or at a distance watching TV, we are active players, often without realizing it. Human nature is the fuel. Even treasured parts of our nature get stirred to inflame, silence and polarize us into violence.

While teaching one afternoon, I had a realization. The field of conflict resolution may be relatively small, but there have always been people – political leaders and warlords – who are expert in their understanding of psychological dynamics of conflict. There are those who know how loyalty and righteousness can polarize communities and lead us to acts of genocide in the name of justice. There are those who use their understanding of human nature to develop torture methods that stretch the boundaries of endurance, and to design terror tactics to dominate their own nation or neighbours. There are those who know how our need to stop the pain of historical trauma can be turned into a deadly replay of the nightmare. There are those who understand how our longing to sense the divine and a bond with humanity can fan nationalism and violence. These (fellow) 'experts' calculate that our naivety and even our urge to awaken can be knitted into war.

When we imagine that our psychology is separate from politics, we support violent conflict. In fact a central assumption of war makers is that this expertise will remain their private turf. The less aware we are of how our individual and collective psychology shapes us, the more malleable we are. If we believe in and agree with this central assumption that we will remain unaware, we are in effect those 'war makers'. Most people believe that forces of war operate outside them. To deal with these forces more creatively, rather than only being swept along, we need to get to know our part.

The structure of this book is built around four main themes: justice, terror, trauma and altered states.[1] Events from past and present hot spots illustrate psychological and political dynamics in these four areas. Examples include the violence during the 1990s in the former Yugoslavia in Croatia, Bosnia and Kosovo, the 1994 genocide in Rwanda, the USA's position of unilateral dominance on the world stage, the Israeli–Palestinian conflict, Hitler's Third Reich, the history of Native Americans in the USA, the history of African Americans in the USA, the Vietnam war and post-communist issues in central and eastern Europe, and others. Many important issues, conflicts and hot spots are not included. Nor do I offer a thorough social, political or economic analysis on any particular zone. I especially draw from my experience facilitating post-war forums in Croatia, after the violence in the former Yugoslavia during the 1990s, as well as other forums of conflict resolution that I have facilitated internationally. In my descriptions of events and psychological dynamics of war, I cannot represent all views. Nor can I bear witness to the boundless suffering of individuals and groups who have experienced the horror of war. The examples therefore weave an incomplete story to highlight only some of the essential psychological dynamics of violent conflict and how we participate. I trust the reader to look elsewhere for more comprehensive analysis of the events in particular conflict zones and fuller accounts of the experience of war, as well as to further explore the vast theme of psychological dynamics in violent conflict and its resolution.

In addition to looking at how our tendency to be unconscious of these psychological dynamics can be exploited in war, I look at how awareness of these dynamics can make a difference. The final chapters suggest that awareness might be the emerging ingredient in humanity, so that we are not only swept along in the violent wheels of history, but also able to facilitate creative alternatives.

The title, *The War Hotel*, appeared in a dream I had when I was in Croatia in 1996. As a part of a post-war project over several years, my colleague Lane Arye and I had just facilitated a forum among a large group of people dealing with post-war issues in their communities. A diverse group of participants (Croat, Serb, Muslim and other national/ethnic backgrounds) was involved with the complex and painful problems of reconciliation in Croatia and Bosnia. We had gathered in a room overlooking the sea near Split. The placid green sea held an endless melancholy for people arriving from all parts of Croatia and also Bosnia, many returning to the sea for the first time since the war. After the intensive forum days, I stayed a couple of extra days in a small hotel. In my dream, I walked out of the hotel, finding myself in a parallel world, an eerie maze of windy streets, with warlords at market stalls. There was a large neon sign 'W A R H O T E L'. I kept thinking I had to find my way back to my hotel. As I studied my dream, I realized I needed to step into the eerie parallel world of the dynamics of war, and find my way through this maze. Writing became a pathway both into this world and back to my 'hotel'. I realized that the more we consider violence as some other, eerie world, and do not become familiar with its dynamics and get to know how we participate, the more readily we are swallowed up.

The link between psychological dynamics and violent conflict is such a vast topic. We often consider our psychology, however, as a kind of excuse for war, a reason to be hopeless or to feel that there is nothing we can do about it. People often say: 'Isn't that just human nature to be aggressive and violent?' The more I study the dynamics of violent conflict, the more I see that the raw material of war is largely made up of qualities that we highly cherish – our loyalty, love, devotion to community, urge to protect the vulnerable, and outrage at atrocity and pain, and our search for meaning that transcends the limits of our personal life and death.

People who bring us the news and those of us who watch the news deal in the foreground with political facts and spin, while in the background immersed in the psychological workings of war. Information and reflection on the psychology of war are needed in public dialogue, so that we do not stand by, unaware of our involvement, responsibility and the possibility that we can make a difference.

Social and political leaders often call for public awareness. But, what do we mean by public awareness? We might consider three sorts. Getting informed involves increasing our knowledge of history and current events within a network of communication full of partial information, misinformation and disinformation. It also means understanding international law and activities geared towards protection of human rights. Roy Gutman and David Rieff point to the importance of this sort of public awareness in the book that they edited *Crimes of War: What the public should know*.[2] They were concerned that journalists did not accurately report the violence in Bosnia and Rwanda, confusing 'genocide' and 'civil war'. In appreciation of the profound impact journalists can make on international affairs, they felt that journalists needed to have a grasp of international humanitarian law, to accurately report on and interpret events whether up close in the field or reporting on violent conflict from afar, and to report on and interpret events within climates of disinformation and strong emotional turmoil. It was soon realized that their important book belonged to a public that also needs access to this information for a better grasp of what is going on in the hot spots in our world.

Public awareness also requires a degree of freedom of thought and the capacity to reflect, rather than just adapt or react. How we engage in community is tied to our relative privileges and worldviews, which we all too rarely question. The women's movement long used the term 'consciousness raising'. Paulo Freire, a beloved figure in education and social movements, described a process of breaking through prevailing mythologies that reinforce oppression, to reach new levels of awareness and the capacity to take an active part in the world.[3,4] Howard Zinn says: 'how we *think* is not just mildly interesting, nor just a subject for intellectual debate, but a matter of life and death.'[5]

Public awareness is also a psychological and spiritual matter – a process of discovering as individuals and collectively what makes us respond and what makes us silent. We are each unique in how we perceive and contribute to this world. We are also each limited and stretch the boundaries of our identities as we meet challenges and grapple with the unknown. Gandhi believed that individuals have a right to perceive and live in their unique manner, and at the same time can dissolve the notion of 'self' and 'other' by attaining identification with humanity and all of creation.[6] Gandhi's political leadership came from the notion that spirituality and politics were identical. He saw our internal and external worlds as part of a single pattern. Politics was a spiritual activity and all true spirituality culminated in politics.[7] Chuang Tzu, an ancient Chinese philosopher, recognized that the same patterns emerge inside us and within the world, and inner development and leadership could therefore not be separated.[8] Arny Mindell's notion of 'deep democracy'[9] suggests that society needs dialogue and interaction that includes not only our political positions, but also our deepest rifts and the emotions of history, as well as access to the underlying creativity that precedes our polarizations of conflict. Awareness of how we identify and what we consider 'other', in both our inner and our outer worlds, allows us to facilitate conflict, rather than only be sunk in it.

So, to recognize our part in violent conflict and to find alternatives, public awareness involves getting informed, developing freedom of thought, and a psychological and spiritual process of becoming aware of the inner and outer dimensions of conflict.

Although some political leaders and warlords have exploited the psychological and spiritual dynamics of conflict for the purpose of power and profit, at the expense of unspeakable tragedy, the responsibility and the possibility to 'profit' from our awareness of these dynamics lie with all of us. Below is a summary of the chapters to welcome you and give you an overview of *The War Hotel*.

SUMMARY OF THE FIVE PARTS

Part 1: Justice and the wheels of history

History repeats and conflicts cycle almost always in the name of justice. In the midst of extraordinary acts of brutality, people readily claim that they are doing this in the name of justice. We identify with being right and just out of both privilege and suffering. Part 1 illustrates how our urge for justice is used to create new rounds of conflict. It looks at how we become polarized around our concern for loyalty and justice and our need for accountability. Accountability is explored as an essential key to interrupt cycles of conflict, throughout all levels of society, from International Tribunals, Truth and Reconciliation Commissions and the Lustration process in the former communist countries, to our grappling with history and the complex issues of personal and collective responsibility in community. Staying out of the loop of accountability supports violent conflict. Exploring personal and social accountability is necessary to know how we replay cycles of violence and to discover that we can step off this wheel.

Part 2: Terror and the spirit that survives

State tactics of terror and acts of 'terrorism' are designed with an astute understanding of our individual and collective psychology. State tactics of terror and acts of terrorism are violent tactics in both directions in a system that is already cracked and holding itself together by power and intimidation. The chapters in Part 2 focus particularly on state tactics of terror: creating or exploiting instability in order to crack down, demonizing, dehumanizing, desensitizing, and the normalizing of violence, torture, targeting leaders, targeting the soul of community and disinformation. We explore how psychology is used to dominate and suppress the spirit at any cost and the spirit that survives.

Part 3: Trauma – the nightmare of history

The effects of trauma are used to ignite conflict. We are vulnerable when we are not aware of how traumatic experience gets locked inside us, such that it reoccurs and continues to haunt us. We will look at the dynamics of trauma in individuals and whole communities and in our global interactions. Traumatic experience not only affects those who suffer atrocity. Feeling distant and silent in the face of atrocity is also a symptom of trauma and an active ingredient in violence. Trauma is a community matter and we need to include our personal and collective stories of trauma into the narrative of history to be able to move forward. We explore how traumatic events replay and reoccur in individuals and communities, including cycles of revenge and the revision of history. If the story isn't told, as when mass graves are not found, our traumatic experience and the stories of our families remain open.

Part 4: The warrior's call – altered states of war

Within the tragic events of war, people feel taken into a mythic battle. Individuals and entire communities are faced with death and loss, thrown from everyday life. After a war, survivors may feel unable and unwilling to 'return'. In the heightened experiences of war, people sometimes feel connected to a sense of spirit or meaning that is awesome and even intoxicating. Contacting dimensions beyond our ordinary lives is an essential part of our nature, as we are propelled and inspired in our search for meaning, whether in the realms of religion, spirituality, the arts or scientific research. Our longing to find purpose and to connect to something infinite, our devotion and our desire to feel part of a greater community, while perhaps among the most beautiful and sacred parts of humanity, are also used to arouse us to violence. With awareness, these experiences are also creative pathways for society.

Part 5: Awareness at the hot spot

Another part of our personal and collective nature is our urge to grow in awareness. Even our urge to wake up, however, when undeveloped, can be exploited in calls to violence. A predominant way of interacting throughout much of history has been based in power, one side dominating the other. In situations of conflict, we often think that one part of ourselves must dominate the other part. Yet, underlying the polarizations of conflict, we might discover a creative potential, allowing us to go beyond our one-sided identities. We look at what people mean by awareness, touching on how our evolving world views influence what we perceive and attitudes towards conflict. We look at things like mapmaking, some basics of systems theory, chaos, complexity theory, non-linear change, and how awareness can emerge at hot spots, making it possible that we don't have to just sleep-walk through history. A hopeful perspective is that we might be on a long-term journey to learn how to not only stand by, observe or participate in destructive conflict, but rather to facilitate our human nature in more creative ways.

PART 1

JUSTICE AND THE WHEELS OF HISTORY

Chapter 1
In the name of justice

Our urge for justice gives us courage to survive and courage to kill. Belief in justice gives purpose to our struggles for liberation and rationale to dominate and terrorize others. How we feel about justice and accountability can be turned into violent conflict, and understanding these dynamics is essential to prevent conflict.

Tapping the vein of justice

We get outraged by injustice and we long for justice, and this passion runs through our veins, easy to ignite. In the midst of extraordinary brutality, we easily claim that we are doing it in the name of justice. Our silence as well as our outrage about injustice is volatile. We might imagine that under pressure this mixture combusts or that in the midst of unfolding events it gradually catches fire. But this fuel is often spilled intentionally and ignited.

In the 1930s, Germans rallied around the idea of being a superior race, because they felt unjustly downed and humiliated after their loss in World War I. People wanted to hold their heads up high. Hitler led the nation to commit systematic genocide and one of the tactics was to promise that becoming powerful was not only possible, but justified, while naming Jews, as well as communists, Roma (Gypsies) and homosexuals, as traitors and scapegoats for past and present injustice. In Germany, people have told me that, when Hitler rose to power, though they were young at the time, they recall the sense of justice due and exhilaration.

During the blood spilling across Croatia, Bosnia and Kosovo, people committing heinous crimes made constant claims of justice on their side. Terms were used to trigger fury about injustices from the past, creating a linguistic and emotional context for fresh violence. A Serb nationalist, Vojislav Seselj, leader

3

of the Serbian Radical Party, began using the term 'Chetnik' to describe the
Serb nationalist movement and to tap memories of the Croatian ultra-nation-
alist Ustase movement of World War II. The Chetniks had fought against the
Ustase regime. The Ustase were responsible for massacres of Serbs, Jews and
Roma (Gypsies). Throughout the war in the former Yugoslavia in the 1990s,
Croats were now regularly called 'Ustase' and Serbs 'Chetniks'. Among other
derogatory names, Muslims were sometimes called 'Turks' to associate them
with invaders of the fourteenth century. With a twist of the tongue, hideous
acts of violence could be considered heroic acts of liberation and justice.

In February 2003 Vojislav Seselj was charged with eight counts of crimes
against humanity and six counts of violations of laws of war.[1] Even so, while in
prison in The Hague, his Radical Party won 82 seats in parliamentary elections
at the end of 2003, more than any other party in Serbia. The acting Radical
Party Chief, Tonisia Nikdic, said, 'We won this victory for Vojislav Seselj and
other Hague indictees and for Serbia's citizens who had enough of being
humiliated'.[2]

In Rwanda, in 1994, civilian Hutus massacred approximately 750 000 Tutsis and moderate Hutus in a period of 3 months, drawing on the experience
of feeling unjustly downed. There is some debate about the historical meaning of the categories of Hutu and Tutsi, but there is agreement that, in the
pre-colonial days, they were not clearly distinct ethnic groups. They shared a
common language and common religious practices. They were distinguished
by social, economic and political position. Hutus and Tutsis intermarried and
a Hutu who acquired cattle could be considered Tutsi. The Tutsis (about 14
per cent of the population) had more social power in the form of holding
political office and raising cattle, whereas the Hutus who made up about 85
per cent of the population were primarily farmers. A third and smaller group,
the Twa or Batwa, considered indigenous people in Rwanda, made up about
1 per cent of the population. They are forest dwellers and hunter-gatherers
who developed particular skills in pottery. It's estimated that 30 per cent of
the Twa were also killed in the genocide in 1994.[3]

When missionaries arrived, they saw Tutsis as superior and, over several
decades, a history was created that accorded with both Tutsi interests and European assumptions that they were distinct and separate ethnic groups. In the
1930s, the Belgian administration issued identity cards, designating a person's
ethnicity. A greater gap was forged in the system of social power. Although
notions of Tutsi inherent superiority at first were used to justify Tutsi control
of Rwanda in the early colonial period, the same inaccurate history became
justification for an uprising in the 1950s. Missionaries now championed the
cause of the Hutus, promoting the notion that they had been terribly exploited and treated unjustly by Tutsis for centuries. In 1959, there was a revolution,

a change of power from Tutsi to Hutu, involving attacks against Tutsis. The injustice carried out by colonial rulers was kept out of the picture and the colonial administrators were not attacked.[4] The injustice towards Hutus, by Tutsis, was again used as the primary justification, as Hutu extremists orchestrated the genocide of Tutsis in 1994.

INFINITE JUSTICE

When we face atrocity, our ideals and feelings about justice are naturally and easily stirred and silenced. After 11 September 2001 (9/11), President Bush vowed to punish those who had committed this evil. The military response against Afghanistan in the first round of the 'war on terror' was designated 'Operation Infinite Justice'. Muslim groups protested the name on the basis that their faith teaches that Allah is the only one who can provide 'infinite justice'. The name was changed to 'Operation Enduring Freedom'.

Before bombing Iraq in 2003, the US and UK governments said the reason to go to war was to protect against Iraq's weapons of mass destruction. As more and more people insisted on seeing the missing evidence, they began to emphasize Saddam's gross injustice towards the Iraqi people to arouse outrage and offer a moral premise to attack. In turn, we were asked to put aside grave concerns about the justice (and sense) in a pre-emptive, unilateral strike to impose 'democracy'. Much of the world watched this unfold, aware of being asked to join a fairytale of good and evil, and outraged by the injustice of the US government's presumed dominance on the world stage.

JUSTICE – WHAT IS IT?

As dynamics around justice are central to understanding how violent conflict is stirred, let's look at some of the things justice means to us. Justice is an interplay between sustainability of society (or any community, group, family or organization) and individual responsibilities and rights. Justice means administering law. Ideals of justice underlie political systems, whether the democratic ideals of liberty and justice or a socialist philosophy of fair distribution.

Justice is a code of relationship. Justice is a code for a civil society. Some of us believe in an eternal justice, beyond our personal limits, and the apparent limits of this painful and unjust world. We may feel justice is in the hands of an all loving and all knowing God (whether the God of Christian, Jewish or Islamic traditions) or, as in the Hindu concept of Karma, a law of nature by which we are all related and held accountable in a field of interactions. In Buddhism, the

↑ **Figure 1.1** Athena flying her owl represents wisdom in matters of justice and civil law, about 460 bc. (By courtesy of the Metropolitan Museum of Art, Harris Brisbane Dick Fund, 1950.)

→ **Figure 1.2** Dipankara Buddha, © Nancy Jo Johnson. In Nepal, large Dipankara Buddhas are paraded during the Samyek festival every 5 years. Samyek means the oneness of all sentient beings and the festival denotes the path of Bodhisattva (Shakya MB, Dipankara festival: www.nagarjunainstitute.com – accessed May 2004). (With permission from Nancy Jo Johnson.)

↓ **Figure 1.3** The Buddha Matri ('Mother of Buddhas') Vajravarahi/Kadgha Dakini, about the eighteenth century. As Vajravarahi, she manifests the female aspects of the *heruka* (peaceful/wrathful) Buddhas. As Kadgha Dakini, with her sword of wisdom, she severs delusion. (Gift of Mr and Mrs John C. Rezk. With permission from Southern Alleghenies Museum of Art, PA (97.074).

Bodhisattva has compassion for every sentient being, and vows to remain engaged in this world until we are all freed or enlightened. Wrathful aspects of Buddha cut through the bonds of our illusion.

Our different religions, cultures and political philosophies influence the way that we think about justice. Yet, we also have the idea of a universal justice, a code of human rights that transcends cultural, religious and political differences. International justice systems and democratic secular governments aim to

ensure our diversity and freedom of religious values. The notion of a universal justice system is used, however, by some people to insist that their particular fundamentalist religious values define what the universal justice system should be.

Justice brings to mind our favourite superheroes with their extraordinary super powers, ready to take a stand against evil, stand up to the bullies of our world and protect the innocent. Justice

→ **Figure 1.4** *Superman*, Christopher Reeve in 'Superman II'. (By courtesy of Ullstein-Cinetext, Berlin.)

↘ **Figure 1.5** *Tom and Jerry* (By courtesy of Warner Brothers, © Turner Entertainment Co., a Warner Brothers Entertainment Company. All rights reserved.)

↓ **Figure 1.6** 'The Queen never left off quarrelling with the other players and shouting "Off with her head" or "Off with his head"!' (From *Alice in Wonderland*, illustrations by Arthur Rackham, 1907. Thanks to Dave Neal Multimedia: www.exit109.com/~dnn.)

sometimes means getting even. If we've been put down or made small, we feel the need to take a stand or get back. Some of the greatest cartoons revolve around this trait we know in ourselves, the endless episodes of plotting revenge and justice due.

Justice often refers to paying the price. In its day, 'An eye for an eye, a tooth for a tooth' referred to restraint. The punishment for injustice should match the offence. A cry for justice often means vengeance, however, and vengeance usually goes well beyond a 'tooth'. Several psalms request God to bring vengeance upon our enemies. Some people believe that punishing criminals is avenging God.

We look to those who have the capacity or position to intervene in the name of justice, whether judges, arbitrators, religious figures or elders, as some combination of wrathful and benevolent. The Christian figure, Santa Claus or St Nicholas, considered sterner in some countries and jollier in others, knows whether we are naughty or nice and punishes us or gives us a gift accordingly.

Justice is also a judgement call, proclaimed from on high, as in 'Off with his head!' or deliberated by juries after hearing and weighing evidence. We are also called to use our judgement when facing tough choices or ethical dilemmas in our personal lives. Justice has to do with how we each grapple with our responsibility, our personal actions, the actions of our group and even the actions of our enemies.

Calls for justice also include claims of righteousness for groups in power, even as they oppress, exploit and murder others. As just one example, during the period of slavery in the USA, 'slave codes' provided a legal basis in the 'justice' system to use torture tactics to punish runaway slaves.[5]

Justice also refers to a process of accountability needed for society to create closure, to close a chapter of history behind us, to be able to find a way to move on together. Accountability sometimes demands punishment. Sometimes it is a matter of reparation. It requires finding the missing information, and the graves. Sometimes, our cries for justice are for truth and forgiveness.

In Chapter 3, we look at accountability in Tribunals and Truth and Reconciliation Commissions and we also look at justice as a process of wrestling with issues of accountability – in community forums, inside of our own hearts as individuals, in relationships and within our organizations.

TIME WARPS

During the 1990s in the former Yugoslavia, historical injustice was excavated in order to carry out ethnic cleansing and genocide. In Bosnia, a teacher, a Serb fighter holding Sarajevo siege, said to a reporter, 'Before this summer ends we will have driven the Turkish army out of the city, just as they drove us from the field of Kosovo in 1389'. David Rieff writes:

> The man looked down at the city of Sarajevo, into which he had been shooting his fifty calibre machine gun for the better part of a year and did not see what had once been a magnificent city . . . but rather the campsite of the Turkish army that had conquered the Balkans in the 14th and 15th centuries. Somewhere he must have known that the people he was shooting at were civilians – after a year of siege, 3500 of the dead were children – but he could not see anyone in that urban bowl except armed invaders. His job was of course not to murder. One cannot murder invaders. One defends oneself against them. 'We Serbs are saving Europe', he said.[6]

Many people have said that, although it was never easy to get the current news during the war in Bosnia, you could always hear about the events of Kosovo in 1389, as if they had happened yesterday, when the Serbs lost the famous battle of the 'field of blackbirds'. The technology of nationalism tapped and exploited the wounds of history. In southern Bosnia in 1996, the acting

Republic of Srpska President said that Serbs who decide to live with Muslims 'will no longer be Serbs, but Turks or Catholics [Croats]'.[7]

The ease and speed with which people develop a fantastic, quasi-logic within a time warp give an eerie impression of paranoia, psychosis or science fiction. Interventions to try to put a stop to the escalating events in the former Yugoslavia were stifled in part as a result of the difficulty of disentangling ingredients such as: the linear events – what happened when in different time periods – the stirring of collective memories of injustice and trauma from other time periods, and fear, suspicion and hatred injected through propaganda.

From 1996–2002, my colleague, Lane Arye, and I facilitated large forums of people from all war-affected areas in Croatia, dealing with post-war issues of reconciliation and community building. Four day forums made up of 60–85 participants were held twice a year in different regions of Croatia. While there were always many new participants, there were also many people who attended more than one forum, and some who came to almost every one. Over these years the project was coordinated by a non-governmental organization in Croatia and supported by the United Nations High Commission for Refugees (UNHCR) and other international and European Union organizations as well as private Foundations involved with post-war reconciliation and community building. The participants were from government organizations and heads of municipalities as well as non-governmental and international organizations. They were educators, doctors, mayors, social workers, lawyers, psychologists, working in direct service and community planning. The forum participants were diverse including Croats, Serbs, Muslims and people of other ethnicities, such as Hungarians and Roma, and of mixed backgrounds and mixed marriages. Each participant had unique war experiences and many were themselves refugees, displaced or returnees. All had experienced loss during the war and many excruciating trauma. Groups gathered to discuss and process together the kinds of tensions and issues that they meet in their work and lives. One idea underlying the project was that people could work in their communities only as far as they were able to go among themselves. Issues of community tensions and violence and problems of accountability involved heated dialogue that was painful and emotional. A discussion around a particular community issue escalated rapidly into a heated interaction about what happened when, whether in a very specific and narrow time period of weeks during the war, during the months directly preceding the war – or including events from World War II, World War I and back to the fourteenth century.

I've had a yellow Post-it on my wall to remind me, 'Either everyone is completely crazy or history is not in the past.' The viewpoint that history is happening along a linear axis makes it very difficult to grasp, let alone intervene in a multi-layered, apparently intractable conflict. Begin from a different perspective – that history is present[8, 9] – and many things that seemed incredibly complex become much more readily understandable, including how masses are manoeuvred into war, why the altered states of killers and torturers are so readily accessible, and how average people can be turned into killers, as well as how to intervene and begin to facilitate communication or to mediate in situations in which everyone is convinced that their side is right and has the facts to prove it.

JUSTICE AND POWER

Conflict is rarely a simple matter of two opposing positions. One position may have social, political, institutional or military power used to dominate the other. History is always important and sometimes the power dynamics have shifted according to the period of history. Hungarians in modern-day Slovakia, for example, suffer discrimination. Prejudice stems in part from hatred towards Hungarians for when they dominated the region.

'Hegemony' means the predominance of one group, social class or culture over another. More than political, military or economic control, it refers to an institutionalized attitude that makes this seem 'normal', common sense.[10] Just as calls for justice support liberation from oppression, claims of justice and moral superiority support hegemony. Bush said at West Point, the military academy in the USA, 'America is the single surviving model of human progress.'[11] Although such comments make many people roll their eyes, this notion of 'Manifest Destiny' is generating deadly international conflict.[12] Even in the human rights movement, superiority seeps in. Bielefeldt comments, 'sometimes our American friends tell us they are fighting for human rights, and in the next breath, for the American way of life. This can lead to absurdities.'[13]

HEGEMONY AND PEACE

Just as conflict involves unequal power relationships, the term 'hegemonic peace' describes a peace process between two significantly unequal powers.[14] Some consider the Israeli–Palestinian peace process this way.[15] Negotiations concern whether Israel will accept returning refugees, whether Israel will dismantle settlements, whether Israel will return land, and if so how much. There is no comparable leverage on the Palestinian side. The only leverage Palestinians have had was the autonomy to say 'no' to Israeli proposals.[16] Although Israel has military and economic power in relation to the Palestinians, Israel has a very different experience concerning the power differential. Israel sees itself as a small Jewish country in the middle of a vast Arab world that has been and continues to be hostile to their existence.

Political scientist and author, Glenn Robinson describes how a 'hegemonic peace process' can destabilize both parties. Following World War I, the allies were powerful enough in relation to Germany to extract a one-sided peace at Versailles. The result, however, was instability and another world war.[17] The hegemonic peace process produces instability within each group, between the government and its own society, as well as between the two sides. In the side with less power, there will be opposition against the government for considering a peace agreement that in any way compromises the full vision of rights. In the more powerful party, there will be dissent against the government for making any concessions. By definition, the powerful party may think that it should not be compelled by the weaker party to concede anything. The opposition thinks concessions are unwarranted and signs of weakness and betrayal by their government. The assassination of Israeli Prime Minister Rabin in 1995 reflected this kind of instability. The reactionary turns in Israeli public discourse since Oslo, and since the negotiations of 2000–2001, can also be considered in this light.[18]

POLARIZATIONS FOR PROFIT

Unresolved events of history do not slip into the past. If you want to polarize a group for profit, you need to know how to exploit these unresolved events and the psychological dynamics at play. Understanding these dynamics is also necessary if we want to be less easily manipulated, less reactive, and more able to stay awake and afloat within the tides of our times.

Nelson Mandela tells how there were attempts to tap into and exploit the ready polarizations in South Africa to create violence in the tense atmosphere at the end of Apartheid, by those who preferred to have war than to lose their power in South Africa. Mandela had the spiritual, psychological and political awareness and capacity not to be provoked, and took active leadership to make sure these dynamics would not be manipulated.

Issues that can trigger the polarization of a field are turf for profiteers. Before the wars during the 1990s, in the former Yugoslavia, Milosevic saw his chance to gain power. In Kosovo, the minority Serb population had grievances towards the Albanian majority there, though the Albanians lived in an oppressed position. In a calculated series of events, Milosevic fanned the fuel, and step by step rose to power in Serbia, polarizing the confederation of the former Yugoslavia in his call for a 'Greater Serbia'.

The Croatian leader, Tudjman, with support from Croat Nationalists at home and abroad, then took this opportunity to profit from the situation. Tudjman used the momentum to renew Croat nationalism, leading his country into an independent Croatia.

CALCULATIONS AND THE MYTH OF REPRESSED ANIMOSITIES

One common myth about the cause of the wars in the former Yugoslavia is that repressed animosities between ethnic groups surfaced and erupted when Tito died.[19] Tito had proclaimed 'Unity and Brotherhood', repressing ethnic difference, and once he died, so the logic goes, long-standing hatred returned. But, this isn't true. Animosities did not sort of bubble up and explode.[20]

All groups and societies, organizations and communities are situated within a field of collective, historical issues. Collective conflicts concerning gender, class, ethnicity, colour, culture, physical ability, religion or age are present and pertinent in all our interactions. Injustice that is unaccounted for stays in the fabric of our daily interactions. This does not mean that resentments from past injustice simply fester and finally erupt. It is absurd to think that people in Croatia and Bosnia were repressing pent-up urges to burn each other's homes, and murder their neighbours and had opted instead to go dancing or fall in love, in a region in which there were many mixed relationships and marriages.[21] This erroneous idea that violence bubbles out of ancient hatred supported the world in viewing the violence as a 'civil war'. Add to this the idealistic notion that justice means being 'neutral' and people around the world could sit back, 'neutral', letting the people in the Balkans 'fight it out for themselves'.

Before the war, many people, particularly young people who were later involved in the fighting, had very little concern about ethnic or national differences. In the very beautiful city of Vukovar, people huddled together underground for weeks as the city was reduced to rubble. As they emerged into a city in ruin, a journalist asked a young woman about her classmates in high school: how many were Serb and how many Croat? She said, 'Really I have no idea. We did not ask. We did not care. We were all the same.'[22]

Ten years after the war, when my colleague, Lane, and I were in Vukovar, the town was still in rubble. The whole town, street after street, is a monument to war, every house burned and charred, blackened window frames exposing remnants of a beautiful tiled kitchen, trees and brush growing through the floor, rock and dust. Almost everyone lives outside the town, because the homes in town are burned and few are rebuilt. Croats and Serbs live in almost complete apartheid, with separate playgrounds and bars. Along the Danube, on a beautiful evening, eating with friends, someone from Vukovar told us, 'When there was first word of trouble in Croatia, we were absolutely convinced there was no way there could be trouble in our town. There were 20 different ethnic groups living here in Vukovar and there was a great sense of pride in being such a multi-cultural city.'

It took carefully planned terror tactics to tap the vein of past injustice and stir up terror and righteousness. 'It was not the inability of different ethnic groups to live together that brought on the conflict, but the political aim of separating them.'[23]

To tear apart communities, you need to make calculations and predictions about how people react. Memories of past injustice stimulate our sense of righteousness. Calls for justice make us loyal. Fear makes us loyal to those who offer safety. We give up our humanity to hang on to our privileges. If this is insufficient, terror tactics enforce our silence and cooperation. All of us are considered in these calculations – those up close in the emotional turmoil, those of us at a safer distance and those of us across the world, watching TV.

HOW WE FIGURE

We participate with our own calculations, although we rarely reflect on how we calculate or its consequence. We measure where our feelings are roused, in order to determine our loyalty. When we can't feel anything, we figure we don't care. When we cannot figure how to intervene, we determine that our position is neutral. We get confused by how complicated it is and retreat from the issues altogether. We weigh the privileges we have. Our sums indicate we cannot make a substantial difference anyway.

LOYALTY

Both fear and privilege can lead to loyalty. Loyalty is a fundamental and deeply held value in most people. Our biggest crises are often when loyalty has been betrayed, whether in personal relationship, in family, or in an organization, community or nation. Betrayal of loyalty may be felt as a profound injustice. Loyalty is linked to existential issues of survival, and a sense of heart when you know you will watch someone's back, and they will watch yours.

Loyalties – former Yugoslavia

More than a decade on, communities in Croatia are split apart by suspicions about one another's behaviour during the war. Questions and doubts cloud and disrupt community relationships and community building. Questions concern loyalty. Why did you flee? Why did you stay? What were you doing? Where did you go? On top of the experiences of surviving atrocity, injustice, expulsion and loss, for some having to endure suspicions is too much to bear.

War trauma often stems from the feeling that one's trust and loyalty has been deeply betrayed by neighbours, family, friends, community and government. Some of the greatest trauma I have seen has been in people who felt that they betrayed their own friends, family or community, by not doing enough, by making a mistake or by giving advice that turned out to be deadly.

In the descent into war in the former Yugoslavia, everybody was pulled apart, inside their own hearts, within their families and throughout community. The polarization of Serbs, Croats and Muslims, and the pain and outrage around issues of loyalty fuelled suspicions and terror.

Choices had to be made. You had to protect the safety and welfare of your family. As the region descended into war, concerns about loyalty influenced people's actions in countless subtle ways, contributing to the polarizing field, like kindling to keep a fire hot. A Croat friend, living in Croatia, described how she wanted to write a letter to her good friend, a Muslim, who fled suddenly to Bosnia when war broke out in Croatia, but she never did. She said she was afraid the letter might not reach her friend, or her friend might not write back, because it was harder for people to send mail from Bosnia. These were her thoughts, she said, but, underneath, she knew she was afraid her loyalty would be questioned. What would her mother say? Her sister? Would they question her Croatian loyalty if she wrote to her Muslim friend? Now she always wondered why she had not been loyal to her friend, whom she never saw again.

Loyalties – Israel

During the renewed Intifada at the start of the new millennium, many people commented on how Israelis became increasingly conservative, many losing their belief in the peace process. Some Israelis told me they began to feel they were not free to question Israeli policy at all, 'even among formerly free thinking friends'. Increased attacks had led to a code of loyalty. 'In danger you stick together.'

This bottom-line expression of loyalty is part of our nature and one of the greatest weapons of war. It's great to know who your friends are and who you can count on in times of danger. Yet, if we stick together without awareness, we contribute to the polarizing field and contribute to violence. This can happen rapidly, with very little reflection on the part of the players, who believe they are following only what is 'just' and 'right'.

Loyalties – gangs in LA

In the early 1990s, during a period of lots of violence among gangs in LA, I worked together with my husband, Jean-Claude, and a colleague, David Crittendon, with a large group of young people in gangs, aged 6–18.[24]

Some were in opposing gangs. Many had been involved in shootings and eagerly pulled up their T-shirts to show us their scars. We had a very intense interaction about their experiences in gangs and their reasons for being in gangs. At one point one of the adults who worked with the kids spoke out against violence, passionately trying to educate the young people. Then a 10-year-old began to speak about what gang life meant for him. He said he would do anything for his gang. He spoke at some length, articulately and emotionally, of his memories of being 5 years old and how his brothers and the other homeboys took care of him, gave him cookies, made him feel warm and loved. A hush grew over the group as we listened, feeling the atmosphere of love and protection he described. The kids felt spoken to, and among the adults there was a sobering recognition that, for the kids, the gangs were not about violence, but about love, loyalty and protection.

PULLED BY A MAGNETIC FIELD

Lane always likes to describe Mindell's theory about fields, polarizations and roles[25] by recalling his science class, when as a kid he put a bunch of metal fil-

→ **Figure 1.7** Sign to Osijek (photo: www.osservatoriobalcani.org). (By courtesy of Osservatorio sui Balcani, Rovereto, Italy.)

ings on a plate and then, with a magnet under the plate, he could move those filings around. If you study your experiences in any field in conflict, even your own family, it's astounding to realize how easily we experience ourselves pulled into opposing loyalties. The expression 'devil's advocate' describes how easily we can take an unpopular point of view, or the one opposite to our usual position, when we find ourselves in a dialogue in which that position is underrepresented. We feel compelled to represent both sides of the argument, perhaps so a more whole and potentially creative dialogue can take place.

The more unconscious we are of how our personal and collective history influences our emotions and views, the more open we are to feeling sucked into playing out the polarized forces of collective conflicts, even against what we feel are our own personal values. As fields polarize, most of us don't know ourselves well enough to know what motivates us into action and inaction, how we get possessed by ideals and righteousness, or grow complacent, cynical, hopeless or terrified. We do not know ourselves well enough to realize how our needs in a situation of crisis or our privileges at a distance may lead us to identify with logic that doesn't make sense in our heart, but we don't check out. We feel sucked into this field of conflict, in high emotion or in a kind of fog.

In Croatia, I have often heard people say that one of the most painful aspects of the war was not knowing if there was something more they might have done to make a difference, and later realizing how they had been taken, unwittingly and unconsciously, well before everything escalated beyond the point of no return.

INNOCENCE AND BUNGLING

Most of us declare either righteousness or innocence. If we act, we usually believe we are doing the right thing. When we do nothing, we tend to believe we are innocent, or are utterly unaware of the possibility that we are players at all. Believing we are outside of it all and can't make a difference anyway can make us oblivious to how we are taken in the tide.

Or we develop complex rationales for our stance or for our inaction. Vaclav Havel, the playwright, activist and political leader of the Czech Republic, wrote a play called *Protest*.[26] It is a one-act play, a dialogue between two men in Czechoslovakia, under communism. One character is a political activist and the other shared his ideals at one time, but was now in a privileged position within the repressive society. They discuss a petition. The activist cannot directly ask his old friend to sign it. They talk around it, considering the impact a signature or a petition could have on the repressive political regime and the risk involved to life, safety and privileges. Their dialogue reflects the life-threatening reality of the repressive regime they lived in, and how attempts at rationalization to reconcile our conscience can sometimes mask our collusion.

We also fall into violent conflict by bungling along as events unfold. A film called *How the War Started on my Island*[27] is a beautifully made, bittersweet comedy about how people naively played out their parts as tragedy developed. It's a story about how the war started in Croatia, a parody about how absurd events unfolded on a small island, between the army and the community, between Croats and Serbs, while everyone was absorbed in hilarious nationalist and personal antics and vanities.

BEYOND NAIVETY

After the travesties of the last century, the last decade of the century, and the beginning of the new millennium, it is evident that our innocence and naivety, whether as a nation or as an individual, whether felt or feigned, whether close to or far from the conflict, cannot take away the reality of our personal and collective involvement and responsibility.

In community forums dealing with post-war conflict and reconciliation in Croatia, I have seen that, although people do readily identify with their own naivety, they are also fed up with it. Left with a legacy of profound tragedy, in which everyone has suffered, staying only with the belief that we were all innocent lends itself to a bleak outlook. It furthers an attitude that my actions don't make a difference and a sense of hopelessness in facing the current challenges of building community. Participants in community forums are thirsty and ready for something more satisfying, an orientation to the past and future that is more promising, through assuming responsibility for their community together.

HIGH AND LOW DREAMS OF JUSTICE

Ideals of justice can make us swell in emotion. 'High dream' is a term used by Mindell to refer to how we are buoyed in a sense of confidence, even elation, when we are moved by our greatest ideals.[28] A part of something meaningful, we feel on top of the world, carried by a positive mood and charge. When we lose touch with a high dream or ideal or feel that our ideals have been betrayed, we may fall into a 'low dream' – a mood of depression, anger, bitterness, resignation.[29] High and low dreams can both be used as fuel for violent conflict. High dreams gather us together and make us feel connected in an atmosphere of meaning, purpose and energy. Low dreams also gather us in a shared feeling of hopelessness, impotence, outrage or determination to right the wrong. We tend to fall into high and low dreams, like falling in and out of love, full of emotion, and with little awareness of what's going on with us.

If we get to know our emotions and behaviour around our high and low dreams, we can begin to communicate and interact, rather than only be pulled into acting them out unconsciously. Becoming aware of ourselves around our high and low dreams means getting to know about our ideals. What are our deepest feelings and beliefs about humanity? It also means trying to live by these ideals, encountering inner and outer difficulties along the way.

Most people are very shy to actually express their ideals, and have great trouble trying to live by them, but are more easily outraged or hopeless when others do not fulfil them. When we do not grapple with our ideals outright, they remain in the background, guiding our reactions and behaviours in peculiar ways. To teach children to be well mannered and make less noise, we shout at them. Who hasn't done that? Have you ever been upset by someone who did not live up to your ideal of kindness and then viciously attacked that person for it? And in this world, out of our ideals of justice, we commit unspeakable acts. While our behaviour might be puzzling to an observer from another planet, to us it is normal.

We support our leaders in the belief that force is necessary to defend our high dreams. Unaware of what happens to us when our dreams are dashed, we easily act out of our own bitterness, hopelessness, outrage or vengeance. Sometimes it is possible to catch the moment we feel our own high dream being dashed, and at that moment, retrieve our dream, by standing for it, and trying to live by it. Noticing when our high dreams are dashed, we can also recognize pain or helplessness originating in our personal and collective history.

High and low dreams are like collective high and low tides as well as aspects of our personal psychology. Regions and periods of history rise in a high dream. As the civil rights movement grew in the USA, many people were in a high dream about the great gains for human rights. Martin Luther King is famous for his words 'I have a dream'. After the assassinations of Martin Luther King and Bobby Kennedy, many people throughout the USA entered a 'low dream'.

CHAPTER 2
SUFFERING, PRIVILEGE AND BEING RIGHT

Most of us identify with our innocence and sense of justice, and are convinced that we are right. Around issues of justice and conflicts generally, usually all sides identify as the victim. It is remarkable to watch our capacity to see ourselves as victims, while persecuting others. In physically abusive relationships, people who beat their partners almost always feel that they are victims of their partners, even while beating them up. They feel unable to deal with conflict, with their frustration and rage, and identify as weak, with no relationship to their power. This capacity to not identify with our use of force leads to abuse of power. This dynamic is a central feature of violent conflict and how it cycles. It happens collectively as well as individually. We saw how Serb paramilitaries could shoot civilians, describing themselves as victims. Snipers felt that they were 'defending' not attacking.

We all identify more easily with where we feel troubled than with our awareness of how we impact on others, through our action or inaction. Our ability to know our part, our position, in relation to a conflict is often obstructed by privilege on one side and pain and rage on the other.

PRIVILEGE SUPPORTS BEING UNAWARE

By definition, having privilege in a particular area supports us to be unaware of what's going on for others who do not share the same privileges. The accompanying attitude that 'it is not my concern' reinforces the isolation that occurs between people around dynamics of privilege. Privilege combined with naivety or disinterest and the certainty that we are right perpetuates the very problems that we think have nothing to do with us. When unchecked and unconsidered, this dynamic creates institutionalized oppression of all kinds, such as homophobia, racism, sexism or discrimination against people with disabilities.

If you are physically able-bodied, you are probably more likely to worry about traffic or a small blister on your toe than be aware of the privilege to walk. Although this is natural, the result is that we tend to be unaware of issues facing physically disabled people in our neighbourhoods and think that issues of disabled access are 'their problem', rather than our community's problem.

We isolate ourselves and discriminate against others by resting in areas in which we have privilege and siding with our comfort. We usually don't mean to and don't notice it. If we are a part of a group that has been oppressed, we may not notice how we, too, made choices internally to side with those parts of personality or culture that were favoured in the dominant culture and gave us privilege, or how we have grown to favour those parts of ourselves that helped us to survive our own suffering, such as toughening up, rationalizing or staying in control. Whether we have lots of privilege, or have suffered oppression, or both, we may feel isolated internally, cut off from large parts of our own personality and history.

PRIVILEGE, PLAYING FIELDS AND POLITICAL CORRECTNESS

In the USA, many whites think racism is a problem of the past. Affirmative action has been a practice aimed to right the playing field in some small way, in an attempt to build a more equitable future, by making more opportunities for groups that have suffered discrimination. By actively seeking diversity within our educational institutions or spheres of employment, the hope has been not only to give opportunities to individuals, but also to give society a chance to turn around institutionalized practices that perpetuate racism and inequality.

Talk about affirmative action and there will naturally be many different points of view. Some people feel that it is one essential step on a journey to turn around history. Some people feel that affirmative action constitutes reverse discrimination and perpetuates social inequality, rather than helping to repair it.

In the USA, I turned on the radio in my car and heard the speech of Martin Luther King in 1963. It was his fervent call – 'I have a dream. I have a dream that my four children will one day live in a nation, where they will not be judged by the color of their skin, but by the content of their character. I have a dream today . . .'. When the radio host suddenly came on, I realized I'd been transported, my eyes full of tears. The radio host then used King's illuminating speech to condemn a university that intended to continue its policy of looking at race as a factor in trying to create a diverse, multicultural student body. Being against affirmative action is one thing. To use King's speech to make the point that affirmative action discriminates according to colour was despising and showed an absence of any feeling for the immense struggle against oppression in American history and now. It was inflammatory, intentionally so, and an example of how a privileged group may try to enforce its assumptions about what is fair, based on its institutionalized advantages, built on the backs of others who continue to suffer for it.

We can never be aware of all our relative privileges. Yet, when we are asked to reflect on issues, we tend to feel defensive and 'corrected'. The term 'political correctness' gets tossed around when people are unaware of their privileges in relation to others and so have no real feeling for the actual experience of those who do not share these privileges. It thus seems like just a matter of 'correctness', impersonal, with no emotional value. At the same time, the term 'political correctness' reflects our dissatisfaction with this superficiality. We talk about political correctness because we need more in-depth dialogue in society about issues of discrimination.

People often speak of the importance of seeing each person as an individual only. This notion, often stemming from a good-hearted ideal of equality and justice, will in turn be understood by others as a lack of awareness about how we are not only individuals, but are situated in a social role, which has suffered, or has benefited from privileges in relation to another role. It can be useful to recognize both how we are individuals and how we are imbedded in certain roles with history and its corresponding privileges and suffering.

Unconsciousness comes with the territory of privilege. In a coffee shop of a big city you will probably worry if the service is fast enough before you worry if the person who grew your coffee gets to eat today. If you have enough to eat everyday, you are probably more apt to worry about being overweight, even if by a few pounds, than about world hunger. If you live in a neighbourhood or in a country without violence or war, you will be more concerned about whether your alarm clock will wake you up for your meeting in the morning, and less aware of your privilege to put your head safely on a pillow to get some sleep. If you are white in America and head off to the store in the evening, you don't count your blessings that a cop doesn't stop you just because of your colour and make you spread against the car for a search. If you grew up and live in a democratic society, you may not recognize or use your right and privilege to free speech. If you are heterosexual and you hold your loved one's hand in public, you will tend to notice your loved one's warmth and tend not to be aware of all the people who cannot focus on the warmth of their loved ones' hands in public, for fear of being bashed if they show their sexual orientation.

WE TEND TO NOTICE WHERE WE FEEL TREATED UNFAIRLY

Whether we have privileges or have endured suffering, or both, we tend to notice where we feel treated unfairly much more easily than how we may have made others feel this way. And this identification with feeling treated unfairly anchors our sense that justice and righteousness are on our side. To observe this dynamic you don't have to go very far past your own conversations at the kitchen sink.

And we go to war around our sense that justice is on our side. The atrocities of 9/11 made many people throughout the USA strongly believe that justice and righteousness were with them. For many, it was unbearable to even consider questions about the US government's response or how and why so many people around the world could possibly be so angry at the USA for its actions in the new 'war on terrorism'. Particularly while the shock and outrage about the terrorist strikes was fresh, any dissent against the US government's response was easily squelched, out of 'respect for the victims'. The highly emotional atmosphere for Americans provided a window of opportunity for the US government to use claims of justice to dampen dialogue and serious questioning about the course of action.

PASSING IT ON

With fewer social privileges in a certain area, you tend to be more aware about dynamics of privilege in that particular area. If you do not speak English fluently and you go to an English-speaking event, you will be more aware of the tendency for people who do speak English fluently, particularly if it is their first language, to be unaware that language is an issue at all. People of colour will tend to be more aware of issues of racism than white people. Gay, lesbian and bisexual people are more aware of discrimination based on sexual orientation.

When we have suffered oppression, our awareness of injustice and understanding of dynamics of privilege may lead us to a feeling for other oppressed and minority groups. If we have been oppressed, we may be dedicated to tackling the wider problem of oppression, beyond just our 'own issue'. Yet, when we have been oppressed, we may also pass on our oppression in situations where we find ourselves in the opposite role. The internalized oppressor gets acted out. It is well known that people who are abusive usually have a background of abuse, and are taken unwittingly into the same story, this time as a perpetrator, acting out the internalized abuser. (Though, clearly, not all people who have been abused will become abusers.) And if we have been oppressed in one situation, have fewer privileges in one particular area, we may have privileges in other areas and will tend to be as unconscious as the next guy in those areas in which we do have privilege.

FACETS OF PRIVILEGE: SEXISM AND EAST–WEST POLARIZATION

In a large international gathering in Slovakia, we were working one afternoon on gender and sexism. It was a few years after the collapse of communism in the eastern bloc countries. At one point, the group decided to separate into two sub-groups, men and women, to work separately on issues of gender. In the women's group, an east–west debate developed. It became evident that, with all the best intentions, women from western Europe and the USA were trying to educate women from Poland, Slovakia, the Czech Republic, Romania, Bulgaria and Russia, with the idea that the women from the east had fewer opportunities to understand and develop a feminist movement. Full of ideals, emotion and good intentions, and trying to bring across their ideas and experiences, these women inadvertently became patronizing, as the 'eastern' women increasingly resisted. Women from the former communist countries felt annoyed, misunderstood and put down. They were not invited to share their personal, political and cultural experiences. At one point, a western European woman was explaining sexism and injustice towards women in terms of skewed social power, using the example of lack of equal pay for equal work. Although sexism is certainly a huge issue in the former communist countries, equal pay had not been an issue. This difference in reference systems was not the root of the problem, however. What was missing in the interaction was a spirit of self-reflection on the underlying roles concerning oppression and privilege. While fighting for an issue where you feel you have knowledge and justice on your side, rooted in your experience of oppression, you are likely to be simultaneously unconscious of your behaviour in areas of your privilege. The western women, identifying with their oppression in respect of gender roles, were unconscious of how they had inadvertently been swept into the role of 'oppressor', and how their style of communication and righteousness was in turn dominating and downing the women from central and eastern Europe and Russia.

THE OPPRESSED AND/OR OPPRESSOR: THE ZIONIST MOVEMENT AND PALESTINE

The Zionist movement arose in response to anti-Semitism and pogroms in Russia and Europe in the late nineteenth century.[1] Jews were seeking refuge, hoping to create a new home in the land of Palestine, fleeing danger and life in ghettos, where they were brutalized, expelled and killed. The second wave of immigration (1904–14) was also made up of refugees seeking asylum from persecution. During these periods, tens of thousands of eastern European Jews immigrated to Palestine.[2] During these waves of immigration, it was clear to many that it would not be possible to assimilate in Europe, which was later proven to be the case in the Holocaust, in which 6 million Jews were killed in the culmination of pogroms and anti-Semitism in Europe.

Britain was given mandate of Palestine after World War I, when the League of Nations assigned territories (formerly German or Ottoman colonies) to Allied powers. The mandated territories were neither colonies nor independent countries. In 1917, the Balfour Declaration of Britain supported a Jewish national home in Palestine and legitimized Britain's own presence there, as a protector of Jewish self-determination.[3] In 1937, the Peel Commission recommended the partition of Palestine to form Jewish and Arab states. The Arabs rejected the idea.[4] Later, the mandated territories were replaced by the UN trusteeship system and, with the recent legacy of the Holocaust, in 1947 the UN proposed a plan to partition Palestine, creating the basis for a Jewish state. Accepted by Israel, it was rejected by the Palestinian and Arab states.

In 1948, war broke out. From the Palestinian point of view, along with their Arab supporters and neighbours, the establishment of a Jewish state was an invasion of their territory, and they were protecting themselves from this invasion. From the viewpoint of the new Israeli state, Palestinians and the Arab nations started a violent war against them, refusing to acknowledge their right to exist.

Imagine the extent of loss, tragedy and hope as Jews, both in the Zionist movement and as survivors of the Holocaust, moved into Palestine and the new state of Israel. With a history of oppression and injustice towards their people, the Israeli Jews now faced a new question of survival in Israel. As a result of their history of oppression, they were usually unable to consider how they were perceived and how they acted in the role of oppressor in relation to the people who had been living in Palestine. A collective memory, emotion and history evolved in which most Israeli Jews identified with the threat to their survival, without recognizing the brutal experience of the Palestinian people. During the war in 1948, between 520 000 and 900 000 people (Palestinians) fled or were expelled from their homes[5] and since the creation of Israel have lived as refugees and under occupation.

OVERLAYING VERSIONS OF HISTORY

In situations in which all sides identify with the pain of oppression, or in which there are overlaying historical periods in which injustice occurred, as is the case in the Israeli–Palestinian conflict, and in the former Yugoslavia, each side strongly identifies as a victim, and orients towards those who will support their version or interpretation of events.

On both sides of the conflict, we almost always know the details of where we've been wronged and have little or no awareness of where we've wronged others. Although this in no way implies that each side has equal power or justification in a conflict, violent conflict clearly escalates and replicates around this dynamic. On each side, we identify in the role of being hurt and right, and refer to certain events and periods of history that support it. This psychological dynamic is familiar to all of us and is exploited to create war. It is the dynamic in which most of us feel helpless to intervene. We tend to join in, convinced of one side, unable to grasp the history and the bigger picture in which we are all imbedded.

REDEMPTION

A common pattern through history is that, when a group or nation have been put down and suffered loss, they share and participate in a collective mood of despair. A shared history has mythic proportion and binds people together around the tragedy that occurred and allows them to germinate the seed of redemption. The 'low dream' gives life to the 'high dream'. We will not be oppressed again. We will not be defeated again. We will seek liberation. We will show the world who we are. Or, we will seek vengeance. Stories of loss mix with stories of heroism and can carry us through generations, spurring on a dream of justice and righting history. The dream of redemption touches a deep sense of dignity, yet easily mixes with vengeance.

Serb nationalists in the late 1980s and early 1990s tapped the low dream and the heroic stories that accompanied their loss in the 1300s in Kosovo, to give birth to a new mythology of a Greater Serbia 600 years later. We have seen how Germans after World War I, humiliated from defeat, were in a collective 'low dream' and easily awakened into a high dream of redemption and power in the 1930s under Nazi rule. The legacy and horror of genocide of Jews in Europe emerged into a high dream of hope for refuge and the new state of Israel. The struggle of the Palestinian people under occupation has created a high dream of liberation.

Dreams of redemption are stronger than time. They help us to endure the long road of suffering, to continue to fight the fight, to feel hope and a part of a long-term movement of social change, transcending our personal stay on earth. Religious, political and philosophical ideals nourish the dream of a greater justice and a refuge from oppression.

When we identify with this greater justice, we are absolute in our righteousness. Our redemption may be for this life or the next, a personal redemption or our community's redemption. The dream of redemption can be exploited to keep people quiet. The promise of redemption in heaven was often nourished to encourage people to accept the conditions under which they suffered, in this way replacing social action with institutionalized religion. Missionaries often helped to pacify a population into accepting colonial occupation of their regions.

Promise of redemption in the afterlife has also been used, conversely, to fuel political or social action. We are faced with the reality that suicide bombers are

← **Figure 2.1** German election poster, 1928: 'Two million dead. Did they die in vain? Never! Front Soldiers! Adolf Hitler will show you the way!' The claim is that Hitler will redeem Germany from the loss of World War I. (By courtesy of Randall Bytwerk, German Propaganda Archive: www.calvin.edu/cas/gpa)

→ **Figure 2.2** The Sunday *New York Times* after the Versailles Treaty, 29 June 1919. The article announces the war debts Germany will pay 'solving Europe's greatest problem'. In hindsight, we see how Germany's debt from World War I leads to the rise of Hitler. (Courtesy of the *New York Times*.)

willing to die, with a promise of redemption. Righteousness and a sense of contact to divine justice can also be exploited to suppress potential concern about whether it is right to inflict violence on others, because the motivation of violence, whether terrorism or bombing, is claimed to be pure.

CYCLES OF VIOLENCE: MATTER OF FACT

As long as past and present stories of injustice remain open and unaccounted for, they are used as a motivating point by one or both sides to tip the field into a renewed cycle of violence. (Revenge is discussed more fully in Chapter 17.) This cycle of violence, to settle accounts, is sometimes experienced as something very matter of fact. One motivation for revenge is to 'settle accounts'.

Fratricides

I remember spending a beautiful week, during my 20s, on a tiny island off Crete, where only a handful of people stayed through the winter, and a few hundred lived in the summer. One young woman from the island began to describe intergenerational disputes. She said this was the material from which Kazantsakis' book, *Fratricides*, was written. She described in great detail how someone from one family or 'side' would get killed, and how that side would then 'have to' kill someone on the other side. She said there was no urgency. It did not have to happen immediately. In fact many years could go by, even a generation, but eventually it had to happen, and then it would be the other side's duty to take revenge. Her description was of a highly ritualized intergenerational series of murders in a cycle of revenge.

Gang life

In our work with young people in gangs from south central LA, the 10-year-old, who described the love and care he was given from his homeboys and his loyalty to them, went on to speak about killing. He said being in a gang is not for the killing – it's about love and watching each other's backs. The killing side of things is just business. It's business that needs taking care of. If someone did something against somebody in your gang 'you just had to take care of it'.

Israel

In Israel, as I write, tensions are at their highest point in years. Jews speak more and more of the Palestinians as murderers. And the Palestinians speak more and more of the Jews as murderers. On both sides, the use of violence is being increasingly condoned and justified as the only possible way to try to stop these murderers. A matter-of-fact tone seeps into the atmosphere of violence, such that it is an increasingly mainstream attitude on both sides to support what would have earlier been considered extremist positions.[6] Although everyone is capable of seeing the inevitable spiral and madness of a logic of revenge, everyone is locked into it.

The 'settling of accounts' in search of justice, and the way this cycles, is one feature of violent conflict throughout the world. This dynamic of settling accounts is familiar to most of us if we just look at our conflicts at home. One way for us to intervene in this cycle of destruction as a society and as an international community is to grapple with our accounts.

CHAPTER 3
TRIBUNALS, TRUTH COMMISSIONS, LUSTRATION AND COMMUNITY FORUMS

STOPPING THE WHEEL: ACCOUNTABILITY

Accountability is vital to the possibility of reconciliation and to prevent new rounds of violence. This notion is now a well-accepted part of international law, and also increasingly enters our mainstream social and political dialogue.

Accountability takes many forms. It involves public acknowledgement and public record that events have taken place. Those responsible for crimes against humanity may be brought to trial in International Tribunals. Accountability includes telling and hearing what happened in Truth Commissions. Accountability includes filling in holes of information concerning missing people, and finding remains of people who were killed, so they can be returned to their families and given a burial. Accountability may include reparations. Accountability involves hearing and responding to the emotional force of what has happened, and exploring the meaning of personal and collective responsibility throughout society. Accountability also means finding closure, to be able to return to community and build a future.

Accountability may ultimately be a process of self-reflection, for individuals, communities, nations and our international community, taking stock and taking account of how we are active participants in this world.

THE TRIBUNALS AND INTERNATIONAL COURT

The need for accountability to resolve conflict and prevent its cycling is at the premise of the International Tribunals set up to deal with crimes against humanity after the wars and genocide in the former Yugoslavia and Rwanda, as well as the International Criminal Court (ICC) or 'World Court'. In the spring of 1993, the UN Security Council created an International Tribunal for the prosecution of persons responsible for serious violations of international Humanitarian Law committed in the territory of the former Yugoslavia since 1991, as a crucial step towards the restoration of peace.

Soon after came the genocide in Rwanda in 1994. There was discussion about whether there should be an expansion of the mandate of the existing Tribunal for the former Yugoslavia to include Rwanda, or to create a separate entity. The International Tribunal for Rwanda was established as a separate entity, but linked in such a way as to promote coordination in the interpretation and evolving norms of international law for war crimes and crimes against humanity, in the first cases on trial since the post-World War II war crimes trials in Nuremberg and Tokyo.

The UN General Assembly first recognized the need to prosecute mass murderers and war criminals in 1948 following the Nuremberg and Tokyo trials. Since then, there are many treaties, laws and conventions, but there has not been a system to enforce the norms through holding individuals criminally responsible. The Tribunals differ from the 'World Court' in geographical jurisdiction and time frame. The Tribunals are ad hoc, temporary, dealing with specific regions over specific time periods, and the ICC or World Court, which came into force on 1 July 2002, is set up as a permanent court.[1]

THE PURPOSE OF TRIBUNALS

The Tribunals were established to partially fill the critical need for accountability and closure. The Tribunal's mission for the former Yugoslavia was to promote reconciliation through the prosecution, trial and punishment of those who perpetrated war crimes, crimes against humanity and genocide. By ensuring that people are held individually responsible for crimes they committed, the International Tribunal aims to prevent entire groups – be they national, ethnic or religious – from being stigmatized, and to ensure that others do not resort to acts of revenge in their search for justice. Hearing the voices of victims in a public forum also contributes to lessening of the suffering and helps in the reintegration and reconciliation of society. By establishing legal truth on the basis of which society can take shape, the International Tribunal aims to prevent historical revisionism.[2] The International Tribunal in Rwanda was described as urgently needed to exorcise the long-entrenched culture of impunity and collective guilt in Rwanda, to achieve a sense of justice necessary for reconciliation, to stem vigilante retribution and facilitate the return of refugees, and to deter a new round of violence in Rwanda and Burundi.[3]

LIMITS

At the same time, there are limits to the Tribunals' capacity to deal with the magnitude of societal needs concerning accountability. The president of the International Tribunal in the former Yugoslavia spoke about these limits.[4] He said that it is impossible for the Tribunal to try all the perpetrators of serious violations of humanitarian law committed during a conflict that lasted more than 5 years. The Tribunal cannot hear the tens of thousands of victims and is limited in its mandate to review what happened from the specific angle of criminal responsibility of the perpetrators, and is not involved in all of the historical, political, sociological and economic issues. Therefore, he said, this work must be complemented by the work of national courts, and initiatives such as the setting up of a truth and reconciliation commission, which derive from civilian society. (The interplay and potentially complementary as well as conflicting interests of Tribunals and Truth and Reconciliation Commissions are discussed below, as well as the role of grassroots community forums.)

The limits of a Tribunal or court are also evident in Rwanda. Officials of the new Rwandan government estimated as many as 20 000–30 000 potential defendants to be tried for genocide and war crimes. These have been described in three tiers – the central core of about 100–300 people who planned and organized the genocide, known as the 'zero network'; the second tier would be local leaders (1000–3000) who were not part of the zero network but who were able to personally order local killings, including a number of municipal officials and administrative authorities; the third tier included all who have killed, including many who were themselves victimized and forced to kill or be killed. This number would far surpass 20 000–30 000.[5] It is expected that the International Tribunal will need to limit its prosecutions to some portion of the first tier, which will leave tens of thousands of additional cases for consideration by the Rwandan government, judiciary and society.

IMPUNITY AND DOMINANCE

Tribunals and the World Court must function in a complementary way with national courts, Truth and Reconciliation Commissions, and with other forums and methods for grappling with the vast issues of justice and reconciliation throughout society. An increasingly clear framework for international human rights is emerging that supports global human rights standards, while also supporting the autonomy of national courts, and respecting local development of community organizations.

An International Criminal Court agrees upon shared standards of human rights and protection against crimes of war and crimes against humanity at the root of all our systems of justice. Those in 'power' cannot expect to get away with human rights violations towards their own and others' citizens, just because they are in control of their own police, military or national courts.

The USA has attempted to block the development of the ICC, because it does not want its own citizens held accountable in this way. The USA signed the statute for the ICC in December 2000. On 6 May 2002, the Bush administration announced in a foreign policy address and letter to the UN Secretary, General Kofi Annan, that it did not recognize the US signature, which occurred during the Clinton presidency and had no intention of becoming party to the statute. The signature of the USA now appears in the UN records, marked with an asterisk to this effect.[6]

The USA is increasingly criticized for talking about 'human rights' and 'humanitarian aims', while wielding its power to break international law. There's a long list of human rights violations carried out by the USA in the name of 'humanitarian' aims in Nicaragua, Guatemala, El Salvador, Honduras, East Timor, Vietnam, Argentina and more. The USA claims impunity, based on its position of power, repeatedly defying international agreements and holding itself outside the perimeters of international law.

The US refusal to be accountable to a world community reflects a more general tendency within us to dominate when we can, while resting in the naive belief that we are righteous or uninvolved. Issues of accountability and human rights, at the roots of our systems of justice, belong in our social interactions and community organizations as well as in the courts. How our international justice system evolves will be dependent on whether we can talk about issues of accountability across many levels of society, as individuals, organizations, communities and societies, and reflect on difficult questions concerning our responsibility. The USA will probably continue to hold itself apart, as the world's only superpower, unless a strong movement develops within the country to insist on grappling with events of history both at home and throughout the world.

INTERNATIONAL COURTS AND NATIONAL COURTS

One concern about the Tribunals and World Court is that it would be wrong for international prosecutions to interfere with national justice systems. The International Tribunals are meant to establish a backstop for national efforts, however, not to replace them. By making clear that violence or intimidation aimed at national prosecutors or judges can no longer guarantee impunity, the national justice system should be bolstered, not impaired.[7] The International Tribunals and World Court are not intended to interfere with local democratic processes. Concerns that international prosecutions might replace national justice systems mask attempts to protect war criminals. In the former Yugoslavia, there were consistent attempts to protect Serb and Bosnian Serb war criminals. In Croatia, there has been pressure from people within government and from various levels of community who did not want to see Croatian war criminals tried because they were seen as Croat defenders, not criminals.

REACTIONARY VIEWS AND SUSTAINABILITY

Someone told me that 'outbreaks of violence in Croatia and reactionary views against taking Croat war criminals to trial were being inflamed and manipulated, as they had been all along, by former warlords and some people in politics, who had plenty at stake'.[8] A purpose of International Tribunals is to relieve a generalized collective guilt and a cycle of revenge, by trying war criminals, rather than those who were swept along in the reign of terror. Yet, a significant part of the population in Croatia believed that, if warlords were considered criminals, the soldiers would also be made to feel like criminals, instead of defenders who risked their lives and gave their lives for their country that was under attack in 1991, and in their view liberated in 1995. And in Serbia, even as war criminals are brought to The Hague, there has been huge popular support for them.

If our goal is to build a process of accountability within society towards sustainable reconciliation, such views must be seen not only as reactionary and extremist, but as actual and legitimate perspectives of some of the citizens of a country. If these views are not included into society's dialogue, these views can easily be stirred up to block the process. Sustainability requires dialogue within society that includes all views. If 'extreme' positions are only criminalized, they will remain to haunt us and make themselves heard through violence.

An effective international justice system needs to develop in tandem with national courts, Truth and Reconciliation Commissions and other social and community forums of dialogue around issues of accountability. In post-conflict zones, intolerance of human rights violations and intolerance of impunity of those who were in power needs to be matched by thorough dialogue concerning accountability within society, to include all perspectives and experiences, including the most extreme views (see pp. 38–39).

TRUTH AND RECONCILIATION COMMISSIONS

Truth Commissions are established and given authority by governments, international organizations or non-governmental organizations to research and report on human rights abuses in relation to a particular period of time or a particular conflict. They provide an official forum for victims, their relatives and perpetrators to give their personal accounts on human rights abuses. Their aim is to account for past abuses of authority, end them and promote reconciliation. Truth Commissions have taken place in many countries.[9]

South Africa: truth and reconciliation

Most well known is the Truth and Reconciliation Commission in South Africa. It was set up to promote a process of healing for the nation, with the idea that everyone had in some way been victims of the oppressive and racist regime and widespread trauma under Apartheid. For some degree of closure to be possible, the whole story about what happened across society had to be told. It was a big experiment, filled with good will and commitment from many individuals and groups, and much of society. The success of the Truth and Reconciliation Commission in South Africa was in the way that it was set up, cooperating with various parts of the community and public, getting feedback on its design, and in its passionate hope to bring healing to the whole country. If South Africa's Truth and Reconciliation Commission is used as a model for such commissions to develop elsewhere, it is important not to just copy the commission, but to model after its spirit of creating a community-based design.

Another important feature of the Tribunals in South Africa was that there was amnesty for people whose crimes were politically motivated, and consonant with policies of either the state or a liberation movement, and that there was full disclosure. This invited people to come forward, to fill in the holes of information crucial for a society to establish as complete a picture as possible of the nature, causes and extent of gross violations of human rights.

In many of the hearings, hundreds of people entered the halls to listen to testimony. Some of the hearings were also televised. First there were hearings for victims. The Amnesty hearings involved perpetrators asking for amnesty and telling what happened in great detail. There was no blanket amnesty. Amnesty was determined by a panel, in the public hearings, and on a case-by-case basis.[10]

THE QUESTION OF AMNESTY OR TRYING CRIMES IN COURT

The principle behind giving amnesty is to encourage people to come forward to tell the story. The hope is for society to tell and hear as complete a story as

← **Figure 3.1** Amnesty hearing, South Africa (photo by Jillian Edelstein). (With permission from Jillian Edelstein.)

→ **Figure 3.2** Exhumation at Boshoek, near Rustenburg, Northern Province, South Africa, March 1998 (photo by Jillian Edelstein). (With permission from Jillian Edelstein (2001) *Truth and Lies*. London: Granta Books.)

possible. When perpetrators acknowledge what they have done in a public forum, this can be healing for victims. It can be helpful to see the person who harmed you acknowledging the wrong doing. And, when loved ones disappeared, it helps in some deep and essential way at least to know what happened. In one testimony, a man told of how he had brutally kicked and beaten a prisoner. As he answered question after question about the details of the crime he had committed, his voice became quiet and began to crack. A hush fell over the crowded room, and then someone called out 'we will forgive you' and the room erupted in applause.[11]

Detailed testimony was given in case after case, by both perpetrators and victims. Many thousands of hearings occurred throughout South Africa. To tell the stories and to listen to them was horrifying and exhausting.

Jillian Edelstein, photographer and author, told me that, although she encountered some cynicism about the process, almost everyone she met who was directly involved, whether giving testimony or going to listen to hearings, found the experience essential and meaningful. One ANC veteran, Singolawan Malgas, gave testimony and at first avoided speaking about how he was treated on Robben Island. As he finally told the details of his torture and why he was currently in a wheelchair, he began to cry. Desmond Tutu, presiding over the hearings, was so moved by the telling of his story, he also wept.[12]

Although some Truth and Reconciliation Commissions are based in the premise of giving amnesty to those who testify, others work in tandem with criminal courts at a national and international level, passing on the collected information for the courts to follow up. Some consider Truth Commissions as complementary to a criminal justice system. Others consider Truth Commissions and criminal justice systems to have conflicting interests.

Amnesty is sometimes considered a bottom line for Truth and Reconciliation Commissions, to ensure that the complete story can come forward. A criminal justice procedure could obstruct this fundamental aim. Conversely, the bottom line

↓ **Figure 3.3** Archbishop Desmond Tutu (photo by Jillian Edelstein).
(With permission from Jillian Edelstein.)

for international or national courts or Tribunals is to stop impunity for those who were most responsible for war crimes and atrocities. Amnesty conflicts with this.

Some believe punishment is a deterrent, and amnesty in effect removes this deterrent against future crimes and human rights abuse. Another idea, however, is that amnesty is geared towards deterrence. If a country can create closure and reconciliation, that will deter further cycles of violence.

One reason to try war criminals is that, once the main players have been identified and tried, society is free to begin a process of self-examination and reflection. By ensuring criminal justice for the main players, others can face complex issues and greyer areas of accountability and problems of rebuilding society, without fear of being criminalized for their actions. An opposite view is that society will not deal with issues of accountability if people fear being seen as criminal. Nor will society grapple with accountability if people can project all issues of accountability on those assigned with criminal responsibility.

RESTORATIVE JUSTICE AND CRIMINAL JUSTICE

Desmond Tutu said that the system of 'restorative justice' in South Africa reflected a fundamental value of African culture, 'Ubuntu', which refers to healing and nurturing social relationships versus vengeance. The goal of the Truth and Reconciliation Commission was to effect a healing process for society that could not begin until there had been public acknowledgement of what had happened. Tutu said, 'You cannot forgive what you do not know'.[13] At the hearings, professional 'comforters' looked after those who testified, both victims and perpetrators. Comforters would hold and stroke those who were suffering from telling and hearing the stories, bring water or dry tears. Pumla Ndulula worked as a comforter in Johannesburg and in Pretoria. When asked about her 'big cases', she said she 'looked after' Colonel de Kock, the security commander at Vlakplaas, known as 'Prime Evil'.[14]

'Restorative justice' is distinct from 'criminal justice'. Restorative justice focuses on truth seeking and potential reconciliation. Critics of restorative justice have gone as far as saying that a democracy that includes widespread amnesty is a 'culture of impunity'.[15]

VENGEANCE AND FORGIVENESS

In community forums dealing with political and social conflict, we see that, if no one stands accountable for an injustice, mutual accusations will escalate, fed by further vengeance and retaliation. Demands for forgiveness before issues of accountability have been taken seriously can also exacerbate and escalate conflict.

TWO PATTERNS: ENDING IMPUNITY AND TELLING THE TRUTH

These are two essential patterns for conflict resolution, represented by the Tribunals' focus on 'ending impunity', and the Truth and Reconciliation Commissions' focus on 'truth'.

The call to end impunity is to take a stand for humanity. We set a boundary and say, as an international community, we will not tolerate the human rights abuses that have been perpetrated and protected by state 'power'. The aim is to stop the legacy of tyranny. Having a bottom line frees society to begin a process of accountability, reconciliation and democracy building. Within community, demanding accountability and standing accountable can also be a way of saying the buck stops here. Let's you and I change the course of history now. Ending impunity means taking a collective and personal stand against the revision of history.

Focus on telling the 'truth' is aimed towards community reflection, for community to tell and hear its story, its collective story and individual stories, with the idea that everyone was a part, some perpetrators, some victims. This does not mean everyone is equally responsible. Acknowledging events creates some shared version of history between perpetrators and victims, no matter how horrible, which is also aimed at avoiding the revision of history and the long-term damage this can cause to individuals, community and societies. Telling the story, telling the truth, also suggests the necessity for many voices to be heard and multiple truths to be told. Telling the story is a process of reckoning, taking stock, remembering, including and moving forward.

Both patterns are useful to society's struggle with accountability issues. Ending impunity might mean more than criminal responsibility. It involves recognizing responsibility more generally. We cannot just use our privilege to claim we are uninvolved. Focus on truth telling may point to the importance of telling our stories more generally, understanding how our personal lives are shaped by the events of history and contribute to the future.

GRASSROOTS ACCOUNTABILITY

It is insufficient to leave all our issues of justice and accountability with our legal and political systems, whether in society generally or in particular conflict zones. Grassroots community interaction around issues of accountability is essential to democracy building and to the development of civil societies interested in self-reflection, self-determination and sustainability.

In post-conflict situations, in addition to Tribunals and Truth Commissions, there is a need for people to gather in community forums to deal with questions of accountability, reconciliation and community building throughout various sectors of society.[16] People need the opportunity to tell the story, interact around the high emotions involved, and questions of accountability, in order to find some shared sense of history and future. We need to update our notion of democracy, so that issues of accountability are addressed in an active and thorough way, throughout all levels of society. In the words of the president of the International Tribunal for the former Yugoslavia, there is a need to 'repair the fabric of society thread by thread'.[17] In situations of long-standing conflict, in addition to negotiations at the political level, there is a need for far more attention on community interaction around the central issues of the peace negotiations, including those extreme views that will threaten the outcome of negotiations. In organizations, neighbourhoods and community everywhere there is a need to interact around issues of history, oppression and accountability, for our future as diverse and inclusive societies.

Both Tribunals and Truth and Reconciliation Commissions emphasize the importance of victims and perpetrators giving testimony in a public arena. Testimony is often very passionate and personal, and is considered to be meaningful and emotionally healing for both the individual and the community. Yet, there can be very little interaction encouraged within these structures. Community forums, however, when well facilitated, can be highly interactive.[18] There are opportunities to relate about different versions of 'truth', different points of view and intense emotional experiences. Interaction is a crucial dimension for transformation and potential closure to occur around issues of accountability.

Facilitation of forums involves supporting interaction just at the point that communication usually breaks down, or threatens to erupt or escalate. This point is a 'hotspot' (a term from Mindell's Process Oriented Psychology, discussed in Chapter 25). Hotspots may arise around issues of accountability, where outrage about injustice and past trauma are triggered.[19] We have a tendency to try to repress the most controversial subjects around these hot spots, to criminalize or ostracize those with extreme views, or highly structure and ritualize our interactions.

Yet it is when we are able to sit at the hot spot, and when people can hear and feel their viewpoint expressed, that they also become interested and able to hear and feel their 'opponent's' point of view and experience. The emotional interactions, complexities and capacity for people both to strongly express their experiences within community and to hear others and feel into the shared tragedy can lead to a genuine wish to move on as a whole community.

When people are able to discuss their different views thoroughly, when emotions are welcomed in, and interaction occurs, a transformation occurs in people's relationship not only to the issues, but also to their feeling for one another and their shared history. Where there are relationships, people begin to care about the sustainability of community, and to dare to believe that it is possible. Groups transform as they begin to identify not only with one point of view, but also with one another, the whole of their interaction and its creative potential.

ACCOUNTABILITY WITHOUT REPEATING WAR

In our forums in Croatia, accountability was a hot topic. People differentiated criminal responsibility from what it means to look at personal and social responsibility, as a member of a national or ethnic group, and as a member of the human race.

The subject of accountability among Serbs, Croats and Muslims was strongly hushed throughout society. In our forums, the participants felt that when their discussions broached the topic of accountability, they were frightened that touching on such complex issues and such hot and traumatic territory could set off violent conflict.

Some people felt that accountability should remain solely the territory of Tribunals, and were reluctant to consider issues of personal and collective responsibility at a grassroots level, for fear of aggravating tensions. Some expressed the viewpoint that accountability was solely a political issue of criminal justice and that the forums should revolve around 'humanitarian' issues only, such as the physical, social and emotional aspects of helping people to rebuild their lives and communities. Others pointed out that progress in rebuilding lives, community and the possibility of living together was clearly blocked around issues of accountability, and the discussions were absolutely needed to build community together.

One afternoon, Lane and I encouraged people to speak about their fears concerning the volatility of discussing issues of accountability. We then invited people to sit in small groups to discuss the following: Do you think it's a good idea to discuss issues of accountability in this forum or not? Do you think it is possible to do it without 'recreating war', and if so how? Regarding this latter question, we had not meant 'recreating war' literally, but were referring to the tense atmosphere in the forum and the fear of touching on these explosive issues. Each small group then shared a summary of their discussions within the large forum. Each small group had taken the question literally, concerning whether it was possible to discuss accountability without re-triggering an actual war. Each small group determined that it was essential to address the issues, and suggested ways to make it safer for everyone.

As war criminals were brought to the courts in the former Yugoslavia, and with the subject increasingly in the news, some of the 'hush' and 'silence' around the subject of accountability was lifted. The subject could perhaps come to the table more easily and some degree of collective blame, guilt and defensiveness was eased. What appeared to be most useful to forum participants was the recognition that it was possible to enter the difficult territory, to have the most difficult conversations, without just falling into a replay of escalating mutual accusations. If the replay began, we could stay with the hottest issues and find a way forward together. A task for society is to support forums where such difficult dialogue can be facilitated – towards finding pathways forward. When participants were able to work emotionally with issues of personal and social responsibility, it was both relieving and transforming for everyone present. It was clear that, when these issues were not taken into account, they blocked efficient social and economic progress in community building.

In an early forum, two friends, a Croat and Serb, sat face-to-face in the centre of the group. With facilitation, they discussed their feelings in relation to one another, as Croat and Serb, concerning what had happened in their devastated community. Though they identified as friends, they had never discussed the war or any of their feelings with each other until now, concerning their sense of personal and collective responsibility in relation to one another. They were courageous and said they felt very relieved to have talked so personally about their feelings. The rest of the group looked on, riveted. I remember that Lane and I viewed this interaction much as we would any relationship work within a group. After their interaction, people said that it was astounding that such a dialogue was possible. The other participants expressed deep appreciation to the two people, underscoring that it was still potentially life threatening as well as life changing that such discussions were taking place.

POST-COMMUNIST ACCOUNTABILITY

The former communist countries of central and eastern Europe have faced the question of how to deal with issues of accountability from the past communist regimes, while moving ahead to create democratic societies.

Several of the former communist countries used a 'lustration' process. Lustration authorizes a government to solicit information, investigate, try, and disqualify from office and important positions in society those people who were most complicit in the past regime. The term derives from the Latin word 'lustratio', which means to purify, in a spiritual, religious or moral sense. Lustration is an alternative method to criminal prosecution or unconditional amnesty in a truth and reconciliation process. Lustration involved assessing people's involvement in the past regime based on accounts from the former regime's secret police files. Laws differ in terms of who initiates the process, how the lustrated individual is treated, such as whether the former collaborator has an opportunity to explain his or her activities, if the individual is removed or barred from public office or other critical positions, and if the lustration process provides public access to files, or not.

The idea was to face the past and for people who terrorized the nation and violated human rights to be removed from positions that they were still holding.[20] In Poland, Lech Walesa advocated that the best way for former collaborators to make amends is to have them maintain their positions and use their bureaucratic expertise to build the new democratic state.

The 'thick line' philosophy illustrated the attempt to draw a line between the past and the present, and to move forward as a society. In some cases, decisions were made to destroy the files, so that people could not dig up the past, or enact a renewed purge of the state. One reason for the thick line philosophy is that huge segments of society were complicit with the former regime, making it impossible to determine who should be punished, or how to determine 'active' as opposed to 'passive' collaboration, and what circumstances legitimized 'active' compliance. For example, people were often forced to collaborate under threat.[21]

Another reason for the choice of lustration was that, in post-Stalin communist regimes, the crimes were less about overt crimes such as torture and murder, and more about widespread mistrust and suspicion among fellow citizens and between neighbours and family members. Particularly after the failed hardline coup in Russia in 1991, there was fear of a communist revival, which brought popular support for lustration.[22]

One of the biggest criticisms of the lustration process was that it involved trying to end the identification with the past regime while using the secret police files from the past regime to do so. Michnick and Havel write: 'It is absurd that the absolute and ultimate criterion for a person's suitability for functions in a democratic state should come from the internal files of the secret police.'[23]

Another criticism of lustration was that it could unjustly punish individuals, undermining rights to due process and individual liberties. Human rights groups have spoken out against lustration laws for violation of individual liberties. Havel and others argued that a flawed lustration process is better than no lustration.

A top-ranking Czech official said, 'I believe that those who knowingly collaborated, even if they did nothing harmful, even if just playing games, should be lustrated. We are attempting some kind of moral cleanup here, to clean the society of those who morally compromised themselves.'[24] This kind of remark raises ethical questions concerning the relationship of means to end. Interestingly, the notion of a generalized moral sweeping for the good of the 'collective', with less concern for individual rights and responsibilities, in some ways mirrors principles of the regime that was being cleansed.

In moving to an increasingly democratic system, in which leadership is more decentralized, the practice of lustration may be understood in an actual and a metaphoric way as the need to try to remove our identification with an old regime, and an old attitude of centrality and power. To develop democracy at a grassroots and political level, we need to radically change our old notions of leadership and power. Vaclav Havel said: 'We are all in this together, those who directly, to a greater or lesser degree, created this regime, those who accepted it in silence, and also all of us who subconsciously became accustomed to it.'[25] This statement offers a more global view of accountability and has relevance beyond the situation of the former communist countries.

CHAPTER 4
ACCOUNTABILITY AND RETURN TO THE GANGES

IMPASSES TO JUSTICE AND THE JUSTICE SCALE

When working with issues of justice around community and social issues and historical injustice, as well as in our relationship conflicts at the kitchen sink, a first and crucial step is to acknowledge the injustice that has taken place. Many conflicts cycle at the point that someone or some group cries out in outrage about a past injustice, and the group who was involved in carrying out this past injustice does not acknowledge what it has done, or individuals within that group may know nothing about it. Or, it is felt to be irrelevant because it was in the past. At the moment of denying a past injustice a new injustice is committed.

It can be useful to study your own behaviour to learn how conflicts escalate around dynamics of 'justice' (Table 4.1). Think of a conflict that you had recently or in the past. It might be a small issue or a more major one. Choose one. What happened? Did you feel the other person treated you unjustly? What did you want from this person? Did that change over time? You can also try it the other way round and ask yourself if the other person thought he or she was treated unjustly. What did the person want from you? Often we want things from the top portion of the list, such as acknowledgement of what happened, along with an apology. When we don't get that, we get interested in things at the bottom of the list, like wanting the other person to suffer, to feel humiliated or even to die.

THE 'POOPOOER': A GHOST OF PERPETUAL CONFLICT

One way we do not acknowledge what happened is through 'poopooing'. It wasn't so bad. It's ridiculous, exaggerated. It never happened. It's in the past. You are making an unnecessary fuss just to get attention. Think of a time you

TABLE 4.1 THE JUSTICE SCALE

I was treated unfairly and I wanted the other person to:

- Acknowledge my feelings
- Admit that an injustice has occurred
- Confirm my version of events, rather than a completely different version
- Apologize for his or her actions
- Feel and show remorse for his or her actions
- Acknowledge his or her misuse of power or rank in the situation
- Acknowledge it and apologize publicly
- Offer reparations
- Be punished for what he or she did
- Suffer and feel humiliated, to feel the same pain that he or she inflicted
- Be publicly humiliated
- Be killed

felt an injustice was done to you and when you spoke out about it you were 'poopooed'. If and when an acknowledgement comes, it may be inadequate if there is no real feeling of understanding for your experience or feeling of remorse. The acknowledgement comes formally, but the 'poopooer' hovers near by.

Another block to acknowledging our personal responsibility and our part of collective responsibility is that we fear, if we acknowledge where we are accountable, that our version of the story will in turn never be acknowledged. We act defensive instead of also standing for and congruently defending our version of the story to be heard. We like to insist that the other person or group must be the first to acknowledge responsibility. Personal and social conflicts often are at an impasse here, though it's surprising how readily people do want to listen to each other once someone has taken the first step to acknowledge some responsibility. In a situation in which a facilitator is present, sometimes the facilitator can even take the first step.

VALIDATION OR ISOLATION

Accountability involves recognizing and validating each others' experiences, to include it in some way into reality or history. When our experience is not acknowledged, we feel that history is revised, and we are no longer included in the flow of history. Our deepest experiences are not included in this world. If the reality of our experience is not acknowledged, it can create a feeling of isolation and anxiety, and the experience of losing our grip on reality.

In an international conference in Slovakia on conflict resolution, participants from 30 countries dealt with many issues from gender, sexual orientation and racism to east–west issues, problems facing post-communist societies, and more. After several days, a woman from Croatia began to feel terribly anxious, dizzy and disoriented. She said, 'I was so frightened. I thought I was losing touch, going crazy.' My colleague spoke with her. They talked about how this international group that had gathered to deal with pressing world issues had not yet spoken about the war in the former Yugoslavia. This was in 1994. My colleague suggested to her that her reactions of anxiety and disorientation were tied to this group dynamic. That we had not yet spoken about the war in the former Yugoslavia made her feel that the group did not take the war as a priority. The silence about the war in the former Yugoslavia during the first few days of the conference also reflected a larger global issue during this period concerning the international community's silence and 'neutrality'. As the reality of the war in Croatia and Bosnia was not being acknowledged, felt and grappled with in this group, she felt isolated in her experience to the point of feeling she was losing her mind and grip on 'reality'. She later told me that, as she discussed this with my colleague, her feelings of anxiety and disorientation were immediately and almost completely relieved. Learning how one's personal responses connect to the larger collective dynamics can be extremely important and potentially relieving. The following day, she and others brought this to the foreground as a focus for the conference.

The wide problem of abuse in our society is another area where the problem of validation and accountability is crucial. When abuse (that has taken place) is denied, people often experience severe anxiety and a sense of fuzziness, as if living behind a veil of truth.

As long as we do not validate history, we all live in this kind of disassociation, feeling cut off from our own story and from ourselves. This dynamic supports widespread isolation in our society. This subject is dealt with further in Part 3 with respect to collective dynamics of trauma.

Conflicts often revolve around the fight for which version of reality is true. When people are validated in their experiences, they are often able to in turn validate others' experiences, even if the content of the experience is very different from their own. Apparently intractable conflicts can give way at this point to understanding and a desire to move forward. One task of the facilitator in communities or organizations in conflict is to validate all sides. This is not 'neutrality'. Rather it's the ability to feel and step into all viewpoints and to support a thorough interaction.

REPARATIONS

Acknowledgement may be insufficient if no reparations are made. Yet, at times, the crucial step of acknowledgement may not be made, precisely because we fear that, if we admit our wrong doing, reparations will be called for. Intractable and long-standing political, social, organizational and relationship conflicts frequently come to an impasse around these dynamics. One reason there has been so little public reckoning in the USA with the legacy of genocide of the Native Americans is that people fear opening up issues of land rights or the need to consider reparations. To avoid this territory, we keep the issues out of public dialogue.

ACCOUNTABILITY AS A FEEDBACK LOOP

Injustice does not gradually retreat into history. It can be passed through generations and stays current until someone stands accountable. When we refuse to assume accountability, the accounts stay open. Refusing to be accountable repeats the injustice.

When we are able to reckon with past and current injustice and assume some responsibility for it, interactions can shift dramatically to new levels of understanding, discourse and capacity to work together for community building. Being accountable creates a feedback loop for some sense of closure to be possible.

This can occur when political leaders stand accountable for their country. Willy Brandt knelt at the Warsaw Ghetto Rebellion Memorial to acknowledge and apologize for the German nation for the Holocaust. In community forums dealing with social and political conflict, an intractable and cycling conflict may transform when someone is able to assume responsibility and express feeling about their part in an injustice.

OUTSIDE THE LOOP

In personal relationships, when we refuse to be accountable, we feel isolated. On a political level refusal to be accountable leads to isolationism. Groups who have perpetrated injustice as well as those who have suffered injustice need a process of accountability. Staying outside the loop we contribute to a lack of closure.

On the world stage, the USA holds itself out of the loop of international accountability. Many Americans do not understand why the world is so upset about this and complain of anti-American attitudes.

American society has barely discussed its accountability concerning injustices carried out on their own soil, towards Native Americans and African–Americans, as well as injustices carried out by the US government's support of terror tactics in regimes around the world, from Nicaragua and Guatemala, to Greece, Argentina, Chile, Turkey and Indonesia.[1] Many Americans either do not know about interventions in these places or believe that the interventions were for humanitarian aims.

In 1986, the 'World Court', which was at that time the UN agency known as the International Court of Justice, considered Nicaragua's charges and ruled that the USA had violated International Law by training, equipping and financing the contra forces. Specific acts the Court found to be illegal included mining of Nicaragua's harbours and publication of a training manual instructing the contras in acts of terror that violate humanitarian law. The USA was called to desist and to pay reparations. The US response was to ignore the ruling and the whole thing was considered so insignificant in the USA that it was barely in the news.[2]

A lot of people in America know nothing about the existence of international conventions and treaties, let alone grapple with US refusal to take them seriously. One important example is the death penalty.[3] The USA refuses to acknowledge the goal of the UN to abolish the death penalty. Moreover, the USA continues to allow the execution of child offenders. The only other countries to continue this practice since 1990 are the Congo, Iran, Nigeria, Pakistan, the Yemen and Saudi Arabia.

ACCOUNTABILITY TO CONSCIENCE AND GOD

People with fundamentalist religious practice may insist on following religious law over secular law or international law. Although Islamic countries accepted secularism in government at the beginning of the twentieth century, in the late twentieth century there has been one trend towards returning to 'Islamic law'.[4] Some Islamic fundamentalists believe they are accountable only to Allah and will be rewarded for their actions in heaven. In the USA, there are large numbers of fundamentalists who believe that President Bush is following the word of God and his actions are therefore righteous and just, and there's no need for further questions of accountability or even discussion. Accountability is understood as a matter of doing what 'God' says is right, rather than a community process involving debate and democracy.

A leader who claims to be following God's word, and therefore does not have to be held accountable for any actions either at home or within the international community, is a great threat. Yet, it is interesting to consider the atrocities and injustice in our world that have occurred precisely because most of us do not dare to follow our own sense of morality, conscience or spiritual values enough.

We all too rarely follow what we believe is right, when it goes against collective norms. Yet, many of us believe that ultimately we must be accountable to our own conscience and/or to God, and must be prepared to challenge the law on ethical grounds. Those leaders and individual citizens who have risked their lives to take a stand against their own group or to speak out against oppression or act to protect the oppressed have often been able to do so out of a sense of accountability to their own conscience and spiritual values.

MEDIA AND ACCOUNTABILITY

The media face deep ethical issues concerning their accountability for accurate reporting. The media are controlled by economic and political dynamics within society and in turn set the pace of society's dialogue. As one example, the US government's complicity in terror tactics throughout Central America, to squelch democratic movements and support dictators, only appeared in bits and pieces in the US news over the years in such a way as to be readily covered over and denied. The full picture never emerged in the mainstream media, so that US citizens could reflect upon it.[5]

As a society, however, it's easy in turn to blame the media as another method of avoiding our collective struggle with issues of justice and accountability. We partially project our own lack of accountability as a way of taking ourselves out of the loop. We blame the 'system' not only out of hopelessness, but because we lack feeling for the stories that we would rather believe have nothing to do with us.

'THEIR' STORY

For groups that have suffered injustice and oppression, one of the most painful and chronic problems is that those who were directly responsible or those who stood by passively and/or benefited from the oppression feel uninvolved, as a result of dynamics of social rank and privilege. The story of an oppressed group is considered 'their' story, instead of 'our' story. In the USA, the histories of African American people and Native American people are increasingly included into history, but often in a limited way and only begrudgingly after strong advocacy from these groups, as 'their' history, rather than grappling with 'our' history.

People from Bosnia and Croatia have often told me that what was most excruciating during the war was their sense of invisibility, knowing that the rest of the world was just going on, business as usual, and didn't seem to care. The silent as well as active complicity of Germans, Europeans and Americans in the Holocaust left world Jewry to realize that no-one will care if they are sent to the gas chambers. This has certainly influenced the reactionary stance that is current in Israel. Nor has the world offered much feeling or awareness for the plight of Palestinians until recently. While Jews and Arabs in the Middle East are in a locked conflict, the Christian world has only occasionally broken its silence concerning its responsibility and accountability towards the history of anti-Jewish attitudes and atrocities towards Jews over generations, which in turn contributed to the current predicament in the Israeli–Palestinian conflict. As long as brutality and human rights violations go unaccounted for, as long as 'their' story (whether African American, Native American, Jewish, Palestinian, East Timor, Central American, Afghanistan) is not considered 'our' story, 'our' shared history cannot move forward. Without accountability, and without a feeling for and identification with our human community, the veins of history are clogged.

RETURN TO THE GANGES RIVER

Together with my husband, Jean-Claude, I learned a lesson about accountability one day in Benares or Varanasi, India. We were with a man who lived there, walking along the many Ghats, the wide steps leading down to the River Ganges. We sat on the steps on a Ghat in the late afternoon sun, feeling part of the flow of life along the river. Hundreds of people were bathing, doing yoga, kids splashing and laughing, boldly coloured saris laid out along the steps to glisten in the sun and dry, people brushing their teeth, praying, shampooing, chanting or carrying someone who had just died to the burning Ghat. In the blur of activity and stillness of the afternoon sun, there was suddenly a great commotion. A man shouted forcefully. Another shouted, and within a fraction of a second about 40 people stood together in a circle, surrounding one man and shouting loudly and fiercely at him, vigorously shaking their fists. It looked like we could expect an eruption of violence at any moment. Then, after about one minute of sustained shouting, as suddenly as it had all started, without any signal of de-escalation, everyone dispersed, and the afternoon along the Ganges continued.

We turned to the man we were with – what happened? He said that the man had stolen something. He said this was not like a theft elsewhere. Here, it was worse. An essential taboo was betrayed, because everyone came to the

Ganges to bathe and pray, and everyone had to undress and leave his or her things along the Ghats to enter the holy river. The community had to shout at him forcefully and quickly, in order to publicly humiliate him, so that the man would be able to return to the Ghats tomorrow. Otherwise he would be castigated and never be able to return.

The emphasis on 'so that he could return to the Ghats tomorrow' touched a chord in me, deepening my understanding of 'accountability' and justice. Along the Ganges in Varanasi or Benares, society looks much like it has looked for thousands of years. The continuity of community is what matters. Accountability was handled on the spot, in community, forcefully and speedily, and then life went on. The goal of 'justice' was for everyone to be able to return to the river.

SUMMERHILL TRIBUNAL

We were giving a seminar on conflict resolution in Suffolk, UK and discovered our seminar location was a few minutes away from Summerhill, one of the first and very renowned 'free' schools. We were invited to come to observe their

↓ **Figure 4.1** Return to the Ganges. (By courtesy of Laurenz Bobke, Wiesbaden, Germany: www.travelphoto.net.)

community meeting one afternoon, and scheduled a long afternoon break to make it possible for those who wanted to go. I was especially excited to visit the school, because as a child I had the book *Summerhill*[6] and kept it near my bed, reading and re-reading it, and looking at the pictures. I was taken by the notion of 'free schools' and the belief that children learn and are creative when supported to follow their own interests and make their own decisions, rather than to follow only outer discipline and authority. An essential philosophy of A.S. Neill, the creator of Summerhill, was that freedom did not mean infringing on the freedom of others and, in the school's beginnings and still now, community rules and the community meeting had a central role.

The meeting was already under way when we arrived, and we were ushered into a large room that was crowded with young people as well as their teachers, sitting on the floor, chairs and tables. We filed into the back and I found enough space to sit, crunched up on the floor. A girl or young women of about 16 was leading the meeting, which was in the form of a tribunal. In what was perhaps the most rapidly paced and efficient meeting I have ever seen in my life, for over an hour, situations calling for accountability were brought up for community review. These included things like someone squeezing toothpaste on someone else's mirror, taking a teacup out of the tearoom, smoking in front of the school and saying 'Fuck off'.

Everyone in the community had the right to say something, regarding the 'accusation', the relative importance of the offence, or to defend the person accused, or to explain why the event had taken place, as well as to make suggestions for retribution or contribute any other points of discussion. The kid who took the teacup out of the tearoom lost the right to drink tea for a couple of tea breaks, after a discussion about how many lost tea breaks was reasonable in relation to the offence.

At one point, a more serious problem of accountability came to the foreground involving some older students who had sent some younger students into town to buy something, which involved them being in town after dark. The girl leading the meeting quickly and fluidly said that she needed someone else to fill her role as moderator, because she was one of the older students being held accountable. After someone took her place to moderate, she then asked for permission to speak. She said she did not want to defend what they had done, but wanted to explain the situation fully. The whole community, including the young people who were involved, carefully looked at all angles of the situation, including the fact that a community rule had been broken concerning being in town after dark, whether the situation had actually been dangerous, the responsibility of the younger kids who knew the rules themselves, and particularly noting the responsibility of the older students who should have been models for the younger kids, but had misused their position of trust and rank. It was stunning to observe how the group dealt fluidly with all of the issues and had a very thorough discussion of the ethics involved.

Throughout the whole meeting, the kids were able to evaluate each situation thoroughly and incredibly quickly, without attacking one another, never 'poopooing' or acting defensive, yet standing for themselves and one another and assuming responsibility. After the meeting, as everyone left the hall, I saw a stream of kids running out to play, with all the energy, radiance and freedom I had remembered in the pictures of my *Summerhill* book. We returned to our seminar, and moved on to what was next on our agenda, the subject of 'accountability'. We felt lucky and really honoured to have received such a timely invitation to witness this tribunal.[7]

↓ **Figure 4.2** Summerhill meeting, 1930. (By courtesy of Zoe Neill Readhead, Summerhill School, Leiston, UK.)

BIG SERB, BIG CROAT

In 1996, in a large group of people of mixed ethnicity and war experience, a Croat, from a war-torn region said: 'How are we supposed to go now to the bakery and kiss our neighbours good morning on the cheeks, when that neighbour was probably a sniper shooting at us?' 'And how is everyone suddenly innocent, when we know that every man of a given age was involved?' He said there is no comfort in seeing the 'Big Serb' (referring to a warlord) and the 'Big Croat' embracing each other in the bars. An eerie feeling went over everyone, in his description of the warlords who had profited from the whole affair.

This unsettling picture of warlords getting rich and happy and feeling off the hook, while others are clouded in trauma and suspicion of their neighbours, reflects the urgency for accountability at various levels of society.

On one hand, it illustrates one of the ideas of the International Tribunals, that war criminals need to be held accountable, rather than be seen hanging out in the bars, in order for society to be able to begin a process of reconciliation, for life to go on at the bakery.

It is also eerie because it represents the tendency in us as individuals and as societies to try to smile and move on. Those of us around the world, who barely know or care what is involved in the aftermath of such tragedy, and barely grapple with any of our responsibility and lack of intervention, move on. All the people taken in the tragedy also must go on, holding all the pain inside in symptoms of trauma and chronic depression. With all good intentions, people speak of forgiveness, reconciliation and moving forward, without dealing with the thick atmosphere in the bakery and the complex issues of accountability throughout society. The international community moves on to the next country, the next war, and all but ignores the tragedy in its wake.

This group discovered that the 'Big Croat' and 'Big Serb' are in that sense inside of all of us. As important as it is for war criminals to be held accountable so that the rest of society can begin to interact again, so is it important for the whole society to interact and grapple with issues of accountability and responsibility, along with discovering more about our attitudes of dominance, refusal to take responsibility, and understandable wish to avoid and forget the whole business.

WHEN HISTORY STOPS

Just observe your own relationships to discover how keen you are to keep a conflict going one more round. Yet, you can also observe how much you wish to resolve conflict, to find closure, to resolve past hurts, and to find sustainability and reconciliation in relationship and community.

As facilitators in Croatia, Lane and I have been very moved by the extraordinary welcome we received. Naturally, participants may also be at first cautious, suspicious or hopeless at the thought of addressing the conflicts that have ripped apart their communities, personal lives and hearts. Yet, the welcome is immense, along with a willingness to get fully involved after this initial scepticism. I have come to realize that the openness of heart that we have been given as facilitators goes beyond hospitality. It reflects a hope and heart within the group that it's possible to find a way forward and the recognition that we must and can find a way forward. A sense of possibility is welcomed. At the end of the tether, people may be bitter, hopeless, angry, hurt and traumatized, but they have also seen more than enough of this, and are ready and willing to try something new. At a hot spot, a point of deep contention, when tensions are at their most extreme, when people are supported to stay with the interaction, awareness emerges from within the group that transcends and includes the opposing views, and facilitates a path forward.

When people have the opportunity to face issues of justice in a relational way, in actual 'real time' interactions among themselves, concerning past and present issues, conflicts can and do transform. Participants involved in such forums have frequently described the impact this has on their lives, making them feel a sense of hope in humanity that they never dreamed they would feel again, and an ability to work in new ways in their communities around the most difficult issues that they had thought were hopeless, intractable impasses.

DISENTANGLING GORDIC KNOTS

In our forums in Croatia, it seemed as though participants were trying to disentangle a gordic knot, discovering and pulling at the central threads of their emotions and perspectives, linked to personal war experience, community pain and trauma, pleas for accountability, and the need to explore individual responsibility and group or national responsibility and accountability. All the while, they also focused on humanitarian needs and concrete issues of community building from their fields of social services, education, law, human rights, medicine, psychology, economics, and community leadership and politics.

Some felt that the human and legal rights of return meant that no further discussions about accountability were needed. Yet, as mentioned earlier, how society actually dealt with reconciliation was intricately tied to community attitudes. If community attitudes and emotions were ignored, they appeared in constant blocks, red tape and episodes of violence. Reconciliation requires discussion about accountability, and the complex interplay between individual and collective rights and responsibility.

Accountability issues stemmed from different periods in the war. In 1991 Serb paramilitary backed by the JNA, the Yugoslav army, seized large regions of Croatia, regions that had majority Serb populations. In the ethnic cleansing that followed, Croats were killed and fled. In 1995, the Croat army seized these regions back, and at this time Serbs were killed and fled. In both periods, there were atrocities and war crimes. During all these years of war Croats, Serbs, Muslims and others suffered. In Bosnia, Muslims were victims of genocide from Serb paramilitaries and at times from Croats. Bosnian Croats (people from Bosnia with Croat ethnicity) were also targeted and fled to Croatia. Huge numbers of people were uprooted from their homes and communities, and after the war the region faced complex problems concerning issues of refugees, displaced people and rights of return. These issues often concerned housing. For example, during the war, many Bosnian Croat refugees, expelled from Bosnia, moved into Croatia and into houses that were vacated by Serbs expelled from Croatia. Returning Serbs therefore could not return to their homes, inhabited by Bosnian Croat refugees, unless they too returned to their homes in Bosnia. Many homes were also burned or ruined. The great difficulty in resolving the complex practical matters of housing clearly reflected deep problems of accountability and reconciliation.

In our forums, there were heated interactions about personal and collective responsibility. If someone spoke about the ill treatment of Serbs and also Muslims as minorities in present-day Croatia, someone else might counter that Serbs are actually getting special treatment as minorities in present-day Croatia, with support from NGOs (non-governmental organizations) and the international community. Some people found it aggravating that Serbs could consider themselves downed as minorities in Croatia, after having attacked Croatia and starting the war and ethnic cleansing in 1991. This was countered by the point that government agencies (as opposed to the NGOs) were purposely blocking the return of Serbs, by making complex tangles of red tape and by perpetuating hatred. Others might say that it is inadequate for Serbs to identify only as victims and minorities in Croatia, and that it is important to assume responsibility for the predominant Serb role in the destruction of the former Yugoslavia and for its attacks on Croatia, and understand why Serbs are not greeted warmly when they return. Others might express outrage at the request to assume collective responsibility, feeling this as an affront, based on an assumption that individuals have done something wrong solely because of their 'national' affiliation. They felt that each person should be seen only as an individual, with consideration of personal suffering and war experience, and basic human and legal rights of return. The outrage at identifying people with their nation ran very deep in a country that was torn apart through the manipulation of notions of ethnic/national identity.

A reply might be that communities simply cannot welcome people home without relating to collective/group responsibility. 'How can you expect our community to welcome you home as an individual, if you do not understand our need to ask questions, to get answers, and to provide answers to members of our community who don't know where their sons and lovers are buried? As a leader of my community, what shall I tell them?' Or 'Lead me to the war criminals in your community. Lead us to the mass graves still hidden, to the bodies we haven't found. Lead me to people in your communities who can answer these questions – only then can I stop being suspicious of the whole group, stop imagining the worst when I see you and treat you with the individual rights you deserve.' Someone might answer, 'But, even if we have leads, we will be too afraid to speak, afraid you will consider us guilty and further ostracize us.' Or, 'We will be seen to be betraying our own group.' The lack of accountability created distress, awakening symptoms of trauma. Similarly, the questioning and suspicion and the inability to return 'home' could also awaken war trauma.

ACCOUNTING FOR BOTH SIDES OF THE CONFLICT INSIDE US

In one group process, there was an atmosphere of suspicion and anxiety as such questions and accusations came forward. One person was in extreme distress. In a sweat and panic, he jumped up to leave the room. When we asked him if he could say something, he was able to say that he was terrified that treading on such volatile issues and painful territory could lead to a violent escalation of conflict that he could not bear. His own war trauma was triggered. We slowed way down to find out if this participant wanted to stay and if so what he needed to be able to say, as well as what each participant needed for the whole group to go forward in a way that would not exclude anyone, would take care of ourselves and would not re-traumatize. He said he wanted to stay. He also said he very much wanted this discussion to happen, but he did not believe it was possible. He wanted there to be a way that took care of everyone and the past trauma so many have suffered.

We appreciated him and valued his message as protective and important for the whole group. At this point, someone asked if she could speak. She described the tense atmosphere in their home communities and within this group created by the questioning and suspicion. She then said that she knew both the questioner and the questioned inside herself, the accuser and accused. She spoke movingly about a shocking and traumatic situation during the war, in which she had been forced to make a choice that did not only involve her own life, but had put her friend's life on the line. They had both lived through it. She described the pain of self-questioning that goes on to this day, about the risk she had taken with her friend's life. The group was touched, and then, one by one, others began to speak about their inner questions and doubts, and how they grappled with their own conduct under the pressure of the times.

Some spoke of their feelings of guilt about not having done enough to stop the atrocity. Several spoke about the terrible doubts and suffering they endured as they were faced with impossible decisions affecting not only them, but also their family and loved ones. One man spoke about being in the role of a public authority, having to make decisions that would have life or death repercussions for his whole community. As the group process went on, and as people shared the experience of their inner questioning – as both the questioner and the questioned – they talked very personally and intimately about the ethical questions and struggles they had concerning personal and collective responsibility.

The highly tense and explosive atmosphere of suspicion and judgement, the panic and jumpiness, the fear of opening old wounds and tripping on volatile issues transformed into a sense of deep concern and respect for one another and all they had gone through, in a process of reflection and accountability that was at once collective and deeply personal. The participant who had been so anxious was incredibly relieved, even elated, saying he never dreamed in his wildest imagination that this level of dialogue could ever happen in a group of Serbs, Croats and Muslims.

ACCOUNTABILITY TO OUR CHILDREN

In a group process one afternoon, some people began to talk about how, if they interact with people of another ethnic/national background (Croat, Serb and Muslim), or try to communicate and mediate between communities, they are seen as disloyal or traitors. Many people in the group recognized this experience and agreed to explore it further. The group jumped into an animated representation of how this occurs in their communities. The speed at which almost everyone jumped into this 'role play' represented the shared experiences they knew all too well. They rapidly formed two groups, and one person would try to physically cross to the other side, or communicate to the other side, and was quickly pulled back or expelled for being disloyal. Another would try, and the same patterns cycled and escalated. Then someone would try to suggest a new way of dealing with the problem, only to be rapidly and abruptly blocked.

This enactment of the roles became very real as anyone who attempted to suggest a new way forward was stopped cold. Everyone felt trapped in the stand-off between the two sides, in which no one was permitted to cross over. Tensions rose. Then a couple of people sat on the floor between the sides. They said, 'We are your children.' A moment of sober quiet came over the group and one by one several people, Serb, Croat and Muslim, told very personal stories about their own children and how they were split apart terribly by the post-war climate, and hurt in their neighbourhoods and schools. With tears in their eyes, they spoke about how their children had known only war. In that moment, everyone was on the same side and everyone wanted to be accountable to their children, for the world they were passing on to their children. They vowed to work together to find ways to take the risks needed to stand up within their own separate communities, in a way they had been unable to do during the war and until now. They were not only standing accountable to their children, but to one another for their past and future. They spoke about how they had often been unable to stand up to their own communities, as their communities were first aroused, preceding the war. They wanted to stand accountable to each other now and lend each other emotional support for the day-to-day choices they face and make in their communities, in order to build pathways to reconciliation and sustainable community.

SOLOMON AND THE BABY

The Old Testament story of wise King Solomon and two women in conflict about a baby is still contemporary. Two women fought over a baby, each saying the baby was hers. So, whose baby was it? King Solomon was asked to arbitrate, to decide whose baby it was. He meditated on the problem and said, 'I can't figure it out, but I have an idea – let's cut the baby in two'. One woman said, 'Sure, that's okay by me' and the other woman said, 'No, let her have the baby' and pleaded to spare the baby's life. Solomon then knew she was the real mother, because she was willing to give away the baby to save the baby's life.

This story holds a pattern for remembering that justice and accountability are intended to nurture community sustainability – much like the story of the Ganges, and the group process in which people stood accountable to their children. We have a 'wise one' and a 'mother' in us that can keep our eye on the baby, on sustainability for the future. One tendency in us is to take a strong stand, and to remain firm in this position at any cost, often in the name of justice. Solomon wisely knew that there is a different sort of justice and mothering that arises, just at the highest point of tension, when there is a threat to cut the baby in two. The mother chooses to save the baby's life over a decision in her favour. A task remains open about what to do with that part of ourselves that would cut the baby in two, that does cut the baby in two – that part of us that is not yet a 'real mother'. She also needs our care, to be mothered, challenged, her story heard, and given new patterns and pathways to deal with issues of accountability out of an interest in our sustainability.

FROM NUREMBERG TO SELF-REFLECTION

At the Nuremberg trials following World War II, Nazis claimed that they were doing their job, following orders. Most shocking was perhaps when there appeared to be no flicker of uncertainty, no mixed signals, no apparent self-doubt, remorse or soul searching.[8]

The horror of humankind's ability to follow orders was etched with a new dimension into modern history. Essential ethical discussions are raised when we stop to recognize that following orders is no cause for impunity. Ethical discussions about personal and collective responsibility have barely begun in our society. What does this mean for the rest of us who follow the mainstream logic, do not question too much and do not like to get involved? What about those of us who are not interested ('It's just politics'), are confused ('It's so hard to get adequate information') or feel hopeless ('There's nothing I can do about it anyway'). These attitudes can lead to gross violations of human rights. But, are they acts of injustice?

What we can say is that if we do not have such discussions fully as a society, we do an injustice to ourselves. To facilitate dialogues around accountability, we need to develop a fluidity of awareness around the positions in which we find ourselves, so that we can facilitate rather than remain stuck in conflict. Ethical and legal discussions are needed throughout society, concerning retribution, reparation, amnesty, multiple truths, filling in missing information, as well as grappling with personal and collective responsibility. Many of us are needed in a process of self-reflection, in our own hearts, in relationships, and within our organizations and communities.

INCLUDING HISTORY, RELATIONSHIPS AND RETURNING TO THE RIVER

During one forum in Croatia, a woman, usually outspoken, now spoke with a halting, and trembling voice. She spoke about the deep work they had done together, with accountability, reconciliation and community building. She said how much she appreciated the extraordinary friendships and closeness that had developed both during this particular forum and among those who knew each other from several forums. She said that their relationships meant everything to her. She needed to talk with the group about if – God forbid – such political events were to happen again, could we dare to believe we could depend on each other, on our friendships and all our work together? Another participant challenged her very strongly, 'How can you doubt our friendship or suggest that we could be divided again after what we have been through together in these forums?' The participant who raised the question said that she did not doubt their friendships and relationships, which now transcended ethnic or national boundaries, and which arose out of extremely deep experiences dealing with their most heated and difficult conflicts together. Still she wanted to point out that it was essential that they remembered to stay aware of their national and ethnic differences and history as Croats, Serbs, Muslims, Hungarians, Roma, Jews, and people of other or mixed backgrounds.

I remember these two courageous women, crossing the room to hug each other. Each carried an essential and far-reaching message of accountability and love. The woman who asked if they can dare to believe that their relationships could sustain political events brought a message that relationship and community must never be taken for granted. The strong feeling and friendship that arose from working deeply with issues that had split entire communities apart led to the realization that it is essential to be vigilant in heart and in an ongoing practice of awareness in relationships. Relationships and communities will be safer if we are aware of our diversity, including awareness of our collective history and accountability in relation to one another.

Her friend also carried a crucial message. She was vigilant in that moment, taking a stand for their friendship and against the ghost of doubt that can undermine us. There is a time to acknowledge what we have accomplished as individuals, in relationship and in community. That is also a form of taking stock, taking account. In this region, it was the manipulation of doubts that had set neighbour against neighbour into hell. We can stop history from repeating by working deeply with the dynamics of history, and noticing the transformation and new territory that we touch, when we step right off the wheel, in our own hearts, in our relationships and in our actions in community.

Part 2

Terror and The Spirit that Survives

CHAPTER 5
TERROR

To intimidate individuals, groups and society, you have to know what makes them tick. Tactics of terror are designed with an astute understanding of our individual and collective psychology. Tactics of terror have been used throughout history and throughout the world. Warlords and governments use tactics of terror in order to gain power, to stay in power, and to intimidate their own citizens or neighbours. The term 'terrorism' usually refers to tactics of terror carried out for political aims by groups that do not hold state power.

Terror tactics involve creating fear and instability and/or exploiting instability and our need for safety in order to crack down. Tactics of terror include demonizing the enemy and dehumanizing individuals and groups. Tactics of terror include torture techniques, designed to break the spirit. Tactics of terror include desensitization to atrocity, normalizing human rights violations, targeting leaders, targeting the soul of community, and the use of disinformation to suppress, dominate and arouse violence. This section begins by looking at the aims of terror and definitions of terror and then goes on to look at the specific dynamics of each one of these terror tactics and examples of its use.

Terror tactics are closer to home than we usually realize and include all of us. We take part in the experience of intimidation and terror when we feel we are without choice, without information and influence, forced or a part of a group forcing others.

We may be standing at the edge of a worldview defined by power and intimidation. This worldview may be crumbling. In addition to looking at how terror tactics are designed with expert knowledge of our individual and collective emotional lives, we touch on what it might mean to not feed and replicate this monstrous system, and to honour the spirit that survives it.

AIMS OF TERROR

Terrorism aims to destabilize society. State terror is used to destabilize a social uprising or revolutionary group, to take away its influence and feared or actual momentum. Terrorism is aimed at an audience, an attempt to be seen and heard[1] at any cost. State tactics of terror are also aimed at an audience, to get the message out, that movements of dissent will be suppressed by any means and at any cost. All through history, terror tactics have been used by governments and warlords, those seeking power and those in power with the aim of domination, by subduing the spirit and the capacity to resist of an actual, potential or imagined enemy, whether citizens of their own country or neighbours.

Empires and dominating regimes have always used tactics of power and intimidation in the name of ideological purposes. Our last century has seen unspeakable atrocity from Nazi occupation of Europe and the Holocaust, to Stalin's rule in the former Soviet Union, Mao's Cultural Revolution, the devastation of Vietnam, disappearances and terror in Central America, murder and atrocity in East Timor, and the genocide in the former Yugoslavia, Rwanda, the violence in the Middle East and the list goes on. International law and human rights organizations help to increase worldwide awareness about regimes that use tactics of terror in order to dominate, suppress and kill their own people or neighbours. Although the purpose of terror tactics is to dominate at any cost, the extraordinary level of violence in our history may paradoxically attest to a human spirit that will not be easily dominated.

DEFINITIONS

There is no agreed upon definition of terror or terrorism.[2] A point of agreement tends to be that terror is politically motivated and can be distinguished from violence within conventions of war. Definitions usually include that civilians are the target of the terror, though there is variation as to whether terror must be directed towards civilians or if it can include such things as an attack on a military base or a pipeline, and if it can include threats as well as actual violence.[3] The term 'terrorism' usually refers to terrorist strikes from extremist political groups, such as suicide bombings or the events of 9/11. In most discussions about how to define terrorism, state use of terror is not even mentioned. The words 'state-sponsored terrorism', and 'counter-terrorism' are often used, oblivious to or avoiding the question of state use of terror.[4]

It's interesting, however, if we return to the *Oxford English Dictionary*. The definition of terror is 'Government by intimidation'.[5] The definition of terrorism from the US State Department is 'Premeditated, politically motivated violence perpetrated against non-combatant targets by sub-national groups or clandestine agents, usually intended to influence an audience.'[6]

A definition of terror from the US Department of Defense is 'The calculated use, or threatened use of force or violence against individuals or property to coerce or intimidate governments or societies, often to achieve political, religious or ideological objectives.'[7]

The FBI definition is 'The unlawful use of force or violence against persons or property to intimidate or coerce a government, the civilian population, or any segment thereof in furtherance of political or social objectives.'[8]

A UN Resolution in 1999 reiterates that 'criminal acts intended or calculated to provoke a state of terror in the general public, a group of persons or particular persons for political purposes are in any circumstance unjustifiable, whatever the considerations of a political, philosophical ideological, racial, ethnic, religious or other nature that may be invoked to justify them.'[9]

All of these definitions from the US State Department, the US Defense Department, the FBI and the UN could be applied to state use of terror tactics as well as to acts of terrorism against states.

STANDPOINT OF TERROR

What may be more important than the ins and outs of definitions is to look at how 'terror' is understood according to one's standpoint. From the viewpoint of the state and perhaps much of society, terrorism is seen as the violence or threat of violence, usually targeted at civilians, by extremists. From the viewpoint of a political or social movement, uprising, revolutionary group or marginalized groups of citizens, terror is first understood as the use of special illegitimate and violent tactics on the part of government to suppress these movements, people and/or their messages.

States may use violent terror tactics against extremists or revolutionary groups that are armed or threatening terrorist strikes. Terrorists often identify as freedom fighters, fighting for their ideals, and are willing to kill and die for them. States may also have long-term violent conflict with such groups. States also use terror tactics against non-violent political movements, uprisings and normal unarmed citizens. We will see that one common tactic of state terror is to 'counter' terrorist threats by either exploiting the emotional reaction around a terrorist attack, or even creating a terrorist threat, in order to counter it, and to have reason to crack down. Sometimes a non-violent uprising later becomes violent, because the movement has faced state terror and suppression to such a degree that they come to believe there is no alternative other than to counter the state terror tactics with violence.

Nelson Mandela, in his autobiography, writes candidly about the period in which he determined and was in the end able to convince the African National Congress, the ANC, to let go of their absolute principles and policies of non-violence, because he deeply believed there was no other way to continue their work in response to the violent state terror tactics against the ANC.[10]

Terror tactics might be understood as an attempt to suppress what in fact cannot be suppressed. The despicable techniques used in torture suggest just how far we will go to try to break spirits that ultimately won't be broken. After the terrorist attacks of 9/11, people in the USA honoured a spirit that could not be broken by such a horrific atrocity. The so-called 'war on terror' has, in turn, emboldened a spirit that aims to topple the unilateral dominance of the USA.

TERROR AS A SYMPTOM OF A SYSTEM IN UPHEAVAL

It may be useful to look at terror tactics from a system's perspective. Terror tactics are a violent symptom of a system that needs renewal or is in upheaval. Terror tactics are brutal acts of intimidation and violence for political purposes which occur in both directions at the edge of an enforced political or ideological system.

When terror is aimed at suppressing social and political movements to maintain control, keep society 'stable' and enforce dominance, we need to take notice of the degrading and illegal tactics that are keeping this control. Yet, we might also ask ourselves as individuals and as society, how is government representing our need to assume control at any and all costs? What are we protecting? How do we suppress our own and others' dissent? What messages are being so strongly suppressed inside us as individuals and society?

When acts of terrorism aim to bust up the control of a dominating system, the system is already breaking apart at the seams. We have a tendency to become afraid, look for a sense of control, and get interested in power and retaliation with far too little interest and public discussion about the underlying processes of upheaval and change that are occurring. One way or the other, terror is a sign that the system is cracking and has been glued together by force.[11] The tragedy lies in the violence, atrocity and loss on all sides as the shell cracks. Talk of 'good' and 'evil' can only be expected, but as everyone identifies as the 'good guy', meanwhile a large public instinctively knows this fairytale is insufficient, if we are to stop cycles of violent conflict and begin to develop a civilized world.

STATE TERROR – IMPLICITLY OR EXPLICITLY SANCTIONED

An important distinction between state terror and terrorism is that, when states use tactics of terror, they can claim impunity more easily. The power lies with the state, which controls the legal institutions and military, and explicitly or implicitly sanctions terror methods. As we've seen, a main purpose of international, humanitarian law, however, is to not tolerate state tactics of terror. From the Nuremberg trials after World War II, which held Nazi commandos accountable, to the International Tribunals, trying warlords and national leaders in the aftermath of the ethnic cleansing and genocide in the former Yugoslavia and Rwanda, there is a movement for an international community to insist upon accountability and to not accept state power as an excuse for 'impunity'.

THE DIMENSION OF 9/11

9/11 changed the dimensions of terrorism and 'state terror'. The dimensions were altered because the terrorist strikes were aimed at the world's only superpower. The stakes were raised by the magnitude of the attack and the recognition that terrorists represent a significant threat and, because of the nature of the US government's response, its war on terror, its proclamation of an axis of evil and its subsequent amplification of tactics of intimidation on a world scale.

Images of planes flying into the World Trade Center and the Pentagon, and the towers collapsing, are etched into most people's memories. The US government seized upon 9/11 to declare its right and justification to use any tactic it wished in its 'war on terror', without concern for international law and international opinion. US domination on the world stage and disregard for international law is nothing new. Yet the unabashed exaggeration of this attitude post-9/11 accelerated concern and increased public awareness and dialogue about it.

Throughout history, when a state has wanted to impose its power, terror tactics have involved exploiting instability, cracking down and suspending or ignoring civil liberties, deemed necessary for purposes of seizing control and creating safety. This scenario is now played out in broad strokes, such that the USA, under the Bush Administration, claimed to be seizing control to make the whole world a safe place. The USA sees itself in the role of the controlling government of the world, and anyone or any country that disagrees is seen as dissident, on the side of the terrorists. 'On an axis of evil, you are with us or against us.' What at first seemed absurd, as Osama Bin Laden and Saddam Hussein blurred into one evil demon, soon meant the UN, the EU, French government or anyone else who would dare to disagree with US dominance was also demonized. When the UN Security Council resisted the US plan for a pre-emptive attack on Iraq, the US government used this as verification that the UN is 'weak' and 'irrelevant', further reason for the USA to see itself as the only powerful player on the world stage. And the USA expects to get away with impunity, because it has the might.

From one perspective the US-led 'war on terrorism' puts the USA in the role of the 'state' cracking down not only on terrorism, but on any disagreement by the world community, to prove its dominance. From another perspective, the USA, in its pre-emptive strikes on Iraq, in its calculated use of force for political purposes, is in effect acting as a terrorist, defying international law. To boot, President Bush identifies as a freedom fighter.

THE TACTICS

I use historical and current political examples to illustrate various tactics of terror in this section, while emphasizing how our individual and collective psychology is used as the raw material in their design. For example, when we don't know much about how the Bogeyman operates in the back of our minds, we easily swell with fantasies and fear along with the desire to give him a name and to know that he is being eradicated. Terror tactics, including torture, are not the cruel methods of shadowy figures that have lost their minds. These methods are calculated, tried and true, written up in manuals.

Chapters 6–14 in this section explore these terror tactics.

CHAPTER 6
TERROR TACTIC: CHAOS AND CRACKDOWN

CREATING OR EXPLOITING VIOLENT EVENTS TO CREATE AN EMERGENCY

At points of instability, we look for order and explanations. To gain control and power, one tactic is to create a crisis or capitalize on a crisis and the feeling that we can't afford the luxury of discussion, dissent or democracy. We're told that there is a state of emergency. We need heightened security. The government has to take secret action, or needs our solidarity for any and all decisions and actions it deems necessary.

EMERGENCY, AUTHORITY AND PROTECTION

Particularly when we feel insecure, we look to outer leadership and authority for guidance and protection, and put our judgement in the hands of experts who we believe can weigh things up better than we can. Even on a hiking trip, or working within an organization, at moments of crisis we know we may not have time for a debate, and naturally shift to a mode of doing what's necessary, either assuming leadership or assuming the willingness to follow someone else's lead. The problem is not that we naturally seek leadership, or that we rely on each other for expertise and protection. Our diverse opinions, often derived and distilled from trusted sources, are a potential for creativity and at the essence of democracy. The problem lies in our tendency to give over to authority without knowing it and without debate. The emotional and psychological factors that influence our judgement as to where we place 'authority' are largely unconscious. This psychological tendency is systematically anticipated and exploited to promote public terror.

We get frightened by erratic events. We panic. Once a sense of emergency is stirred up, it is followed by an explanation and/or a solution as to how to control it. Alternatively, 'unexplainable' events are used to amplify uncertainty, to make us seek analysis and reassurance from authorities. It also sets up an insurance of impunity of those involved. Later, no one is sure exactly what happened. Or 'it never happened'.[1]

State terror tactics can include planning and carrying out 'terrorist' events, designed to look like they have been carried out by the enemy group. Provocateurs and manufactured incidents are used to create an atmosphere of terror, for the purpose of making us feel that a crackdown is justified and any and all methods are acceptable, even if undesirable, to create order.

HITLER AND THE REICHSTAG FIRE: INSTABILITY AND CRACKING DOWN

Adolf Hitler became chancellor in January 1933. A rule allowed for the parliament to be dissolved, and new elections were set for 5 March. In the midst of intense election campaigning, a fire was set in the Reichstag building on the night of 27 February. A tremendous explosion occurred and the fire raced out of control. Immediately, the communists were accused of setting the fire. A Dutchman, a communist, was arrested on the spot and later tried and executed, accused of being part of a communist plot. There is still debate as to whether or not the fire was actually set by the Nazis. But what followed is clear. Hitler convinced the 86-year-old President von Hindenburg to proclaim a state of emergency. Freedom of speech and assembly were banned and death or imprisonment was ordered for crimes, including resistance to the decree itself. There were no guarantees for legal trials or counsel. By morning some 4000 communists as well as intellectuals against the Nazi party were arrested.

It was also decreed that the Reich could assume full powers if the federal government was unable to restore public order. On 2 March, a correspondent of the *Daily Express* asked Hitler whether the suspension of liberties was permanent. He answered that full rights would be restored as soon as the communist danger was over.[2]

All campaigning was silenced. Even the meetings of the Centre party politicians were broken up by brown-shirted SA thugs. Still, the Nazi Party fell far short of the two-thirds majority needed to change the constitution. Hitler now turned the decree of 28 February against those states where significant opposition existed. Using the argument that local authorities were unable to maintain order (while order was being disrupted by Brown-shirts and SS

← **Figure 6.1** Reichstag fire, Berlin 1933.
(By courtesy of Photo Archives: US
Holocaust Memorial Museum.)

members), the legally constituted governments of Wurtemburg, Baden, Bremen, Hamburg, Lubeck, Saxony, Hessen and Bavaria were replaced. With the support of the Centre, Catholic and Bavarian People's Parties, the Nazis gained the passage of the Enabling Act. Adolf Hitler became the dictator of Germany on 23 March, free from any restraint. The SS and SA had police power for state-sponsored torture and concentration camps were established for dissidents. Following on these acts of terror was the genocide of the Holocaust and the full tragedy of World War II.

The world watched what was happening as Hitler created and capitalized on instability in order to crack down in a bold claim to dictatorship that degraded (amid active and passive support within Germany and around the world) to one of the most atrocious periods of human history. Right at the beginning the signs were there, yet the world showed little concern or put aside concerns until much too late to avoid the horror to come.[3] In Germany, as Hitler swelled in power, so much of the public adored him, loved his power and with him swelled in a regained sense of pride. Hitler offered what the public wanted to hear, a promise of economic improvement in a terrible depression, as well as security, strength and the chance to be once again a mighty nation, after their defeat in World War I.

MILOSEVIC'S TACTIC OF CREATING AND EXPLOITING INSTABILITY IN THE BREAK-UP OF THE FORMER YUGOSLAVIA

Under Marshal Tito's leadership, Yugoslavia had become a virtual confederation after 1974, consisting of Slovenia, Croatia, Bosnia, Macedonia, Montenegro, Serbia, and the Serbian provinces of Vojvodina and Kosovo. Tito's leadership was pivotal and when he died, in 1980, he left a revolving 'collective presidency' to deal with political complexities and a climate of economic crisis. In Yugoslavia in 1981, Serbs represented about 36.3 per cent of the population, Croats 19.7 per cent, Muslims 8.9 per cent, Slovenes 7.8 per cent and Albanians 7.7 per cent. Other groups included Macedonians, Montenegrins, Hungarians, Roma (Gypsies), Slovaks, Romanians and Turks. The Serbian provinces of Vojvodina, a multi-ethnic region with a large Hungarian minority, and Kosovo, with a strong Albanian majority, were part of Serbia, but had some autonomy and voting powers in the federation.

Although Albanians were a majority in the province of Kosovo, they suffered from a long history of human rights abuses and lack of civil liberties. While Albanians looked for increased rights, and the federation was offering increased rights of representation, a Serbian nationalist movement arose in Serbia, with strong sentiments against the autonomy of these provinces. Serbia's economic problems relative to Slovenia and Croatia were blamed on 'anti-Serb' attitudes among the other federal states. The confederation was felt not to serve Serbia's interests. The rising nationalist movement, represented in the famous memorandum of the Serbian Academy of Sciences, and other nationalist publications, presented Serbs as victims of genocide, mixing together the genocide that had been carried out against Serbs by the Nazis and Croatian Ustase regime in World War II, and the Ottoman invasion of the Balkans in the fourteenth century, with the minority (in numbers) position of Serbs in Kosovo, and declarations that the Serbs were victims of a conspiracy to rob them of historical lands.[4]

Slobodan Milosevic rode and directed the surge of nationalism, rising to power in the League of Communists of Serbia in 1986. In Kosovo, Serb nationalists organized mass demonstrations by bussing in Serbs from Serbia proper. Milosevic realized that such mobilizations along with actual and manufactured street violence were keys to capitalizing on Serb frustrations and rising nationalist fury, creating the need for someone to come and seize control and power.

In 1988, the 'Workers Power' stated in anticipation of what was to come:

> The Serbian Communist Party has embarked on a pogromist crusade to end the partial autonomy of both Kosova and Vojvodina. At its forefront has been Serbian party leader Slobodan Milosevic . . . [who] has authorized a series of anti-Albanian and Greater Serbian demonstrations in Kosova, Montenegro, Vojvodina and Macedonia. He is campaigning for Kosova and Vojvodina to be brought back under direct Serbian control on the road to building a Greater Serbia within Yugoslavia. His politics are quasi-fascist.[5]

When the provinces called for republican status in 1990, Milosevic cracked down on the provinces' existing limited autonomy. When pressure mounted to hold multi-party elections, he called a snap election. He changed the name of the League of Communists to the Socialist Party of Serbia (SPS) and, with control over media and use of police force, ensured that no electoral rivals remained, taking 194 of the 250 seats in the Serb parliament.

Milosevic continually stepped up and initiated crises that enabled him to further his nationalist agenda. Milosevic's block to a multi-party political system in Serbia also played out on the federal level. The federation leaders refused to sanction Serbian repression of Albanians in Kosovo. Clashes and divisions escalated rapidly and led to the collapse of the League of Communists' Party of Yugoslavia in January 1990 and, over the next 12 months, the federation collapsed too, as the republics declared sovereignty. Few Serbs lived in Slovenia, but both Croatia and Bosnia had large Serb populations. Slovenia was the first to become an independent state with relative ease while the subsequent tragedies unfolded in Croatia and Bosnia.

EXPLOITING INSTABILITY IN THE DESCENT INTO WAR IN CROATIA

The tactic of exploiting instability continued. Croatia claimed independence. There was concern for what this would mean for the large Serb minority in Croatia. This concern was stirred into terror and violence.

In the Krajina region, Serb paramilitary leaders took over the police station in Pacrac. Croatian authorities and military stepped in. The Serb Army (previously the army for the whole of the former Yugoslavia and now controlled by Serbs) moved forces into Croatia saying it needed to 'separate the two sides'. Creating instability allowed for a crackdown to follow, all in the name of protecting the region. Milosevic organized an attack by Serb paramilitaries, and then had reason to go in with the army to stop the Croat authorities, in the name of supposedly protecting everyone from an ethnic dispute.[6] In 1991, as war moved into other towns and regions in Croatia, large numbers of Croats were killed and forced to flee, in what was to be the first round of 'ethnic cleansing'. Towards the goal of creating a Greater Serbia, and to ensure Serbian domination and control, Milosevic had set out to clear whole areas of existing populations. Tudjman in turn used the unstable situation to rise to power and further the Croat nationalist agenda.

LIVING WITH TERROR UP CLOSE

Tactics of terror did not create just the political instability needed for war, with the personal tragedies that followed of atrocity, torture, death and forced expulsion. Terror tactics caused instability in everyone's lives, inside minds and hearts. The terror tactic of creating and exploiting instability is internalized and creates unbearable anxiety, loss of orientation to community, loss of faith in humanity, depression and, within the uncontrollable stream of events, uncertainty, paranoia, attempts and failures to take control of one's own thoughts and emotions. Terror created distrust of others and of one's own mind and motivations, suspicion of neighbours, schoolmates, friends and loved ones. Friends, loved ones and families were torn apart. Terror tactics led to a plague of accusations, self-accusations, doubts and questions: Why did you leave? Why did you stay? Where did you go? What did you do? Could I have done more? Worries about survival, one's children and ageing parents were accompanied by long periods without sleep and living in heightened states of stress for days, weeks, months or years. Outrage at losing one's chance for an ordinary life was compounded by constantly being thought of only in faceless terms of one's ethnic background as 'Croat', 'Serb' or 'Muslim' by those close by and by the news in the outer world, as though you didn't have any digni-ty or value as a person, neighbour, professional, citizen or member of this world.

AND AT A DISTANCE

While those of us at a distance believed we were too far away to know what was really going on, and felt powerless to impact on world events, we were rarely aware that those up close, descending into war, may have known even less, and felt even less able to affect the course of events. We were rarely aware that our responses at a distance to the unfolding events are also anticipated and exploited as a tactic of terror. Terror tactics include the calculation that we will feel confused and disoriented and unable to follow the news, and will ignore human rights violations, within the chaos of events, accepting explanations such as 'they are just crazy over there in the Balkans' and 'the region has always been unstable and they are killing each other in some kind of chaotic civil war'.

CREATING INSTABILITY TO CRACKDOWN: MAPUCHE INDIANS IN CHILE

The Mapuche Indians are the largest group of indigenous people in Chile and over many years have been actively seeking recognition, including rights to territory. The government has used the state internal security law against so-called Mapuche 'terrorists' in repressive political actions.[7] The land was symbolically occupied in the autumn 2000, and individuals wearing hoods, supposedly Mapuche, were reported as having committed crimes such as attempted homicide, arson and timber theft. Many Mapuche were promptly arrested with the use of violence, terror and torture to obtain confessions. Houses were ravaged and many people were hurt. The Chilean press was primarily concerned with the supposed violent action of the Mapuche, rather than the crackdown.[8] An unverified assumption is that the hooded (supposed) Mapuche were not Mapuche extremists or 'foreign terrorists' or 'infiltrators' as propagated by the right-wing politicians, but provocateurs of 'conflict' for the purpose of a crackdown by the Chilean government.[9]

In May 2000, an article by Sr Villalobos describes the 'pacification' of the Mapuche as inevitable, because a 'meeting between a highly developed culture and a less developed one will always result in the former dominating the latter.'[10] This statement exemplifies the racist rationalization that has been used to support the use of terror tactics to dominate indigenous groups and oppressed peoples all over the world.

INSTABILITY AND CRACKDOWN IN GENOA – OVERREACTION OR TERROR TACTIC

Many people suffered terror at the anti-globalization demonstrations in Genoa, during the G8 gathering in the summer of 2001. About 100 000 people gathered in Genoa for the demonstration. Just after the demonstrations, which ended in one person killed and approximately 200 injured, and many more traumatized by what they witnessed, the reports from the mainstream news tended to describe demonstrations that had been taken over by violent protesters, ending in tragedy. Soon the reports of police brutality could no longer be overlooked, because of the number of reports being filed. But, even as the police brutality in Genoa came more into the open, it was seen as an 'overre-action' of the police against violent protesters.[11]

There were numerous reports about an incident in which a school building serving as the premises of the Genoa Social Forum, which was an umbrella group for some 700 groups in Genoa, was raided by police at around midnight. It was being used as a place to sleep, and many people had just bedded down in sleeping bags or were fast asleep as police came in and began to beat people up.

People who were there described a bloody scene in which people suffered heavy blows, including broken bones, broken ribs and a punctured lung. All photographic and video equipment was confiscated.[12] There were reports that police also removed hard disks from computers, indicating that the raids may have been for the purpose of getting the database and disrupting the organiza-tion. Some people were taken to the hospital and some to prison. Reports described people who were taken to prison with broken bones, forced to stand spread-eagled against a wall, spat on and urinated on by the police, along with other acts of intimidation.[13]

Four British demonstrators were kept for 4 days in prison, in inhumane con-ditions, without access to the consulate or lawyers, and then released without charge. One of the demonstrators, who had been severely injured, said that police had beaten people indiscriminately with batons, and that the people they were beating were offering no resistance. Police also sang fascist songs and threatened protesters with violence and rape.[14] One police source confirmed that demonstrators had been lined up and their heads banged against walls, and that police urinated on someone.[15]

Although these incidents did appear in mainstream news, some mainstream newspapers, particularly in the USA, barely mentioned the events. Several reports from demonstrators appeared on internet sites.[16] I heard a first-hand report of someone who was among those sleeping, who was woken up to a scene of terror, with people being beaten and blood splashed on the walls.[17] In the mainstream news, there was mention of 'police brutality'. Some journalists implicitly defended the police, attributing their 'overreaction' to the unruly demonstrators. European governments expressed outrage towards the Italian police and wanted to know why the police weren't better trained to deal non-violently with a protest. What I have not seen questioned in the mainstream news is how events in Genoa could possibly be explained by a police force overreacting. No matter which way I turn the coin, I cannot see how waking up people from their sleep to beat them up and confiscate their videos, cam-eras and files can be seen as a matter of 'overreaction'.

During a gathering of the G8, in which many of the world's leaders were in Genoa and there was a great deal of concern and readiness for violence and terrorism, it seems rather unlikely that policing of the demonstrators was just the responsibility of the Italian police. To describe the brutal attacks on demonstrators as 'police brutality' or an 'overreaction' ignores the likelihood that the police were employing terror tactics designed to create and exploit instability, in order to legitimize a crackdown against a growing anti-globalization movement, with its demonstrations over the past several years in Seattle, Prague, Genoa, Florida and elsewhere.

THE USE OF THE TERM 'TERRORIST' BY THE FBI TO SUPPORT CRACKDOWN

In the USA, the Federal Bureau of Investigation (FBI) was deeply involved in tactics of terror against its own citizens, in attempts to squelch political movements, notably the civil rights movement, the Black Panther movement and AIM (the American Indian Movement).

The Counter Intelligence Program COINTELPRO was a secret, nationwide campaign conducted by the Bureau from 1956 to 1971, for purposes of destroying 'politically objectionable' organizations. COINTELPRO's activities came to light in the early 1970s, with the release of FBI files that documented more than 2000 incidents of tactics used to 'neutralize' political dissidents. These included explicit acts of violence and degrading attempts to stir up hatred and instability within and between groups, making use of all manner of terror tactics to destroy movements and leaders of these movements. COINTELPRO was investigated by a special Senate committee, and the report from 1976 is now available to the public.[18] It says that, although the claimed purpose of these tactics was 'to protect national security and to prevent violence, many of the victims were concededly non-violent, were not controlled by a foreign power and posed no threat to national security'.[19] Many believe that COINTELPRO closed only in name.[20] (COINTELPRO is discussed further in Chapters 10 and 13.)

Immediately after the closure of COINTELPRO, the term 'terrorist' was applied to members of the Black Panther Party who had only months earlier been called 'agitators'.[21] Other terms, such as 'guerrillas' and, in the case of the AIM, 'insurgents', were also used. Some think that, although Americans were not happy with the FBI interfering in political diversity, they would accept the need for the Bureau to protect them against 'terror'.[22]

One striking example that illustrates the attempt to linguistically blur the notion of a 'terrorist' with social dissidents was the use of the term 'counterterrorism' to describe activities geared against the devoutly pacifist Silo Plowshares organization – committed to anti-nuclear/anti-militarism.[23] Several Plowshares' 'terrorists' were ushered into long prison sentences for such things as conspiring to trespass on a US nuclear facility.[24]

'Terrorist' investigations included many non-violent groups such as the Committee in Solidarity with the People of El Salvador (CISPES), Clergy and Laity Concerned, the Maryknoll Sisters, Amnesty International, the Chicago Inter-religious Task Force, the US Catholic Conference and the Virginia Education Association – opposed to US policy in Central America.[25]

9/11 – INSTABILITY AND CRACKDOWN

The emotional instability set off by the horrendous act of terrorism on 9/11 created a window of opportunity for reactionary leadership of the USA: 'You are with us or against us' on an 'axis of evil'. Mythic, archetypal stories of good and evil fit the collective dream-like state after being jolted from our everyday world. President Bush encouraged an urge for revenge, claiming that retaliation was justified and necessary to 'smoke Bin Laden from his cave'. Dissent was there from the beginning, but was slow in coming out, because there was a tendency to make people feel that they were not showing sufficient respect for the victims. As President Bush moved to bomb Afghanistan, he created a coalition, but refused to consult the UN Security Council. If we put aside the questions of whether or not the bombing was necessary, whether it was wise or foolish, justified or unjustified, whether we must consider and weigh the outcome of deaths and devastation from bombing or consider the lost lives as 'collateral damage' in a necessary intervention, the US government refused to share these questions with the international community. It determined to act independently and unilaterally, refusing to follow international law. It appears that President Bush could have got support from the UN Security Council and therefore his reason not to consult them was a declaration of unilateral decision-making.[26] The actions of the USA in the 'war on terror' can be seen as a clear example of exploiting instability to crack down, but on a massive and international scale. The USA claimed that it needed to crack down on the world stage, unilaterally.

In response to the events of 9/11, the USA detained 'enemy combatants' incarcerating them secretly and indefinitely without their being charged with any crime or having the right to legal counsel. Several hundred people were imprisoned in Guantanamo Bay, with the defence secretary declaring that they would not be released even if they were someday tried and found to be innocent.[27] Early on, Mary Robinson, head of human rights in the UN in 2002, and former president, Jimmy Carter, condemned these actions. Mary Robinson criticized that the 'T word' was being used as an excuse to crack down. She said that the USA, Russia and China were among the nations ignoring civil rights in the name of combating international terrorist groups.[28] Jimmy Carter said that a core group of conservatives is realizing long pent-up ambitions under the cover of the proclaimed war against terrorism.[29]

WEAPONS OF MASS DESTRUCTION

The work-up around 'weapons of mass destruction' in Iraq seems to have also been a tactic to exploit instability in order to crack down. The Bush Administration first mixed Bin Laden's attack of 9/11 and Saddam's tyranny in Iraq into a single evil force that had to be eliminated. Weapons of mass destruction gave cause for a pre-emptive and immediate bombing of Iraq. The USA made it clear that it would take this action, even if on its own. The UN and the international community tried to insist on continuing inspections to determine whether or not Saddam had weapons of mass destruction. Some questioned the wisdom of launching a pre-emptive strike on a country, even or especially if you think they have weapons of mass destruction that can be quickly deployed. Many assumed the real reason that the USA wanted to bomb Iraq was for political power and for oil. A huge anti-war movement gathered momentum as the USA prepared to attack. Yet many people were made anxious enough by the prospect of Saddam having weapons of mass destruction to consider that bombing might be necessary. Many Americans assumed that the urgency of the Bush Administration reflected a real and pressing danger. They wanted to put their trust and authority in the Government to evaluate the situation based on their intelligence and expertise. They had no trouble understanding that sometimes you have to take a stand. If we see this as a tactic of exploiting or creating instability to impose dominance and control, it was geared not only towards Iraq, but towards the American people and the international community.

MAGNIFYING OUR RESPONSE

Terror is aimed to terrorize, to magnify our reactions. It is aimed to create instability and loss of orientation. It is aimed to make us search for someone in authority to protect us. Our response to terror is extremely vulnerable to exploitation. Getting to know our responses to terror tactics is vital to not being unconsciously and neatly swept along. It is essential to explore how terror works on us psychologically, as individuals and communities. Knowing our response to terror means investigating how we react when afraid, the personal and community trauma that is touched, as well as our relationship to authority, how we adapt and follow what people say, or how we rebel or act against the authority. Getting to know ourselves in this way is necessary to be able to have thorough dialogue and debate within society about the essential meaning of our civil liberties along with our need for protection, rather than letting such issues get polarized and acted out between radical groups and reactionary leadership, while others quietly accept emergency measures and new laws that take away more civil liberties.

EXCESS FORCE: AN ISOLATED EVENT OR PATTERN?

In a country with strong ideals of democracy, when we hear a report about terror tactics on the part of police or prisons or in political violence, we tend to think it's an isolated event of excess force, rather than a cause to suspect that it may be pervasive and possibly policy. When we hear of civil liberties being removed, we may think it is temporary and probably needed. If we are members of a targeted group, the opposite is generally true. We may have heightened sensitivity to such patterns. When we hear of an isolated event, we consider the broader pattern. We may also err on the side of assuming a pattern when there isn't one. In fact, one of the problems that people who have been marginalized as a minority group often describe is that they have to continually worry and ask themselves if they are overreacting, over-generalizing when they suspect a prejudiced attitude or action.

If we tend to see a crackdown as an anomaly, it probably comes out of privilege, naivety, even an innocent good-heartedness. We may believe those on the receiving end of such human rights violations or brutality must have somehow deserved it. Or, we think tactics of terror and torture are wrong and we simply don't believe that they could be carried out by trusted authorities. Or, we think 'it must have been unavoidable in the current emergency' or 'it was a mistake'.

These responses feed and maintain a vicious system and are included in the calculations of terror tactics. A leader or warlord can speak the language of positive values, while committing atrocities, and large segments of the population will hear only the high ideals. Every fascist leader has done this. The USA is famous for talking of democracy, freedom and humanitarian aims, while committing human rights violations at home and abroad, and supporting dictators in acts of brutal oppression. Talking about humanistic values while ignoring our own actions and inaction is something we all do. We easily identify with our good intentions, while unaware of our own behaviour. This tendency, as individuals and communities, when unconscious, leaves us susceptible to 'leaders' who do the same.

We may take part in such tactics, out of our own need for safety and protection and our own need to feel innocent. We don't want to question our protector. Use of tactics of terror and torture on the part of government and police are not only horrifying in the actions themselves. The individual or group targeted is left with no protection. This also creates a climate for warlords or gang leaders to rise up, who often recreate the same oppressive dynamics, demanding compliance for protection.

CHAPTER 7
TERROR TACTIC: THE BOGEYMAN AND DEMONIZING

THE BOGEYMAN IS OUT THERE

The 'Bogeyman' is out there, and he will eat you up. Come inside and lock the doors and windows!

The Bogeyman is a part of our inner dreamscape, our fairytales and mythology, fantastic theatre and child's play. The Bogeyman embodies all that creates terror! The Bogeyman lies out there lurking, while we try to protect our innocence, lest we be eaten.

The Bogeyman story is of course a favourite for creating an environment of terror, demonizing an individual or group and proceeding to carry out human rights violations, or ethnic cleansing and genocide. Tactics are designed to stir up terror of the Bogeyman, to create and feed fear against and despising of a given group and the need for protection against their evil.

One way to understand the 'Bogeyman' is that we disavow and try to get rid of parts of ourselves that frighten us, parts of our own attitudes and behaviours. We project these parts of ourselves onto another individual or group, preferably someone or some group who is different from us, somehow unknown, or marginal to our group or society – who we must shut out at all costs. It's the premise of prejudice and xenophobia. We all do it. It's a part of our nature. When we have no awareness of it, this part of our psychology is easily stimulated. The Bogeyman looks to us like Jews, Blacks, Roma (Gypsies), homosexuals, the homeless, large corporations, Croats, Muslims, Serbs, Osama Bin Laden, Saddam Hussein and President Bush.

Before turning to the terrible stories of how our internal Bogeyman has been exploited to turn whole communities and nations into willing murderers, let's look at how our belief in and denial of the Bogeyman shape us.

Most of us grown-ups, the world over, imagine or pretend that the Bogeyman existed only in our childhood. Growing up, we deny the existence of the

Bogeyman. We lose access to mythic reality. The problem does not lie in believing in the Bogeyman. The problem lies in denying the Bogeyman's existence within its world of dreaming. The problem lies in not recognizing that this mythic dimension shapes our emotion and perception. The problem lies in our denial of the existence of the Bogeyman and the terrifying and exciting interior of our dreamscapes. Trying to act grown-up, we split off the Bogeyman story and its rich emotional substance into a notion of 'child's play', out of conscious reach, while we replicate the myth in our relationships and social and political interactions.

Children so easily join the world of mythological creatures, monsters, imagination and dreaming, full of passion and fun. They know these creatures are real, and yet they almost never mix things up, confusing the 'real monster' with the 'real person'. While killing the monster, they don't kill the person who is play-acting the monster. Children can also awaken in their healthy, loving parents and grandparents the urge to playfully gobble them up, without actually doing so.

In cultures in which ritual theatre and dance honour and enact the mythic realm, with all the awe and seriousness that it deserves, your neighbour might wear the mask of a demon in a terrifying dance, and you believe in the reality of that demon. It's not a game. Yet, after the ritual, you still go and borrow some flour or milk. He is still your neighbour.

← **Figure 7.1** Bogeyman, by Laura M. Anderson. (Bogeyman, terracotta H9' × W8' × L7, artist Laura M. Anderson, HC50 Box 5301, Red Lodge, MT 59068, USA: www.lauramarieanderson.com.)

In *No Go the Bogeyman*, author, Marina Warner, tells a story:

A mother who took to heart urgings that adults should always treat children's imaginings with respect responded seriously to her daughter's worries one night that there was something under the bed: she looked under it, then made believe she found an intruder, hauled him out, hustled him down the stairs, opened the front door threw him out, slammed the door, and came back up again, dusting off her hands and saying 'Well, we truly got rid of him', only to find her little girl whey-faced in the bed, asking 'Mummy, was there really someone under the bed?'[1]

The mother's attempt to join the world of make-believe of her daughter is at once touching and sobering. One way to understand this is that the daughter needs to know that her mother is safely in the world of 'reality', in order to be free to dream. By making the threat 'real' in order to play along, and to get rid of the threat for her daughter, she inadvertently terrified her daughter who trusted her to know the difference between mythic threats and consensus reality threats. By making it 'real', the daughter's 'pretending' or dreaming was not supported at all! She temporarily lost her freedom to dream about scary things. She could no longer play-act the scary monster, or hide from it under the covers, or cuddle and feel the warmth of her mother or Teddy bear. It became dreadfully 'real'.

This little anecdote of make-believe and reality is far-reaching. Our problem does not lie in the myths of the Bogeyman. If we could nourish the mythic and emotional world, we might develop a relationship to it, fighting our nature, embracing our nature, making contact with ourselves, and our deepest experiences of fear, courage, the capacity to be 'bad', and to protect ourselves. The problem – and it is a very 'real' problem – lies in the fact that we lose access to the richness of our dreaming and emotional world, and are easily duped into actualizing Bogeyman scenarios, in which they become terrifying political, social and personal realities.

It's a mix-up of parallel worlds. Now get under the covers and shut the windows, while I tell you this: the Bogeyman, like all mythic, dream and ghost figures is real. The most exciting thing of all is that the Bogeyman is free-floating, travels through time and history, floats through every village and nation of

→ **Figure 7.2** *Max and Moritz*, a 1925 children's book by Wilhelm Busch (original images hand coloured 1870). 'Mischievous Max and Moritz fall in the dough. The baker doesn't notice and puts them in the oven.' (Diogenes Verlag AG, Zürich; published 1977.)

this world. He slips through your window, into your heart, just when you thought you were finally feeling safe. He appears in your neighbours, your partner or the news, and in your own urge to tear someone apart. The mythic world is real and it governs our individual and collective emotional responses and interactions. If you get to know yourself, your deepest fears under the covers, and that scary part of you lurking under your bed, and if you engage with friends and community, going into the things that you fear, with courage and trepidation, shyness, nastiness, unpredictability and heart, the 'real world' transforms. It becomes richer, less two-dimensional, more mythic and passionate in dimension. You feel in touch with life and with people in your life. And the mythic dimension alters too. It becomes more human, as we take responsibility for its forces.

The Bogeyman appears in legends, crossing cultures, touching our deepest fears about our own wild and unknown nature, what lies under the bed, around

→ **Figure 7.3** The Bogeyman, Doyle R., about 1890. 'The Bogeyman collects his victims in a basket.' (By courtesy of The Fitzwilliam Museum, University of Cambridge, UK.)

the corner. The Bogeyman appears as the devil, goat men, satyrs and trolls. Windigo is a tall forest-dwelling wild man from a North American Algonquian legend, who eats people, especially naughty children. This mythic reality is readily exploited in the name of morality, to intimidate kids and get them to behave. The child is warned, if you are a naughty boy, the Bogeyman will eat you! Naughty children in Russia and eastern Europe were threatened that Baba Yaga was coming to take them away. Baba Yaga was also a wise woman, but, in her ogress form, she would steal children and cook them in a pot – reminiscent of the witch in Hansel and Gretel. Santa Claus knows whether you are naughty or nice. In the Netherlands, St Nicholas had an assistant 'Black Peter'. St Nicholas and Black Peter bring gifts and candy to good boys and girls, but Black Peter takes away the bad boys and girls. (The Bogeyman status here is assigned to a black man.)

The threat of the Bogeyman goes beyond threatening naughty boys and girls, as we begin to look at how the myth of the Bogeyman is used as a terror tactic to incite hatred, expel communities and promote genocide. The dynamic and potentially creative interconnection of our mythic reality and our consensus reality are exploited intentionally and ruthlessly.

↓ **Figure 7.4** Propaganda slide entitled 'Punishments of Hell', Berlin about 1936. Lecture given by 'Der Reichsführer SS, der Chef des Rasse und Siedlungshauptamtes' (the Leader of the SS, Chief of the Race and Settlement Main Office). The lecture was called 'Das Judentum, seine blutsgebundene Wesenart in Vergangenheit und Gegenwart' (Jewry, Its blood-based Essence in Past and Future). (By courtesy of the US Holocaust Memorial Museum.)

EATING CHILDREN – JEWS AS THE BOGEYMAN

In the middle ages and even to this day, in a classic Bogeyman tale, people thought that Jews killed and ate children. A friend in central Europe told me that he still met people in his psychotherapy practice who believe this today, literally.

Jews were charged with ritual murder of Christian children. Norwich, England in 1144 saw the first recorded case of an allegation of ritual murder of Christian children. A century later, the myth of blood libel grew out of the ritual murder belief. The claim was that Jews used the blood of Christian virgins on Passover for ritual purposes, in baking matzo (unleavened bread) or to drink as wine.[2]

This myth is still perpetuated today. An article in a recent Saudi daily newspaper described how Jews use blood to bake pastries for the holiday, Purim. It reads: 'I chose to [speak] about the Jewish holiday of Purim, because it is connected to the month of March. This holiday has some dangerous customs that will, no doubt, horrify you, and I apologize if any reader is harmed because of this.' It goes on to say that Jews prepare pastries that require a special filling made of blood from a Christian or Muslim. It goes on and on in excruciating detail about how the pastries are made and the blood extracted. This article could only have been intended to arouse Bogeyman fears and intense hatred. The article was translated in the western media, and after harsh criticism the editor published an apology.[3]

RACE, VIOLENCE AND THE BOGEYMAN

A children's book, from Germany, dated 1936, concludes: 'The devil is the father of the Jew. When God created the world, He invented the races: the Indians, the Negroes, the Chinese, and also the wicked creature called the Jew.'[4] The Bogeyman myth was used not only to condemn a race, culture, religious or ethnic group, but was imbedded in the very development of theories of racial groups and the use of racial theories to condone exploitation and genocide of groups considered racially inferior. Social Darwinism supported the notion that some groups were less evolved and incapable of civilization. Howard Winant writes: 'Though intimated throughout the world in innumerable ways, racial categorization of human beings was a European invention. It was an outcome of the same world-historical processes that created European nation-states and empires.'[5] Swallowed in a Bogeyman myth, we become the Bogeyman without awareness of our own violence, projecting 'wildness' on to those who we are killing. Indigenous people all over the world have been considered 'wild' and 'primitive', while being ruthlessly exploited and killed for the development of so-called 'civilization'.

← **Figure 7.5** 'Murder of Miss Jane McCrea AD 1777', an 1846 painting by Currier and Ives. (The event from 1777 became mythic, demonizing Indians.) (By courtesy of the Library of Congress, Washington DC, USA.)

BLACK MEN AS THE BOGEYMAN

In the USA, black men were frequently falsely accused of raping white women. Without trial, they were routinely lynched. Those doing the lynching committed unspeakable acts of violence, while identifying as protecting the innocent from the Bogeyman. To this day, projections and stereotypes of the black man as wild and violent make blacks the targets of harassment, false arrests and being despised.

THE BOGEYMAN AND HOMOPHOBIA

Members of disliked minority groups are often stereotyped as representing a danger to the majority society's most vulnerable members, particularly women and children. Gay men have often been seen as the Bogeyman, considered criminal, mentally deranged and, above all, child molesters. The fear of the Bogeyman is aroused as a result of fear of homosexuality and fear of children losing their innocence. The unsubstantiated claim and outright lie that gay people are more prone to child molestation (with plenty of research to show otherwise[6]) has deeply hurt gay people, who are anyway faced constantly with homophobic attitudes and stereotypes in families and community.

When Anita Bryant campaigned successfully in 1977 to repeal a Dade County (FL) ordinance prohibiting anti-gay discrimination, she named her organization 'Save Our Children', using the myth of the Bogeyman who threatens to snatch children away. Anti-gay activists have routinely asserted that gay people are child molesters. In debates about the Boy Scouts of America's policy to exclude gay scouts and scoutmasters, this stereotype is raised.[7]

THE BOGEYMAN AS COUNTER-REVOLUTIONARIES

In the Cultural Revolution in China, in the 1960s,[8] Mao urged students to take part in the People's Revolution. These young people had grown up with Mao almost a God. What Mao said was right. Now, he was declaring that the communist party and much of the current leadership were blocking the progress of his revolution. He urged young people to topple the local leadership in their communities. Those people to be targeted were named counter-revolutionaries. They were the Bogeyman. They threatened the values of the people and of the revolution. Young people ransacked old people's homes, humiliating them and killing them. One interviewee described how she arrived at the home of an old man who had been beaten to death by a group of her peers. She saw him just after he died. She said she did not give it much thought at the time, because this was common and wasn't questioned. But, later, she said the question haunted her, whether or not she would have participated in the beating and murder had she arrived some moments earlier. She felt she was never able to answer this question. Yet, later, when she disagreed with friends about the statement that Mao was always right, she was castigated by her peer group and didn't speak to anyone for a long time.[9] She became the Bogeyman, the outsider – the one who doesn't identify as one of us and is a threat to our community or movement.

IN CAHOOTS WITH THE BOGEYMAN

The Bogeyman myth is exploited as a tactic of terror for political purposes. It works not only to arouse hatred and despising of a particular group to be blamed and accused for the problems of a community, but also to demand loyalty to one's own group. If you do not stay in line with the predominant movement of the community, you will be suspected of being a Bogeyman, or being in cahoots with the Bogeyman. This also takes place within social activist movements, in which

←↓ **Figure 7.6** Cultural Revolution, China, about 1966. Cartoons depict crimes of intellectuals. Text reads 'The Cultural Revolution Magazine' 'Zhang Zheng, an agent guilty of most heinous crimes' 'Doctors pretend to cure women but molest them' 'The cause of illness is due to owning the land'. (By courtesy of the Hoover Institute, Stanford University, CA.)

members may fall under suspicion for undermining the movement, as outsiders/Bogeymen. This dynamic is then exploited through the common use of infiltrators in social movements, as a tactic of state terror. Not knowing much about one's own Bogeyman makes us more easily susceptible to such tactics.

CARTOONS, JOKES AND SPORTS MASCOTS

A favourite method of stirring up the Bogeyman myth is the use of caricatures and cartoons. The use of cartoons with amplified, humorous or distorted features touches on the mythic source of the Bogeyman. The traditional use of masks makes use of distinctive facial features or ritualized movement to access an archetypal character, and a charged, mythic atmosphere, transporting the participants and observers into mythic reality. Cartoon images blend the mythic world and the targeted individual or group to be despised. They may appear light-hearted in style, playful, funny, covering the violence underneath. Perhaps for this reason, jokes that put down women, blacks, gays and other ethnic communities are often thought of as 'just a joke'. Often people are insulted that their joke is considered oppressive, and think such reactions stem only from political correctness.

In slogans, catch phrases and cartoons, the native inhabitants of North America were referred to over time, and still now, as wild savages. A current issue in schools around the USA concerns the use of Indian mascots to represent sports teams. One such team, with a 'wild' Indian mascot, is called 'the Savages'.[10] The local small community became riled at the idea that this should be seen as racist or even insulting, taking pride in their sports team and the long identification with the mascot. Although Native American and civil rights groups speak out against the use of mascots, their use persists both naively and defiantly.

→ **Figure 7.7** 'Where is the Honor', Committee of 500 Years of Dignity and Resistance. (Chief Wahoo is a mascot of the Cleveland major baseball team. They persist on using it, although there is active demonstration against its negative stereotyping.) (By courtesy of Committee of 500 Years of Dignity and Resistance, PO Box 110815, Cleveland, OH 44111: www.geocities.com/com500years.)

Bogeyman effigies

Cartoon characteristics of the appointed Bogeyman appear in large posters and signs, and in effigies, also reflecting the mythic and numinous Bogeyman. After 9/11, Osama Bin Laden and President Bush were respectively seen as the Bogeymen of our times. Just as Bin Laden was demonized to arouse a spirit of retaliation, effigies of the Bogeyman Bush were set on fire and stamped upon.

Bogeyman terms and slurs

Racist slurs reflect racist attitudes and perpetuate racist attitudes. Slurs refer to the Bogeyman, not to an individual. Racist remarks are like propaganda, used to identify an individual or group with the Bogeyman. African Americans have endured an endless range of racial slurs. In the former Yugoslavia, as we've seen, Croats were called 'Ustase' to associate them with the fascist Ustase regime, arousing Bogeyman fears, and Muslims were sometimes associated with the Bogeymen invaders of the fourteenth century.

The term 'Balkanized' is defined as 'to divide a region or territory into small, often hostile units'.[11] The term comes from the political division of the Balkans in the early twentieth century. The term also reflects ingrained attitudes that people in the Balkans have a hostile character, feeding the kind of misinformation and disinformation that occurred throughout the war in the Balkans in the 1990s, that the war was somehow a result of simmering ethnic rivalries and long-suppressed hatreds, clichés that supported the world to assume it was inevitable, and nothing could be done.

Many of us, who are good-hearted and intelligent, upset about the violence in our world and devoted to peace, see ourselves as without prejudice. We see the Bogeyman now in the 'racist', the 'fascist', the 'state', 'politicians', and we easily let go of the problem of reckoning with what makes us tick, and how we take part.

TAKING ON THE BOGEYMAN

One way to understand the Bogeyman myth is that in our identification with innocence, we split off and feed our own violent nature, while acting at the mercy of it. Another way to consider the myth is that we are that Bogeyman, behaving in very dangerous ways, threatening our children and future. We need to grow out of this naive identification of being as innocent as children, in relation to the violence in our world. We need to 'eat up' the identification with being 'good', while 'evil' lurks outside. We need to step into the unknown, with some combination of innocence and courage, to get to know ourselves, each other, and our dreams.

Chapter 8

Terror tactic: dehumanization

A widely used terror tactic is to dehumanize, to portray an individual or group as an infestation that has to be exterminated. Demonizing stimulates our fear of the unknown. Dehumanizing urges us to kill or makes it possible to do so.

Cockroaches and rats

In Rwanda, 7 and 8 April 1994, the RTLM (Radio Television des Milles Collines) set off the genocide, broadcasting, 'You have to kill [the Tutsis], they are cockroaches . . .'. On 2 July: 'I do not know whether God will help us exterminate [the Tutsis] . . . but we must rise up to exterminate this race of bad people. . . . They must be exterminated because there is no other way.'[1]

The Nazis depicted Jews as an infestation of rats in a propaganda campaign with the aim of dehumanizing Jews and preparing the German nation for their exclusion and extermination. The film *Der Ewige Jude* ('The Eternal Jew'), a well-known propaganda film, was produced at the insistence of Joseph Goebbels.

The film shows rats and says: 'Wherever Rats appear, they bring ruin, by destroying mankind's goods and foodstuffs. In this way, they [the rats] spread disease, plague, leprosy, typhoid fever, cholera, dysentery and so on. They are cunning, cowardly and cruel and are found mostly in large packs. Among the animals, they represent the rudiment of an insidious and underground destruction.'

The film then goes on to show pictures of a Jewish man and smiling boy, and says: 'Just like the Jews among human kind.'

At another point the film says: 'Under the leadership of Adolph Hitler, Germany has raised the battle flag of war against the eternal Jew.' With pictures of statesmen and cheers by young Germans, it promises 'the annihilation of the Jewish race in Europe!' It says 'the eternal law of nature, to keep one's race pure, is the legacy which the Nationalist Social movement bequeaths to the German people for all time.'[2]

← **Figure 8.1** *Der Gift Pilz* (*The Poisonous Mushroom*), an anti-Jewish children's book, published by Julius Streicher. (By courtesy of Randall Bytwerk, German Propaganda Archive: www.calvin.edu/cas/gpa/.)

„Wie die Giftpilze oft schwer von den guten Pilzen zu unterscheiden sind, so ist es oft
sehr schwer, die Juden als Gauner und Verbrecher zu erkennen…"

← **Figure 8.2** *Der Gift Pilz* (*The Poisonous Mushroom*). The caption under the picture reads 'Just as it is often difficult to separate the poisonous mushrooms from the good ones, it is also often difficult to distinguish the Jews as crooks and criminals'. (By courtesy of Randall Bytwerk, German Propaganda Archive: www.calvin.edu/cas/gpa/.)

RAT ON A RAT – A LONDON DRUG PROGRAMME

In London, I was walking down the street one afternoon and saw a large poster with a cartoon-like picture of a rat. The poster said 'Rat on a Rat', 'Drug Dealers Ruin Lives'. I got upset. It's a great thing that a community is trying to deal with its drug problem and it turns out this was a large and successful campaign in London, according to the Metropolitan Police over a period of a couple of years – 2000 and 2001.[3] The campaign later went to other places in the UK. I could easily imagine that the design was meant to counteract the problem of people holding back information that could be crucial to the life and safety of the community. I assumed it was intended to counteract the way kids are enticed and coerced into using drugs, which are wrecking community, ruining lives and killing people. At the same time, I was alarmed to see an image of a rat used in this campaign. I don't believe such tactics can help in the long-term building of a humane community. The use of images and descriptions of rats is reminiscent of tactics of dehumanization. The campaign dehumanized drug dealers. Probably no one would disagree with that. Some might say, why not?

↑ **Figure 8.3** Poster for 'Rat on a Rat' Campaign to crack down on drugs. Metropolitan Police, London. (Courtesy of the Metropolitan Police, London.)

DEHUMANIZATION OF NATIVE AMERICANS

Native Americans were dehumanized throughout history to support and excuse their extermination. Stannard says that, in 1492, it's estimated that there were no less than 75–100 million people in the hemisphere, with approximately 8–12 million north of Mexico. He says some well-respected researchers estimate around 145 million for the hemisphere and 18 million for the area north of Mexico.[4] Churchill states the hemispheric figure was approximately 125 million. Population loss among native societies routinely reached 90–95%.[5]

George Washington, the first president of the USA, said that Indians 'were wolves and beasts who deserved nothing from the whites but total ruin'.[6]

Thomas Jefferson urged the USA to 'pursue Indians to extermination, or drive them to new seats beyond our reach'.[7, 8]

By 1717, all New England colonies paid bounties for scalps of Indians. Massachusetts rescinded its Scalp Act in 1722 on grounds that it was 'ineffectual', but later reinstated it by popular demand in 1747.[9]

Andrew Jackson was elected president in 1828. He boasted that he had 'on all occasions preserved the scalps of my killed'.[10] He supervised the mutilation of some 800 Creek Indian corpses – men, women and children whom he and his men had massacred. He cut off their noses to count and record the dead, 'slicing long strips of flesh from their bodies to tan and turn into bridle reins'.[11] It's revolting to even write such stories. Yet, people in the USA have all too rarely reckoned with the reality of this history and the ongoing story of human rights violations, while ignoring questions of land rights. Jackson urged American troops to root out from their 'dens' and to kill Indian women and their 'whelps'.[12] In his second annual message to Congress he said that, while some people get 'melancholy' about Indians being driven by white Americans to their 'tomb', an understanding of 'true philanthropy reconciles the mind to these vicissitudes, as it does to the extinction of one generation to make room for another'.[13] This attitude won him elections. When he took land from the Cherokee, they managed to resist, and even won their case before the US Supreme Court. Jackson challenged the court saying, 'John Marshall [of the Supreme Court] has made his decision, now let him enforce it.'[14]

Theodore Roosevelt in a speech in 1886 said: 'I suppose I should be ashamed to say that I take the western view of the Indian. I don't go as far as to think that the only good Indians are dead Indians, but I believe 9 out of 10 are, and I shouldn't like to inquire too closely in the case of the 10th.'[15]

The abominable expression persisted over time – 'the only good Indian is a dead one'. The image of the savage Indian not only reflected Bogeyman fears. These 'savages' inhabited the land and stood in the way of the white man's right to expansion.

In March to April 1971, 3 years after the My Lai massacres in Vietnam, a congressional committee took testimony on war crimes. Congresswoman Mink asked Robert B. Johnson, Captain, US Army, West Point Class of 1965: 'You made a statement that in your opinion the My Lai massacre was the inevitable consequence of certain policies. Would you specify what policy you make reference to with regard to the killing of POWs?' Johnson replied: 'First, the rational policy, that is "the only good gook is a dead gook", very similar to "the only good Indian is a dead Indian" and "the only good nigger is a dead nigger" ... "We used the term Indian country". The notion of killing "savages" was part of an attitude of bombing villages, forcing civilians into detention camps, and that one should kill "anything that moves" in free-fire zones.'[16]

In the Aberdeen *Saturday Pioneer*, a weekly newspaper in Aberdeen, South Dakota, 15 December 1890, just after the assassination of Sitting Bull, an article reads:

> *Sitting Bull, most renowned Sioux of modern history, is dead. He was an Indian with a white man's spirit of hatred and revenge for those who had wronged him and his. In his day he saw his son and his tribe gradually driven from their possessions: forced to give up their old hunting grounds and espouse the hard working and uncongenial avocations of the whites. And these, his conquerors, were marked in their dealings with his people by selfishness, falsehood and treachery. What wonder that his wild nature, untamed by years of subjection, should still revolt? What wonder that a fiery rage still burned within his breast and that he should seek every opportunity of obtaining vengeance upon his natural enemies.*

It continues:

> *The proud spirit of the original owners of these vast prairies inherited through centuries of fierce and bloody wars for their possession, lingered last in the bosom of Sitting Bull. With his fall the nobility of the Redskin is extinguished, and what few are left are a pack of whining curs who lick the hand that smites them. The Whites, by law of conquest, by justice of civilization, are masters of the American continent, and the best safety of the frontier settlements will be secured by the total annihilation of the few remaining Indians. Why not annihilation? Their glory has fled, their spirit broken, their manhood effaced; better that they die than live the miserable wretches that they are. History would forget these latter despicable beings, and speak, in later ages of the glory of these grand Kings of forest and plain that Cooper loved to heroism. We cannot honestly regret their extermination, but we at least do justice to the manly characteristics possessed, according to their lights and education, by the early Redskins of America.*[17]

Sadly, the editor and publisher of *Aberdeen Pioneer*, who advocated genocide, was L. Frank Baum. A decade later, his book *The Wizard of Oz* (1900) would become a beloved classic.[18] Robert Venables wrote that he first received the microfilm of this *Aberdeen Pioneer* article in 1976 and believed he would find editorials that protested the massacre at Wounded Knee. After mulling the documents over for 14 years, he says he tried to read the terrible articles as satires or parody, but they are not. He notes that he still loves the Oz books and movie.

Venables also comments that we can guess that calls for genocide were not aberrations but widely held. Yet, such an attitude cannot be only passed over, as part of another time. As far back as the 1500s, Europeans in America spoke out against treating Indians in subhuman ways. When the army massacred Indians in the west, newspapers reported the crimes and many people were outraged. Commissions were established to investigate.[19]

Another reason we sadly cannot assign such attitudes to the past is because they are still current. A feature of Baum's article is the way in which he simultaneously romanticizes and dehumanizes Native Americans. Attitudes that simultaneously romanticize and dehumanize still exist, in relation to Native Americans and other groups. Although there is very little public outcry about the history and current treatment of Native Americans, there is a great deal of romanticizing of their spiritual traditions. The use of Indian mascots – symbols of 'wild' Indians – for sports teams uses a combination of romanticizing and dehumanizing. As mentioned above, some people have a sentimental attachment to what they see as purely a symbol representing the 'wild' spirit of their team. They act unaware that their naivety in projecting wildness on Indians is bound to a story of genocide. They ignore the wishes of Native American communities, complain that it is all just an issue of political correctness and refuse to grapple seriously with the issue. This twisted tendency to romanticism and exoticism of groups that are simultaneously dehumanized, and then 'poopooing' that there is any issue, extends to various groups, and makes the issue of cultural appropriation a very serious one. (See also Chapter 12.)

DEHUMANIZATION IN THE ISRAELI–PALESTINIAN CONFLICT

Dehumanization tactics urge us to focus on a perceived or actual threat to our existence and to take away feelings for the personal and collective humanity on the other side. Israel continually portrays Palestinians as threatening Israel's survival, but all too rarely takes on board the terrible and inhumane conditions of the occupation and the reality of its responsibility.[20] Dehumanization of Palestinians has occurred within Israeli Defence Forces and it occurs in the media and throughout society.[21] In the autumn of 2001, Amos Elon wrote that a newspaper in Israel considered 'dovish' had a cartoon depicting the Intifada as an infestation of a human body by a pack of vicious vermin. He mentions there was one letter to the editor protesting about the cartoon from a German resident in Jerusalem who protested the dehumanization of the Palestinians implied in the drawing, reminiscent of Nazi cartoons.[22]

In Palestinian society, Israelis and Jews are dehumanized. The Palestinian Media Watch looks out for dehumanization in cartoons, music and film clips. There are many. In one cartoon, Prime Minister Ariel Sharon eats Palestinian children out of a bowl. One depicts a rat wearing a prayer cap and Jewish star. There's a photo of a donkey dressed up in a Jewish prayer shawl.

Dehumanization is the language of threat and violence. Rabbi Michael Lerner, an American and editor of *Tikkun* magazine, who advocates ending the occupation of the West Bank, received threats to his life. In one such threat, someone wrote: 'You subhuman left animals should all be exterminated.'[23]

While researching dehumanization tactics, I saw how each side will some-times use the other side's dehumanization tactics as a reason to dehumanize them. As if to say: 'Look at how inhuman they are. Look at their dehumaniza-tion tactics! They are ruthless and will stop at nothing. They want to eliminate us. You cannot live with such people or negotiate with them.' Journalist Carolyn Glick expresses outrage about the dehumanization of Israelis and goes on to conclude, along with many Israelis: 'Once we understand that this is the situation of Palestinian society, we reconcile ourselves with the fact that we are not in a struggle against a political movement for national sovereignty. We are being victimized by a genocidal campaign for our violent elimination sup-ported by the overwhelming majority of Palestinians.'[24] This assessment in turn supports an atmosphere that justifies violent crackdown, assassination and use of terror tactics against Palestinians. The dehumanization on all sides feeds a general hopelessness throughout the world that the conflict is intractable. Our hearts begin to grow cold.

A cold logic of terror takes holds that is indifferent and calculating. The *Her-ald Tribune* reported on Israeli officers referring to Palestinian suicide bombers as 'a new kind of "smart bomb"'.[25]

> The suicide bomber has become the Palestinian version of a smart weapon, Israeli military officers say. Moreover, the bomber is cheap, unpredictable and abundant. He or she is relatively easy to hide, transport and store, and therefore difficult to detect and defend against, despite the Israeli military's high-tech prowess and long experience.

Some will find this clever. But when we can talk about Palestinian suicide bombers as 'smart bombs', without serious reflection or comment, we have in effect legitimized referring to a person as a bomb. It contributes to the process of legitimizing and normalizing violent crackdown on civilians. Civilians are weapons. While the writer of this article probably did not mean to support dehumanization tactics, this article shows how, as we read the news, dehuman-ization tactics are replicated within our society and within our awareness as individuals.

We make the 'enemy' faceless as a way to dehumanize, in order to commit violence. People have to be trained to torture and to kill, to not see a person with a family, culture, political philosophy or future. Soldiers practise thrusting their weapons, dehumanizing the enemy they are readying to kill. Hoods on torture victims aim to disorient the person being tortured (see Chapter 11), but also to make it easier for the torturer to humiliate and terrorize the faceless person. Among the atrocious pictures of tortured Iraqi prisoners, the world saw faceless naked prisoners, one with a dog collar and leash, held by the American military person.[26]

INTERNALIZED DEHUMANIZATION

Tactics of dehumanization not only dehumanize the targeted group. The strategy dehumanizes all of us, so we will be increasingly unmoved, uninvolved and indifferent, even actively despising and willing to support and carry out atrocities.

Individually, we internalize and repeat this strategy when we cut off our humanity, cut off our sensitivity and responses to our experiences and those of others in our community and world. When we break off contact with what matters to us, our deepest feelings in life, sometimes in subtle ways, we cut off our compassion, our troubled feelings of shock, despair or grief concerning tragedies in our environment and world. We cut off from the life source that unites us. We isolate ourselves and ignore others. We refuse to learn what is going on.

My point is not to equate dehumanization as a terror tactic used in war and genocide with what are natural and human tendencies to cut off our feelings in more subtle ways. Yet, dehumanization tactics dehumanize all of us. Noticing where we lose sensitivity internally, and noticing our strong and subtle reactions and responses, can lead to greater 'humanizing', not only of our personal lives, but also of our communities and world.

Large-scale violent conflict is preceded by terror tactics and human rights violations. Lack of response to human rights violations is a way to support large-scale violence. Responding to human rights violations in our own hearts and in our own neighbourhoods and communities can make a profound difference, for the individuals involved and for the wider picture. More of us will contribute to necessary political changes and community interventions that protect human rights. As a society, we will also pay attention when we hear how people are demonized and dehumanized in 'jokes' that are racist, homophobic or sexist. We will notice our reactions and sensitivity, rather than toughening up, whether we flinch a little or are outraged, or notice the tendency in us to want to pass it by and let it go. We will want to learn about how our responses arise, and how to intervene and talk about it as a society.

CHAPTER 9
TERROR TACTIC: DESENSITIZATION AND NORMALIZATION

Create or exploit instability so there will be need for control. Stir up fear of the Bogeyman. Dehumanize everyone to make ready for murder. All the while, make it seem normal, natural and acceptable.

Desensitizing and normalizing doesn't happen 'naturally'. It is a terror tactic, often carefully planned and carried out for the purpose of control and domination.

DESENSITIZATION IN SOUTH AFRICA

We have an enormous capacity to adapt or conform to our environment. We can get used to how things are. This is of course particularly true if we are in a privileged position. In South Africa, whites all too rarely questioned their supremacy. The state enforced Apartheid through brutally silencing anyone who spoke against the system, as well as providing extreme economic advantages for whites. The more you profit from the system, the more 'normal' and 'natural' it seems to become.

White people in South Africa have told me how they can recall strange and strong feelings that they knew something was wrong when they were young children and how their concerns and questions were unspeakable and suppressed. Someone told me she remembered the exact moment her concerns were split off on the other side of a wall that defined her 'normal' world. As a child, she expressed concern why a black household servant did not get to live with her own husband and kids. She received an awkward and curt answer and never asked again. Those who did go on to question and tackle the situation in any significant way were at profound risk from the repressive regime. Awakening to human rights violations and speaking out about it always puts the 'messenger' at risk in regimes where the premise is dominance through terror.

The constant threat of the regime was in itself normalized. Just before the end of Apartheid, my partner Jean-Claude and I were teaching in South Africa. In one group, made up of only white people, a woman began to speak about how she was being followed. She reported on various signs and signals and strange events. Speaking at length, she added more and more detail, in a highly agitated state. We have lots of experience with people with mental health difficulties and realized she must have a problem of paranoia. I remember thinking that we needed to find a way to respond that would respect her and perhaps be useful to her, while taking into account her vulnerable, possibly psychotic state and considering the needs of the large group. As this group knew that my husband and I work a lot with people who have acute and chronic mental health difficulties, they would be looking to us to support her and the group in what could be a difficult situation. I looked out to the large circle of participants. I will never forget the faces I saw. Everyone was nodding and listening to her story, as if it was not the least bit exceptional. The intricate and strange details of her story were facts. She was not paranoid. It was my husband and me who were caught in an alternate reality.

NORMALIZATION OF RACISM

Many people feel that racist attitudes of despising and superiority are a somehow 'natural' and unavoidable response to our innate differences and fear of the unknown. Prejudice is often seen as a fear of the unknown, fear of the Bogeyman and an inability to accurately perceive another person as a result of our preconceived myths. Racism can be understood as prejudice that is presumed accurate and enforced by social power. Yet, the very notion that prejudice and racism are a 'natural' human response can normalize it. Zinn questions that the feelings and actions that we call 'racism' are a result of 'natural' antipathy of white against black. He suggests that this question is not only relevant for the sake of historical accuracy, but any notion of 'natural' racism lightens the responsibility of the social system.[1]

Desensitization and slavery

Racism in America is in part a result of terror tactics, including desensitizing whites. Terror tactics enforced slavery. After slavery, terror tactics continued to enforce the oppression of African Americans.

For slavery to work, white people had to be 'dehumanized' along with blacks and desensitized. After escaping slavery, Frederick Douglas jeopardized his freedom to publish the story of his slave experience. He describes how his second owner's mistress was 'a woman of the kindest heart and finest feelings'.[2]

She had never owned a slave until Douglas arrived. He describes how she transformed. 'But, alas! This kind heart had but a short time to remain such. The fatal poison of irresponsible power was already in her hands, and soon commenced its infernal work. That cheerful eye, under the influence of slavery, soon became red with rage; that voice, made all of sweet accord, changed to one of harsh and horrid discord; and that angelic face gave place to that of a demon.'[3] One way to understand Douglas's description is to recognize the psychological dynamic of desensitization to violence. When we identify only with our sweetness, we project the demon on to the individual or group that we oppress. The demon simultaneously appears in our own brutality, acting freely and autonomously. We don't have a feeling reponse and reaction to our own violence, because we simply don't identify with being violent, projecting this instead on the people we attack or oppress.

The first Africans were brought to Virginia in 1619. The slave trade emerged from 1640–70. By 1800, 10–15 million blacks were brought into the States, as the plantations grew. Only one in three survived the trip, because of the vile conditions of the ships. It's estimated that the African continent lost approximately 50 million people to slavery, death from the crossing or from trying to escape capture.[4]

The Africans brought to the shores of America were not easily enslaved.[5] The Virginia slave code legitimized tactics of terror and compliance at any cost. Through the 1700s, the Virginia slave code read:

> *Whereas many times slaves run away and lie hid and lurking in swamps, woods, and other obscure places, killing hogs, and committing other injuries to the inhabitants . . . if the slave does not immediately return, anyone whatsoever may kill or destroy such slaves by such ways and means as he . . . shall think fit . . . . If the slave is apprehended . . . it shall . . . . be lawful for the county court, to order such punishment for the said slave, either by dismembering, or in any other way . . . as they in their discretion shall think fit, for the reclaiming any such incorrigible slave, and terrifying others from the like practices . . . .[6]*

Zinn writes that Mullin found over 1000 advertisements in newspapers for runaways between 1736 and 1801. The slave system separated families and didn't allow marriage. Runaways often risked their lives to get together with loved ones.[7]

Slave owners developed a system of control through terror. Zinn writes:

> *The system was psychological and physical at the same time. The slaves were taught discipline, were impressed again and again with the idea of their own inferiority to 'know their place,' to see blackness as a sign of subordination, to be awed by the power of the master, to merge their interest with the master's, destroying their own individual needs. To accomplish this there was the discipline of hard labor, the breakup of the slave family, the lulling effects of religion . . . the creation of disunity among slaves by separating them into*

field slaves and more privileged house slaves, and finally the power of law and the immediate power of the overseer to invoke whipping, burning, mutilation, and death. Dismemberment was provided for in the Virginia Code of 1705. Maryland passed a law in 1723 providing for cutting off the ears of blacks who struck whites, and that for certain serious crimes, slaves should be hanged and the body quartered and exposed.[8]

Slavery had to become normalized to prevent revolt or uprising. A common state terror technique to squelch any possibility of uprising is to ban assembly of the group concerned. Examples of banning assembly included forbidding slaves to assemble for dances, playing cards or religious purposes, and creating curfews. By creating laws and codes, such practices are legitimized by society and become 'normal'. Laws banning assembly in 1812 were a part of 'Washington's Black Code'.[9]

Desensitization and dehumanization of the slave owner

One way to desensitize the oppressor group to the atrocity of slavery was to focus on material 'needs' while dehumanizing the slaves. The plantations needed labour. There needed to be a way to settle disputes and preserve estates. In October 1705 an act declared 'the Negro, Mulatto, and Indian slaves to be "real estate", for the purpose of better settling and preserving estates within this dominion'.[10]

Black and white servants of the seventeenth century were noted to be unconcerned about their physical differences and worked and socialized together.[11] Whites sometimes joined the slave resistance.[12] There was a fear that discontented whites would join black slaves to overthrow the system. 'As early as 1663, indentured white servants and black slaves in Gloucester County, Virginia, formed a conspiracy to rebel and gain their freedom. The plot was betrayed, and ended with executions.'[13]

What tactics could prevent such an uprising, while furthering the normalization of slave holding? 'In 1705, about the same time as the Slave codes authorizing punishment to slaves, a law was passed requiring masters to provide white male servants whose indenture time was up with ten bushels of corn, thirty shillings and a gun, while women servants were to get 15 bushels of corn and forty shillings. Also, the newly freed servants were to get 50 acres of land.' In this way white servants could feel the slaveholders were protecting their interests.[14]

Normalization of apartheid: from abolition of slavery to segregation

After slavery was abolished, there was a decade of advancement. African Americans worked for pay, acquired land and voted. In 1866 the 14th Amendment promised citizenship and protection of civil liberties. In 1875, a Civil Rights bill was passed. These gains were lost as states began to legitimize segregation with the 'Jim Crow' laws. The Civil Rights Act was overturned in 1883, and America was not to see a Civil Rights Bill passed until 1964. Blacks could not ride the same railcars, sit in the same waiting rooms, use the same toilets, eat in the same restaurants. Blacks were denied access to some hospitals and to public areas such as parks and picnic areas. Apartheid in the south was legitimized and enforced through law and terror. Lynching went unchecked by government. While some victories in the Supreme Court paved the way, 1954 legislation that segregation of schools was unconstitutional marked for many the beginning of the civil rights movement.[15]

THE CIVIL RIGHTS MOVEMENT: NON-VIOLENCE AND STATE TERROR

The Montgomery bus boycott of 1955–56, the 1961 Freedom Rides, the massive march on Washington in 1963 – these events moved history. Facing state terror tactics and terrorist threat from groups such as the KKK (Ku Klux Klan), the civil rights movement in the USA rose up and changed the course of his-

↗ **Figure 9.1** Sign from the Jim Crow years. (By courtesy of the Jim Crow Museum at Ferris State University, Big Rapids, MI, USA.)

→ **Figure 9.2** Sign from the Jim Crow years. (By courtesy of the Jim Crow Museum at Ferris State University, Big Rapids, MI, USA.)

tory with its practice of non-violence, a powerful means of uprooting a violent system. Civil rights laws were finally passed in 1964.

NORMALIZATION OF STATE TERROR TACTICS

The struggle went on. Martin Luther King was assassinated in 1968 after horrific harassment by the CIA. The Select Committee of the US Senate to study intelligence activities wrote in their report in 1976 that 'the sustained use of such ("Counter Intelligence Program") tactics by the FBI in an attempt to destroy Martin Luther King violated the law and fundamental human decency'.[16]

In 1960, Malcolm X called for a radical upheaval of the system of white supremacy. He was killed. The Black Panther Party was formed in 1966. Just 2 days after King was shot, Bobby Hutton (17 years old), of the Black Panther Party, was shot down by Oakland police. A few months later, J. Edgar Hoover, head of the FBI at the time, announced the Panthers as the greatest threat to internal security of the country. State terror tactics to block the Panthers went on to include assassination of party leaders, infiltration, false arrests, imprisonment, wire tapping and disinformation campaigns designed to split the movement.[17] (See Chapters 10 and 13 for more information and documents about FBI activities against King, and also the Black Panthers.)

American society has made great gains in the area of civil rights and human rights and in recognizing African Americans' historical struggle, but the violence continues. A characteristic sign of state terror tactics is brutality within state institutions such as the police and prisons, such that there is no protection on the part of the state for our fundamental right to safety. There have been efforts to clean up the brutality of police and prison systems, but a legacy and reality remain of 'police brutality' or explicitly and implicitly legitimized tactics of terror in the legal institutions of the USA, particularly towards blacks. The brutal beating of Rodney King was captured on video and the acquittals of the police who beat him led to the uprising in LA in 1993.

The high rate of African American men in prison could be looked at as both a result and a continuation of this history of terror. Violence is committed against African Americans, and it has also been internalized within the African American community. African Americans are portrayed as violent while white (and black) Americans identify as having to protect against that violence. This is normalized along with the violence within the African American community. If, as a society, we do not fully grapple and struggle with the historical and ongoing violence inflicted on African Americans, we perpetuate it. We split off our brutal history. The tendency to disown and project violence is deadly and and in effect replays our violent history.

NORMALIZATION: GERMANY AND THE ROAD TO THE HOLOCAUST

Laws make the process of genocide simpler. If it is legal, we think it must be okay, as long as the state is still protecting 'our' interests. By the time Jews, Roma (Gypsies), homosexuals and other so-called 'non-Aryan' groups were rounded up and deported to death camps, their exclusion had long since been normalized. If your neighbours were no longer part of mainstream community life, could it have seemed in some way natural when they no longer lived in their houses or disappeared entirely? Those who watched trainloads of Jews taken 'east' assumed there must have been some legitimate reason for the authorities to do this.

In the midst of unfolding events, we gradually reduce our sensitivity to the events that will follow. This tactic can ready societies to tolerate atrocities, expulsion and genocide. Though evidence now suggests that the 'final solution', the plan to systematically exterminate millions of people in death camps, may not have fully culminated until 1941,[18] the legitimization and normalization of expelling Jews and other 'non-Aryans' that occurred from the very beginning made it possible. Browning describes the dedication of Hitler and the Nazis to the so-called 'Jewish question'. He writes 'Jewish policy could evolve no further in concept. It remained only to be implemented through action'.[19]

↓ **Figure 9.3** *Der Stürmer*, Julius Streicher's anti-Semitic paper, established in the 1920s and one of the most widely read newspapers by 1939. A young man looks at a poster taped to the daily's Danzig office, Poland on 10 July 1939. The poster reads: 'The Jews are our misfortune.' (Thanks to the US Holocaust Memorial Museum Photo Archive and with permission from Associated Press, London.)

↓ **Figure 9.4** Sign over entry to University says 'Juden sind hier nicht erwünscht'
(Jews are not wanted here), Germany, about 1934. The sign below it says 'The USU
helps. You help too. Become a member'. (By courtesy of the US Holocaust
Memorial Museum Photo Archive.)

Below is a compiled time-line of some of the events of the Holocaust from
1933 to 1945.[20, 21]

January **1933**   Hitler became German Reich Chancellor. On 28 February, the German
government took away freedom of speech, assembly, press and freedom from
invasion of privacy and house search without warrant. On 4 March, the first
concentration camp was established in Dachau. It was for political opponents of the new regime. On 1 April, the Nazis initiated a national boycott
of Jewish shops. On 7 April, Jews were dismissed from public jobs, including schoolteachers and university professors. On 25 April, a law against
'overcrowding' of German schools and universities restricted Jewish children. On 10 May, books written by Jewish authors and opponents of the
regime were burned in public. On 14 July, laws permitted forced steriliza-
tion of Roma (Gypsies), handicapped, Afro-Germans and others considered
'below the level of the Aryan race'. On 19 October, Germany withdrew
from the League of Nations (which was the forerunner to the UN).

1934   Hitler proclaimed himself Fuehrer of the Third Reich. The first major
wave of arrests of homosexuals throughout Germany occurred. In **1935**,
Jehovah's Witnesses were banned from civil service jobs and arrested. In
May, signs saying 'Jews not allowed' were posted outside German villages
and outside restaurants and shops. In September, Hitler said that the government needed a framework to establish 'tolerable relations' with the
Jewish people.[22] This included the Citizenship law to distinguish between

'citizens' and 'subjects'. You had to have German blood to have full political rights. It also included the law for the 'protection of German blood and honour' prohibiting marriage and sexual relations between Jews and Germans. Jews could also not employ German women under the age of 45 in their households.[23] In **1936**, German Gypsies were arrested and sent to Dachau concentration camp. In 1936 and **1937** the concentration camps of Sachsenhausen and Buchenwald were established.

May **1938**   Romas (Gypsies) without a fixed address, living in Austria, had to register. In June, all Roma children aged above 14 had to be fingerprinted, as a part of the growing racial definition of Romas as 'criminally asocial'. Also in June, 'Operation Anti-social' meant Jews with a criminal record were sent to concentration camps. In July there was an international conference in Evian. Most of the participating countries refused to receive Jews from Germany. In July, Jews had to carry identity papers at all times. In August, Jewish men had to take the name 'Israel' as a middle name for identity papers. Women had to take the middle name 'Sarah'. In October, Jewish passports were stamped with a red 'J'; 9 and 10 November was 'Kristall-nacht' or the 'Night of Broken Glass', following the assassination by Herschel Grynszpan (a Polish Jew) of a German diplomat in Paris. This was a centrally directed pogrom against Jewish synagogues, shops and homes. Synagogues were burned and ransacked; 30 000 Jews were arrested and placed in concentration camps; 90 Jews died. German Jews were ordered to pay compensation for the damage done to them. In December, Jewish driver's licences were invalid. Jews were forced to sell businesses and real estate and could no longer study at universities.

June **1939**   Cuba refused to accept Jewish refugees aboard the ship SS St Louis. The USA refused the refugees and the boat was forced to return to Europe. In October, doctors were given the right to go ahead and kill mentally ill and physically disabled people. In November, all Polish Jews had to wear a yellow Star of David or a blue and white armband. In December, all Jewish males in Poland aged between 14 and 60 were conscripted for forced labour. In May 1940, more than 160 000 Polish Jews were confined to the ghetto in Łodz. The concentration camp of Auschwitz was established. In October, the Warsaw ghetto was established

September **1941** German Jews are forced to wear the yellow Star of David. In October, deportations of German Jews to eastern Poland began; 34 000 Jews were murdered by mobile killing squads in the Ukraine. At Chelmno, there were mass killings of Jews and Romas with the use of exhaust fumes in mobile gas vans. After the Wannsee conference in January 1942, Nazis deported Jews to six extermination camps in the former Polish territory – Chelm-no, Belzec, Sobibor, Treblinka, Auschwitz-Birkenau and Majdanek.

May **1944**   440 000 Hungarian Jews were deported to Auschwitz-Birkenau and gassed to death. In January 1945, the Nazis evacuated Auschwitz and sent the prisoners on 'death marches' to Germany. The Red Army liberated Auschwitz. In April and May, US troops liberated concentration camps at Dachau, Bergen-Belsen, Buchenwald and Mauthausen.

NORMALIZATION, CLOSING DOORS AND LEARNING FROM HISTORY

We are easily unconscious of the significance of a given event as it is occurring. And, even when we see its significance, it is easy to turn our heads. It is possible, however, to learn from history. To study how we turn away and close doors, we need to understand how we grow insensitive to our own questions and our own urge to make a difference. To wake out of our tendency to feel absorbed in the momentary bubble of passing time is a challenge to our psychological, spiritual and political awareness.

On 26 June 1940, an official memo in the State Department of the USA described effective ways of obstructing the granting of visas to refugees, particularly from Germany. One suggestion was to 'simply advise our consuls to put up every obstacle, to require additional evidence and to resort to various administrative devices which would postpone and postpone and postpone the granting of visas'.[24] Whether administering our own personal lives or administering the immigration system of our countries, we often say that our closed doors are the result of limited resources and poor management. There is of course truth in it. As a society, we all too rarely stop to grapple with the situation of refugees from all perspectives. We project the problem onto administrative delays, while not recognizing the reality of our closed borders and our responsibility.

NORMALIZATION OF LONG-STANDING CONFLICT

In long-standing, repeating conflicts, we get desensitized. Up close, people suffer ongoing anxiety, terror, grief and outrage, and yet learn to desensitize themselves to their own pain.

At a safe distance, we read the news about the Israeli–Palestinian conflict, or the conflict in Northern Ireland, and begin to find the conflict normal, along with our inability to intervene in it. We forget about it. We may feel uncertain about what the conflict is all about. With gaps in our knowledge and without an overview, we may be embarrassed to ask. Limited access to our history through partial information, misinformation or disinformation supports the desensitization process. We stop questioning. We stop reacting.

NORMALIZATION OF DOMESTIC VIOLENCE

Violence towards women, including domestic violence and rape, has been so normalized in much of the world that, when feminists first spoke out in the early 1970s in the UK and America, their concerns were considered radical and disruptive of social norms. Although there has been a great increase in awareness about domestic violence in the last 30 years, the normalization of violence against women persists. Violence against women includes battering and sexual assault within the family, violence in community and violence perpetrated or condoned by the state or by state actors, such as police, prison guards or soldiers.[25] The 1990s and the new millennium have seen significant advances in human rights for women and this issue is increasingly on international agendas, encouraged by international law and standards.

The normalization of violence towards women has been the backdrop of the women's movement. If we are to develop new norms concerning gender roles while respecting diversity of culture, we must begin by challenging how violence towards women is normalized. Violence towards women is a pressing human rights issue internationally. Pressure from social groups and grassroots' changes in attitudes can lead states to implement new policies, which in turn further stimulate changes in our attitudes and norms. These policies may become new international standards (before they are internationally accepted norms), thus influencing the development of human rights norms internationally.[26]

DESENSITIZATION AND DEPRESSION

Desensitized, we feel numb within the status quo. We say there is nothing we can do. By way of desensitizing ourselves to our human reactions to the atrocities of our world, we dehumanize ourselves and then normalize it. We get depressed without quite noticing it. We may feel it is all too much or that it's wiser to just take it easy. We are unable to find our way out of the soup, and can't quite recognize the soup we are in. Depression is a widespread social phenomenon and is in part a response to the anaesthetization of our responses. Our depression is needed for the effective and widespread use of this tactic that normalizes degrading treatment of individuals and groups. At the same time, depressions often lift when we break free of this desensitization that is internalized. We break free of the trance and get involved in our own hearts and in our world.

CHAPTER 10
TERROR TACTIC: TARGETING LEADERS

Another tactic of terror involves targeting leaders in order to topple a social or political movement. This method of terror has been used pervasively across the world. Leaders are arrested, assassinated, disappeared and tortured.

There are many incidents of this tactic historically and currently. The OMCT, the World Organization Against Torture, as well as Amnesty International and Human Rights Watch are resources for up-to-date information.

The leader is a target in an attempt to cut off the impulse, heart or centre of an organization or movement. Human rights advocates, who bring awareness to these issues within their own countries and internationally, may become targets themselves.

Studying the dynamics of leadership is essential to understand and prevent violent conflict and has great bearing on both our individual psychological development and our collective development as a world. We need more public awareness about how leaders are targeted as a method of collective terror and intimidation. We also need to grapple with underlying questions about the nature of leadership, considering what it is that leads us and what we follow. Our concepts of leadership, so often imbedded in notions of power, authority and dominance, are a significant, social, political and spiritual matter.

SYSTEMATIC SUPPRESSION BEGINS WITH TARGETING LEADERS

To target a leader is to disorient and terrorize a wider community that is influenced by that leader. Another aim may be to demonize the individual and his or her movement. The execution of leaders may be accompanied by references to myths of good and evil, which glorify the killer for protecting society against the evil ones – whether these are particular individual leaders, an entire

network of leadership, broad categories such as 'intellectuals', or civilians associated with a particular religious, social or political group, which are seen to
endanger the progress of the dominating or emerging regime. When we are not
alert to this tactic of targeting leaders, we may blur the claim that a terrorist
needs to be captured or assassinated in order to protect civilians, with justification for targeting civilians who may be politically threatening or even in the
neighbourhood.

Systematic suppression often begins with targeting leaders who might resist
or speak out. Leaders may include political opposition, intellectuals or spiritual leaders. Targeting leaders may be just the beginning of wide-scale genocide,
used as a way of making the process technically simpler. If a government is
ready to kill a dissident leader, or individual members of social uprisings, it may
be ready to kill whole groups or even a whole population.

TARGETING LEADERS ON THE WAY TO GENOCIDE

A first step in ethnic cleansing is to target those who might lead a rebellion or
slow down the process.

Bosnia

In Bosnia, Muslims were killed or sent to starve and be tortured in concentration camps, in the systematic ethnic cleansing of towns. In Prijedor, 'Serbs were
first targeting for actual deportation the elite . . . political leaders, judges, police-
men, academics and intellectuals, officials who had worked in the public
administration, and artists'.[1]

The Armenian genocide

In 1915, over 2000 towns and villages were emptied of their Armenian inhabitants. Over 2 million Ottoman Armenians were sent to their destruction. First
the young men and community leaders were murdered, followed by women,
children and elderly people. Some were killed at the outset and others were
killed through disease and malnutrition in concentration camps. There were no
Armenians left to speak of in what became modern Turkey in 1923.[2]

Kurds

The Turkish government adopted a sustained programme of forced assimilation
of Kurds, banning any legitimate opposition to the Turkish government's

programme, including cultural organizations, political parties and media out-
lets, along with the violent repression of any Kurdish resistance. Hundreds of
thousands of Kurds have been murdered by Turkish state authorities. The Turkish state has imprisoned Kurdish members of the Turkish parliament, human
rights activists and many academics advocating Kurdish rights. The Turkish
government has also assassinated scores of journalists and intellectuals.[3]

COLONIZATION AND TARGETING LEADERS

Colonization involved targeting leaders. If you wanted the people you were
invading or dominating to assimilate, they had to be freed of their old ways,
their old Gods, their elders. This was carried out in the name of missionary
work. In Australia, missionaries targeted Aboriginal medicine men. Discrediting the medicine men was a way to destroy the fabric and values of
community.[4] Medicine men were considered men of knowledge, who moved
between the world of spirit and the world of men. The nineteenth century settlers described them as charlatans. But, these 'charlatans' were blocks to the
settlers' presumed authority and dominance. It was these men of knowledge
who they first tried to discredit in order to subjugate a tribe. Medicine men
were targets for ridicule. If their 'medicine' could be shown to be ineffectual,
then their hold upon a tribe might be loosened.

EXECUTIONS AND MARTYRS: IRELAND AND THE EASTER RISING

In the long history of English subjugation of Ireland and the Irish resistance to
subjugation, there were ongoing attempts to squelch the leadership of Irish
opposition to British rule.

The Easter Rising of 1916 is an important story in Ireland's history and in
our subject of targeting leadership. The Irish Republican Brotherhood and the
Irish Citizens Army referred to themselves now for the first time as the IRA,
the Irish Republican Army. At the last minute, the planned uprising against
British rule was almost cancelled. They thought this attempt to overthrow
British rule had no chance of success whatsoever. None the less, it did go forward and, after several days, the rebels surrendered. A series of trials of 16 of the
leaders, each lasting only a few minutes, resulted in 14 executions, the first execution taking place just a few days after their surrender.

The purpose of targeting leaders is to squelch a political or social uprising, yet
it can have the opposite impact, creating heroes and martyrs. That's what

happened in Ireland. There was a surge of support for the rebellion. Pictures of these martyrs hung on kitchen walls and the British underestimated the magnitude of the suffering and the spirit of the Irish people in resisting oppression. By 1918, Sinn Fein won 73 of 105 seats. Alarmed, Britain sent the army to reassert British control, resulting this time in war. The war was over in 1921, with a treaty dividing Ireland into two parts; 26 of the 32 counties became the present Republic of Ireland, and 6 were partitioned off and remained under British Rule, Northern Ireland. The Easter Rising and its martyrs led to the overthrow of British rule in Ireland and the continued struggle in Northern Ireland.

'SPECIAL ACTS' TO MAINTAIN ORDER: ARRESTS

Special Acts and decrees 'legitimize' arrest, outside legal process. We have seen how this may begin with a process of creating and/or exploiting instability, demonizing and dehumanizing the targeted individual or group, and normalization of the violation. Leaders who threaten the existing order are arrested and often tortured.

'Special Acts' legitimize state use of terror tactics, to target leaders to suppress violent uprisings or non-violent ones, often creating and furthering the belief that violence is the only way forward for a suppressed movement.

Shortly after the war and partitioning of Ireland, on 7 April 1922, the 'Civil Authorities Act' or 'Special Powers Act' came into force. It gave the local government and police free rein to take any measures they deemed appropriate to maintain order in Northern Ireland. It allowed for new regulations to be made at any time without needing to consult parliament. There was free rein to suspend civil liberties. People could be arrested without warrant and flogged. The power to intern without trial was repeatedly put into effect. Originally introduced as a temporary measure, this legislation remained in effect for half a century.[5, 6]

Catholics made up two-thirds of the population, but were excluded from political and social power, and discriminated against in housing, health and jobs. In 1968, a civil rights movement, in part inspired by Martin Luther King, arose. 'The Troubles' began. The Northern Ireland Civil Rights association organized a march in 1969 and met with police force. In 1971, a policy of internment was called for, and people could be arrested and held indefinitely without charge. On 30 January 1972, a huge march was planned to protest the internment policy. The march was supported by every civil rights and nationalist organization. Some 20 000 people marched. This was 'Bloody Sunday'. Soldiers fired first rubber bullets and then gun fire, killing 14 and wounding another 28. The British army was exonerated, claiming self-defence. Many claimed, and journalists who were there reported, that the police shot into the crowd with no provocation.[7] There have been demands for a proper investigation, and more than 30 years later, as I write, debates about what really happened are current in the news.

The Civil Authorities Act was finally repealed in 1972 and replaced in 1973 by the 'Emergency Provisions Act'. This was equally repressive and shifted the burden of proof to the accused and allowed for trial without jury.[8]

Under the Emergency Provisions Act, the Royal Ulster Constabulary (RUC) were given the power to arrest, detain and interrogate suspects, getting confessions through torture in interrogation centres.[9] Many people suffered horrific acts of torture. In 1977, Amnesty International arrived in Belfast and conducted an investigation, publishing a report about the use of torture tactics in 1978. Also a RUC doctor, appalled by the injuries he saw, spoke out.[10]

Creating special laws and suspending civil liberties is a state terror tactic. As we've seen, portions of the public, seeking safety, will often excuse, even welcome and demand crackdown, and may be unconcerned with the loss of civil liberties, unaware of its ramifications for human rights, unaware that rebellions arise because of such crackdown, or the possibility that the unrest has been created and/or exploited in order to legitimize the crackdown.

The ongoing conflict in Northern Ireland has been shaped by ongoing state terror tactics on the part of the British state and military, the RUC and loyalists, as well as tactics of terror(ism) used by the IRA.

MEETING IN PRISON

Another terror tactic involves banning leaders from gathering and meeting together. Meetings may be infiltrated or wire tapped. South African leaders of the African National Congress (ANC) were regularly arrested and tortured, to try to squelch their movement against the racist and fascist Apartheid regime in South Africa. Nelson Mandela describes a kind of paradox that in his memoirs he's even able to laugh about. Early on, all the leaders of the ANC were arrested at the same time and they were all put together in one area in prison, where they had their first unbanned meeting.[11]

KILLING THE 'LEADER' – RAZING THE OLD IDEOLOGY

If you want to impose a new regime and new ideology, the old one needs to be wiped clean. That's one idea behind targeting political, intellectual and spiritual leaders who practically or symbolically stand for the old regime or might resist. Old authorities block progress and must be toppled. For the new idea to take root, opposition must be weeded out. This idea has been the premise of massive terror and executions.

Razing the old ideology: the Cultural Revolution in China

The Cultural Revolution from 1967 to 1977 engaged the grassroots, especially young people, into a revolution aimed at ridding the country of 'old ideas, old customs, old culture and old habits of mind'. Teachers were persecuted under the maxim 'the more knowledge you have, the more counter-revolutionary you are'. Non-conformists were imprisoned in mental hospitals. Lists of who should be targeted and persecuted were put on walls. In Chapter 7, I mentioned how 'counter-revolutionaries' were demonized. The Red Guard, made up of many young people, verbally and physically attacked elderly people and 'intellectuals', often resulting in their death. Tens of thousands of people were killed.

In 1967, Sam Marcy, a Marxist thinker and founder of the Workers World Party, criticized the Socialist Workers Party and the Communist Party in the USA for their disagreement with the tactics of the Cultural Revolution in China.[12] He wrote:

> The cultural revolution was launched last August by decision of the Central Committee of the Party. . . . It proposes, among other things, to root out all 'old ideas, cultures, customs and habits of the exploiting classes' and 'to transform education, literature and art and all other parts of the superstructure that do not correspond to the socialist base . . .'.

> How can any genuine Communist quarrel with this? Has it not been an integral part of the understanding of all Communists that the old order, with its old ideas, old culture, and habits of the exploiting classes should be abolished and that new, revolutionary, socialist ideas, customs and habits be instituted to conform to the socialist foundation of the new regime? . . . What is really new about all this is the inflexible determination of the leadership of the Chinese Communist Party to make an earnest effort to really bring it about in practice. That is what is new! The August Decision proclaimed the necessity – 'to struggle against and crush those persons in authority' who are actively opposing the Cultural Revolution.

He goes on:

> Notwithstanding all that has been said, there is, nevertheless, grave and serious concern among many sincere and honest friends of the Chinese People's Republic over the form and method that the struggle has taken. . . . They view with growing alarm what appears to them the extra-legal and extra-governmental activities of the Red Guards.

Then, normalizing the tactic, he writes:

> *It must, however, be remembered that the cultural revolution is after all a revolution, and as such, is subject to the same general laws as all revolutions. Rarest of all social phenomena is the revolution that can be fully developed strictly within the confines of the existing social and political framework! Here, in the U.S. such presumably polar opposites as The Militant, spokesman for the SWP [Socialist Workers Party] and The Worker, spokesman for the CP [Communist Party] find common ground in hostile attacks against the Cultural Revolution . . . . What counts is that they lined up on the other side of the class line in this momentous struggle.*
>
> *For our part, whatever the shortcomings and however serious and profound the differences over the problems that are raised by the overall character of the current struggle, we believe that no real progressive or socialist, let alone a genuine Communist, can fail to give unequivocal support to the cultural revolution and the leadership at its head.*

These comments of Marcy are interesting in that they point clearly to the grave concerns of socialist and communist parties in the USA, who spoke against the tactics of the revolution and at the same time demonstrate a pattern of thinking that justifies and normalizes such tactics. He considers intimidation and violence as unavoidable in the name of transforming society. He also uses a tactic of loyalty, suggesting that his colleagues were hostile and on the wrong side of the class line. To be a 'real' or 'genuine' progressive, socialist or communist, unequivocal support to the movement and the leader was required.

In 1976, after Mao's death, the so-called 'Gang of Four' led by Mao's wife, and supported by Mao, were arrested. They found themselves bearing the guilt of a nation. 'The 1980 trial of the four, televised throughout China and designed to humiliate its members, was turned into a public rite aimed at closing this chapter in China's history book.'[13] They were sentenced to execution, though this was changed to life imprisonment.

In a report of this history on ChinaWN.com, it states: 'It was politically wise to shift the blame to the Gang of Four, as it seems that they were a sacrifice that the society had to make in order to feel they had departed from the past.'[14] I find it interesting that, on the one hand, principles of accountability were used, a kind of lustration process or accountability needed for society to put some closure on history. On the other hand, the same terrible philosophy and practice are repeated – the 'old authority' needs to be got rid of, in order to depart from the past.

TARGETING THE INFRASTRUCTURE: VIETNAM'S PHOENIX OPERATION

During 1967, the same year as the Cultural Revolution in China, during the Vietnam War, the CIA (Central Intelligence Agency of the USA) launched an operation called Phoenix. Phoenix was a programme aimed at 'neutralizing' – through assassination, kidnapping and systematic torture – the civilian infrastructure that supported the Viet Cong insurgency in South Vietnam. It targeted the Viet Cong leadership, to 'neutralize' key players.[15]

On 19 July 1971, William Colby,[16] the CIA officer in charge of Operation Phoenix, testified before a Subcommittee of the House Committee on Government Operations that between 1968 and May 1971, 20 587 alleged Viet Cong sympathizers were executed as a result of the Phoenix programme. The government of South Vietnam credited Phoenix with 40 994 deaths. Vietnamese who were taken into custody were regularly tortured before being executed.[17] Phoenix offices were set up from Saigon down to the district level. The Phoenix or Phuong Hoang Operation was originally designed to 'neutralize', i.e. assassinate or imprison, members of the civilian infrastructure of the National Liberation Front (NLF). Their functions were to: (1) collate intelligence about the 'Vietcong Infrastructure'; (2) interrogate civilians picked up at random by military units carrying out sweeps through villages; and (3) 'neutralize' targeted members of the NLF. This third task was often carried out by CIA-led Vietnamese organized into Provincial Reconnaissance Units (PRUs).[18]

US officials, led by Colby, established quotas of numbers of Vietnamese to be neutralized each month. These quotas, combined with the difficulties in identifying the NLF infrastructure and the impossibility of proving membership of NLF, resulted in vastly increased numbers of people being rounded up, tortured and murdered. At some points, the quota ran at 1800 per month. As a result of the numbers of detainees, the 'security committee' was given special powers to jail any South Vietnamese citizen for up to 2 years, renewable, with no right to legal proceedings. Interrogation was marked by brutal torture. In a testimony given before US Congress, in July/August 1971, Osborne, a Phoenix agent, testified to Congress: 'I never knew an individual to be detained as a Viet Cong suspect who ever lived through an interrogation.'[19]

Douglas Valentine who has collected and studied the documents from the Phoenix programme said that Nelson Brickham, most responsible for the creation of the Phoenix programme, kept copies of documents. Otherwise there would be no documented evidence. During the evacuation of Saigon in 1975, the CIA destroyed most documents about the assassination programme.

THE CONVINCING OF 'MR BA', AMERICAN SOLDIERS AND THE AMERICAN PUBLIC

An interesting element of the Phoenix programme was the widespread use of propaganda, from loudspeakers on trucks to dropping leaflets, as part of a broad 'Psychological Operations' (PSYOP) offensive. This included the use of comics. *Mr Ba's Family and the Phoenix Operation* depicts 'Mr Ba', who is convinced and eventually rewarded for informing the US military about where the Viet Cong are hiding in his village.[20]

↓ **Figure 10.1** Psy Ops comic book from the US Phoenix programme in Vietnam. From a cartoon book titled *Mr Ba's family and the Phoenix Operation*. Declassified US government document. (See Douglas Valentine (2000) *The Phoenix Program*. www.iuniverse.com.)

'See, there are so many leaflets'.

'Honey, what do they say in those leaflets?'

'They are the same as those wall posters, as well as the announcements on the radio yesterday. The two Communists Ba Luong and Hai Goon are presently hiding in our village in order to collect taxes. I am determined to report to the Phoenix Operation Committee because I know their hiding place.'

'What does the letter say?'

'Dear Mr Ba, since you helped the government by providing information and undermining the local structures of the Communists, you will be rewarded accordingly. You are invited to attend the coming meeting of the Phoenix Operation Committee to receive your reward. Sincerely yours.'

Colby, the architect of Operation Phoenix who later directed the CIA, believed that, with a little more patience, a lasting settlement could have been reached on US terms. He apparently claimed vindication for Phoenix, believing its potential success to be more relevant than its criminality.[21]

International law tells us that illegal combat operations, such as torture and targeting civilians, are considered crimes of war. Outside the context of war, such abuse, also towards one's own people, is a crime against humanity. Although voices call for accountability and for the truth to be told, others consider such tactics as logical and legitimate, for the difficult task of trying to topple a system or conduct a war.

In an article 'The Vietnam syndrome', Richard Falk[22] refers to former Senator, Bob Kerrey, who had commanded a small unit of the Navy Seals on assassination missions, as part of the Phoenix programme, and who was upfront about the fact that the soldiers in Nam were never trained about laws of war. He learned of the prohibition concerning killing civilians (contained within the US Army's Field Manual) only long after the war.

THE LOGIC OF TARGETING CIVILIANS

The tendency for soldiers to not know is mirrored in an uninformed public. Operations such as Phoenix stay partially hidden. When they come to light, atrocities against civilians are often thought of as one-off 'screw-ups', tragedies. Falk points out: 'Proper training of soldiers concerning laws of war would have contradicted the main lines of counterinsurgency warfare which rested on a criminal premise. In those parts of the country where the revolutionary side had societal support, soldiers were told that the entire civilian population, including women, children, the infirm, and wounded should be treated as the enemy.'[23]

At its root, this way of thinking suggests that what society's members want is of no concern. In trying to root out the infrastructure of an opposing movement, not only are individual leaders of such movements considered targets. Whole groups and movements may be considered targets for interrogation, torture and death, and even large civilian populations who support such movements. This thinking led seamlessly into the massive civilian casualties in Vietnam, which to this day go largely unacknowledged. This history in Vietnam is clearly relevant to the investigations into torture and military tactics in Iraq.

In a study at the University of Massachusetts on attitudes about the Gulf Crisis (in the 1980s), one question was: 'How many Vietnamese casualties would you estimate there were during the Vietnam war?' The average response in this study, among Americans, was 100 000. The official figure is about 2 million. The actual figure may be much higher. The people who conducted the

study raised the question about what we would think about the German political culture if you asked people how many Jews died in the Holocaust, and they
estimated about 300 000.[24]

Discussion about accountability for what happened in Vietnam is still limited, and compounded by the long-lasting affects of trauma of Vietnam vets and
the way vets were victims as well as perpetrators of these policies. There are
currently a wide number of books about Vietnam, as the story and history are
still being shaped. But the complex issues of accountability on an individual
and societal level come only slowly to the forefront of American dialogue.

We have seen that arresting, torturing or executing a leader of an uprising,
in order to try to stop a movement, is a terror tactic, often called a 'counter-
terrorist' tactic. If the political dissident is criminalized (often through false or
trumped-up charges), this can also serve to 'legitimize' his arrest. If there is a
threat of violence, many people will consider the use of terror tactics to stop
potential violent activities as justified. (This is the rationale offered by the USA
concerning political prisoners in the war on terror.)

An extension of this logic leads to arresting, torturing and executing large
numbers of civilians,
because they support
or might support the
enemy's infrastructure
and activities. Leaders
of movements are tar-
gets. Whole groups
within such move-
ments are targets, and
even large sections of
civilian society who
agree with those
movements are targets.
Anyone along the way
to targeting these indi-
viduals may be
considered 'collateral
damage'.

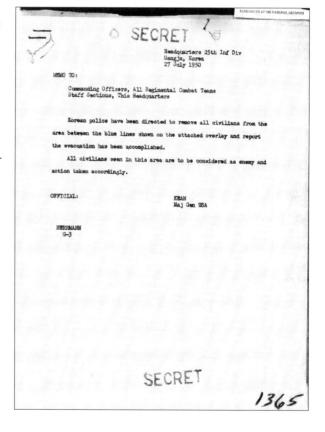

→ **Figure 10.2** Approval to kill
civilians, Korean War, US military,
July 1950. (Declassified US
government documents, thanks to
Charles Hanley, co-author of *The
Bridge at No Gun Ri*, Owl Books.)

In 1999, the Associated Press reported that ex-soldiers confirmed the claims of South Korean Villagers that some 400 civilian refugees were killed by American soldiers during an incident at No Gun Ri, in July 1950. Military documents showed that US commanders had issued orders to shoot civilians so as to not risk infiltration by disguised enemy soldiers. With this report, the story was coming into the open for the first time. Full investigations were set in motion.

In 2001, the US Army confirmed the story, but did not assume accountability, saying that what happened in 1950 at No Gun Ri was a 'tragic and regrettable accompaniment to war'. The journalists, Charles Hanley, Sang-Hun Choe and Martha Mendoza, went on to fully research and write a book about this event.[25]

In April 2004, several hundred civilians were killed in Fallujah, Iraq. According to the head of the local hospital, these were largely women, children and elderly people.[26] Then, newspapers around the world reveal the despicable photographs of US military personnel torturing Iraqi prisoners in the Abu Graib prison near Baghdad. Although many at first tried to say that these events were the outrageous behaviour of a few military personnel, many began to look into what appeared to be systematic abuses. The International Red Cross released a report saying that this abuse and torture in US-run prisons was systematic.[27] The reality of torture tactics used against Iraqi prisoners is accompanied by the knowledge that tens of thousands of Iraqis were put in jails and prison camps without charge.[28]

TARGETING LEADERS: FBI AND COINTELPRO

In the USA during the 1960s, the FBI targeted the civil rights movement and black nationalist groups using vicious terror tactics. According to the 1976 US Senate's 'Final Report of the Select Committee to Study Governmental Operations with respect to Intelligence Activities', also known as the Church Committee report,[29] The Counter Intelligence Program (COINTELPRO) attempted to destroy Dr Martin Luther King as the leader and inspiration of the civil rights movement. At the same time the FBI made plans to find his replacement, someone to assume the role of leadership once King had been discredited.[30] When they were unable to destroy his reputation, and when it was announced that King would receive the Nobel Peace Prize, 2 days later, a composite tape was produced, supposedly taken from taps of his hotel rooms, with sexual material. The tape was sent to Dr King with a note urging suicide (Figure 10.3).[31] It said 'The American public, the church organizations that have been helping – Protestant, Catholic and Jews – will know you for what you are – an evil, abnormal beast. . . . You are done. King, there is only one thing left for you to do. . . . You know what it is. You have just 34 days . . . . There is but one way

Date: December 1, 1964

To: Mr. W. C. Sullivan

From: J. A. Sizoo

Subject: MARTIN LUTHER KING, JR.

Reference is made to the attached memorandum DeLoach to Mohr dated 11/27/64 concerning DeLoach's interview with ████ ████ and to your informal memo, also attached.

████████ stated to DeLoach that he was faced with the difficult problem of taking steps to remove King from the national picture. He indicates in his comments a lack of confidence that he, alone, could be successful. It is, therefore, suggested that consideration be given to the following course of action:

That DeLoach have a further discussion with ████ and offer to be helpful to ████ in connection with the problem of the removal of King from the national scene;

That DeLoach suggest that ████████ might desire to call a meeting of Negro leaders in the country which might include, for instance, 2 or 3 top leaders in the civil rights movement such as James Farmer and A. Philip Randolph; 2 or 3 top Negro judges such as Judge Parsons and Judge Hasty; 2 or 3 top reputable ministers such as Robert Johnson, Moderator of the Washington City Presbytery; 2 or 3 other selected Negro officials from public life such as the Negro Attorney General from one of the New England states. These men could be called for the purpose of learning the facts as to the Bureau's performance in the fulfillment of its responsibilities under the Civil Rights statute, and this could well be done at such a meeting. In addition, the Bureau, on a highly confidential basis, could brief such a group on the security background of King ████████████████████████ The use of a tape, such as contemplated in your memorandum, together with a transcript for convenience in following the tape, should be most convincing.

The inclusion of U.S. Government officials, such as Carl Roweh or Ralph Bunche, is not suggested as they might feel a duty to advise the White House of such a contemplated meeting. It is believed this would give us an opportunity to outline to a group of influential Negro leaders what our record in the enforcement of civil rights has been. It would also give them, on a confidential basis, information concerning King which would convince them of the danger of King to the over-all civil rights movement. ████ is already well aware of this. This group should include such leadership as would be capable of removing King from the scene if they, of their own volition, decided this was the thing to do after such a briefing. The group should include strong enough men to control a man like James Farmer and make him see the light of day. This might have the effect of increasing the stature of ████ ████ who is a capable person and is ambitious.

There are refinements which, of course, could be added to the above which is set forth in outline form for possible consideration.

KING,

King, look into your heart. You know you are a complete fraud and a great liability to all of us Negroes. White people in this country have enough frauds of their own but I am sure they don't have one at this time that is any where near your equal. You are no clergyman and you know it. I repeat you are a colossal fraud and an evil, vicious one at that.

King, like all frauds your end is approaching. You could have been our greatest leader.

But you are done. Your "honorary" degrees, your Nobel Prize (what a grim farce) and other awards will not save you. King, I repeat you are done.

The American public, the church organizations that have been helping – Protestant, Catholic and Jews will know you for what you are – an evil, abnormal beast. So will others who have backed you. You are done.

King, there is only one thing left for you to do. You know what it is. You have just 34 days in which to do (this exact number has been selected for a specific reason, it has definite practical significant. You are done. There is but one way out for you. You better take it before your filthy, abnormal fraudulent self is bared to the nation.

←↑ **Figure 10.3** COINTELPRO FBI memo about how to eliminate
Martin Luther King's influence, urging him to suicide.
(Declassified US government documents. See Churchill and
Vander Wall, *The COINTELPRO Papers*, South End Press.
Thanks to Paul Wolff: www.cointel.org.)

out for you. You better take it before your filthy, abnormal, fraudulent self is bared to the nation' (the 34 days referred to the days before the Nobel Prize ceremony). When King did not respond, they offered the recordings to several major news agencies. The media refused to take them.[32]

One technique of COINTELPRO was to 'neutralize' activists by obtaining false convictions against them. COINTELPRO framed Black Panther Party leaders for murder with fabricated evidence and perjury, involving local police.[33]

Wesley Swearingen (a former FBI agent) testified that Geronimo Pratt, former head of the Panthers' LA chapter, was framed by the FBI as part of its campaign to destroy the Black Panther Party. Louis Tackwood said that detectives and FBI COINTELPRO personnel sat down one afternoon with a stack of unsolved cases, looking for a murder with which Pratt might be most feasibly charged. They then orchestrated appropriate 'evidence' and had him prosecuted.[34]

Much later, in 1980, Patrick Gray, the former FBI Director, and Edward Miller, one-time head of Squad 47, the domestic counterintelligence unit in the Bureau's New York office, were convicted of having 'conspired to injure and oppress the citizens of the United States'. Neither spent any time in jail. In 1981, President Reagan interrupted their appeals to pardon both men for excesses during the political conflicts of the era, during an especially turbulent and divisive period of American history. The victims of COINTELPRO were, however, not pardoned.[35]

Pratt had been charged in 1970 with a 1968 murder that occurred in Santa Monica, California (near Los Angeles). Pratt always said he was attending a BPP meeting in Oakland, California (near San Francisco) at the time. He said the FBI had bugged their meeting, so its electronic surveillance logs would verify that he was not at the scene of the crime. Under oath, an FBI official denied such surveillance occurred. Years later, when it was confirmed that the surveillance had been conducted, the FBI claimed to have 'lost' the relevant logs. Pratt's conviction was overturned only in 1997, when it was proven that the state's star witness – a paid FBI informant – had perjured himself on key points. By then Pratt had served over 27 years.[36]

A once prominent New York Black Panther Party leader named Dhoruba bu Wahad, or Richard Moore, was finally released in 1990 after spending 21 years in prison on a wrongful conviction. There are many more documented cases of terror tactics used against the Black Panther Party and many that remain mysteries.[37]

COINTELPRO's activities came to light through the rigorous investigation by the Senate Committee in 1976, in response to leakages around Watergate, the Pentagon papers and the COINTELPRO files. (As a result of the Freedom of Information Act, the report is now available to read.[38]) It is clear that the FBI was not limiting its tactics to people whom they regarded as violent. King, the leader in non-violence, was dangerous because he was so inspiring in his call for civil rights. The Church Committee report stated that nearly quarter of a million first class letters were opened and photographed by the CIA between 1953 and 1973, providing an index of one and a half million names. At one point, at least 26 000 individuals were catalogued on an FBI list of people to be rounded up in the event of a 'national emergency'.[39] The history of the FBI and these Senate Hearings is crucial in creating a perspective on the current Bush Administration's steps to remove civil liberties.

TARGETING LEADERS: STALIN AND THE SOVIET UNION/IDEOLOGY AND ABUSE OF POWER

In the 1930s, Stalin launched a purge of the Party, aimed at expelling opposition or counter-revolutionaries, in what went on to be known as the Great Terror, in which millions were killed or sent to the Gulag. The whole of Russia lived in terror. The numbers of people killed in Stalin's Great Terror are controversial and quoted as anywhere from 700 000, to 2 million, 20 million and 40 million, depending in part on whether only political executions are counted, or deaths in rural areas and whether these are considered murder or due to famine. Roberta Manning, who headed a research team that investigated Soviet archives, says that people think Stalin's terror took place mainly in cities against political opponents, but that half of the executions took place in rural areas. 'Sometimes the local authorities had a different agenda, like clearing out people they might have to feed.'[40]

Marxist historian, Rogovin, describes the tragedy and terror of 1937. He says the aim of the terror was to annihilate what was indeed a substantial opposition to Stalin's regime. He places Leon Trotsky and his followers at the centre of these purges. Despite years of repression, Trotsky's influence had remained a powerful current with revolutionary potential.[41] He states that Stalin's mistrust of many people in the Communist Party during this period was well founded in the fact that there was indeed a great opposition to him, and that, had these people had a chance, they would have gladly deposed Stalin.

Rogovin describes Stalin's terror as initially targeting Communist leaders who would have opposed him and brought communism in another direction. Hundreds of thousands of people were torn away from their apartments, thrown into prison, tortured and in the Show Trials made to confess to crimes against the Communist Party, and then were either exterminated or sent to concentration camps.

One Socialist position is that one of the greatest lies maintained in this century was the identification between Stalinism and socialism. In this view, western historians are seen as having tended to use the crimes committed by Stalin's regime to discredit socialism. Stalin has been portrayed as a logical development of communism, rather than as a dictator who used terror tactics against Communist leaders and intellectuals who wanted to take communism down a different path.

In turn some historians and authors strongly condemn what they feel is a leftist tendency to cover up awareness and public reaction and outrage about what occurred in communist countries throughout the last century, out of a wish to support the underlying philosophy of communism.

The *Black Book of Communism* chronicles the atrocities of communist regimes throughout the century. Several claim that the book lays to rest the 'myth of the well-intentioned founders'.[42-45] McShea writes 'a great number of people still cling religiously to the fantasy that Marxism–Leninism is innocent at its heart, that Stalinism was a corruption and not an outgrowth . . . among leftists who still believe strongly in the (pseudo) science of human history and who refuse to see that Marxism–Leninism is a deadly brew.'

Although an overview of the legacy of the Soviet Union is not within the scope of this work, this particular issue about whether the ideology was inherently at fault or whether it was the abuse of power by dictators in the name of a particular ideology that was at fault, is a fundamental question of more global and general interest in trying to understand patterns of violence in our world and communities, and our part in the perpetuation of this violence.

KILLING THE LEADER AS A PSYCHOLOGICAL PROCESS

What leads us – ideology or power?

Our capacity to dream and change the world and our tendency to enforce the status quo are both projected onto leaders. We talk about ideology with passionate feelings. Although our fights may look like they are about ideology, they are more likely to be about power.

In the Cold War between the USA and the Soviet Union, what appeared as a fight between two ideologies (capitalism and communism, or democracy and socialism), played out as a mythic polarization of power. Great ideals have always been used as the reason for dominating and colonizing others. Almost any great idea (or less than great idea) can be used to arouse our ideals and high emotions, and eventually our compliance and capacity to terrorize others.

A broad question is what leads us, collectively and individually? Is it ideology? Or is it the power to enforce and dominate in the name of a particular ideology? We regularly confuse our ideology with the enforcing of our ideology, whether as parents, teachers, lovers or citizens. The more we are unconscious of this tendency, the more readily we support a leader or government in the tactic of using our ideals and our strong emotions about these ideals to gain power and to dominate.

Dreams bring possibilities and pathways for society. People carry dreams. Or we could say a leader is a dream personified.[46] If the leader is identified with a dream that threatens the predominating worldview, the leader may be a target. Leaders who identify with the predominating or competing worldview are also targets.

Democracy and power

We routinely talk about democracy in terms of power. Sometimes we talk about balancing power. We think that one idea or person leads or wins over another. We even imagine we can impose a democracy by force. We say 'majority rules'. Arnold Mindell recognizes that what leads us is not one idea or the other. Our tensions, emotions and long-standing conflicts lead us. What leads us is the atmosphere between us and the underlying field that not only pulls and pushes us, but joins us ultimately to one another.[47] What leads us is the voice, the idea, just on the outskirts of our awareness, that has not yet been heard. What leads us is the interplay between old and new, between that which dominates and that which is marginalized. History leads us. We need leaders who can facilitate this encounter, who welcome diversity, conflict and the feelings and dimension of our experience. Mindell calls this 'deep democracy'.

The tip of the iceberg

A worldview based in power, one side dominating the other, is sustained only through intimidation and terror. If you are terrorized, you might do whatever is demanded. We often heard people say: 'The fear of getting killed didn't get me, but it was when they threatened to kill my friend or my child, my family or my community.'

Terror tactics are just the tip of an iceberg that is historical, chilling and in the marrow of our bones. It is important to look at the psychology of leadership and what leads us, because we participate in terror tactics long before they become so extreme. We easily freeze within a limited worldview based on one side dominating the other and intimidation.

The leader as a role

Many social and political movements recognize that the leader is not only an individual, but also a 'role' that will be filled by someone, for better or for worse. Although leaders may stir movements, movements also stir up leaders.[48]

↑ **Figure 10.4** 'Reunion at Sera', Lhasa, 1993. © Nancy Jo Johnson.
Sera Monastery, a Tibetan labourer cradles a photo of His Holiness the
Dalai Lama. A photo of the exiled leader is an illegal possession in Tibet.
(With permission from Nancy Jo Johnson.)

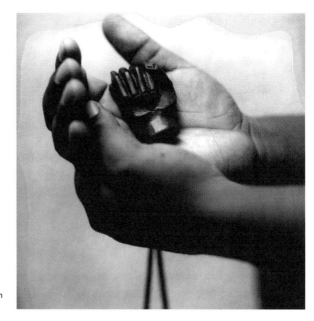

→ **Figure 10.5** Steve Biko's son holds
the wooden fist that belonged to his
father. Steve Biko was killed in South
Africa. (Photo by Jillian Edelstein, with
permission.)

The terror tactic of targeting leaders presupposes a centralization of leadership, with the idea that a movement will flounder without its leader. But a leader is much more than an individual. Targeting the leader is only 'useful' as a tactic of terror in so far as it might slow down the expression of that leadership role.[49] Someone else will eventually fill it. Or the spirit of the leader is far greater than any individual and it is that spirit that is kept close to people's hearts and can persist over generations.

The Dalai Lama fled Tibet in 1959. In exile, he remains both the religious and political leader of Tibet. The devotion of Tibetans towards the Dalai Lama, also in his physical absence, holds their deepest spirit and dream of freedom and independence.

Many social activist movements recognize that leadership is a role that many people can fill together and understand the importance of decentralization for a movement to thrive. Social movements use 'affiliate' groups to avoid centralization. Leadership is dynamic and involves relationship. If leadership is decentralized, if everyone is a leader, or carries that 'leader' in their heart, there is no 'leader' to target, no centre to aim for.

In a related vein, the 'war on terror' faces problems of decentralized leadership among terrorists. When one terrorist is killed, we can anticipate that many more will appear, particularly if the targeted terrorists are considered freedom fighters and heroes. We can anticipate, as one terrorist cell is eliminated, that more terrorist cells will arise. In this way, targeting terrorists can increase the problem of terrorism.

The anarchy movement decentralizes leadership. The word 'anarchy' comes from an ancient Greek word meaning the absence of a leader. Anarchy rejects the idea that we need centralized authority.[50] In the late 1880s in the USA, anarchists wanted to destroy the capitalist system, abolish class rule and eliminate central leadership of the state.[51] A 'New Anarchism'[52] has been pivotal in the anti-globalization movement. Anarchy is often associated with chaos, but a high level of organization often occurs through the interaction of 'affinity groups' and largely peaceful and also celebratory gatherings of workers, youth, environmentalists, peace activists and many other groups.[53] Because of the tactic of 'targeting the leader' to uproot an old system, sometimes with violence, 'anarchy' is often associated with violence. The underlying ideology of anarchy, however, is based on the notion that we can assume responsibility in filling the role of leader and it is not necessary to project responsibility and power onto centralized authority.

Many of us moan, joke and are outraged by the behaviour of some of our leaders. If we understand that leadership is a role, we may be more prone to step up to the task, rather than leave the role to be filled in such unsatisfactory ways.

To rebirth our notions of leadership

We tend to think about leadership with a governing belief that one side wins over the other. Even inside of us as individuals, one part tries to assume control of our personality, forcing other parts to comply. A serious problem throughout societies across the world is that so many people are unwilling to lead, unable to see their own ideas and feelings as central to their communities. One reason we resist leading is that we equate leadership with dominance. We feel we must adapt or rebel, or we retreat into a limited sphere of thought and activity. The authoritarian leader is internalized and rubbishes our thoughts and impulses. Or we think we have to be strong and powerful, to overcome authority and, in so doing, we dominate others. Our personal and collective psychology concerning leadership takes on particular forms, based on our family, culture and political history. For example, we have had interesting discussions among colleagues in former communist countries, about their particular concerns when stepping into a leadership position in a group, resulting from a deep-seated belief in collectivity that makes it sometimes difficult to support individual expression, as a well as an experience of leadership as tyranny.

We might consider 'killing the leader' as a psychological challenge, to revisit our notions of leadership. Leading as dominance has had its day. It is not possible to dominate others, without using terror tactics to enforce it. We might imagine that what actually leads us is an underlying creative field and polarizations that drive our interactions. This is a leader you cannot kill, intimidate or lock up. This leader needs our awareness.

CHAPTER 11
TERROR TACTIC: TORTURE, BREAKING BODY AND SPIRIT

The aim of torture may be to obtain information or a confession, to incriminate a third person, to punish or to establish a reign of terror within a community, by breaking the body and mind of the torture victim. Torture is a central tactic in the systematic violence towards targeted individuals and ethnic, religious or political groups, as a part of ethnic cleansing or genocide, or trying to squelch a potential uprising. When members of targeted ethnic, religious or political groups or leaders of movements are arrested, the aim of torture is to erase the spirit of resistance in the individual, and his or her community or movement.

We often think of torture as the use of extreme methods to extract information or for punishment. What is less commonly known is that torture is a tactic of intimidation, intended to destroy individuals and communities and to erase the possibility of a social and political movement resisting oppression. Torture follows on from the tactics of exploiting instability to call for a crackdown and special legislation eliminating civil liberties, tactics of demonizing, dehumanizing, normalizing and desensitizing, and targeting the leader. Many people think that torture is something that happens sporadically and somewhere far away. The reality is that it's happening frequently and probably close to home.[1]

Before the 1980s, torture was addressed only in a limited and sporadic fashion. Inge Genefke, from the Rehabilitation and Research Center for Torture Victims in Copenhagen, describes how it was considered a rather local and random phenomenon. She says one thing is certain: 'Torture is neither local nor random – and systematic torture can only take place with the knowledge and support of government. Torture is an instrument of power that governments use to stay in power.'[2] Systematic violation of human rights and methods of terror and torture are used to destroy individuals and communities, in order to achieve and maintain dominance, in states around the world.

Genefke said (in 1997) that one-third of the world's governments remain in power exclusively because they use torture to assume dominance over their own people.[3,4]

Torture does not originate with a few evil people. Torture methods are systematic and a part of planned tactics for assuming dominance and for killing the spirit of potential resistance. Torture aims to destroy the personality, leave the victim ruined, unable to function. Torture is used to violate the deepest fibres of what holds us together as human, as individuals and as communities, to humiliate, erase the spirit and stop any possibility of resistance to those wielding power. Manuals are written to provide instructions for effective torture methods.[5] Similar patterns are used worldwide in prisons and paramilitary operations. Methods and equipment are exchanged. Torture equipment is sold worldwide.[6]

TO CRACK PHYSICAL AND PSYCHOLOGICAL LIMITS

Torture methods are physical and psychological and aim to crack the boundaries of human tolerance of pain, sensation and emotion. Torture aims to destroy identity. Torture has been described as an attempt to kill people, without them physically dying.[7] Methods include the most brutal of physical injuries imaginable, such as repeated trauma to the body, burns, electric shocks, suffocation, extreme physical conditions, such as hot and cold, forced body positions over long periods of time, no rest or sleep, sexual harm, humiliation and rape, and mental torture such as sensory deprivation, threats and mock executions, threats to arrest or rape a family member, forcing the victim to observe the torture of someone else or to torture someone else.

Methods of torture are designed according to knowledge of the physical and psychological limits of a human being. Torture methods aim to push the limits of what we identify as human, erase the personality, and take away any reference point that might rebuild a sense of identity. If released, a torture victim may be unable to return to everyday life. Or, a torture victim returns and his children cannot recognize him, cannot believe he is the same person.

TO NEVER GO HOME – THE UNSPEAKABLE

To prevent the torture victim from 'returning' home, or to his or her previous identity, torture methods use everyday objects and everyday activities. Telephones, chairs, plastic bags, boiled eggs, water and electric wires become objects of torture. Walking or running and other repetitive movements are turned into torture. The victim's relationship to all daily activities and the environment is violated.[8] Torture might occur within a 'medical' set-up. Interrogation might occur in a bureaucratic environment. In this way, refugees who have been tortured may be severely traumatized and unable to go to the doctor, or to face bureaucracy, without symptoms being triggered. This is the goal of torture, to cut off the spirit and possibility of refuge. Torture victims might not speak about what happened. They don't want those close to them to suffer. All sense of humanity has been violated. Torture victims may feel isolated, their stories unspeakable or, if told, met with blank faces, not believed, not wanted.

When people are illegally detained and arrested, they may be tortured, as a way of getting across the message that any resistance will not be tolerated. After 'Kristallnacht', in Germany, in 1938, some 25 000 Jewish men were arrested and taken away for short stays in concentration camps – this was before the full-scale rounding up to concentration camps and death camps. What happened during these stays is not spoken about much, but many were tortured and some randomly beaten to death.

Torture is used to squelch and counter resistance, even non-violent protest, in conflicts around the world. The UN Convention against Torture and Other Cruel, Inhuman or Degrading Treatment or Punishment was adopted in 1984, with entry into force in June 1987. Out of approximately 20 million people worldwide who are refugees, displaced or internally displaced, studies indicate that 20–30 per cent have suffered torture by their own governments.[9] Asylum seekers who have been tortured have to deal with the long-lasting trauma, on top of great personal loss, being forced into exile and meeting a new country, a new culture, a new language, while often being faced with suspicion and racism, if not closed doors.

One way in which we participate in the problem of torture is by not recognizing how pervasive it is or the suffering that many asylum seekers have endured. The torture victim is silenced and society goes blank. Torture is hard to fathom, precisely because it targets the boundaries of what we identify as 'human'. Particularly hard to fathom is how such tactics become institutionalized and remain institutionalized, within those social structures set up to protect society and civilization. A terrible and interesting feature of torture is that the infrastructure used to carry out torture, within prisons and policing, is often the most constant aspect of society. A regime change can occur, with resulting change in political, social and cultural attitudes, and the torture system is passed on intact.[10]

The photographs that first emerged from Iraq in April and May 2004 tell a story of American military personnel torturing Iraqis in the very prisons where Saddam Hussein's regime used torture.

Torture has been used widely in police stations, prisons and detention centres, across the world, including democracies throughout Europe and the USA.

Torture is used against 'common' criminals as well as political prisoners. Although international recognition of this problem has grown dramatically in recent years, and there have been significant steps made to discover and eliminate the use of torture and other cruel and degrading punishment, it has often been misunderstood as one-off events, rather than an institutionalized problem, implicitly and explicitly sanctioned.[11]

AT ANY COST AND BEYOND ALL BOUNDARIES

The brutality of torture, often thought of as extreme aggression and violence, extra-legal, or outside the perimeter of the justice system, historically and currently is often actually the perimeter of our justice system. Many governments maintain 'order' through suppression of dissent by intimidation and force at any cost, including torture. Tactics of torture lie outside international law and conventions of war, yet continue to be used as military strategy.

I ask myself if the nature of torture tactics is not only a reflection on our violent nature, our urge to dominate and willingness to do so at any cost, but is also a reflection on the spirit that doesn't break. (If we 'broke' more easily, the tactics we have concocted to suppress the spirit might not be so horrific.) One cannot dominate without resorting to terror. Even then, terror tactics ultimately don't work.

Survivors of torture sometimes attest to that spirit, the spirit that survived. After the torturer attempts to erase the personality, to humiliate and brutally destroy the limits of physical and emotional identity, and take away the possibility to resist or to return to normal life, those who survive often suffer from trauma throughout their lives. Yet some tell of their experience of a spirit that survived the atrocities, connected to something sacred, beyond personal history, beyond this rule of power and intimidation, no longer in its clutches, no longer its victim. It is as if our ordinary attachment to power, taken to its outlandish and hideous extreme, releases its hold.

CHAPTER 12
TERROR TACTIC: TARGETING THE SOUL OF COMMUNITY

RAPE

Rape is a tactic of war, expulsion and genocide. When political prisoners are arrested, rape is a tactic of terror, particularly targeting women and children.

Why is rape a tactic of terror, a method of torture and weapon of war? Rape targets the soul of a community and intends to hurt what is sacred and to shred the bonds of community life. Rape aims to humiliate, create depression and cut off the spiritual and relationship ties of community that sustain us.

The similarity of atrocities in town after town in Bosnia suggests that means of terror were predetermined in detail. In *Rape Warfare*, Beverly Allen quotes a document written by the army's special services, including experts in psychological warfare:

> *Our analysis of the behavior of the Muslim communities demonstrates that the morale, will, and bellicose nature of their groups can be undermined only if we aim our action at the point where the religious and social structure is most fragile. We refer to the women, especially adolescents, and to the children. Decisive intervention on these social figures would spread confusion – thus causing first of all fear and then panic, leading to a probable retreat from the territories involved in war activity.[1]*

In both Kosovo and Somalia, large numbers of women were raped and these women are often unable to speak about the suffering they endured. The taboo is too great. They may be blamed or expelled from family. Rape is a systematic tactic of terror, designed to strike a community where it is most sensitive and fragile.

TEAPOTS, PHOTOGRAPHS AND SACRED THINGS

Why was the old teapot smashed and the flowerpot on the windowsill? Why were the irreplaceable photographs in a small community centre thrown on the floor and set alight? Why are cherished monuments, cathedrals, churches and temples bombed, looted and burned? The target is the soul of community, anything that touches the sacred, what connects us to 'home' and a sense of belonging to community and to history.

MONUMENTS AND THE ROOTS OF COMMUNITY

In Croatia, Serbs damaged or destroyed more than 500 monuments and historical buildings and more than 370 museums, libraries and archives in the period between July 1991 and January 1992, including an eleventh-century church and a fourth-century Roman palace in Split, historical sections of Dubrovnik and Karlovac, and the entire city of Vukovar. These buildings, which had survived Turkish occupation and World Wars I and II, were now shelled as a deliberate policy of targeting other's cultural treasures. In Bosnia, after burning an old town, mosques and Catholic churches were frequently destroyed. Croats blew up a famous 400-year-old arched bridge in Mostar, and a Serb Orthodox monastery in Herzegovina.[2]

In Kosovo, in 1998–99, there was large-scale damage to the Islamic culture: 600 mosques were destroyed or damaged. Mosques were left with racist graffiti and Korans ripped up and smeared with faeces.[3] Serb nationalists saw this as their holy land that had been ransacked and taken away from them during the Ottoman invasion in the 1300s.

→ **Figure 12.1** Vukovar, Croatia (photo: www.osservatorio-balcani.org, by courtesy).

The date 9–10 November 1938 became known as 'Kristallnacht' ('Night of Broken Glass') in Germany. Nazis organized nation-wide pogroms, with looting and destruction of Jewish schools, community offices and stores. Hundreds of synagogues were vandalized and burned down. After Kristallnacht, 25 000 Jewish men and several thousand women were arrested.

Chinese forces invaded Tibet in 1949, and over 1.2 million Tibetans have died as a direct result of the occupation. Over 6000 monasteries have been destroyed. Thousands of people have been imprisoned and tortured because of religious and political beliefs. Approximately 130 000 Tibetan refugees live in exile around the world.[4]

→ Figure 12.2
Kristallnacht or 'Night
of Broken Glass'
('Die zerstörte Synagoge
in Eberswalde').
The destroyed Synagogue
in Eberswalde (near Berlin).
(By permission of
Bildarchive, Abraham
Pisarek, Berlin.)

↓ **Figure 12.3** Shide ruins, Lhasa, 1993 © Nancy Jo Johnson. Shide Monastery, one of Tibet's most venerable Buddhist monasteries, was destroyed during the Chinese invasion of Tibet in the 1950s. (With permission of Nancy Jo Johnson.)

Throughout history, destroying culture is a major tactic of terror. When a new regime wants to dominate, the old regime's symbols are destroyed. The loss of culture of oppressed or targeted groups is often forgotten or seen as a side effect of the events of history. Our capacity to forget is calculated in this tactic. The goal is to remove memory that bonds us in community, not only for the group in question, but also for the wider collective psyche. One way to erase memory and revise history is to smash old gods, monuments, statues and temples, and replace the old gods with new ones. When Moses received the Ten Commandments and came down from the mountain, he saw people dancing and praying to Babylonian deities and these 'false idols' were smashed.

BOOK BURNING

Burning books aims to burn ties to culture and to a shared history and contact with the river of life. Book burning celebrates a new ideology that must not be disputed or debated. Where there is book burning, there is an attempt to revise history. Freedom of information jeopardizes control. Book burning is a grand gesture to humiliate the community, a grand sweep to defy the lifeline to our

↓ **Figure 12.4** Book burning: a sixteenth century woodblock by Jost Annan.
(Thanks to Denis Gouey: www.bookbinding.net.)

ancestors. It is symbolic and actual, cleansing old ideas that might block the progress of a new ideology or regime.

Nazis burned books on 10 May 1933. Among the books burned was a book by Heinrich Heine, a German Jewish poet. A century earlier he had written: 'Where they burn books, they will end up also burning human beings' ('Dort, wo man Bücher verbrennt, verbrennt man am Ende auch Menschen').[5]

The largest single act of book burning in modern history took place in 1992 when, on 25 August, Serb nationalist forces began a 3-day assault on the National and University Library of Bosnia. Despite sniper fire, many people of Sarajevo risked their lives to form a human chain and pass books from the flames. Nearly 1.5 million books – including 155 000 rare books and manuscripts – the state archives, and all the Bosnian periodical literature published since the mid-1800s were lost.[6] The targeting of monuments, burning of books, expulsion and genocide go together.

In China, during AD 842–845, 4600 temples and some 40 000 shrines were destroyed, along with expulsion of more than 200 000 Monastics. The destruction of libraries and books deeply impacted on Buddhist study.[7]

There are many examples of the destruction of books, libraries, museums, knowledge and treasures of history. During the US attack on Iraq in 2003, museums and libraries were left unguarded and were looted and ransacked, as were historical archaeological sites. Amid discussion about who is at fault and how this happened, the situation has been portrayed as a matter of mismanagement, a tragedy. Even if this were true, the lack of foresight and protection offered by the American military for these treasures must be considered, in context to its pre-emptive attack, as the willingness to erase the soul of a civilization as part of the plan to install a 'democracy'.

WITCH BURNING

Witch burning aimed to purge society of 'evil'. I've included this under 'targeting the soul of community', and with the discussion of book burning and genocide, because this tactic of torture and killing was designed to target practices that might not conform to the dominating Christian theology. It aimed to control and to eradicate knowledge associated with women and 'pagan' practices. Many of the women targeted and killed possessed spiritual knowledge, healing and midwifery practice.

In 1326, the church authorized the Inquisition to investigate witchcraft, and developed a theory of its diabolic origin. In 1486–87, a book called *The Witches Hammer* described the activities of witches and methods for extracting confessions.[8] Witch hunts occurred in Europe from 1450 and declined after 1680. Executions ended in Europe by 1792.

In what is known as the 'burning times', 1550–1650, many tens of thousands were executed, and outrageous methods of torture were used to get confessions. Exact numbers killed are unknown. Some researchers estimate 30 000–50 000.[9] A Neo-pagan movement places the figure at 9 000 000. Germany, France, Switzerland and Austria had the most witch burnings. Witch hunts were a tactic of 'demonizing'. If God was 'all good', some speculate that a scapegoat was needed for the evil in the world.[10] Witches were considered 'pagan', worshipping other gods and goddesses, and in league with demons, meeting in the night, and causing all manner of evil, such as male impotence. 'Witch hunting was typically part of broader campaigns to repress unruly behavior and impose religious orthodoxies.'[11] Eighty per cent of those accused of being witches were women and many were children.

COLONIZATION, LANGUAGE, RITUAL, CUSTOMS

Targeting the soul of community was a central tactic of colonization. Cut the essential threads that weave the fabric of community together and it's easier to come in and take over. If you can get people to ignore their own rituals, customs and language, you might convince them to adapt to you. The more they lose faith in the knowledge and spirituality of their own culture, the more they will accept you and your gods. While actively targeting the pulse of community, missionaries often identified as doing God's work.

We have seen how discrediting elders is one method of cutting people off from the roots of their own culture. Another tactic is to remove children from their families and communities. From the late 1870s to the early 1970s, the US government forced thousands of Native American children to federal or religious boarding schools. The idea was supposedly to help children to assimilate. This was done through eradication of their culture, language and custom. Children were brutally beaten for speaking their own language and there was rampant physical and sexual abuse. Native communities now deal with the legacy of this abuse, which has 'infected, diminished and destroyed the lives of Indian people decades later, generations later'.[12] In Canada, thousands of children were forcibly placed in boarding schools where there was widespread physical and sexual abuse. Testimony in Canada documented that children were beaten, sexually abused, and killed by way of beating, poisoning and electric shock.[13] Stories of abuse are coming to the foreground within Native communities in an attempt to heal the past and move forward. Public acknowledgement by the government and church has been minimal.

SYMBOLS AND SOUL AS POINTS OF ATTACK

To dominate, we suppress the culture, rituals and symbols of others and replace them with our own. We often assume that loss of cultural symbols is but a side effect of changing power relationships, or that some cultures get lost in the shuffle, whereas others predominate. We may think that the group in power is prejudiced and doesn't value other cultures, or sees their rituals as foolish, if a little exotic and out of date. But we destroy culture more actively than this. Customs and symbols are seen for what they are, meaningful and pivotal for community life. Loss of culture is not just a side effect of oppression. Rituals and symbols are seen in their value and are points of attack.

SYMBOLS AND SOUL AS WEAPONS

Not only is the soul of community a point of attack. The soul of community is also used as a weapon. After bombing, burning and raping, we use our symbols, political ideologies and religion to intimidate and dominate. In this way the soul of community is taken away from the dominating group, too – by turning its cherished ideals and sense of meaning into weapons of war.

TARGETING THE SOUL OF THE 'MAJORITY' COMMUNITY

Everyone is targeted. We lose contact with our roots, our sense of community and meaning. Loss of soul in community is linked to isolation and widespread depression in our communities. Lack of awareness of our own ethnic and cultural background contributes to prejudice and racism. In societies with a white majority, ethnicity and diversity are regularly projected onto colour. The word 'ethnic' is regularly used these days in the USA and in parts of Europe to refer to a group that is felt to have some connection to culture and customs that are different from the mainstream. 'White' people often act as though they don't have an ethnic or cultural background of their own. When all notion of diversity is projected onto colour, this supports prejudice and racism. In favour of privilege, a great 'we' or 'majority' swells out of the lost richness of diversity and lost contact with history.

THE SOUL OF COMMUNITY AND CULTURAL APPROPRIATION

The term 'cultural appropriation' refers to taking from other cultures, without recognizing our relationships and history. How we make use of rituals and symbols is a serious matter, because of our legacy of violating others' values and cultural symbols as a tactic of terror. We target symbols at the heart of community in acts of systematic terror. After the community has suffered, died and/or been expelled from their home and their history revised or erased, these symbols emerge again. They are like artefacts from a plundered archaeological site, in which no one recalls the history of what happened there. Yet, we may innocently just like the artefact. We borrow and enjoy elements of other cultures. If asked to consider how these cultures have been violated, we may be unconcerned, annoyed and even hostile, muttering about political correctness.

Such symbols are charged. We might consider that they are emerging in an unconscious attempt to revive the sacred and even to grapple with the atrocity in our history. Yet, we more often romanticize and trivialize these symbols without reckoning or considering our story together.

In the open-air market of Warsaw, in the early 1990s, you could see stall upon stall of little carved wooden knick-knacks of Jewish Rabbis with Torahs, the Hebrew religious scripts. Weirdest of all, the word 'kosher' and Jewish stars were on the labels of candy and even Vodka bottles. Kosher refers to particular dietary rules and rituals followed by Orthodox Jews. Poland lost almost all of its large Jewish population and was also the location of Auschwitz–Birkenau and other death camps. These items marked kosher were clearly not kosher. The word 'kosher' and the Jewish star seemed to mean this candy or Vodka was exotic. It was a fad.

Cultural appropriation often links to a need to see the group who has been put down as exotic, wild or sexual. It's a characteristic of racism. We have seen how, in the USA, images of the 'wild' or 'savage' Indian are celebrated, the same 'wild' Indian who had to be killed in the 'manifest destiny' of Europeans in America.

We borrow from each other's cultures all the time. Sometimes this is in respectful and creative ways. Sometimes it is in a long-term process of mixing and tumbling. Sometimes it is a defiant exploitation. The issues involved are not always cut and dry, but definitely call for dialogue and deep consideration.

LONG-TERM AIMS AND LONG-TERM EFFECTS

Tactics that target the soul of community have long-term aims and effects. A huge amount of movement and migration arises from global conflict, global economics, and transportation and communication possibilities. We are increasingly a multicultural society. A question for our future will be how the soul of community can survive. Will we continue to use our ideology and culture as something to strike with and something to strike at – or will society's dialogue begin to include the possibility of relating to one another in the richness of our diversity.

CHAPTER 13
TERROR TACTIC: DISINFORMATION

DISINFORMATION AND THE MEDIA

Spreading false information is a tactic of terror. The media are a mighty weapon of war. If a government supports tactics of terror, chances are it controls the media, whether to a lesser or a greater extent. The *Oxford English Dictionary's* definition of disinformation is 'the dissemination of deliberately false information, especially when supplied by a government or its agent to a foreign power or to the media, with the intention of influencing the policies or opinions of those who receive it'.[1]

All media were controlled by the state in the former Soviet Union and those countries under Soviet domination. Nothing could be said against the wishes of the regime. As a result of a widespread system of informants and intelligence, you risked your life if you spoke out against the system, even in private.

As there was only one source of 'news' in the former communist countries, people learned to follow the party line. At the same time, people were keenly aware that all dissent was suppressed through terror, and few people could be trusted. In democracies, on the other hand, many people trust that they are getting a free flow of information and a diversity of views, even when they are not.

At the heart of democratic ideology is freedom of speech and a free flow of information to ensure that the will of the people will be the basis of authority in government. The control of the mass media by small numbers of private companies threatens the very tenets of democracy. The European Commission of Human Rights has recognized 'excessive concentration of the press' as an infringement on the rights guaranteed by Article 19, calling on states to prevent such abuses.[2] In *Media Monopoly*, author Ben Bagdikian wrote in 1983 that 50 corporations dominated most of every mass medium. In a 1987 edition, that number was 29. In 1990 it was 14. In 1997 it was 10.[3] In

2000, the sixth edition of *Media Monopoly* documented that only six corporations were supplying most of the nation's media. 'It is the overwhelming collective power of these firms, with their corporate interlocks and unified cultural and political values that raises troubling questions about the individual's role in the American democracy.'[4]

Where information ends and disinformation begins is sometimes a blur. Information is constantly interpreted to fit our worldview or to sway opinion or to obtain an advantage. Partial truths, misinformation and spin are part and parcel of information. The fact that a blur exists is also handy to mask disinformation. When someone blows the whistle, there is usually enough blur to leave an atmosphere that no one is sure what happened. We let it go. Half-truths and spins are formulated to intentionally mislead us. We know this. We debate it and let it go again. Even with the best intentions, limited or skewed reports contribute to the flow of disinformation, which is self-perpetuating.

Disinformation ranges from explicitly inciting violence and genocide through spreading of false information aimed to arouse sentiments of nationalism, and the deliberate manipulation of information to shape or coerce public opinion. The UN chief weapons inspector in Iraq in 2003, Hans Blix, said that the Bush Administration leaned on his inspectors to produce more damning language in their reports. He also said he was the object of smear campaigns by elements of the Pentagon.[5] The USA and the UK are both investigating the disinformation leading to the unilateral attack on Iraq in 2002.

Noam Chomsky documents how the Wilson Administration established a government propaganda commission in the USA before World War I. The 'Creel Commission' succeeded in rapidly turning a pacifist population into a population wanting to go to war against the Germans. A 'liberal democratic' theory supported the new techniques to 'manufacture consent'.[6] The idea was that an elite, intellectual community could figure things out and assume responsibility for decision-making; the rest of us would be involved by voting, but then step back into the spectator role.

Chomsky points out the similarities with a Leninist view, that a vanguard of revolutionary intellectuals should take state power, using popular revolution as a force to get it.[7] State propaganda, when supported by the educated classes, can have powerful consequences. In addition to the problem of a very small number of corporations owning the media in the USA, there's concern over a relatively small 'elite' group governing journalism, particularly in the USA, where a few newspapers such as the *New York Times* and the *Washington Post* have strong influence over the whole country's news.

This is a hot issue. Academics and intellectuals initiated and stirred the Serb nationalist movement in the late 1980s and early 1990s. Academics wrote about racial purity in Nazi Germany. Throughout history, 'experts' and journalists have been the arms of violent conflict, used to poison community, to incite killing and silence. As we have seen, the reverse is also true. Throughout history, many people have risked their lives to speak out and these journalists and 'intellectuals' have been targets of terror, in order to stop any potential or actual resistance to the imposing regime.

The internet was originally relatively free from political control and commercialized interests. This immense network of information exchange is an extraordinary and exciting counter-tendency to that of concentrated economic, social and political power, offering endless possibility in its freedom of information and for mobilizing cultural and political activities. At the same time, the web is now very much influenced and controlled through global marketing, and government intelligence certainly must join the large companies and hackers in monitoring us.

THE RECEIVER OF DISINFORMATION

Disinformation is not only about the sender of lies, misinformation and spin. Information involves a sender and a receiver. All of us are involved with the news – agitated, polarized, turned off or hopeless. If society wants to address the problem of disinformation and the role of the media, we need to look into how we pick up, sort and use information.

Disinformation targets our emotions, our limitations of awareness and capacity to sort information, our tendency to believe whatever version of events fits our personal and collective history and emotional attachments. Disinformation targets our capacity to believe anything if it supports our privilege. Disinformation is used to smear key activists and leaders, discredit social and political movements by arousing suspicion and hatred of individuals and groups, stir a sense of loyalty, touch upon old wounds and spurn the urge to retaliate. But, all information is as good as disinformation, if we only absorb it and simply accept or reject it, based on whether it makes us feel superior and convinced (again) that our view is the right one.

THE THOUSAND HILLS – INCITING TO KILL IN RWANDA ON THE RADIO

In Rwanda, in 1993, the media blatantly incited people to kill. The most popular radio station, RTLM (Radio Television des Milles Collines), 'The Thousand Hills Radio Television', was founded in 1993 by family members and friends of President Habyarimana. People liked the music. This radio station played music people liked to hear and began to preach Hutu supremacy.

Minutes after the downing of Habyarimana's plane, the incident that triggered the violence, this radio station accused the Belgian UN peace-keeping troops. The next morning, 10 Belgian soldiers were brutally killed and UN forces withdrew. RTLM began inciting massacre, using dehumanization tactics, as we have seen: '. . . they are cockroaches' or 'All those who are listening to us, arise so that we can fight for our Rwanda . . . fight with the weapons you have at your disposal, those of you who have arrows, with arrows, those of you who have spears, with spears . . . take your traditional tools . . . we must all fight [the Tutsis], we must finish with them, exterminate them . . . there must be no refuge for them, none at all.' They stayed on the air until the very last moment of the Rwandan genocide. Ferdinand Nahimana, RTLM's director, was arrested and delivered to the Rwanda Tribunal, on the charge of incitement to genocide. The same slogans entered another radio station in Zaire, to incite hatred against Tutsis in Burundi.[8]

DISINFORMATION AND GENOCIDE IN CROATIA AND BOSNIA

In the former Yugoslavia, the media were one of the most powerful weapons of war. During the descent into war in Croatia, in the Krajina region, when Serb paramilitary leaders took over the police station in Pacrac in February 1991, and Tudjman ordered that the Croatian army retake the police station, 180 men were arrested and many took to the hills. The town was left with broken windows and pock-marked walls and roofs. The Belgrade press erupted, reporting a flood of refugees, 20 000 strong, pouring into Serbia. In the mass-circulation Belgrade daily, *Cecernje Novosti*, a special edition reported on the front page that an Orthodox priest had been killed, on page 2 the priest had been wounded, and page 3 carried a statement from him.[9] That day a rally of Krajina Serbs was told that Croatia had declared war on the Serbs. The JNA (Yugoslav/Serbian) army intervened in Croatia for the first time.[10]

Throughout the war, the same events were reported on, not only with different spins, but with radically opposing versions of events. When Serb paramilitaries forced Bosnian Muslims from their homes in 1992, including executions and forcing Muslims to execute their own neighbours under threat of death, or forcing them into unbearable conditions and torture in the brutal concentration camps such as Omarska,[11] Serb authorities sent out reports that they were acting out of self-defence. Fabricated stories awakened fears that Muslims were intending to carry out genocide against the Serbs. People heard and believed this version of events, official news of the Bosnian Serb television and radio.

Misinformation about the genocide in Bosnia in the western media

As evidence of mass deportation, concentration camps, torture and massacre increased in Croatia and Bosnia, as mentioned, the western leaders and media referred to a 'civil war'. We were told that people in the Balkans could no longer live together because of longstanding ethnic rivalries, rather than that a conflict had been incited and created with the political aim of ethnic cleansing and genocide. As atrocities did occur on all sides, journalists often painted a picture of a war in which it seemed that everyone had gone mad and started killing one another. The term 'civil war' instead of 'genocide' supported avoidance of obligations under the UN Charter. An exhaustive report to the UN concluded that globally 90 per cent of the crimes in Bosnia were the responsibility of Serb extremists, 6 per cent by Croat extremists and 4 per cent by Muslim extremists.[12] Although we must expect these figures to vary significantly according to source, this was not a 'civil war'. What is crucial here is to consider how we can influence the course of history by how we receive and grapple with information.

Affiliation and poisonous documents: COINTELPRO

A common tactic of disinformation is to plant documents. The Counter Intelligence Program (COINTELPRO) tried to provoke or exasperate existing tensions between the Black Panther Party (BPP) and groups with which it was affiliated. A memo's stated objective was to provoke a vendetta between the Black Panthers and a group called 'United Slaves' by sending a letter attributed to the Panthers, revealing a fictional assassination plot (Figure 13.1). The same memo had plans to create discord between the BPP and the Peace and Freedom Party (PFP) and within the BPP.[13]

COINTELPRO also tried to provoke a split between the BPP and the SNCC (Student Nonviolent Coordinating Committee), by creating documents to give to news sources with volatile insults against Black Panthers, apparently originating from the SNCC.[14] Another COINTELPRO memo proposes a fictional letter to be sent to a Jewish group, as if from a black person favourable to Jews, claiming that the Black Panthers are extremely anti-Semitic and must be stopped (Figure 13.2).[15]

In one story, the FBI determined to smear the reputation of the BPP and Jean Seberg, a (white) woman, an actress, who was supporting the BPP financially (Figure 13.3). FBI records show a memo that requested permission and

```
                OPTIONAL FORM NO. 10
                MAY 1962 EDITION
                GSA GEN. REG. NO. 27

         UNITED STATES GO    MENT
      Memorandum
      : DIRECTOR, FBI (100-448006)        DATE: 11/29/68

ROM : SAC, LOS ANGELES (157-1751) (P)

UBJECT: COUNTERINTELLIGENCE PROGRAM
        BLACK NATIONALIST - HATE GROUPS
        RACIAL INTELLIGENCE
```

Re Los Angeles letter to Bureau dated 9/25/68.

I.   OPERATIONS UNDER CONSIDERATION

The Los Angeles Office is currently preparing an anonymous letter for Bureau approval which will be sent to the Los Angeles Black Panther Party (BPP) supposedly from a member of the "US" organization in which it will be stated that the youth group of the "US" organization is aware of the BPP "contract" to kill RON KARENGA, leader of "US", and they, "US" members, in retaliation, have made plans to ambush leaders of the BPP in Los Angeles.

It is hoped this counterintelligence measure will result in an "US" and BPP vendetta.

Investigation has indicated that the Peace and Freedom Party (PFP) has been furnishing the BPP with financial assistance. An anonymous letter is being prepared for Bureau approval to be sent to a leader of PFP in which it is set forth that the BPP has made statements in closed meetings that when the armed rebellion comes the whites in the PFP will be lined up against the wall with the rest of the whites.

It is felt that this type of a letter could cause considerable disruption of the association between the BPP and the PFP.

In order to cause disruption between the BPP of Oakland, California, and the BPP of Los Angeles, an envelope is being prepared for Bureau approval which appears

```
      REC-9
(2) - Bureau (RM)
 1 - Los Angeles

LWS/dl
(3)
```

↑ **Figure 13.1** FBI letter planning disinformation to create a 'vendetta' between the BPP (Black Panther Party) and the US (United Slaves) as well as to disrupt the relationship between the BPP and PFP (Peace and Freedom Party) and to disrupt relationships between the BPP of Oakland and Los Angeles. (Declassified US government documents; see Ward and Vander Wall (1990, 2002) *The COINTELPRO Papers*. Cambridge, MA: South End Press.)

```
                                                              ●
         UNITED STATES ●  ₍NMENT
         Memorandum.

    TO   :    DIRECTOR, FBI (100-448006)        DATE: 9/10/69

    FROM :    SAC, NEW YORK (100-161140) (P)

    SUBJECT:  COUNTERINTELLIGENCE PROGRAM
              BLACK NATIONALIST - HATE GROUPS
              RACIAL INTELLIGENCE
              BLACK PANTHER PARTY (BPP)

                   Re NY report of █████████████, captioned
         "JEWISH DEFENSE LEAGUE, RACIAL MATTERS", NY file 157-3463;
         Bu letter to NY, 7/25/69.

                   Referenced report has been reviewed by the NYO
         in an effort to target one individual within the Jewish
         Defense League (JEDEL) who would be the suitable recipient
         of information furnished on an anonymous basis that the
         Bureau wishes to disseminate and/or use for future counter-
         intelligence purposes.

                   NY is of the opinion that the individual within
         JEDEL who would most suitably serve the above stated purpose
         would be Rabbi MEIR KAHANE, a Director of JEDEL.  It is
         noted that Rabbi KAHANE's background as a writer for the
         NY newspaper "Jewish Press" would enable him to give wide-
         spread coverage of anti-Semetic statements made by the BPP
         and other Black Nationalist hate groups not only to members
         of JEDEL but to other individuals who would take cognizance
         of such statements.

                   In order to prepare a suggested initial communi-
         cation from the anonymous source to Rabbi KAHANE which would
         establish rapport between the two, it is felt that this contact
         should not be limited to the furnishing of factual information
         of interest to the aims of JEDEL because the NYO does not
         feel that JEDEL could be motivated to act as called for in
         referenced Bureau letter if the information gathered by the
         NYO concerning anti-semitism and other matters were furnished
         to that organization without some embellishment.
```

↑ **Figure 13.2** FBI memo planning to create split between the Black Panther Party and the Jewish Defense League. Continues opposite.

(Declassified US government documents; see Ward and Vander Wall (1990, 2002) *The COINTELPRO Papers*. Cambridge, MA: South End Press.)

For example it is felt that JEDEL is aware
of the majority of information concerning the factual
views of the BPP and other Black Nationalist groups through
public sources of information such as the BPP newspaper,
"The Black Panther", and to furnish such information from
an "anonymous source" would either be dismissed by JEDEL as
trivial or attributed to some other party who may have an
interest in causing JEDEL to act against such groups as
the BPP.

In view of the above comments the following is
submitted as the suggested communication to be used to
establish rapport between the anonymous source and the
selected individual associated with JEDEL:

"Dear Rabbi Kahane:

I am a Negro man who is 48 years old and served
his country in the U.S. Army in WW2 and worked as a truck
driver with "the famous red-ball express" in Gen. Eisenhour's
Army in France and Natzi Germany. One day I had a crash
with the truck I was driving, a 2½ ton truck, and was injured
real bad. I was treated and helped by a Jewish Army Dr.
named "Rothstein" who helped me get better again.

Also I was encouraged to remain in high school
for two years by my favorite teacher, Mr. Katz. I have
always thought Jewish people are good and they have helped
me all my life. That is why I become so upset about my
oldest son who is a Black Panther and very much against
Jewish people. My oldest son just returned from Algers in
Africa where he met a bunch of other Black Panthers from
all over the world. He said to me that they all agree that
the Jewish people are against all the colored people and
that the only friends the colored people have are the Arabs.

I told my child that the Jewish people are the
friends of the colored people but he calls me a Tom and
says I'll never be anything better than a Jew boy's slave.

Last night my boy had a meeting at my house
with six of his Black Panther friends. From the way
they talked it sounded like they had a plan to force
Jewish store owners to give them money or they would
drop a bomb on the Jewish store. Some of the money
they get will be sent to the Arabs in Africa.

They left books and pictures around with Arab
writing on them and pictures of Jewish soldiers killing
Arab babys. I think they are going to give these away
at Negro Christian Churchs.

I though you might be able to stop this. I
think I can get some of the pictures and books without
getting myself in trouble. I will send them to you if
you are interested.

I would like not to use my real name at this
time.

A friend"

It is further suggested that a second communication
be sent to Rabbi KAHANE approximately one week after the
above described letter which will follow the same foremat,
but will contain as enclosures some BPP artifacts such as
pictures of BOBBY SEALE, ELDRIDGE CLEAVER, a copy of a BPP
newspaper, etc. It is felt that a progression of letters
should then follow which would further establish rapport
with the JEDEL and eventually culminate in the anonymous
letter writer requesting some response from the JEDEL
recipient of these letters.

another memo that granted permission to create a false story about her and disseminate it to news sources. The story was that she was pregnant by a BPP leader and not her husband. The disinformation was aimed to capitalize on racist and sexist attitudes, as well as to tear at relationships within the movement. She became distressed, had a stillbirth (her baby was her husband's) and later committed suicide.[16]

As an anecdote, while I was writing this chapter on disinformation, I went to an internet site considered politically left and well respected. They announced on their homepage that emails with extreme views were being sent around, ostensibly from their website. The emails were not from them and did not reflect their views. They said nothing more, but it appears to have been an attempt to smear their growing reputation and to turn off their growing audience, making them appear extremist.

THE PATH OF A LIE

Austrian scholar Karl Kraus wrote: 'How is the world ruled and led into war? Diplomats lie to journalists and believe those lies when they see them in print.'[17] First there's a lie or distortion. The original piece of disinformation is amplified and becomes a 'given' around which analysis and commentary emerge. Once the lie is implanted, anyone who suggests any discrepancy or doubt might be considered a conspiracy theorist, radical or liar. When a lie is brought to light, it may be seen as a one-off event that doesn't put the larger system into question. Disinformation is normalized. Truth is a kind of collateral damage.

The USA bombed Iraq based on the claim that Saddam Hussein certainly had weapons of mass destruction. As the bombing was under way, reports turned to the theme of liberating Iraq and installing a democracy. Then people asked, but where are those weapons of mass destruction? With a broad grin on his face Secretary of Defense Donald Rumsfeld said: 'We haven't found Saddam either, but no one's saying he didn't exist.' Asking for verification about weapons of mass destruction was made out to be foolish.

DISINFORMATION AND THE FILES OF OUR INTERNAL AUTHORITIES

To do something about disinformation, as a society, we need to learn more about the psychology of how we get disinformed. We easily believe what we are told if it matches our preconceptions, suspicions and ideals. In Process-

Date: 4/27/70

Transmit the following in _____

(Type in plaintext or code)

Via _____ AIRTEL _____   REGISTERED MAIL

(Priority)

TO: DIRECTOR, FBI (100-448006)

FROM: SAC, LOS ANGELES (157-4054) (P)

SUBJECT: COUNTERINTELLIGENCE PROGRAM
           BLACK NATIONALIST HATE GROUPS
           RACIAL INTELLIGENCE - BLACK PANTHER PARTY

           Re San Francisco airtel to the Bureau dated 4/23/70,
entitled, "BLACK PANTHER PARTY (BPP), LOS ANGELES DIVISION,
RM-BPP."

           Bureau permission is requested to publicize the
pregnancy of JEAN SEBERG, well-known movie actress, by
███████████ Black Panther Party (BPP) ████████████
████ by advising Hollywood "Gossip-Columnists" in
the Los Angeles area of the situation. It is felt that
the possible publication of SEBERG's plight could cause
her embarrassment and serve to cheapen her image with the
general public.

           It is proposed that the following letter from a
fictitious person be sent to local columnists:

           "I was just thinking about you and remembered
           I still owe you a favor. So---------I was in Paris
           last week and ran into Jean Seberg, who was heavy
           with baby. I thought she and Romaine had gotten

2 - Bureau (RM)
2 - San Francisco (Info) (RM) REC- 51
2 - Los Angeles   100 - 448006 - 1766

RWH/fs   17 MAY 1 1970
(6)

                                       RACIAL INT. SECT.

Approved: _____   Sent _____ M ___ Per _____
          Special Agent in Charge

U. S. GOVERNMENT PRINTING OFFICE : 1966 O - 245-486 (11)

LA 157-4054

together again, but she confided the child
belonged to ████████ of the Black
Panthers, one ████████ The dear girl
is getting around!

           "Anyway, I thought you might get a scoop
on the others. Be good and I'll see you soon.

                    "Love,

                         Sol"

           Usual precautions would be taken by the Los
Angeles Division to preclude identification of the Bureau
as the source of the letter if approval is granted.

↑ **Figure 13.3** FBI plans to smear Jean Seberg resulting in her baby's stillbirth and her suicide. (Declassified US government documents; see Ward and Vander Wall (1990, 2002) *The COINTELPRO Papers* Cambridge, MA: South End Press.)

Oriented Psychology, the concept of the 'edge'[18] or the perimeter to our identity defines who we think we are, what we think is possible, what we believe about the world. Inner and outer authorities define this 'edge' of identity. Inner authorities are usually internalized from our personal and collective history, whether parents and teachers, religious figures, representatives of political ideologies or 'experts'. Edges govern our perception and cognition, what information we are able to pick up, what information actually makes it through our filters, the way we accommodate and understand the information, as well as the way we value and respond to it.

Information is received, interpreted and filed by internal authorities. We mark some files urgent, others less important, some as belonging on someone else's desk or as junk mail. We sift and file information according to our belief systems and ideals. If we believe that this is a fair and democratic country, when we hear the 'news' that someone has been convicted of murder, we assume there has been a fair trial and the person is a murderer. If we are immersed in a racist belief system that black people are violent, when we read that a black person was convicted of murder, we absorb the information in two filing systems – 'we are a good and democratic country, in which people have fair trials' and 'black people are violent'. Disinformation is readily swallowed when it matches those internalized authorities or files. Unnoticed and easily digested, it's poisonous. In this case, the receiver does not suspect that the event was fabricated. Not only do those planting disinformation get away with the lie, but the lie becomes fuel for further ignorance, further lies and further waves of disinformation.

When the true story threatens to dispel a belief system or puts our position in question, we easily welcome disinformation to strengthen it again. Disinformation is needed by those in power to uphold a failing myth.

Disinformation is often what we want to hear, so it is fairly easy to slip it in the pie. You don't have to go out of your way to make the fabricated information appear true. Conversely, it's much harder to bring out the truth if it goes against a myth or ideal that is supported by outer and inner authorities.

DISINFORMATION AND IDEALS

We also swallow disinformation so readily because there are essential and genuine dreams and ideals at stake.[19] We can't just put our idealistic tendencies aside to see more clearly. Ideals make us human, give us purpose and connect us to values and forces beyond our personal lives. The more unconscious we are of our ideals, the easier they can be used as sugar to help us swallow disinformation. Becoming conscious of our ideals might mean doing our utmost to live by them rather than only be lulled by them.

THE PSYCHOLOGICAL DIMENSION AND 'INTELLIGENCE'

There is usually not much coverage in mainstream reporting on the use of the terror tactics we've been discussing – exploiting instability, demonizing, dehumanizing, normalizing, targeting leaders, targeting the soul of community, torture and disinformation. These tactics are typically covert and a part of 'intelligence' activities. Further tactics include wire-tapping and other forms of monitoring information. In fascist states, control of media goes hand in hand with secret service, surveillance and the suppression of dissident voices. In democracies, state terror tactics are usually called 'intelligence' and 'counter-terrorism', and lie outside public scrutiny.

Society's debate about civil liberties, disinformation and 'intelligence' needs to include a psychological dimension, regarding how we participate in the flow of information. If we define ourselves as passive recipients of information, we in effect give away our 'intelligence' and our capacity to observe and participate in this flow of information.

Violent conflict almost always involves the suppression of information and interaction, and the arousal of opposing opinions, fed by 'facts' on both sides. Public discourse often encourages us to have one view, rather than an interaction. One problem is that we don't fully differentiate and polarize our views. We stop half-way, feeding conflict, rather than thoroughly debating it. In this way 'disinformation' is self-amplifying. Our curiosity, dialogue and debate stop half-way when we don't consider how internal rules govern our perceptions of information and our emotional reactions. When we stay minimally informed or one-sidedly informed, we are all the more vulnerable to disinformation that further locks us into a polarized position. If we aren't interested in the deepest feelings that guide our perceptions and reactions, we can't know and express our views and interact with others. As long as we don't really believe our own perceptions, we paradoxically stay attached to them, unable to reflect upon them.

Disinformation can be thought of not only as someone pulling the wool over our eyes, but also as a process in which we often isolate ourselves and participate unknowingly in violence. We isolate ourselves from the past, from one another and from our present participation in the world. Disinformation is self-perpetuating. To begin to unravel it, we need a society-wide process of something like a Truth Commission, to intentionally untangle the humanity of our stories. To do that, we'd need more than information. We need access to one another in our own hearts and in relationship and community.

CHAPTER 14
BEYOND TERROR

HUMAN RIGHTS AWARENESS

Human rights violations often pass unnoticed or elicit little public outcry. One reason is because there is a limited understanding of the systemic nature of such violations and their implications and potential consequences. We may assume that an emergency measure such as suspending civil liberties is appropriate to an exceptional situation, in the hope of returning to a sense of security as quickly as possible. We need to develop a broader perspective, connecting the dots, discovering the underlying patterns and warning signals.

When she was UN High Commissioner for Human Rights, Mary Robinson emphasized that human rights violations are precursors to violent conflict. If we respond to human rights violations early on, she believed we might prevent wide-scale violent conflict. Where there are human rights violations, there is already an endorsed practice of using violence to enforce control, and conflict will escalate. Where there are human rights violations seen, there are more underneath, unseen, unreported and covered up. Such violations are often systemic, institutionalized and implicitly or explicitly sanctioned by a government.

If we feel protected in our fundamental human rights, we want to keep it that way. We want our intelligence systems to work effectively in protecting our safety and freedom. Those of us who have experienced threat and terror know what it is like not to be able to turn to authorities for protection. A major purpose and responsibility of government is to protect our safety and fundamental human rights. A major purpose of international law and human rights advocacy is to encourage this to happen, and to make it known when it is not happening.

International law differentiates what can be considered a dispute between two states from a state that is committing war crimes or crimes against humanity, including terror tactics against civilians, who may include the state's own citizens. Although there is no humane war, the distinctions of international law have been paramount in developing an ethical and legal framework to protect individual human rights around the world during war, as well as to protect the human rights of citizens at any time.

After the horror of Nazi atrocities, the 1945 Nuremberg Tribunals set out the principle that there are crimes against humanity – systematic crimes against civilians – that can occur inside a country, but could be brought to trial elsewhere. In 1948, the UN adopted the Universal Declaration of Human Rights, which has served as the foundation for all subsequent human rights work, and is increasingly integrated into national and international ethics and law. The Genocide Convention of 1948 and the Geneva Convention of 1949 differentiated rules governing wars between states from crimes against humanity.

Though issues of human rights are increasingly in the public domain, human rights violations and violent conflict are rampant. Groups such as Amnesty International, World Organization against Torture or Human Rights Watch, along with the Human Rights Commission of the UN, are involved with monitoring and responding to human rights violations all over the world, and raising awareness. Human rights activities involve raising public awareness of human rights violations and violations of international law. The public also needs awareness about how our own behaviours and emotions feed tactics of terror and human rights violations, leading to violent conflict.

US VERSUS INTERNATIONAL LAW

The USA, as the world's only superpower, appears to have taken the stance that it need not be concerned with international law and international human rights conventions, that it is outside and above international bodies.

This is of escalating concern and more in the forefront of public knowledge, as a result of the unilateral actions and rhetoric in the 'war on terrorism' since 9/11. All the while, the USA tries to undermine the International Criminal Court and ensure impunity for US nationals. It has demanded that any US national accused of crimes under the jurisdiction of the International Criminal Court or World Court should be returned to the USA, without any commitment that they be prosecuted by US courts and without any recourse if US courts fail to fulfil their responsibilities. The USA has tried to pressure states to sign bilateral agreements to grant this immunity, by threatening to withdraw aid if they do not. In Europe, this pressure was put on Romania, Georgia, Albania, Macedonia, Bosnia, Croatia, Serbia and Montenegro. The EU appealed to European countries not to sign these agreements and to comply with EU principles – to which the Bush administration accused the EU of 'undercutting all our efforts to repair and rebuild the transatlantic relationship'.[1]

As a result of the military and economic power of the USA, and the way this power is used to claim and ensure impunity, concerns over human rights violations have far-reaching significance. A purpose of international law is to bring international attention to situations where states misuse their power against their own citizens or others and can claim impunity in their own countries, because of their power. The USA, because of its might, is claiming impunity in relation to the whole world. The rest of the world, if they disagree, are considered dissident, and cannot expect to be treated within international conventions of war or international conventions of human rights.

International human rights groups and the UN Commission for Human Rights have been outspoken about the serious human rights violations involved as hundreds of people were detained without charge or trial at the US Naval Base in Guantanamo Bay. Those detained include children considered 'enemy combatants'.[2] The 'war on terror' created a climate where many Americans assumed such tactics must be excused under exceptional circumstances. Yet, as we've seen, this is an age-old tactic of state terror to exploit instability to remove civil liberties. In Guantanamo Bay, none of the prisoners was given access to the courts, to lawyers or to relatives. None had his case brought before a 'competent tribunal' as required under the Geneva Conventions. Along with refusal to consider outside monitoring of trials, plans for military trials proceeded. Some suspected the building of death chambers.[3]

THE MONSTER

As we look at the violence and massive human rights violations over the last century and the last decades, we may feel that our inability to prevent such violence is because the problem is just too big. It is monstrous. We don't know where to begin. We may be disinterested, uninformed, disinformed, unsure, busy, wanting, but not knowing how to make some contribution. Or we may feel restricted for fear that these tactics will be used on us.

Where does the mindset come from that allows us to dominate at any cost, use torture as a means of control and write manuals about it? When we believe that it is just a monster out there, a monstrous leader in a terrible war-torn country, we do not begin to face ourselves and the violence in this world. We stay in a fairytale landscape with a Bogeyman around the corner. We suffer from a spirit of dominance, we rebel against it and we like it a lot. Absorbed in a worldview oriented by power, we stifle the richness of our thought and feeling.

If we disagree with an implicit code, just speaking up among a group of friends can be terrifying, and as difficult as doing so within an organization, community or country. We might learn to barely notice the urge to bring in a difference. By the time we do, we are outraged and flip into rebellion, the other side of the same coin. We easily cut off from our interest in relating our deepest and subtle feelings and perceptions, and our awareness that we are fully able to support the differentiation and interaction of all views. If we don't recognize our capacity to facilitate an interaction of our diverse experiences, we tend to let one mood, belief or idea dominate and then we feel cut off from a sense of meaning and reflection.

REPRESSION AND FREEDOM OF THOUGHT

Many people from Russia and the eastern bloc countries that were dominated by the former Soviet Union, such as the Czech and Slovak republics, Poland and Bulgaria, have spoken to me about the experience that they not only felt they could not speak out freely, but that gradually, through the internalization of this system, they noticed how they had become unable to think freely. I always remember a presentation by a Russian man, who spoke about this dynamic with refreshing clarity. He gave a very detailed and thorough description of the process of losing consciousness and being absorbed in the repressive system. He was able to describe this sense of losing the ability to think freely, with such extraordinary lucidity that he had a group of a couple of hundred of people on the edges of their chairs. There was an implicit and enlightening paradox in his capacity to express the process of losing the freedom to think freely so accurately and articulately. Though he spoke of his experience of losing freedom of thought in Russia, many felt his comments reflected an uncanny freedom and creativity of thought. He seemed to be speaking not only for people from former communist countries, but for many of us who come from parts of the world where we take freedom of speech for granted, but could relate to the description of a gradual deadening of the capacity to freely question and reflect deeply, stemming in this case from privilege and feeling unable or disinterested in sorting an abundance of information (and disinformation).

INTERNALIZED OPPRESSION

The feminist movement has been a global process of waking from a collective trance, governed by the belief that a women's viewpoint doesn't count, her existence doesn't count and that she is someone else's 'property'. Women have led the women's movement. Although this is obvious, it's an essential and far-reaching idea that the oppressed group first 'liberates' themselves. Freedom not only involves liberating oneself from an oppressor, but also involves getting to know that oppressor within oneself. Getting to know the internalized oppressor in great detail is terrifying and freeing, to no longer be unconsciously imprisoned inside one's own mind and heart. Steve Biko, the South African activist, murdered by the Apartheid regime said: 'The most powerful weapon in the hands of the oppressor is the mind of the oppressed.'

Internalized oppression occurs when an individual or group is tied to the internalized voice of the oppressor – the oppressor who now lives in close quarters. The oppressor has an ally not only spying on the oppressed, but living inside his mind. Internalized oppression also fuels rage and rebellion against the oppressor and against oneself.

We might recognize how this internalized domination operates in all of us, by observing our reaction to it – when it reduces our motivation to stay informed or engaged. It might coerce us into feeling isolated and cut off from large portions of our inner life and outer reality. It dampens our creativity and wish to relate. It blocks our curiosity. It asks us to relax, make the most of it, entertain ourselves. It tells us we are stupid or others are stupid. It questions our right to question, to discuss things deeply. A German expression, 'Schuster, bleib bei Deinen Leisten', 'Shoemaker, stay with your shoe soles', tells us to not think thoughts beyond our position in society. This ghost questions everyone's education, gender, class, sexual orientation, nationality or ethnic cultural background and age. It worries about our emotional stability, moods, mental health and loyalty.

THE RIGHT TO DREAMING AND DIVERSITY

Internalized oppression violates our freedom of expression before we even notice. It results in a loss of integrity, a widespread chronic mild depression. This depression helps us to adapt to the status quo, to feel helpless in front of the human rights violations in our communities and world. What we consider to be normal may be a kind of chronic mild depression. We don't notice how we are immersed in dynamics of power, whether adapting, dominating, rebelling, feeling outraged, hurt, intimidated, worthless, or self-assured and powerful.

It's an extraordinary feat to get to the perimeter of this worldview, rather than to assume the world is flat. We have seen how a worldview based on one side dominating is upheld through terror tactics that work on us psychologically and spiritually. This worldview impacts on our political and economic dynamics, the media, and all our community interactions, social relationships, personal relationships and contact with ourselves as individuals.

Whether we are part of an oppressed or dominant group, or find ourselves on both sides of this interaction, there is a part of us that knows something isn't right and longs to get beyond the perimeter that defines a worldview based on one side dominating the other – to discover the richness and spirit in our inner and outer diversity.

AWAKENING

I liked the 'Truman Show'.[4] It was a film in the USA during the late 1990s about what it takes to go beyond the perimeter of our limited worldview. Truman lived inside a television show, in which he was actually born and raised, as the world watched, in a kind of daytime soap. As he began to suspect something wasn't quite right about his world and began to follow his impulse and heart, he got too close to the boundary of his (TV) world. So everyone conspired to stop him at every turn, to hold him inside the TV show. First he was nudged back into his old daily patterns – then, disinformation and lies, including fabricated news events to explain the anomalies he had noticed, and then deception from his (TV) best friend. Increasingly he was faced with tactics of terror and in the end a 'death walk'[5] in a violent storm at sea, intended first to send him back to shore, and then to kill him. The producer preferred him dead than conscious – or a more hopeful interpretation is that, while the producer's role was to stop him at any cost, the task of his TV character was to risk everything, to get beyond his old TV personality, to make it to the other side of the set, and become really human. His two-dimensional character had to become real. All the while, we see the daytime TV audience gripped, rooting for him to escape the set in this great drama. What appeared to be the horizon was in fact the wall, with painted clouds, at the end of the set. And there was a little door. When Truman got there, he just walked out. As it was all 'live' on TV, there was an outburst of cheers, and on a sobering and humorous note everyone changed the channel.

TERRORIZED BY A GHOST: ROLES AND GHOST ROLES

In intractable and cycling conflict, the whole system is caught in a world of terror. Everyone may feel terrorized and each sees the threat and oppressor in the other. The system replays in never-ending retaliation against the oppressor. As no-one identifies as being that oppressor, the oppressor remains a kind of 'ghost'.[6] It's a ghost, because it is non-local, not attached to any region, group or person. It's everywhere. People suffer from it on both sides. And the ghost lives at the perimeter to our worldview, enforcing it.

In situations of conflict, it's very useful to differentiate the opposing positions. In a forum, the positions may be set up as two places in the room, and people can enter these positions to speak. This helps people to see and participate in the interaction of positions, rather than to feel only embedded in the conflict. Arnold Mindell's concept of 'roles' helps to deepen this interaction.[7] Roles are bigger than just one person's viewpoint. Each role needs many viewpoints to be fully fleshed out and differentiated. But, individuals are also bigger than roles. As you are able to express yourself within one role, you may begin to discover the other role within you as well, and might switch sides, even momentarily.[8]

Roles are like nodes in an underlying structure of a conflict. Roles are archetypal – the oppressor and oppressed, the insider and the outsider, the ghosts that expel or welcome.[9] I like to see the interaction of roles as a 'deep structure'[10] that emerges with varying content. When each side has suffered violence from the other side, facilitation requires working, not only with the actual issues of violence that occurred between the different groups at different points of history, and the accountability required, but also with the underlying structure of the conflict between oppressor and oppressed, repeating through history. The roles remain the same, although the people filling these roles change.[11]

A GROUP PROCESS: TERROR, ISOLATION AND COMMUNITY

One afternoon during a forum in Croatia, the group began to talk about how they frequently feel that their contribution in community is unwanted. All of the participants were active in their own communities in developing programmes and working as social workers, lawyers, psychologists, teachers, mayors, etc. Several participants described how they met an attitude within their own professions and within the community that continually put down their ideas as stupid or just useless, renewing a continual cycle of hopelessness within what was a spiritually and economically depressed period in Croatia. After the session came to a close, we realized the dynamics had become actualized in our interactions. We learned that one participant, who had never been to such a forum, was feeling upset because another person was making jokes and sarcastic remarks, making her feel that people were not being taken seriously and she was afraid to say a word.

In preparation for the next morning, my colleague and I looked at the structure of the process. We kept feeling we were missing something and finally decided to sleep on it. I dozed off a while, but kept waking up, feeling very uneasy and queasy. I accused myself of having too much wine over dinner, and was determined to get some sleep so I would be fit to facilitate in the morning. But I couldn't sleep. I felt strange and disoriented. I broke out in a cold sweat. What in the world was going on in me? I focused on my sweat, and to my surprise discovered I was terrified. But, why was I terrified? Was it because I hadn't understood the group process? I knew myself to want to stay up until I have understood something. But this was terror! Then I realized there must be a 'ghost' creating this terror. My disorientation and anxiety vanished, as I understood that my feeling of terror and the ghost creating this terror were roles within the field, still very present in Croatia, and shaping the dynamics of our group.

I took a couple of notes and went straight to sleep. In the morning I discussed it with Lane and, in our short morning presentation, we said a few words about the process the day before, that feeling unwelcome for one's contribution to community can touch into traumatic experience around terror tactics and expulsion from the community. We opened the group discussion, to find out how the group wanted to go forward. The woman who had been upset and frightened to speak spontaneously stood up, came to the centre of the room and asked to speak. She began to tell a horrific story that she had never told anyone before. During the war, she had been arrested for no reason, taken away for 3 days, humiliated and terrorized, and was threatened with being 'disappeared'. She had never told her family or anyone where she had been those 3 days. As she spoke, she was shaking both with the memory of the terror she had suffered and with her fear and shame to speak to the group now. The group said they wanted to hear her story. We mentioned how her fear of being rejected by this group now connected to the story from 10 years ago, when she had been pushed out of her community and almost killed.

With support to choose if and how she wanted to tell her story, she continued and we stood near her.[12] Yet, her shaking persisted. We told her it may be useful to her, and all of us, if we represented the 'role' or 'voice' that was still blocking the story from being told and heard – that part of the group or community, also internalized, that is casting her out, threatening to 'disappear' her. We guessed into the voice of the threatening 'ghost role', threatening her life and expelling her. We also guessed into the voice that does not want to hear the story. Many nodded in recognition of the familiar 'voice' who says: 'We are not interested. It is too hard to listen. We hear too many stories. No more tears. There are many worse stories.'

Then a participant came forward, wanting to stand in the role of the 'ghost' who cannot listen. He spoke personally. 'The reason I can't hear you fully is because there are so many dead people who can never tell their stories.' He said the only way he could express his hurt and outrage would be to go into the main square and set himself on fire. With support from my colleague, Lane, he was able to express some of his rage, not in words, but by following a movement he spontaneously made that evolved into a fiery dance, an expression of rage, passion and life.

The person who had been making jokes the day before then came forward to encourage the woman who had told her story, saying she needed the group's warmth, protection and invitation. She was very touched by the way he and the whole group welcomed her. Her shaking had stopped and her tears too. She said she felt relieved to have told her story, for the first time. The group went on to talk about what had happened, particularly looking at attitudes in community that made people unable to speak and tell their stories. They talked about the importance of processing the traumatic experiences of terror in their communities, and what it meant for them to contribute to building their communities.

STEPPING OUT

Terror tactics are aimed at our tendency to comply or rebel. They are aimed at intimidating and silencing us, or working us up into a reaction, so that there can be further crack-down. To step out of this never-ending story requires awareness of how we perpetuate it.

To break the spell requires awareness that is both personal and political. Process Oriented Psychology, developed by Arnold Mindell,[13] links inner work and community work in unique ways. Through awareness of one's perceptions, reactions and communication, as well as the polarization of roles and ghosts in a system, it is possible to discover systemic interactions at an internal level, in relationship and in community. By bringing awareness to the whole interaction at an internal level, we are no longer stuck, freer to respond and facilitate in the outer interaction. There may also be an experience of a unifying field that precedes and includes the conflict. Inner focus does not replace outer work – rather, it makes it possible. In this way, there is freedom to get engaged with the conflicts of our inner life, relationships and communities, rather than only suffer them and replicate them.

Gandhi believed that 'the Self discovered itself in all its complexity and grew only in the course of trying to meet the powerful challenges of the world. For Gandhi, self-realization was impossible without worldly involvement.'[14] He believed humanity was indivisible, and no man could brutalize another without also brutalizing himself.[15] Non-violence refers to not falling into the violent system, not replicating the violence. It does not mean being passive.

Gandhi was very plain about this. He even said it was better to be violent than passive. Non-violence thus referred to the capacity to not fall into a conflict by being passive or reactive.

In Los Angeles, my husband and I had the privilege of meeting Glen Smiley several times before he died. He had been the teacher of non-violent methods to Martin Luther King and was deeply involved with the civil rights movement, remaining involved in the study of non-violence until the end of his life. I remember his stories about the early days of the civil rights movement, when they would go into cafés in the southern states in the USA, in pairs, a black man and a white man. When they were told that they would not be served or were provoked, they politely insisted on being served, while refusing to engage in a fight. He emphasized the inner work and discipline that was necessary to do this, under threat.

In his autobiography, Nelson Mandela describes several situations in which he refused to be treated with indignity, yet also refused to become reactive, both in his days in prison and as the leader of his country, South Africa.

MANDELA'S GOAL TO GET US ALL OUT OF PRISON

Breaking free from terror, intimidation and oppression is not only a political, social and community task, but also a deeply psychological and spiritual one. Mandela said about his time in prison: 'It was during those long and lonely years that my hunger for the freedom of my own people became a hunger for the freedom of all people, white and black. I knew as well as I know anything that the oppressor must be liberated just as surely as the oppressed . . . I am not truly free if I am taking away someone else's freedom, just as surely as I am not free when my freedom is taken from me. The oppressed and the oppressor alike are robbed of their humanity. When I walked out of prison, that was my mission, to liberate the oppressed and the oppressor both.'[16] Mandela stepped out of his own personal history and South Africa's tragic history of oppression. He set an example that it's possible to walk right out of the prison of history.

THE SPIRIT THAT SURVIVES

Throughout history, our individual and collective psychology has been consistently used as fuel for terror – to control, and to target the limits of what individuals and communities can endure. We've been looking at how tactics of terror exploit instability and need for safety, our fear of the Bogeyman, the dynamics of dehumanization, desensitization and normalization, targeting leaders and the soul of community, and disinformation. The boundary of a system defined by power is enforced through terror tactics.

But, this boundary is kept intact through our agreement to participate in these dynamics as they repeat within us internally, in relationship, in community and politically. If we break this agreement, the system cannot remain intact.

To break the agreement is to face widespread human rights violations, terror tactics and violent conflict, without freezing, growing helpless, hopeless or repeating the cycle through retaliation. To do so we need to recognize that our psychological and spiritual development is an essential part of our political awareness.

We may be inspired by people who have hope and inner peace and resolve, not founded in naivety, but in the experience of having touched the outer limits of what anyone can endure, and at the same time exposing those limits. A spell is cracked, a discovery made of possibilities beyond that horizon, beyond the reign of terror.

PART 3

TRAUMA –
THE NIGHTMARE OF
HISTORY

CHAPTER 15
OUR STORY – THE DYNAMICS OF TRAUMA

Whether we have suffered from atrocity or silently watched, our human story has been traumatic. Trauma occurs when an atrocity is too much to bear. It may be unthinkable, unspeakable, and one response is to try to cut it off as life events move us forward. We cannot begin to grapple with it, respond to it or include it. Yet, we cannot move on. The atrocity refuses to go away from our consciousness. It reoccurs, intrudes and persists. Traumatic symptoms revolve around this interplay between cutting off from the experience to leave it out of our story, and its intrusion and persistence to be included. The experiences of traumatized individuals include both the numbness of cutting off and the violent replay and intrusion of events in flashbacks, nightmares, visceral and emotional reactions, and body symptoms. We all take part in the experience of trauma in our shared story, by both silencing the unspeakable events of history and continually replaying them.

Differentiation and recognition of symptoms of post-traumatic stress disorder are important to clinicians and those who suffer trauma.[1] It can also be important to differentiate individual trauma, community-wide trauma and our collective, historical experience of trauma which also includes those of us apparently at a distance.[2] When we are unaware of how the dynamics of trauma operate inside us, both as individuals and as communities, we may unwittingly contribute to the perpetuation of violence and are vulnerable to exploitation. Traumatic experiences get locked inside us as individuals and communities, and traumatic events reoccur and haunt us. The psychological dynamics surrounding trauma are predictable and systematically exploited to ignite the next round of conflict. How we fall silent in the face of atrocity is also an active ingredient in violence.

The author David Rieff describes how he had at first believed that he had a task to let the world know what was going on in Bosnia.[3] He felt passionate about his responsibility as a journalist. Surely, if the world only knew what was really going on, the world would intervene. He describes how he later realized his naivety. In Hitler's Germany, many thought, surely, if the world knew what was going on, the allies would bomb the death camps, the railway system and/or accept refugees in great numbers. Surely, if the world only knew. . . . But, time and again, we, the world, knew and did not intervene.

Knowing about the horrible things going on in our world does not put a stop to them. In fact, when inundated by the extent of the horror in our world, we may grow increasingly numb. Numbness in the face of atrocity at a social level mirrors the numbness that traumatized individuals often experience. Traumatized individuals need to be able to tell their unspeakable stories to be able to return to and participate in life. Collectively, we might begin to break the silence and the spell of complicity, if we begin to tell this story that is ours, realizing that, even if we feel at a distance from the atrocities in our world, the way we cut ourselves off from feeling and the way we silence ourselves can be understood as part of the dynamic of our collective trauma.

To tell our story as a society, as a world, leads to enormous difficulties in facing issues of personal and collective accountability. Even more difficult is to feel it, to open our hearts to include what we have done to one another and what we have experienced as human beings. It leads us to ask ourselves, individually and as a society, if we can stop cycles of violence. We meet our hopelessness, our depression. When we no longer identify only as bystanders, we begin to witness, to include and grapple with the tragedies of our world and our story. This requires a great compassion for ourselves, how we are linked to one another and to our terrible and beautiful history and life together on earth.

SHOCK

Trauma occurs around a great shock. At the point of shock, life as you knew it was interrupted, in your personal life or in the life of your community. The shocking experience may have betrayed a fundamental value. You may have been forced without control or choice. You may have been taken into a chain of unfolding events. You may have had to make an impossible choice, under threat and terror, risking not only your own life, but also the lives of your children, partner, friend or neighbours. Trauma may originate during combat, torture or when violently uprooted from your home and forced to flee. Trauma may originate when you are abused, terrorized and unable to turn to authority, because it is the authorities who are forcing your expulsion or committing atrocity. Traumatic symptoms can occur in those who observe violence, as well as those who are direct victims of violence. Trauma can occur in people who perpetrate violence, who may themselves be acting under threat and terror. Trauma also frequently arises from the experience that inaction or mistaken action led to a violent and irreversible outcome.

If you have suffered a traumatic experience, you may not recall the shock. This is an important feature of shock. There was no time to react. Life moved on, perhaps in an accelerated series of events oriented around survival. If you have the opportunity to focus at a later point on the events around which the trauma originated, the initial shock may still be there just below the surface as if suspended outside time.

PART OF US GOES FORWARD AND PART OF US STAYS TRAPPED

Not all shock leads to symptoms of trauma, but, where there is trauma, there is an element of shock. Around a shocking event, part of us goes forward, as if on automatic – and a part of us stays behind. As we go on, there may be one shock overlaid upon another. Most of us have experienced at least a taste of this dynamic. A teacher I know said that, when a student asks him a question, he goes into a little shock. A part of him goes ahead and answers the questions without much problem, but another part feels far away, fuzzy, distant. When he investigated this experience, he discovered that it was directly linked to repeated humiliation that he suffered as a child from his teachers when he did not answer a question correctly.

SURVIVAL

In situations of shock, people often recall a strange feeling that part of the personality went ahead autonomously and accomplished some necessary task. After an accident, you cross six lanes of traffic and provide medical assistance. In situations of sexual abuse, it's common to hear someone say she apparently went on with normal life, but with a loss of feeling contact to herself. When war broke out, someone recalls preparing food for the kids. There was no time to deal with the shock or to express the pain, fear and outrage that match the events. In all these cases, going ahead and not reacting with pain or outrage was an actual or perceived necessity for survival.

TOO MUCH TO WITNESS

In everyday life, a part of our personality perceives our experiences, responds, reflects and narrates. Around traumatic experience, witnessing is too much to bear. Judith Herman writes: 'The ordinary response to atrocities is to banish them from consciousness. Certain violations of the social compact are too terrible to utter aloud: this is the meaning of the word "unspeakable".'[4] The experience is beyond the 'edge' of what it is possible to perceive, or what we are able to include in our identities, as individuals or communities. The part of us that witnesses events cannot. That part of us that reacts, responds and grapples with what has happened cannot. While one part goes ahead, the traumatic event remains, as if frozen in time until it can be witnessed.

As one part goes ahead and the other part remains frozen, the memory of events is often separated from the associated emotion. One way this appears is that someone can tell the story in full detail, but with an apparent lack of emotional response to the events. Or someone may lose the details, have gaps in the story and confuse the order of events, while being deeply upset and physically agitated.

In situations of trauma, people lose their sense of control of memory. This can occur as amnesia, the inability to remember the event at all. Or the memory intrudes, without control, flooding consciousness, or as strange inexplicable fragments. The lack of choice, in remembering and grappling with memory, reflects the lack of choice in the original experience. The conflict between denying the horrible event and the will to be aware and communicate about what has happened is the central dynamic of psychological trauma.[5]

REPLAYING

Traumatic events not only remain, they reoccur, hideously. The event replays in nightmares. The event replays in flashbacks. Traumatic events do not replay like a memory. Rather the event may be experienced as if it is happening again. Visceral responses reoccur. There may be a full sensory replay of the event in a flashback or dream. Small fragments of the experience replay. Visceral reactions and powerful emotions of terror and acute anxiety may be relived. Panic and sudden fits of rage or grief may be suddenly triggered or seem to come up out of nowhere. Symptoms of high blood pressure and headaches are frequently chronic. Sleeplessness may be prolonged for months and years. Many people who have been traumatized, particularly in combat, experience ongoing states of extreme vigilance, mentally and physically prepared for danger and attack, in the replaying trauma. All of these experiences are well-known symptoms of post-traumatic stress disorder. (Symptoms of post-traumatic stress disorder are listed in the appendix, along with a corresponding list that I've developed of symptoms of trauma in groups and communities and collective trauma in the broader society.)

There are varying explanations concerning the psychological and biochemical factors of trauma that make for this replay of traumatic events. In addition to looking for mechanisms of how trauma replays, it is useful to consider if there is a purpose for the replay. One way to understand this is that the traumatic event replays as if continually seeking the missing witness, seeking to be perceived, pieced together, included and responded to, included in our own life story and into our collective and communal history.

NARRATIVE

The story repeats where there is a missing perceiver. It is as if the witness had to step out. It was too much to perceive, to bear and all the human responses towards the event had to be kept on hold, to be able to act, to survive. While life apparently went on, the traumatic event remains and replays. Traumatic experience involves being either stuck inside the experience, or split off from it, unable to access it.

At an internal level, it is useful for traumatized individuals to discover an inner witness, who can perceive, narrate and respond to what happened. The term 'metacommunicator'[6] is one name for that part of ourselves that can witness and communicate about our experience, rather than being only at the mercy of repeating events. This capacity to reflect and comment on our experience also brings a sense of choice along with the ability to witness the story, narrate the story, in effect commit it to 'memory', so that we can choose and make conscious contact with the events, rather than the events simply recurring. Telling the story also involves bringing the emotional response together with the story. Reactions of outrage, terror, rage and grief can come

→ **Figure 15.1** '1984', by Arpana Caur.
(By courtesy of Arpana Caur.)

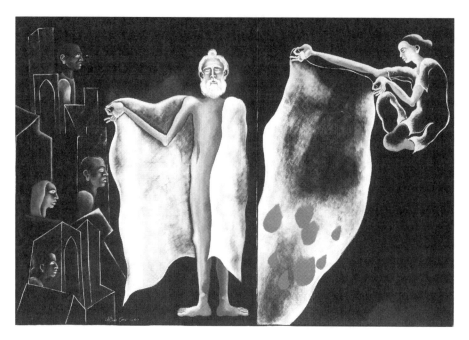

↑ **Figure 15.2** 'Wounds' by Arpana Caur.
(By courtesy of Arpana Caur.)

forward, reactions that may have felt overwhelming or had no space or time to unfold, but remained locked in the psyche and body.

People who have told me their stories about what happened to them during the war in the former Yugoslavia often felt at first afraid to begin telling their story, afraid that, if they told the story, they would begin to cry and, if they begin to cry, the tears would never stop. Jonathan Shay, in his outstanding work *Achilles in Vietnam* writes: 'Severe trauma explodes the cohesion of consciousness. When a survivor creates fully realized narrative that brings together the shattered knowledge of what happened, the emotions that were aroused by the meaning of the events and the bodily sensations that the physical events created, the survivor pieces back together the fragmentation of consciousness that trauma has caused. Such narrative often results in the remission of some symptoms, particularly intrusive symptoms, dissociated bodily sensations, affects and behaviours that inexplicably intrude into the person's life.'[7]

COMMUNALIZING THE STORY: THE MISSING WITNESS

The need for an individual who suffers from trauma to 'metacommunicate' and tell the story, rather than just being trapped in the story, includes telling the story in community, and the need for the story to be heard and felt by others. Narrating the story is healing for the survivor of the trauma, only when there is a community of people who can listen and respond.[8] The need to narrate the story, rather than either split off from it or feel overwhelmed by it, is a community and collective need, not just an individual need.

Often, the community doesn't want to hear the story, and this reinforces the isolation and withdrawal of people who are traumatized, along with fear of sharing the story. The difficulty of community or society to hear and respond to a traumatic story runs very deep and is many faceted. It includes numbness, the incapacity to grapple with the atrocity, protection against triggering trauma in others, hopelessness, guilt, fear of questioning one's own or one's group's accountability, disinterest, ignorance, disdain, and the wish to remain sealed in one's privilege and happier view of the world.

Thus the problem of a missing witness, that part of us that can perceive, reflect and respond to the experience, occurs not only as an inner process, but also as a collective or community problem. We are unable to perceive and witness ourselves, the reality of what has gone on and respond.

In the Balkans, we often heard people struggle with the realization of how easily they grew numb to the extent of trauma in their community, to their own pain and outrage, to their own personal story and the stories of others. There is always one more story, another story worse than the one before. Many people carry an attitude that 'there are far worse stories than mine', 'there are far worse stories than yours', 'it is time to get over it' and 'it is time to move on'.

These attitudes keep us isolated from one another. People are often afraid to tell the story for fear of creating upset in the listener. In war-torn regions,

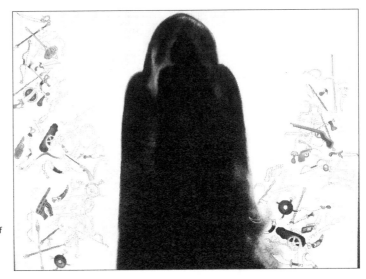

→ Figure 15.3 'Heart of darkness' by Arpana Caur. (By courtesy of Arpana Caur.)

people are often afraid of re-triggering trauma in the listener, who may also have been traumatized. Expressing outrage and grief about one's own story might tap into the collective outrage and grief that is without end.

In our work in large forums, we have come to learn how important it is to attend to these concerns, while at the same time not blocking the individual and community from telling and hearing the story. When working with groups or communities in conflict, traumatic experiences are touched. There is wisdom in the caution people feel about bringing their traumatic story into the public forum. In essence, it is an attempt to take care not to allow the traumatic event to replay once again, even in the telling – unless there can be a sense of choice on the part of both the teller as to when and with whom she or he wants to tell the story, and the listeners as to when and how to hear it. Taking explicit care around the importance of choice, rather than letting the event simply replay in the telling, or re-trigger and replay trauma in others, can lead to compassion and the capacity of community to find a way to witness and respond.

Although it may be someone's choice, and it may be very useful to tell a traumatic story in privacy to someone you trust, it is important to be aware of not repeating the pattern of splitting off the individual experience of trauma from the community. The story also belongs in community. The benefit for both the individual and the community of being able to tell the story in a group setting or a community forum is profound, and regularly overlooked. Most important is that, when a traumatized individual tells his or her story, there are human responses on the other side.

Whether a traumatic story is told in a one-to-one situation, a group or in a larger community forum, it is further isolating and damaging if someone tells a story and is met with a blank face, whether as a result of shock, discomfort or so-called professional distance. In Croatia, a large group of people, who devoted their lives to helping others, discovered how they had often submitted, in part unconsciously, to a belief system that they should not be emotional. They had been taught that this was 'professional distance'. The ability to share their own personal stories, and to express the grief and outrage for all that they have experienced and heard in their own communities, was often felt as recovering their own humanity, the will and reason to go on living, along with the capacity and heart to go on working with others.

A woman told of how she had to give professional testimony in a tribunal regarding a war crime she had witnessed. She said that, as she told of the atrocity she had witnessed in the Tribunal, she became emotional and cried. The judge reprimanded her, saying that surely as a professional she could keep her emotions under control. Luckily she was able to tell the judge that it was her humanity and emotions that made her professional. It was the judge in this instance who behaved unprofessionally. Coldness towards the emotional response to tragedy and atrocity recreates trauma.

I've often seen that blank looks and silence in response to someone's traumatic story are felt to be respect, awe and empathy. We may feel any words would be inadequate, so we say nothing. We hope the person will know that we are feeling with them. Even so, silence is insufficient. 'Without emotion in the listener there is no communalization of the trauma,' writes Shay.[9] At the same time, the listener needs to have a certain strength and heart to be able to listen to the story without being so taken and overwrought by emotion that he or she inadvertently retreats into his or her own emotion and leaves the person alone, unable to share further. The person telling a traumatic story needs to be received with warmth and emotion, but also to feel that you have the strength and capacity to hear it. Feeling with an individual or community's suffering brings humanity and a sense of witness and compassion, rather than a repeat of suffering. Shay writes: 'A listener must be ready to experience some of the terror, grief and rage that the victim did. This is one meaning, after all, of the word compassion.'[10]

Time and again, in forums dealing with conflict, we have seen that, if a conflict is brought out fully, such that each view is expressed in an intensive interaction, at some point the group will be able to feel and accompany someone in the grief, outrage and suffering from the conflict – and at this point there's an experience of going underneath the cycle of accusations, and a transformation may occur that deepens people's commitment to a different future together.

COMMUNITY TRAUMA

To understand how dynamics of trauma contribute to perpetuating conflict, we need to understand how community responds to widespread trauma. When whole communities suffer atrocity, the trauma can stay in the fabric of family, community and society for generations. Consider community as a body. Just as an individual may take many years before being able to tell the story and begin to recover, narrative of the community-wide trauma may begin to be told only in the next generations. If 10 years is not a long time for an individual to begin to grapple with loss and trauma, 50 years or 100 years begins to seem like a short time for a society to begin to face what has occurred.

In Rwanda 750 000 people, Tutsis and moderate Hutus, were killed over a very short period of months in 1994. Tens of thousands of women were raped and, on top of the atrocity, there is now an AIDS epidemic. Families, culture and the fabric of society are destroyed. Just as a traumatized individual may not be able to perceive and respond to the traumatic event as it happened, because of the need to focus on survival, a community that has been traumatized also needs to focus on survival and basic issues of subsistence. The trauma from the gruesome events remains, intrudes and pervades every facet of community life. Communities in Rwanda must focus on basic issues of economic survival, yet community trauma will interfere in that outer work. Even when the focus of post-war community must be on economic subsistence, it's of essential importance to find a way to grapple with the community-wide trauma, in a way that respects the inherent eldership and creativity in the community, in order to be able to recover a spirit and will to rebuild society. Until now, in post-conflict situations there has been very little attention on the impact of community-wide trauma, and its direct bearing on social, economic and political dimensions of community building. Literature about trauma is circling this essential connection between large-scale violence and trauma, and trauma and community. Bracken points out that even the surge in interest in trauma in recent years has been largely oriented and limited by thinking in terms of individual psychology.[11] Robben and Suarez-Orozco emphasize that violence and trauma should be studied together, and with special attention to the effects of violence on both the individual and the group.[12]

In Kosovo, faces are ageless. Eyes have the look of having seen far too much. In the months and years immediately after the genocide of Albanians in Kosovo and the bombing of Serbia, in a situation of great instability, UNMIK (United Nations Mission in Kosovo) was responsible for developing an infrastructure of services and an interim government. Countless humanitarian organizations also swarmed the region, trying and often doing lots of good, but, in a kind of chaos of input, there was very little cooperation and overview. A desperate need for housing, apparently easy enough to fulfil with this amount of resources in the region, was tied up in red tape.

My colleague, Lane, and I met one day with groups from Pristina and Mitrovice, to facilitate conversations among people working in a social service agency in the region, about issues they faced and how they were doing. The trauma from the loss and atrocities they had endured was pervasive. Many found themselves for the first time in social service positions and spoke of being glad to do something useful for those in greater need. One man told a story of how he went on a whole day's travel to meet an elderly couple, just to tell them that the supplies for their housing that they were waiting for were unavailable. He told how he had been afraid to bring this bad news to the couple who were isolated and had lost everything. He said that, when he arrived and told them the news, the couple fell to their knees and kissed him repetitively on his clothes and hands, in gratitude that he had cared enough to travel all that way to tell them this. As he told the story, with tears in his eyes, he said how he'd been stunned by the realization that, even when there is a dire situation of subsistence and survival, what matters most is the feeling of compassion we have for one another.

The group we met was in turn amazingly warm, welcoming and grateful to us for our interest in being with them and for wanting to know how they were really doing. One man wanted to send a message that they desperately needed and wanted people to come to help them in Kosovo, but with an attitude not only of doing something, but of relating deeply in this way to the people there, with interest in their lives, stories and their community trauma, and to join them in their long-term journey ahead.

In post-conflict situations, in which there is so much to do, to begin to rebuild the community socially, economically and politically there is a need not only to move forward, but also to rebuild community through a willingness and heart to connect to the emotional reality of what has occurred. Working with and responding to community trauma in community forums could greatly enhance the cooperation and effectiveness of efforts to rebuild community, by supporting a process of the community's reckoning with how to reweave the fabric or spirit of community. Just as a traumatized individual cannot go about rebuilding his life, if he is trapped in the trauma, and in a feeling of isolation, hopelessness and loss of meaning, a community cannot rebuild if it has lost its spirit and is hopeless, without a sense of a communal bond of meaning.

LET'S PUT HISTORY BEHIND US – THE ATTITUDE OF PRIVILEGE

Another way to look at how a splitting occurs in collective trauma is that one part of society suffers the atrocity and another wants to move on, unwilling or unable to relate to the traumatic story. Often this is played out such that the dominant group within society, or the group with the most social power, will not include the traumatic story of a 'minority' group into their collective identity or their 'narrative' of events. A minority group who suffered atrocity – often at the hands of this majority or dominant group – may be left holding the story, telling it again and again. The shared memory binds the group to one another. Ongoing exclusion of the minority group from the awareness, thoughts and feelings of the wider society and dominating group also recreates the suffering and trauma.

If we are a part of a group who has oppressed another group, or has gained privileges, as a result of that oppression, we are often the first to have difficulty relating to the lasting affects of the story, and may want to forget it and move on as quickly as possible. In Part 1, we discussed how going forward without dealing with accountability does not bring closure to the cycle of conflict. Lack of accountability combines with trauma and remains in the fabric of community, into the next generations. It may be possible to look at issues of accountability where previous generations could not. Yet, often the insistence upon having nothing to be held accountable for only increases with time. The next generation feels innocent and untouched, because it was not their personal responsibility, and it seems so long ago. In this way we remain unaware and split off from a feeling of connection to history, with no awareness of the privilege of being able to say you just want to put it behind you, while those who have suffered cannot, because they are still suffering.

REPARATIONS AND GRAPPLING WITH CONSCIENCE

As we've seen, one thing that keeps us from being able to include the pain of others in our awareness and hearts is our fear of being held accountable if we do, not wanting to feel guilty and not wanting to deal with a demand for reparation. At the root of discussions around reparations is the need for us to go beyond lip service. For the same reason, however, reparations mean little when there is no real feeling and conscience in society's grappling with past and current oppression and atrocities.

The story of Jacob in the Bible is about accountability, conscience and reparations. Jacob went to meet his brother Esau, many years after having cheated him out of his blessing and inheritance. Jacob had tricked his father, who intended the blessing for his first son, Esau. His father had failing eyesight and Jacob received the blessing in the place of his brother, using furs on his arms to pretend he was his hairier brother. Now, many years later, Jacob prepared to meet his brother Esau, bringing elaborate gifts as reparation and to soften the encounter. The night before he was to see Esau, he had a great struggle throughout the night. 'At first he did not know with whom he was wrestling and retained his arrogance. But, as the night wore on, Jacob realized his adversary was God. He then reflected on his own lack of righteousness towards Esau and as dawn broke he asked God's blessing for his new awareness.'[13] In the morning, he went to meet his brother, limping from his night's struggle and laden with presents ('200 she-goats, 20 he-goats, 200 ewes and 20 rams, 30 camels, 40 cows and 10 bulls, 20 she-asses and 10 foals'). Esau refused his offer, saying he had enough himself. 'But, Jacob then said: "Nay I pray thee . . . for . . . I have seen thy face, as one seeth the face of God." . . . He urged him and he took it.'[14] One interpretation of this story is that, for closure to be possible in situations of long-standing conflict, as a society we need to have a genuine struggle of conscience, to face our most difficult history, and see the 'other' as God, as our source of wholeness.

In the USA, the phrase '40 acres and a mule' recalls that, when slavery was abolished, each slave was promised 40 acres and a mule. This promise was never fulfilled and the phrase symbolizes that there has never been a closure to this horrendous chapter of American history, through either a true reckoning and attitude change among the white majority or material reparations. There has never been a full grappling with what it means to be a nation, built literally on the backs of slaves.

With few exceptions, Native Americans are left alone to suffer the abomination that occurred and continues to occur towards them and upon which American society and American history were built. The author, Ward Churchill writes: 'The growth of ethnic consciousness and the consequent mobilization of Indian communities in the Western hemisphere since the early 1960s have been welcomed neither by government forces nor by opposition parties and revolutionary movements.' The atrocity of building a country through a process of murder and ethnic cleansing and, after stealing their land, trying to kill off culture, language and sense of meaning for Native Americans, has never been formally acknowledged as a core problem belonging to every American, or dealt with in any serious way. Native Americans in the USA are living in greater poverty than any group in the nation. In some regions there is widespread illness and malnutrition. Native American land was taken illegally, in many cases governed by treaties that were ignored by the USA. Ward Churchill describes how non-Indian activists: 'with only a handful of exceptions, persistently plead that they can't really take a coherent position on the matter of Indian land rights because, unfortunately, they're not really conversant with the issues [as if these were tremendously complex]. Meanwhile, they do virtually nothing, generation after generation, to inform themselves on the topic of who actually owns the ground they're standing on. The record can be played only so many times before it wears out and becomes just another variation of "hear no evil, see no evil".'[15] Although the tendency to want to move on, to leave the story behind, amplifies with the passing of time, American history remains current, buried, but intact.

COLLECTIVE FROZEN STATES

In many ways, Germany has actively tried to include the reality of the history of World War II and the Holocaust and to make reparations. Yet, on an emotional level, there is a collective frozen atmosphere around the story and trauma, and a general incapacity to relate on a feeling level to history. I've often heard Germans say they cannot hear another story about the Holocaust. They don't want to feel guilty anymore. As in every traumatic zone, it is natural and necessary to try to move on. Still frozen in the collective trauma, however, many Germans are unable to have any feeling of contact with the period of the Nazi regime and the Holocaust. And there are anti-Jewish attitudes, which allowed the Holocaust to happen in the first place, still present. Not infrequently, there's the wish that they had won the war, further cutting off the process of grappling with the atrocities that occurred. Germans often identify with the wish to go on with life and put the past behind them, and yet they still suffer from an extraordinary collective shock and the incapacity to contact their feelings about it. I have had an interest in understanding frozen states of trauma in Holocaust survivors, as well as children of Holocaust survivors, and I recall how a deep compassion grew in me, as a Jew (my parents are both German Jews who escaped the Holocaust), when I came to realize that in many ways Germans were sitting in the same boat, frozen in history.

In my experience in Poland, many young people didn't know much about the events of the Holocaust and had very little feeling about it. They grew up grappling with the terrible tragedies of World War II that their own families had suffered, as victims of Germany and the war. They did not know much about the large Jewish population who once lived in Poland, and the history of anti-Semitism in Poland, and the fact that there are only small numbers of Jews left in Poland, created further alienation from the issue. When there were current acts of anti-Semitism such as people destroying graves or monuments, or anti-Semitic graffiti on the walls, there was little thought or reaction about it, without a sense of context.

Genocide removes the group from the region, so they can be forgotten in the following generation. I recall in a large group forum, a young woman from an eastern European country, which had at one time had a large population of Jews and now very, very few, who began to speak about how she often felt a sense of frozenness, emptiness, as if there were a big gap, something essential that was lost and missing from her land, her culture, her heart. Naively, but very genuinely and personally, she said at one point, how much she missed the Jewish people and their culture, and felt the terrible loss and emptiness left behind. I was surprised by how deeply touched I was by this young woman. My family originates not far from her home and I realized it was the first time I had ever heard that we were missed.

ROMANTICIZING TRAUMA AND MYTHIC TIME

We have seen how there is a tendency not only to keep our atrocious stories of the past hidden when they are painful, uncomfortable or infringe upon our current privileges, but also to romanticize the story. Having romantic sentimentality towards a people who have suffered atrocities is a characteristic of the dynamic of collective trauma. We are often sentimental when our feelings are frozen. Sentimentality can ensure that we don't have to face the situation squarely and have any deeper feelings about it. Another way to understand sentimentality is that, when we are numb and frozen, unable to relate to difficult feelings directly, the sentimentality seeps in, as an attempt to try to warm us up and stir feelings and reckoning about what happened.

In Bratislava, Slovakia, in the previous Jewish section of town, there is a highway pass where the synagogue once stood. There is a small Jewish museum nearby. At the time I visited this museum in the early 1990s, there was an exhibit of Jewish life, with examples in glass cases: 'these are the Sabbath candles', 'this is the Rabbi's shawl', 'this is a Torah'. I had the strong impression that the Jewish people and customs were described as if they were a long-lost race, with no relation to a living story that had occurred on those very streets. Slovakia was the only country that actually paid Germans to take the Jews.

Romanticizing also occurs in relation to loss and traumatic history of our ancestors. The romance touches a mythic history that is poignant and makes meaning out of loss. It brings hope and a longing for redemption. It is accompanied by poetry, song, dreaming, and religious symbols and fervour. The battle of Kosovo, in which the Serb Prince Lazar was killed, became a powerful symbol of Serbia's defeat and its subsequent 500 years under Ottoman rule. This history later became legend in art, poetry, drama and literature. Lazar was portrayed as a martyr, a Christ-like figure who had been betrayed. A Serbian knight, Obilic, assassinated Sultan Murat, in revenge for the death of Lazar and became a hero. Modern Serbian nationalism was built on this history of mythic dimension. As the home to Serbian monasteries and treasures, Kosovo was considered a kind of holy land. As Albanian Kosovars, who suffered discrimination in Kosovo (despite being the vast majority there), advocated for human and civil rights in the 1980s, tensions grew. The Serbian Orthodox Church published a claim in 1986 that Serbs were subject to a plot to ethnically cleanse them from Kosovo. In 1987, Slobodan Milosevic rose to be the spokesperson for nationalism in Serbia. In 1988–89, relics of Prince Lazar were ritually transported through areas claimed to be 'Greater Serbia' and then brought to the Kosovo province. Ritual celebrations surrounded bringing Lazar's relics to the Gracanica Monastery in Kosovo and imbued Kosovo with a sense of sacred space and sacred time, such that 1389 became 1989.[16]

REVISING HISTORY

If finding out about the suffering of others makes us feel threatened in our sense of righteousness or privilege, we have a tendency to want to quickly move on from the story. There are many examples in which one part of society 'goes ahead', while leaving those who suffered to bear their trauma on their own. That part of society that goes ahead bemoans the fact that the survivors of a group that suffered atrocity tell the same story again and again.

In the extreme, one part of society not only goes ahead, but also determines that the event should be written out of history. This is a total 'splitting'. There is an attempt to erase the chapter from history, as if it never happened, or to revise it. In the former Yugoslavia there was a continual revision and rewriting of history, even as the events surrounding ethnic cleansing unfolded.

In the Bosnian town of Foca, all the Muslims were killed or expelled and the town was renamed Srbinje (Serb place). The men who took part in the 'cleansing' were given medals named after Milos Obilic, the avenger of Kosovo. The mosques from the fifteenth and sixteenth century, masterworks of Islamic architecture, were dynamited. When asked why all the mosques had been destroyed, the new Serbian mayor said 'there never were any mosques in Foca'. A similar story happened in the town of Zvornik, when after the Serb nationalists dynamited the mosques the new Serb mayor denied that they had ever existed.[17]

There is a substantial movement to revise the history of the Holocaust, some saying it never happened, that it was a history fabricated by the Jews, or its proportions are significantly altered. For example, the numbers of deaths are questioned and attributed to typhus, and not the gas chambers.[18] The history of colonization around the world is packed with examples of events told as hero and adventure stories, rather than of atrocity and trauma.

Although historical revisionism is often thought of in connection to extremist and nationalist groups, we all revise history when we are interested only in finding a version of events to protect our interests or innocence, rather than finding out and relating to what has happened as our own story. The widespread and complex workings of misinformation and disinformation add to the problem.

TV WATCHING

When people suffering violence, torture, expulsion and genocide call to the world for help and feel the world turn away, it exacerbates trauma more than anything else. Still, we have all experienced reading the news or watching television about a situation of unbearable suffering and then going about our daily business with little reaction. We may feel that the amount of tragedy in our world is just so great that we cannot possibly feel it. We may feel a kind of cool detachment that we cannot quite explain, a distance from horrific events that seem to be happening in a parallel world that somehow don't touch us. We can barely find the energy to focus on our own lives, business as usual. It is interesting that this is a description of the dynamic of trauma. One part goes ahead focused on the need to return to a normal life, splitting off from the events that are too unbearable to witness.

The first time we were in Croatia, in a town that had been heavily affected during the war, people gathered from regions all over Croatia and from Bosnia. It was a mixed group of Croats, Serbs and Muslims dealing with the aftermath of the war. A group from Sarajevo hung out together, becoming friends. They were sometimes a few minutes late to a session, as a result of dealing with the stairs and mobility needs of one young man in a wheelchair. They were a great group, and most of the seminar participants would have said that they had a kind of 'status' in the group, with their warmth towards one another and a city style from Sarajevo. Some even felt that they held themselves apart, but, in a group interaction, what emerged was something very different. The group from Sarajevo felt as though they were being held at a distance because of their war trauma.

Though everyone had lived through the war, and many had suffered trauma, those from Sarajevo had been through a recent living hell.

One woman said to the other participants: 'We feel you keep us at a distance. You treat us as though we were museum pieces.' 'You look at us, but don't touch.' At this point, a woman came forward and sat facing her. She said to her directly: 'I watched the atrocities in Sarajevo on television. At that point, the war in

→ **Figure 15.4** 'World goes on', by Arpana Caur. (By courtesy of Arpana Caur.)

Croatia had stopped, and though I lived only 200 km from Sarajevo, I watched it on TV and it seemed far away, and I remember I couldn't feel it. And I remember feeling I was glad it was there and not here.' As she said these words, sitting close and face-to-face with the woman from Sarajevo, who had suffered excruciating personal loss, tears began streaming from people's eyes. In a situation I have never quite seen before or since, every participant in a group of about 60 had tears streaming down their faces. As Lane and I facilitated, we too wept. The professional translator began to cry, and was very upset that she was unable to control her tears. We assured her it was okay, as she dropped to the floor and wept, and others pitched in to keep translating, as others also spoke about how they had distanced themselves from the pain and isolated themselves from one another, watching television about what was going on even in the next village, exactly as the world had stood by and silently watched it all on television.

SILENCE, DISTANCE AND NEUTRALITY

Our silence in the face of atrocity should be understood not only as the absence of speaking out. Silence is much more than this. It is an active ingredient in the planning and carrying out of atrocity. Silence is a central component of the dynamic of trauma. We fall silent in the face of atrocity. Silence is enforced in various ways through manipulation of our individual and collective tendency to invest our authority in others, demonize our neighbours, seek a sense of safety at any cost, normalize ethnic conflict and focus on business as usual. When our spontaneous silence is not assured, silence is enforced through tactics of terror. Profiteers bet on our silence and complicity, that we will not react. Yet, each of us is also a profiteer when we ignore what goes on in our name in this world, while searching only for our own advantage and privilege at every turn.

The description of ethnic cleansing and genocide as an eruption of conflict between two groups can amount to a tacit acceptance of nationalist claims that certain ethnic groups are a threat. In the transition from multi-national empires to the development of homogeneous nation states, those creating the nation states often turned the horrors of deportation, ethnic cleansing and genocide into a notion of inevitable and unavoidable civil and ethnic conflicts.[19] The author, R.G. Suny, cites a scholar, Bernard Lewis, who wrote:

> For the Turks, the Armenian movement was the deadliest of all threats. . . . The Armenians, stretching across Turkey – in Asia from the Caucasian frontier to the Mediterranean coast, lay in the very heart of the Turkish homeland – and to renounce these lands would have meant not the truncation, but the dissolution of the Turkish state.

Turkish and Armenian villages, inextricably mixed, had for centuries lived in neighborly association. Now a desperate struggle began between them – a struggle between two nations for the possession of a single homeland that ended with the terrible holocaust of 1915, when a million and a half Armenians perished.

Suny remarks how this passage assumes the legitimacy of a nation state, and changes it from a land in which Armenians were the earlier inhabitants into one in which they became an obstacle to the national aspirations of the Turks.[20]

In this way, the genocide of Armenians could be considered inevitable. Although Turkish and Armenian villages had, according to this author, lived in a neighbourly association, suddenly conflict was now expected. This sort of logic has seeped under our skin, allowing us to shake our heads and shrug our shoulders at the inevitability of ethnic conflict and the inability of people to get along with their differences.

In the former Yugoslavia, as we have seen, the violence and genocide were often reported on as a civil war, resulting from age-old tensions among Balkan people, who have a nature and history that make them incapable of living together and who are doomed to repeated vicious outbreaks of atrocity. We may easily think that it's just too complicated to understand, and they have any-way been killing each other for centuries. President Clinton abandoned his commitment to lift the arms embargo, leaving the Bosnians without arms, as the Administration and media described the conflict as age-old ethnic unrest.[21] Similarly, in Rwanda, the western media portrayed the 1994 genocide as age-old ethnic divisions between Hutu and Tutsi tribes. Yet, in Rwanda, too, Hutu and Tutsi had continued to live together and intermarry in most communities, and the genocide was a strategy carefully designed over several years. It was created for the political goals of a nationalist regime, rather than from tribal hatred.[22]

At a distance, our notion of ethnic rivalry fuels the strategy. We act as though it is a good thing to be neutral based on the notion that ethnic conflict is intrinsic and inevitable, rather than recognizing how past issues of justice and trauma are intentionally being used to carry out atrocity. Our so-called 'neutrality' is a necessary ingredient in genocide. On the other side of the coin, calls for 'intervention' for 'humanitarian' purposes are also used as a rationale for attacking or dominating a region. The war in Iraq is an example close at hand.

CHAPTER 16
TRAUMA AND REFUGE

SAFETY

Our urge to find safety is a most basic part of our psychology as individuals, families and communities. It is augmented through our personal and collective memory of atrocity and trauma. Our need for safety is easily exploited. If there is a threat to the survival of our family, we are forced into a position to go along with anything for a promise of safety. It is therefore a simple step for a government or leadership to instil, arouse or cash in on our fear and need for safety in order to implement its power for our 'protection'. Our capacity to demonize and dehumanize are the ticket.

Political leaders and warlords know that for the sake of 'safety' we will turn ourselves upside down to screen out huge chunks of information, give up all sense, close our hearts, close our minds, lose contact with morality and decency, and then create myths to glorify our behaviour, while displaying our loyalty and patriotism to those who will protect us.

In the former Yugoslavia, betting on his rise to power, Slobodan Milosevic in effect 'juiced' past trauma from the period of the Ustase or Croat Nationalists in World War II who committed atrocities against Serbs, Jews and others, and the Ottoman invasion in the 1300s. This went beyond opening accounts of justice, tapping an emotional memory based in past atrocity, to claim protection for Serbs from Croats and Muslims in Croatia and Bosnia. The notion of needing to protect the safety of Serbs was the moral justification that led to ethnic cleansing and genocide.

The protector/betrayer

Absence of 'protection' is an important feature of trauma. Trauma from physical and sexual abuse of children is not only from vicious acts, but also from the act of betrayal by the person who has our trust and responsibility to protect us. Croats, Muslims and Serbs have frequently told me of traumatic memories when those whom they thought to be trusted neighbours now demonized them, and turned on them and their children in vicious ways. For political refugees, often the greatest trauma comes from the betrayal of government in its primary responsibility of protecting the human right of safety. In the midst of the most painful, terrifying experiences, there is no one to turn to, no authority to call. The police or the government is in on your demise. There is no safe haven. The government betrays and turns on its own people.

In Vietnam, as in other combat situations, there was an absolute dependence of the US soldier on the army for everything he needed to stay alive – training, food and water, communications, knowledge of the enemy and skills of his superiors.[1] If soldiers were involved in killing civilians, they knew it betrayed the deepest human and social values, and yet may have been told by their superiors to forget it, not to worry, even to celebrate body count. This betrayal of one's deepest values by the authority you are dependent on is an important feature of trauma. Jonathan Shay writes that he has come to believe through his work with war veterans that moral injury is an essential part of any combat trauma that leads to lifelong psychological injury.[2]

The greatest of trauma may also be caused when someone cannot fill the role of protector him- or herself, towards his or her own children, family and friends. A severely traumatized man told me the story that haunted him. Close friends came to him in a panic, saying they had to flee. He assured them that they could stay, and that he would be able to protect them, because of his position of some authority in the community. This turned out to be a deadly mistake. He could not protect them and they were killed.

Safe havens and refugees

One of the fundamental purposes of governments is to create safety. Yet millions of people have been killed or forced to flee their own countries by their governments. There are millions of refugees worldwide, many deeply traumatized, seeking a safe haven.

As communities and countries debate the treatment of immigrants, trauma is recreated in our refusal to adequately protect the rights of refugees. Many

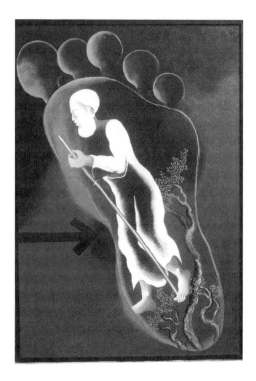

↑ **Figure 16.1** 'Nanak in bleeding times' by Arpana Caur.
(By courtesy Arpana Caur.)

people have no conception of the situation from which refugees come, or what it means to be driven from one's home and from any protection. The prejudice and unwelcome that many immigrants face compound their trauma. A cold unwelcoming bureaucracy, which none of us particularly likes, can trigger the memory of torture. A cold look on the street compounds isolation and trauma. A welcoming attitude towards someone can change his or her life.

TRAUMA AND BORDERS

The strategy of 'protecting' one group and 'demonizing' another group not only creates the rationale and arousal for nationalism and genocide and the plight of refugees. It is the same strategy used to create strong borders and keep refugees out of our countries or homes. Although there are no easy answers to worldwide immigration issues, a tragedy is played out as a result of the high level of public support for policies to limit immigrant refugees. The same dynamics that are used in war arouse people's reactionary level of concern for safety and privilege, while locating a target to demonize and expel.

While 10 000 Jews were being exterminated each day in death camps during the Holocaust, the world knew it. The USA accepted only a limited number of refugees, under special conditions. In the film 'Amen', Costa Gravas depicted the US Ambassador saying that the USA clearly couldn't open up to more Jewish immigrants because it would cause a wave of anti-Semitism. This kind of unabashed double speak illustrates the ability we have to identify with reason and virtue while shutting the door.

As waves of refugees seek refuge, they often meet closed doors. According to the UNHCR (United Nations High Commission for Refugees), as of July 2004 figures indicate that there were approximately 17.1 million people of direct concern to UNHCR activities worldwide in 2003, including refugees,

→ **Figure 16.2** 'Boundaries' by Arpana Caur. (By courtesy of Arpana Caur.)

↘ **Figure 16.3** '1947' by Arpana Caur. (By courtesy of Arpana Caur.)

asylum seekers, returnees and internally displaced people. This is a significant reduction from 20.8 million at the end of 2002.[3] Asia hosted approximately 36 per cent of the population of concern to UNHCR, Africa 25 per cent, Europe 25 per cent, North America 5 per cent and Latin America 8 per cent.[4]

International law requires that refugees, who cannot return to their homes due to the political situation and violent conflict, should be offered refuge in other countries. Immigration policies vary between countries. While there is much general agreement conerning the importance of differentiating economically motivated migration from the situation of political refugees, it is often difficult to determine who is who. Large numbers of asylum seekers from countries known to be in violent conflict are denied asylum due to any number of reasons, such as arriving illegally, failure to fill out forms correctly, being late to interviews. Large numbers are denied or detained.[5]

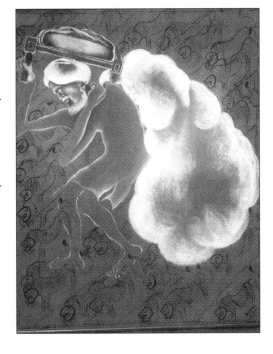

CHAPTER 17
REPLAYS OF VIOLENT CONFLICT AND BREAKING THE CYCLE

We have seen how a traumatic event creates a split in the individual, one part going ahead to survive and function, whereas the other remains trapped in the experience. We've seen how this split occurs collectively and historically, such that one part of the society tries to go ahead and leave the story behind, and another cannot. We have seen how the traumatic event persists and replays, through nightmares, flashbacks and physical symptoms of the individual. Another way that trauma intrudes and cycles is in the replay of violent conflict.

Trauma is usually linked to great injustice. Past trauma is fuel for battle. Violent conflict often cycles as each side identifies with their traumatic history. Trauma and violent conflict replay like a collective nightmare. The nightmare repeats, sometimes in a new location or a new era. Sometimes it replays with the same players. Sometimes there are new players. Sometimes the players switch roles.

Just like a nightmare or flashback, violent conflicts replay, without a witness. The nightmare replays, and we are the players, like dream figures taken along into the mythic drama without capacity for self-reflection. In the Israeli–Palestinian conflict, there is a constant replay of the nightmare, as the Israeli government cracks down on Palestinians, and Palestinian groups retaliate with terrorist strikes, followed by retaliation from the Israeli military, followed by another terrorist attack. Everyone can see this cycle quite plainly. Yet, it's as if we are taken into compulsive, repetitive behaviour, without awareness or control. The trauma continues to intrude and replay.

TRAUMA AND SIX MOTIVATIONS FOR REVENGE

Conflict often cycles around public arousal and support for revenge and retaliation. It's useful and possible to understand and get to know our urge for revenge and its relationship to our urge for justice and to relieve our trauma. We can bring awareness to our urge for revenge and the needs underlying it, rather than simply trying to get rid of this urge, or simply acting out of it, or supporting our leaders to do so. Taking a good look at our motivations for revenge can help us to find ways of taking our needs seriously, without resorting to retaliation and replaying the nightmare. Below are six motivations for revenge. One or more of these motivations may be present in acts of revenge. Motivations for revenge are (1) to demand accountability, punish and settle the score, (2) to create pain in others rather than suffer pain, (3) to make someone understand what it feels like, (4) to relieve internalized oppression, (5) to refuse humiliation and to stand up and (6) to avenge the dead.

To demand accountability, punish and settle the score

In situations of conflict, some people describe their urge for revenge as the wish to hold others accountable. In the absence of accountability, including public acknowledgement, legal or criminal proceedings and punishment, the urge for revenge is easily aroused and stirred. In the discussion about accountability in Chapter 4, a 'justice scale' shows how what may begin as a need for acknowledgement, when not fulfilled, can end in an urge to punish and take revenge or to kill. 'Now you must pay the price for what you have done.' Revenge is an urge to settle the score. The more we insist on being unaccountable, the greater the urge for revenge to hold us accountable.[1]

To create pain rather than suffer pain

Another motivation for revenge is to get out of feeling trapped in pain. It usually happens without awareness of the shift. One way we stop pain, although it is temporary, is, instead of being a victim of pain, we pick up the role of the one making pain. We want to create hurt in others. We will even do this when we stub our toe on a chair, turning to kick the chair. We identify as being hurt by the chair, at the very moment we are kicking it across the room. Sometimes we stop feeling hurt and begin to identify with hurting others. At other times we continue to identify with the pain, and the role switch happens without our realization. All the while identifying with feeling hurt, we flip into the role of hurting others, seeking revenge. This dynamic can make conflicts flip-flop in endless cycles. We flip-flop between occupying the roles, or we are in both roles at the same time. This tendency can easily be exploited to keep people and whole nations recalling the way they have been hurt, while they are in turn hurting others.

Shay records the words of a Vietnam veteran speaking of his closest friend-in-arms who was obliterated by a mine, and his hunger for revenge that followed:

> And we looked and looked and looked. And the only thing that was left was, it almost looked like a wig. It was just his hair. Just his hair. And we put that in the body bag. And I was crying like a baby. . . . And a convoy was going by and there was soldiers and they were looking at me and I just didn't give a fuck. And I cried and I cried and I cried. And I stopped crying. And I probably didn't cry again for twenty years. I turned. I had no feelings. I wanted to hurt. I wanted to hurt. And I wanted to hurt.[2]

Phil Mollon writes about trauma and the violence in our world. 'We appear to be afflicted with some unbearable pain for which we can find relief only by inflicting it on others.'[3] Paradoxically, the urge within us to switch roles, to flip and flop, can be understood not only as a search for relief from the identification with the pain of the victim role, but as an unconscious search for awareness. Just as being a human being makes us prone to flipping roles and seeking revenge, we also have the capacity to become aware. Individuals and groups are readily interested in finding alternatives to falling into conflict, to recognize how we inhabit these roles, what makes us switch or flip roles, and to communicate about our interaction, rather than only being taken in the loop. Thus, if we become aware of this tendency to flip, rather than fall into it, it can become a method of conflict resolution.

To make someone understand what it feels like

Just at the point people have an urge for revenge and retaliation, if you support them to take their urge seriously and ask them what they want, they will often say it's a deep urge to make the other person or group know how it feels. There may be a deep belief that, if only the other person knew what it really felt like to be so hurt and put down, they might wake up and change and do something to stop it.

In a heated conflict, just at the point people are about to lash out in revenge, if you encourage them to express themselves fully, they may cry and shout in outrage and pain about the suffering and atrocities they have endured, about the suffering of their people, until someone can feel it, until someone's heart bursts open and shares even a drop of their suffering. As long as others don't share the pain and outrage, there may be an urge to repeat it, an urge for revenge.

Revenge may be felt as hate. In a large international conference, the group focused on the conflict between Muslims and Hindus in India. At one point focus shifted to the suffering resulting from the caste system among Hindus. A man from the 'untouchable' caste began to speak, and then shout about the horror of the oppressive system that has caused so much suffering. He screamed and he shook with rage, outrage and grief, about how untouchables are treated as less than human. His outrage was immense and his shouting sustained. Then he shouted: 'I hate you. I hate you. I hate you. You have oppressed me for four thousand years, and I will hate you for another four thousand years.' I remember in that moment dropping to the floor, with a sense that he had touched a bottom-line deep vein in the tragedy of humanity, yet by touching it and expressing it in that large group, there was a moment of awe and connection in that room, that gave the sense of possibility for transformation of our history.

To relieve internalized oppression

Another dynamic of revenge is when oppression is internalized, it repeats. The oppressor, whether in the form of racist, anti-Semite, fascist or torturer, is internalized and continues to kick us and haunt us. When we are down, he kicks again. When it is apparently over, he kicks once more. This internalized aggression is acted out both unconsciously towards oneself and one's own group or out towards others. Again, this replay often happens as if autonomously without our awareness.

To refuse humiliation and stand up

When we have been profoundly hurt and humiliated, as an individual or group, a moment occurs when we find ourselves with a sense of power. It's as if the accumulated hurt and suffering suddenly rises up, inflames us, and inspires us to stand up and refuse this time to be put down. After the Six Day War in 1967, Ben-Eliezer, a Knesset member, said: 'We were not so few in number as there is a tendency to believe. By our side fought the six million, who whispered in our ear the eleventh commandment: Do not get murdered.'[4]

The urge to stand up may be acted out in revenge. When facilitating in situations of conflict, it's possible to bring awareness and encouragement to this moment of rising up, catching it just before it flips into revenge, supporting the person to act from this stance, which may often result in the capacity to use this strength to find positive avenues and directions of change.

To avenge the dead and grieve for them

Some people say that their urge for revenge is for the dead. Revenge is for loyalty and love, or even to make contact with the realm of the dead. The urge for revenge counteracts hopelessness, and may be felt as a moral requirement for justice. There may be the goal to avenge the deaths of ancestors or comrades who were killed and even grieve for them. 'Here's one for you, baby. I'll take this motherfucker out and I'm going to cut his fucking heart out for you.'[5]

TRAUMA, THE URGE TO KILL, TO PARTICIPATE, AND TO END THE SUFFERING

One way of understanding cycles of retaliation and violence is that the urge to retaliate and to kill is in fact an attempt both to claim the story and to put an end to it. It's an urge to participate in the story and to no longer endure the pain, to exit the recurring nightmare. Our deepest urge to stop the wheel of suffering, paradoxically, inflames the urge to revenge and the perpetuation of the next round.

BREAKING THE CYCLE OF TRAUMA

In this way, we can understand the replay of trauma in nightmares, flashbacks and even the cycle of revenge as a search for a witness or awareness. The suffering and violence repeat, as if looking for us to perceive them, to include them, to tell the story, and to stop them. It's in some ways a hopeful perspective that it may be possible to deal with the reality of collective trauma and cycles of violence. Trauma is volatile fuel for political and social conflict. Working with the collective dynamics of trauma in post-conflict zones and around chronic conflicts of society can support a level of awareness needed for attempts at reconciliation and conflict resolution. Forums are needed where heated emotional and traumatic history can be burned, as a way of interacting and connecting about the reality of our collective relationships. We need new ways of understanding the replay of conflict, and the manipulation of our deepest emotion, as well as the possibility of connecting to our story as human beings, rather than feeling numb and disassociated.

We have looked at how a traumatized person experiences a shattering of consciousness, as one part of the personality goes forward and the traumatic experience remains, replaying and intruding in debilitating symptoms. There's a need to tell the story, to reconnect to the events and emotion that were too much to bear, this time to witness and be witnessed, rather than only suffer again the repeating nightmare. In this way, a traumatized person finds the possibility of returning to life, not by splitting off the terrible events that then reoccur in symptoms, but by including the story, with the reality of its horror,

↑ **Figure 17.1** 'Where have all the flowers gone' by Arpana Caur. Commissioned by the Hiroshima Museum to commemorate the fiftieth anniversary of the atomic bombing. (By courtesy of Arpana Caur.)

into his or her life. The community or society that witnesses the story also needs to feel it and include it into its collective story, in order to move forward whole, rather than splitting off chunks of reality and revising history. As a world we are full of trauma and the reoccurring flashbacks and nightmares of violent conflict. Humanity's consciousness is shattered. The whole world is our client suffering from trauma. One thing we can do together is to create narrative, telling our collective stories, our history, in a way that links the events in some way with the emotional reality of those events. This needs to include interaction and communication between groups. Otherwise the story falls into the gap that isolates us.

The survivors of the US atomic bombing of Hiroshima and Nagasaki are called 'Hibakusha'.[6] They hold a very important place in Japanese society and for the world, as witnesses and sufferers of the effects of the nuclear bomb. Some 300 000 people were killed in Hiroshima and Nagasaki and tens of thousands lived to witness and suffer the atrocity. The world looked on. Many celebrated the end of the war. Historians debate. Was Japan ready to surrender anyway, making the bombing not only atrocious beyond imagination, but pointless? Or were lives saved? The Hibakusha believe they have an essential role to witness and tell the story for our future as humanity. They believe that no arguments in support of nuclear arsenal can stand up in the face of what they saw. As they get older, they continue to tell the story, with urgency, to encourage society to grapple with itself and not to forget them.[7]

FORUMS

In Chapter 3 we looked at how Tribunals and Truth and Reconciliation Commissions are useful for a society to tell the story, fill in the holes and take account of what happened. An important aspect of the Truth and Reconciliation Commissions is that there is a communal witnessing of the events and the emotion. The story is told, as fully and completely as possible, in order to be able to move forward as a society. We also looked at how Tribunals or Truth Commissions can deal only with a small part of the story, and a small part of society's need for accountability and to process its history to move forward.

Our experience facilitating forums in post-conflict regions and around long-standing conflict suggests the great value that such forums could have if more pervasive throughout society, to address issues demanding accountability in society and to grapple with traumatic history. Forums can occur within governmental and non-governmental organizations (NGOs), as joint projects among and between organizations, as grassroots projects and as a part of international conflict resolution efforts. Such forums are also useful in cities dealing with social conflict,[8] as well as in war zones and post-conflict zones. Community forums are needed both as town meetings, and within and between organizations. Communication between organizations is of critical importance in building community. Organizations working with the public, in areas of health, social work, education, law, human rights, policing and government, naturally run into conflicts and blocks in their own work and with one another. This is amplified greatly in zones of conflict. In Croatia, as is true in many conflict zones, there were difficulties between NGOs and governmental organizations, often with conflicting interests. In our project in Croatia, the sponsoring organization made special efforts to relate to and gather people from governmental organizations, NGOs, international organizations and local authorities.

Understanding that trauma is a collective issue, and needs to be addressed in community forums, is an essential consideration for preventing the repeat of violent conflict from the fuel of past traumas, and is paramount in any serious effort to resolve conflict. When working with conflict in a region that has suffered enormous trauma, I have learned that, every time you touch a hot issue, you touch a reservoir of pain, just below the surface of interactions. The facilitator must be alert to the possibility of triggering symptoms of trauma. Avoiding these hot issues, however, only leaves the trauma intact just below the surface. Thus, conflict resolution facilitators and negotiators require special skills, care and knowledge essential for understanding and working with community trauma, as well as for working accurately with 'hot spots'[9] of conflict.

WHEN COMMUNITIES CANNOT RECONCILE – TRAUMA WORK

In situations in which atrocity has wedged communities apart, it can be crucial for the individual communities to meet among themselves to work with their community trauma. The urge to stay separate is often intricately linked with the need for safety and fear of re-triggering symptoms of trauma and violence.

More than a decade after the war and atrocities in Vukovar, Croatia, the town is still in rubble. People live in almost complete apartheid. From bars to playgrounds for small children, Croats and Serbs live separately. In a meeting here, several comments were made about those not present at this and other meetings to address humanitarian issues in the region. Using a simple intervention of Process Work, we said that, if there was a wish to interact around humanitarian issues with those not present, we could do that by creating a 'role' for those not present, and have that dialogue. We put a chair in the room to represent this 'role'. To the group's surprise, they were quite able to represent the views and experiences of those 'others'. Speaking from that role, one woman began to talk about their devastating trauma. She said: 'when you talk about "us" not coming to meetings, you ignore this reality' and 'When you do not acknowledge what our experience and trauma is really like, we can't come to meetings with you.' There was a shift in the atmosphere. My co-facilitator, Lane, and I paused to acknowledge the trauma throughout the entire region, among those not present, and among those present in the group. Many realized that they did not sufficiently acknowledge their own trauma, out of fear that it is too overwhelming and because of the need to put it behind them and try to stay active and move forward in rebuilding their devastated community. As a result of the extensive trauma in the region and the need to move on, trauma was usually considered to be something to endure, simply part of life. Everyone was traumatized. Some said that, in order to grasp and relate to the traumatic experience of others, they needed to make space to work on their own trauma, and that the notion of just putting the story behind them, while understandable, disrupts their efforts to build community.

We felt that this process indicated that one of the things needed in this region is sub-community dialogues on the extensive trauma in the region and, as sub-communities are ready, they will be able to work increasingly together. Pervasive trauma impacts on all social and economic development.

THEATRE FORUMS

The combination of theatre and forums brings such work into community, in a way that is immediate, actual, while bringing an element of ritual and protection. Theatre is a space to express and process issues and emotions that lie at the very limits of society. Theatre is in itself a forum to communalize events, while discovering something underlying, creative and inspiring. J.L. Moreno, who developed psychodrama, originally worked with community and political issues.[10] Augusto Boal's 'theatre of the oppressed' and 'legislative theatre' actualize our participation in political and social issues.[11] The combination of forums and theatrical skills to work with community issues in live, improvisational theatre is an area of my own and colleagues' current interest.[12] It is at once ancient and modern. A particular challenge and important part of this work involves how to address areas of community trauma. Shay writes how the ancient Greeks revered Homer, the singer of tales and the doctor of the soul. In the Odyssey, Homer paints a portrait of the epic singer whose healing art is to tell the stories of Troy, with the truth that causes the old soldier, Odysseus, to weep and weep again.[13]

PERSONAL, COLLECTIVE AND TRANSPERSONAL ASPECTS TO TRAUMA

Breaking the cycle of trauma involves understanding the personal, collective and also the transpersonal dimension of traumatic experience. There is nothing more private, more personal than the experience of being face-to-face with terror. Shaken to the bone, you are betrayed in your deepest values and belief in what might happen and what you can endure. There is nothing more intimate than sharing such personal experience. Yet, trauma is not only personal. It affects family, community and society. Trauma is communal. Trauma is political. When symptoms of trauma are viewed only as a personal psychological problem, it can exacerbate the effects of trauma, keeping the individual isolated, and her experience split off from the community and considered sick.[14] It can also support the tendency in society to hold the story at a distance, leaving the traumatic experience outside, from where it will continue to intrude and replay.

Trauma also has a transpersonal dimension. It erases a sense of personal history, a connection to whom you were before the traumatic event. After seeing the worst of humanity, you easily feel hopeless and desperate, depleted or cut off, from your old personality and everyday life. Yet, sometimes, traumatic experience brings a contact to something beyond one's old personality and beyond one's personal life, beyond even life and death, to an uncanny source of spirit and compassion. Although trauma is linked to a betrayal of trust and one's deepest values, from this collapse of core values, sometimes a new connection to a deeper, transpersonal source emerges. Acknowledgement of the transpersonal and spiritual dimensions of traumatic experience is vital to recognize the resources and capacities in individuals and communities to deal with their trauma, as well as to work with apparently intractable conflict, involving generations of traumatic experience.

TIME AND TRAUMA

Traumatic events remain locked in time, not as memories, but as present, reoccurring events, transcending our notions of linear time and place. Weird body experiences, disconnected perceptions and memory lapses give an eerie feeling of being outside the agreements of 'consensus reality' and linear time. This experience of being outside time can make people feel a terrible sense of losing grip on reality and losing their mind. Yet it can also relate to an experience of touching outside time, outside the events of history, disconnected, yet connected in moments to something eternal, something that carries one through, something spiritual, outside the polarizations on the spokes of the wheel.

GRIEF, RITUAL AND LETTING GO

The capacity to grieve is essential to be able to move forward, whole, after a loss or traumatic event. Grieving supports a process of both including and honouring the tragedy, keeping the memory alive of the person who died and the capacity to let go. The ritual of burials or cremation is needed both to honour the lives of those who died, to let them go, and to let the living go on. When the bodies of those who died are not found, people cannot find closure. The story remains open, and continues to haunt and reoccur. Mass graves are also symbolic of war and the tragedy of incomplete lives, and chapters of our history that cannot be closed. Worse, when mass graves are not found, when the dead are not found, survivors feel that they cannot go on.

People sometimes say that, when they have lost a loved one, at some point they recognize that they need to let their loved one go emotionally, to let them free from their constant thoughts, grief or unfinished business. It's as if we sense that the dead want and deserve to be freed, to let go of the whole thing. And, if we let go, we may feel in touch with the same freedom of the dead, the freedom to transcend the unfinished story, the part of us that can let go of it, in touch with something infinite. In Hindu religion, when someone dies, traditionally a flame is lit. After cremation, there's a period of prayer. On the tenth day after the person's death, the flame is carried to the sea. The

↑ **Figure 17.2** 'Soldier's mother' by Arpana Caur.
(By courtesy of Arpana Caur.)

↓ **Figure 17.3** A memorial in Vukovar
(photo: www.osservatoriobalcani.org by courtesy).

immersion of the flame into the sea is to let the spirit know that he or she can truly break attachment with the former life and continue in the world beyond.

COMPASSION AND STAYING ENGAGED IN THE WORLD

There is nothing to romanticize and it is impossible to overestimate the devastation that traumatic experience brings to people's lives. Yet, sometimes, people who have experienced trauma in time discover a heart big enough to hear and hold all of their experience and the experience of others – there is room for all that is unspeakable, and still there is room for an uncanny joy of

life and playfulness. In a sense, you have taken a trip to the other side and come back. It can bring a sense of freedom; there is nothing more to lose. You come back out of love for life and, while deeply engaged in this life, perhaps more than ever before, a part of you is already with the ancestors, outside time and free.

Whether we have experienced personal trauma, or have had the fortune not to have personal experiences of trauma, as a world we have all known and been part of the collective dynamics of trauma. Traumatic wounds of history remain present, and cannot be excluded in the process of moving forward. If we try to move ahead by splitting off and forgetting traumatic events, they persist and replay. Just as traumatic experience tends to make people feel both cut off from an event and overrun by it, there's a tendency for any of us to feel cut off from our world, and simultaneously to feel overrun by it, taken along into the recurring nightmare. Compassion may mean having the heart to include our history and to stay engaged.

PART 4

THE WARRIOR'S CALL – ALTERED STATES OF WAR

CHAPTER 18
BEYOND THE ORDINARY

WALKING

A group of us were walking along a pathway by the sea, back from dinner one evening in Croatia on a beautiful warm evening with a star-filled sky. I was talking to one of the forum participants. He had been to previous forums and it was good to see him again. I was asking him how he was doing. He talked about his work for a while. As we walked, I noticed our pace speeding up and we began walking in silence. After a few minutes, we both said something about enjoying walking and then he said: 'After the war, I walked and walked. It was the only thing that kept me alive. I walked miles and miles. When our town was attacked, I was involved in the resistance and didn't sleep. All night, I would be walking, running through the town, back and forth, to meet someone, to carry a message – grenades flew past. It was as if they flew right past me or through me and couldn't hit me. I couldn't die. I knew I couldn't die. It was as if I was already dead. I felt elated, connected to something beyond life and death, to God. After the war, I fell into a depression, and my depression was as low as my elation was high. All I wanted was to die. All I wanted was to be underground. More of my friends were underground than above the ground. All I wanted was to be underground with them.'

And, he said: 'That's when I began to walk. Walking was my only way of feeling connected again to life, to God. I walked every day for weeks and months, for years, for hundreds of miles.' As he told me this story, we continued to walk, my attention at our feet, and inside his story. I glanced back, and our group of friends walking behind us had receded into the distance.

War throws people from everyday life with mythic force. Not only does war cut off people's path of life with terrible loss of family, community, goals and all that once mattered, but also people sometimes experience a connection to something beyond their personal life. Some sense a spirit and feel in contact with a sense of meaning, beyond life and death, that is awesome and even intoxicating. The moment is etched deeper. Within the tragic and traumatic events of war, it's the rest of the world that may seem far away and out of touch.

ALTERED STATES OF WAR

Altered states are perceptions, emotions, moods and experiences that lie outside the boundary of the states we call 'normal'. This is relative to collective 'norms' and to our identity. If we are always depressed, waking up happy could be an altered state. If someone is always drunk, being sober is altered. Altered states are also pathways into the deeper dimensions of our collective psyche, where we fight demons and dragons, and where we feel linked to a sense of the infinite and creative source of life.

As individuals and communally, many of us feel it essential to try to access these deeper dimensions of our lives, as reflected in ritual and spirituality across all cultures. For some, these experiences weave through life as a constant source of meaning. Others rarely experience this contact with something outside the ordinary world. Often just before death, or when faced with a life–death situation, people will experience a shift in perspective, as if both inside and outside of their everyday life, a part of a larger story or eternity.

One way of looking at this is that archetypal forces drive our personal and collective development. These forces have many faces appearing in myths, fairy tales and religious stories across cultures. We find joy in discovering the mysteries and creative patterns of life. We are inspired to create works of art, to make music. We are inspired to research. Our longing to find purpose and meaning beyond the confines of our everyday identities, our longing to transcend the ego and connect to something infinite, our devotion and capacity to feel one with community – these are such splendid aspects of humanity and yet, when unconscious, these qualities are exploited to arouse people to violence and war.

The 'call beyond life and death' appeals to something deep within us. We are ready to abandon the everyday world to accomplish something vital, because it may be our psychological and spiritual task to go beyond the confines of our everyday identity and experience our wholeness, and even the infinite. If we are unconscious of these tendencies, we can be easily exploited in our attraction to 'altered states', as pathways out of the 'ordinary' and into the 'extraordinary' and awesome.

IN THE NAME OF GOD

This tendency is not only exploited covertly. Throughout time, religion has played an essential role in war. We call for violence in the name of spirituality – in the name of God. Institutionalized religions have practised violence against both their adherents and their real and imagined enemies. People turn to God as a rationale for violence, as they also turn to God as a justification to resist or to come to terms with destruction and loss.[1]

We look to leaders to stimulate our sense of connection to a greater cause. Leaders mobilize us, as we mobilize leaders. Some of the most sacred and awesome aspects of life are the stuff of war. We long to be lifted by great dreams and love of community. We are propelled by our devotion and capacity to sacrifice our love, loyalty, joy in unity, and our search for purpose and something more essential than life itself.

INTOXICATION BY 'POWER'

Victory feels good. We get intoxicated. I remember colleagues in Croatia who celebrated in 1995 when the Croat army took back the regions that had been

taken in 1991 by the Serbs. As we have seen, there were terrible atrocities in the 'ethnic cleansing' of 1991. In 1995 the situation was reversed. Serbs were killed and violently forced to flee the region. The emotional high accompanying the Croat victory in 1995 made it difficult for people to perceive the atrocities now committed by the Croat side.

In the 1967 war in Israel, when Israel not only held its own, but seized and occupied what are now called 'the occupied territories', people rejoiced. After a

← **Figure 18.1** Russian poster, Emperor Nicholas II with shield 'God is with us'. (By courtesy of the Hoover Institute, Stanford University.)

legacy of hostility towards the Jews culminating in the horror of the Holocaust, there was now a sense of vindication, elation, returning to the 'promised land', not only of fighting for their survival, but also a land that once was 'home'. The 'altered states' of victory made it difficult for Israelis to see the plight of Palestinians and the future trouble that this 'victory' would mean.

The Intifada renewed its spirit through altered states of possibility, redemption and power. The spirit of resistance is emboldened by a sense of contact to meaning, beyond this life of suffering and beyond life and death. Some people celebrate a brutal terrorist act, despite the human atrocity, and the fact that it will lead to the next crackdown of the Israeli military, and a new cycle of violence. One reason for this is the intoxicating altered states of vindication and power, even if fleeting, that cannot be underestimated and which help to keep people dreaming of a brighter future.

A dramatic sense of victory, freedom and power fans the fires that make us unable to consider repercussions, let alone perceive what it might be like on the other side. Propaganda feeds the flames and makes explicit and intentional use of these altered states.

↓ **Figure 18.2** Charlie Chaplin as Hitler in 'The Great Dictator'.
(© Roy Export Co. Establishment. By courtesy of Association Chaplin.)

SOARING WITH HIGH DREAMS

Touch someone's high dream[2] and you can arouse or restore their will to live and their belief in humanity. You can also arouse patriotism, nationalist fury, righteousness and the capacity to murder.

In a high dream, we feel on top of the world, elated. High dreams make us certain, absolute, invincible and able to commit wholeheartedly to a cause, but easily reduce our ability to see things in perspective. If you have ever fallen in love, you may have found yourself in a 'high dream', intoxicated by what seemed to be a dream come true. At last, the perfect partner! The expression 'love is blind' describes this high dream. We see perfection, and cannot see the pimples or foibles of our partner – not yet. And this is how it should be. The dream allows us to connect beyond the confines of the ordinary world and reason, and if we are lucky to a shared and long-lasting love.

Our high dreams guide us, give us purpose – and yet, when we are seized by these dreams, we rarely live by them. Instead we behave as if we were in a stupor and are easily duped, whether in our personal lives or in our social, political lives. Out of belief in a high dream, many people believe what they are told without question and reflection.

THE ATTRACTION OF LOW DREAMS

We fall or crash from our high dreams into what seems a dreadful reality. We get into moods of despair, bitterness and hopelessness. We are convinced that things will never get better.

We wake up one morning and our partner no longer looks like a reflection of our fantasy. This can be the beginning of a relationship, rather than an affair with our high dream – but this awakening and meeting can be fraught with difficulty.

Moods around 'low dreams' can be terrible to endure, yet strangely attractive. We are drawn into existential depressions, hopelessness and a longing for redemption. Or we become 'cool', jaded. We may feel trapped and anxious. These 'low dreams' are also exploited in the political process and in war.

When we feel we belong, our high dream makes anything possible. When we feel rejected, the 'low dream' begins. Young people who feel rejected by society get into low dreams, whereas gang life stirs the high dream and sense of belonging. Privilege can also contribute to us feeling cut off. Moods of hopelessness, jadedness or serious depression draw in teenagers who are otherwise privileged, cut off from a sense of responsibility and community. In the USA, there were incidents of teenagers going on rampages, shooting classmates and teachers. They identified with hopelessness and mania, ready to die and to kill.[3] Throughout history and all over the world, the low and high dreams of youth and even children are used to send them to war.

PATRIOTISM AND SUPPORT FOR TERRORISTS

Hopelessness can be turned into a commitment to a greater cause for better or for worse, and the willingness to give one's life for it. Acts of terrorism, particularly suicide bombings, arise from the interplay of low and high dreams, and political commitment.

In the USA, the horror of 9/11 led to a surge not only of fear, outrage and grief, but also of feelings of closeness to one another, an urge to unity and to wave flags. Although much of the world expressed its shock and sympathy, there were those who swelled in a high dream, that it was possible to hit, at least symbolically, at the heart of US political and economic power.

NATIONALISM

Similarity of culture

Nationalism is a political principle that maintains that similarity of culture is the basic social bond.[4] In its extreme version, similarity of culture becomes both the necessary and the sufficient condition of legitimate membership; only members of the appropriate culture may join the unit in question and all of them must do so. A further step is that everyone else must be eliminated. To grasp how nationalist movements develop, it is essential to consider the high emotions involved.

That 'nations' are based on membership to a particular culture or ethnic group is offered up as a 'fact'. As described in Parts 1, 2 and 3, historical injustice and trauma may be tapped to provoke fear and outrage, and other groups are demonized, dehumanized and blamed for society's problems. These ingredients are stirred with our deepest emotions around self-determination, a sense of home and land, and our love of community. Nationalist movements are born and carried with our emotional commitment.

Self-determination and pride

Nationalism arises with an urge for self-determination, to be free of domination and threats to our existence. We want to survive, thrive and claim our own identity and autonomy. We want to feel a sense of dignity and pride in our culture, history and future. We want to feel that we have a place on this earth, free to fulfil our nature as an individual or group. When we do not have this privilege of safety and self-determination we tend to feel anxious, without bearing.

Home and land

We long for a sense of ease, to be 'at home'. The sense of having one's bearings comes from having basic human rights of safety and inclusion in society. It also comes from having contact to one's own experience and story. We've seen how trauma can make us lose this orientation, as individuals and as entire communities. When we connect to our personal and collective story there may be a sense of coming 'home'. Feeling at 'home' can also come from a connection to a spiritual source. Some feel at home anywhere. For some, this sense of home is tied to nature or to a particular land. Our love of nature and devotion to our homeland can run very deep in our souls. Some of us experience land as if it is our body, or the body of our mother. Being severed from one's land may feel like losing one's body, losing one's mother or losing contact with the pulse of life. A sense of home can also come from the capacity to be aware of one's own body, and our deepest subtlest impulses and rhythms, and an underlying source and orientation to life.

Nationalism often arises with a historical claim to land that touches upon a poetic, spiritual or sentimental longing. Our lack of consciousness, about the sacredness of land and our and others' connection to the land, can lead us to bitter conflict, and to exploit the land and one another.

LONGING FOR COMMUNITY

Our sense of belonging to community makes it possible for us to serve a cause and care for community. Our urge for community, when unconscious, is also readily exploited for purposes of war. We easily grow romantic and sentimental. Snipers sing folk songs and love songs.

It is important to underline that the various characteristics that are so readily exploited do not spontaneously take the route of nationalism, exclusion or genocide. For this to occur, these qualities in us are carefully, rigorously and systematically misused.

THE ESSENTIAL INGREDIENT – NAIVETY

Thugs and criminals become war heroes during nationalist campaigns of ethnic cleansing. In the Balkans, warlords acted in tandem with the state. In Nazi

Germany, the 'brown-shirted' thugs were the strong arm of the Party to instil terror and compliance.

But force alone would be ineffective. Naivety is needed to help the ball roll with a faster, lighter and uplifted touch. For this reason youth groups are often targeted. In the 1930s, the Nazi youth movement inspired enthusiasm in young people and instilled positive values and discipline, harnessing a spirit of community and loyalty. The extreme right and white supremacists in the USA and Europe aim their propaganda at youth.

Fresh and naive blood is needed to fulfil nationalist goals. Not all young people are naive of course, nor is it only the young who are naive. 'Youth' are symbolic as well as actual. Waking up about our naivety could avert violent conflict. Waking up also involves getting to know this 'youth-like' quality in us.

BEGINNER'S MIND

Let's say naivety is a combination of a high dream and not much awareness. But naivety has a close cousin, a quality of 'beginner's mind', a term used in Buddhist philosophy. The 'beginner's mind' is in the researcher who is open to perceive what lies outside his or her existing theory or paradigm. It is in the freshness of an artist and the open heart of devotion in a spiritual practitioner. It is in the capacity to let go of one's position at a given moment and see the other side. This quality of beginner's mind would allow us to interrupt the status quo and not just be swept along.

SACRIFICE

Sacrifice is linked to giving up our preconceptions. An act of sacrifice involves giving up our identification or ownership. In Hindu philosophy, sacrifice is essential to contact the underlying source of creation. 'The creative impulse requires sacrificing oneself so that the potency and abundance of Spirit can manifest in one's inner life.'[5] In Indian religion and mythology, Ganesh (the god with the elephant head) is the Lord of thresholds. He sits at that place, where we let go of the old and enter the new, the gateway of perception. He stands between past and future and supports the process of change in every new situation that we confront in life. Kali appears as the destructive aspect of time. She destroys the mundane aspect of consciousness to bring forth a new attitude.[6] Acts of sacrifice, including symbolic offerings are also intended to link us to the infinite. To sacrifice the self means to regenerate the self anew through the transforming touch of the divine.

Whatever our particular religion or personal beliefs, our capacity for self-sacrifice is associated with some of the most important experiences of humankind. Hindu religion teaches that, through dedication of oneself and works to God, one can overcome bondage to the world of illusion. In Buddhism as well as Hinduism, 'samsara' refers to our attachment to the continual replay of cycles of conflict, and our delusion when we are sunk in it. Contact with the divine touches a creative energy that transcends and breaks the cycle. Christian religion values self-sacrifice and giving one's life for a greater cause. Islam also values sacrifice for the community and the future. No matter one's religion, meditation and prayer are acts of giving oneself over to the divine and may be symbolized or enacted in ritual 'offerings'.

Self-sacrifice may be essential on a path of personal and spiritual development. Yet it is easy to be taken by a 'high dream' of spiritually, to give up personal responsibility and get intoxicated rather than developing awareness. Chogyam Trungpa described the attachment to goals and outcomes of spirituality, and the accompanying moods, as 'spiritual materialism'.[7] Other situations demand special awareness. In the therapeutic relationship, or in the student–teacher relationship, it's important to work carefully.

Our capacity for devotion and self-sacrifice may manifest as loyalty to a particular group, spiritual leader, political leader or ideology. Our innate tendency

↓ **Figure 18.3** Sacrifice, Puja. (Photo by Alex Johnson.)

↑ **Figure 18.4** Rembrandt Harmensz van Rijn, *The Sacrifice of Isaac.* (By courtesy of the State Heritage Museum, St Petersburg, Russia. © the State Heritage Museum, St Petersburg, Russia.)

↓ **Figure 18.5** 'Father kissing his son goodbye', State Political Directorate Poster, Russia about 1939. (By courtesy of the Hoover Institute, Stanford University.)

to devotion and sacrifice is a great gift that is easily exploited. Nationalist leaders may calculate and depend upon this tendency, to call for absolute devotion.

DEVOTION AND LOVE IN WAR

If you ask people what are the psychological and emotional factors that lead us into war, you will often hear things like hatred, prejudice, rage and aggression. Yet devotion and love are two essential elements of war. Devotion towards our country arises from our capacity to know ourselves as part of the collective, to care for something much more important than our personal survival.

Love between soldiers goes beyond a feeling between comrades and friendship. Shay records one Vietnam vet: 'I became the mother hen. You know "C'mon, c'mon, c'mon, c'mon, c'mon, get over here, get over here. Stay down. All right, now, now, everyone keep, y'know, y'know – the shit hits the fan, hit the fucking ground, don't worry about nothing, just stay down now." It was constant now. I was watching the other five guys like they was my children.'[8]

Shay writes: 'Combat calls forth a passion of care among men who fight beside each other that is comparable to the earliest and most deeply felt family relationships. We often hear that the death of a special friend-in-arms broke the survivor's life into un-healable halves, with everything before his death

radically severed from everything after.'[9]

The bond of passion between soldiers in battle is profound – soldiers often hold the lives of their comrades above their own, and fear the loss of their friends' lives over their own. The willingness for self-sacrifice is part and parcel of battle. The feeling of love, and the devotion we are capable of having, to give our life for another, is a profound and beautiful part of our human nature, needed and exploited to send men and women into war.

← **Figure 18.6** 'Your friends need you', World War I poster to recruit soldiers, England. (By courtesy of the Hoover Institute, Stanford University.)

CHAPTER 19
WITH THE FIELD

UNITY

Difficult and terrible events can shake us free of our everyday routine. At our personal limits, we may connect to a source beyond the personal. Our personal limitations and mundane concerns evaporate and we feel a sense of oneness with community, the earth or the universe. A crisis can have this effect. I was living in LA during the big earthquake in 1994. I remember huddling outside with neighbours, shaken, fiddling with radios and enjoying meeting for the first time. For the next few weeks, a beautiful sense of community, painfully absent most of the time, lifted the city.

Patriotism and nationalism depend on this urge for unity and easily twist it into a quasi-unity. 'We are united. We are glorious. They are not one with us.'

In the Balkans, people gave up differences with former neighbours, as they united based on their supposed commonality now as Serb, Croat or Muslim. Conversely, an old argument or a manufactured one often served to support suspicion or hatred and the capacity to murder someone who used to be your classmate, baker, neighbour or spouse, for being Serb, Croat or Muslim.

KILLING AND DYING

One of the most atrocious things about being a human being is that we kill each other – apparently a unique characteristic that some say differentiates us as a species. Our capacity to kill is not only related to the way we demonize and dehumanize. Our capacity to kill is also linked to our belief in something more important than life itself. This quality is also at the seat of our compassion. It drives human community and civilization and allows us to feel part of a flow of life, transcending our short stay on earth. It makes us able to sacrifice our life for another. Our capacity to give our life for each other is therefore connected to our capacity to kill each other.

Our interest in something more important than life itself can be harnessed and exploited in war. Yet, if we recognize that there are more important things than our attachment to life itself, this might lead us not to kill, but to live fully, to go all the way during our short stay here.

In the *Bhagavad Gita*,[1] Arjuna faces grave doubts on the great field of battle, and has a conversation with Krishna. Krishna teaches us to enter and engage fully with the battle of life, through recognizing that we are ultimately not attached to the different roles and polarizations we play out.

↓ **Figure 19.1** Krishna talking with Arjuna on the battlefield. Early nineteenth century manuscript of the *Bhagavad Gita*. (By courtesy of the British Library, London. OR 13758.)

DAY OF THE DEAD, STOPPING THE WORLD

Another distinctive feature of being a human being is how we bury and burn the dead and have rites and rituals around death. Throughout time and across cultures, there are many views about what, if anything, happens after death. What is consistent is the importance of our respect and contact with ancestors who have come before us and a realm or sense of meaning that transcends our life on earth.

Our beliefs in dimensions beyond life and death, whether spiritual, religious, artistic or intellectual, shape our lives, our interest in grandchildren, our creative work, our contributions in different fields, our search for meaning and our capacity to reflect on life itself.

↑ **Figure 19.2** Day of the Dead, Adam and Eve. (By courtesy of the artist, Bryant Holman.)

In Mexico, the 'Day of the Dead' is a festive time. Families welcome the dead back in their homes. Along with great feasts for the visiting dead, there are images or sculptures of skeletons involved in daily life scenes, such as cooking or selling you something at a kiosk.

It is liberating to be both in the ordinary world and to step out of it or 'stop the world'. It may be just a momentary or fleeting experience. 'Un Ange Passe' is a French expression that describes that moment of stillness and awe that suddenly passes over us. Something essential is touched, perhaps in the midst of conversation, and it's as if everything stops, and something numinous, peaceful, eternal and awesome is in the atmosphere. An angel passes and life moves on again.

The altered states accompanying war sometimes include the feeling of stopping the world. This occurs as tragic loss, but at times as a sense of mystery. As our world falls apart, we are no longer tied to the ordinary.

INITIATION RITUALS: TO DIE IN ONE IDENTITY AND MOVE TO ANOTHER

Initiation rituals celebrate the coming of age – you move from the role of one who is cared for by the community to one who cares for community. You go out on your first hunt, meet a partner or become a parent. At the point of stepping into your new role, you are linked to ancestors who have stood before you in this role and the generations to come who will take your place. Moving into new roles involves taking risks as you give up your old identification, before you know what is coming next. As you give up one role, whether willingly or through life's twists and turns, you may experience a profound sense of loss. You lose a parent. A child leaves home or dies. You lose your partner. You get a job or you retire. You move to a new city. Yet, as you leave one role and move into another, you may be surprised by the experience of freedom and recognition that the former role or identification was just that, a 'role' – and not the whole of you.

'Initiation' ceremonies celebrate passing to a new role, and in some cultures may involve rituals for passing a threshold of pain, which test and challenge the boundaries of your former identification. Calls to war are also an initiation – a call to be ready to give up your own life for the survival of community, and to step over the threshold of your ordinary world in the spirit of being connected to a greater whole.

In Europe, annual ritual enactments still take place of burning effigies of the king,[2] symbolizing the renewal of spring and the renewal of culture. The ritual death of the leader (or leading principle) is needed for renewal of life and the continuity of cycles of life. The Christian practice of Holy Communion involves tasting a wafer and drinking a sip of wine, the body of Christ and the blood of Christ. Christian theology values giving up attachments or one's life for the redemption of the soul. In Hindu religion the devotee transcends the boundaries of ego to unite with Brahma, the great unity that underlies and includes our diversity. Tantric Buddhism teaches that 'out of the symbolic "death" of the body, the spiritual human being arises'.[3]

Longing to connect to something beyond our personal lives, beyond life and death has countless faces and expressions from different cultures and religions. As we age, we may begin to experience not only how short and fleeting life has been, but a sense of detachment from our personal lives, and a part of a longer, intergenerational story, the passage of time or even eternity.

A friend of mine, a young man, was shot and paralysed by a sniper in Sarajevo. He told me how he lay in bed for weeks in the hospital, staring (in an apparent vigil, comatose state). He later learned that, while he lay in the hospital, people worried he wouldn't make it through. While they feared he would slip away, he was wide awake, seeing God, filled with love and awe.

We often heard people say that during the war they sometimes felt a heightened state, connected to God or a 'source' underneath the layers of fear, rage and grief. Yet, others felt they lost a connection to their belief in such a source, to their belief in God. Several times, I heard people say: 'If there is a God, how could this God allow such atrocity to happen?'

TRAINING FOR WAR

Training armies and navies includes accessing 'altered states' that prepare the 'warrior' to meet the extremes of war. Again, it is usually young people who are trainees. Just as in the development of nationalist movements, our emotions

and the field dynamics that shape us are tapped and disciplined, to train people to give their lives for the community and a greater cause, and to be able to
take life. The sound of drums, marching in formation, chanting, shaving your
head, wearing uniforms and conforming to routines that strip away individuality are all part of tapping and bringing discipline to these tendencies. Suicide
bombers are also geared and sometimes trained towards giving up their own
identity, their own life, for their community. An oft-mentioned characteristic of
suicide bombers is that they do not feel isolated, but rather deeply connected
with others with a spiritual purpose.[4]

SEALs

The 'SEALs', a special section of the US navy, are trained to handle extreme situations and emergencies. After each training phase the candidates for the SEAL
units are tested. Those who cannot 'go the mile' are deselected. In a report about
SEAL training, a trainer said that a bottom-line criterion for selecting a candidate was that he, the trainer, would feel personally willing to go on a mission
with the candidate. He said: 'Could I put my life in this trainee's hands?' Training and testing of the SEALs involves submersion in cold water for long hours
at sea, sleep deprivation and heavy exertion. All personal limits are crossed, until
people lose their identification with their individuality, and experience themselves as a part of a unit – pulling in the same direction as the rest.

The tactics mirror terror tactics and have been criticized, checked and
revised. The tactics are not designed to strengthen will power. Rather the individual will must be broken, aligned with the group's will. The slightest
individual impulse that might separate the individual from the unit is dangerous. Training involves giving over to a force that is greater than the individual.
Physical and spiritual resources are tapped beyond the limits of the trainee's
imagination, to connect with a 'field' and to be able to serve the unit.

ASCETIC PRACTICE

SEAL training has similarities to certain ascetic religious practices. Some
Sadhus in India, for example, who live away from civilization, survive and
thrive in extreme conditions. Extreme ascetic practices may involve going
without food and water for extended periods, or inflicting pain on the body,
as a method of transcending the limitations of the ego that are bound to human
comfort, and connecting the practitioner to a deeper underlying source of life,
unity and creation.

SOCIAL MOVEMENTS

We are aroused to social activism in our outrage about current injustice and in response to the traumatic stories of our personal and collective history and the belief in a better future. Our search for contact to a greater cause and our devotion in community is good fertilizer to grow social movements. Once more, youth are often central to social movements. As a movement gains momentum, it may further differentiate and polarize the conflict and potential crackdown in a process of raising awareness.

FEELING THE TIDE: PRAGUE SPRING AND THE VELVET REVOLUTION

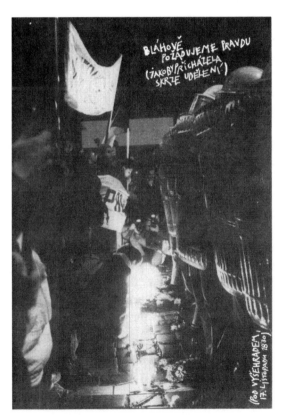

↑ **Figure 19.3** The Velvet Revolution, 17 November 1989, Pod Vysehradem, Prague. 'Naively we dare to ask for the truth (although ultimately no one has it).' The second part of the sentence has a double meaning that the truth used to be owned and put on us by government. (By courtesy of the National Museum, Prague.)

We feel buoyed in a sense of possibility. To feel part of a movement is exciting. Alone we are limited. Together we can accomplish anything. Yet, this elated feeling doesn't come just from the power of numbers. It comes from a sense of contact to a deeper pulse of life. As a young teenager, I was in a demonstration against the war in Vietnam. Moving up a long hill in Seattle, I recall looking ahead and looking back, and there was no beginning and no end to this great crowd. I felt part of a great wave of change. Czech and Slovak friends have told me about the excitement of the Prague Spring in 1968, the promise of opening out to the world and liberation from tyranny, the pulse of the atmosphere. Songs of Marta Kubisova lifted spirits and the sound of

Bob Dylan, heard for the first time under communism, brought the feeling of being part of an international wave of freedom.

Then there was the terror, sadness and depression following the tanks that rolled in during the crackdown of the Communist government in 1968. It was 20 years later, as Communism collapsed across Europe, when Marta Kubisova sang again in front of thousands gathered in freezing temperatures at Wenceslas Square in Prague. She sang 'Prayer to Marta', the unofficial anthem of both the Prague Spring (1968) and the 'Velvet Revolution' (1989).[5] The Velvet Revolution recalled the excitement of the Prague Spring, this time without the crackdown.

SONG

Many rituals involve letting go of the boundaries of your individuality to connect to community spirit. We may enter a mythic, timeless, shared space through rhythmic chants, song, dance and prayer. Some sports not only stretch the limits of individual skill and endurance, but also help us discover ourselves as a member of a team, in touch with an underlying source. If we dance in a group, we may sense the meaning of transcending the boundaries of being an individual to feel the joy and pulse of being moved by a greater field.

As I am working on this section, it is Christmas Eve, actually Christmas Day, close to 2am in Kauai, and, across the field, there is a great party at the neighbours, a Hawaiian family. I'm in a hut with all screen walls, and find myself grinning, as one song after the other booms and floats across the field. Everyone is singing, chanting and drumming. Deeply romantic songs, Hawaiian songs, and then the Beach Boys and the Beatles, 'I wanna hold your hand'. Now a Caribbean song, 'I wanna go home'.

I'm reminded of nights in Croatia, and feel a longing for those nights under the stars, with home-brewed fresh wine and friendship. We would gather at the beach or at the hotel. People would start singing together around 10 at night and go all night until 4 or 5, sometimes 7 in the morning. And there was never a break, not for a moment, one song flowing seamlessly to the next. Someone would always begin a new song and everyone would join in, and this group never ran out of songs – folk songs from Croatia, Serbia, Bosnia, Montenegro, Macedonia, Slovenia, romantic, sad, stunningly beautiful and silly. My colleague, Lane, pitched in a little blues and rock and roll. Once, around 5am, this group ran out of folk songs. After a moment's pause, fishing for the next song, they started up with patriotic Russian songs, until the police showed up! By 10am, we'd all be back in the meeting room, in suit and tie, ready for our closing morning together in the forum.

Songs in the Balkans have been strongly associated with nationalist movements. In a party during the first workshop we gave, people were dancing in one room and, in the other, a few started playing the guitar and singing. After a while, everyone gathered and sang together. During one particular song, there was lots of feeling in that room. I remember having goose bumps. Someone whispered that this was a song from a beloved Serb singer who had been outlawed in Croatia and no-one had heard since the war.

ALCOHOL: BEER, FULLNESS AND COMMUNITY

During a forum in Croatia one afternoon, the group told Lane and me about problems that they faced in trying to lead projects in their communities. They described how everyone needed money, and how the international agencies with money held the power. A wild scene emerged with everyone hamming up a 'scene' of what it is like, buttering up to the international aid agency, trying to get your picture taken, arm over the shoulder. Every time someone tried to suggest a new pathway forward, or a useful idea or project, the role of hopeless 'beer drinkers' showed up. In a playful, almost drunken, yet deadly serious enactment, the whole group showed how passive resistance, burn-out and hopelessness were killing off projects and community leadership.

We spoke about how alcoholism is linked to the pain and trauma of war and to the constant hard work against all odds to rebuild community. We decided to explore the altered state that is so attractive in 'beer'. One participant spoke about how she is seen and knows herself to be a community leader, but struggles with burn-out. We asked her to step into the role of the 'beer drinker', and to feel into what it's like to drink beer, to access the state of having had a few beers and to describe what she loves about it. She began to make slow movements to accompany her altered state of 'beer', and to focus on her internal state. She described how beer brings her a feeling of connection with people, with community and a sense that she is 'filled up'. This experience 'could make life worth living'. As she accessed this sense of fullness right then in the group, she expressed it by saying she was very touched by this group and felt filled up with a deep sense of community that had developed over the past few days. The atmosphere shifted in the group as everyone felt appreciated, and we acknowledged the new quality of leadership in her that emerged from this state of fullness.

We discussed the widespread problem of alcohol in the aftermath of war and how this is a major issue in Croatia and in much of the world.[6] We discussed how the capacity to access this sense of fullness and connection to community (in ways other than alcohol) was essential, as community leaders, to not suffer from burn-out, amid the high level of personal and community stress from past trauma and the long-term and continuous work of rebuilding community. One thing the group learned was that, without access to this state of 'fullness' (within the altered state produced by beer), community leaders enthusiastically try to launch projects, or 'make things happen', which is then blocked by burn-out and beer. In this process, some of the group discovered a new dimension to their personal leadership, coming from a place of 'fullness', which made them feel heartened, enlivened and also inspiring to others, such that long-term and difficult tasks could be more sustainable.

CHAPTER 20
OVER THE EDGE

SUICIDE

In the post-war years in the Balkans, the suicide rate among former soldiers was high. The urge to commit suicide after surviving a war arises from grief and loss, self-blame for not having been able to save a friend, depression, loss of meaning and apparently insurmountable challenges to build a new life. Yet another reason for suicide among former soldiers is the longing for the acute and heightened experiences of life felt during the war. Return to everyday life is sometimes experienced as a fall or crash into the mundane. Or, sometimes a soldier cannot find his way home – he never imagined he would be home again, and may feel that he already died in battle. He cannot bridge his war experience with his relationships and activities at home. And, as we have seen, he may feel isolated, returning to a community that shows no interest or understanding of his experience. He longs for the communion that he felt with other soldiers. There is a longing for something beyond life and death. Suicide is often the attempt to go back to that place, to that place beyond life and death, where he once was with his buddies. And, when these buddies died in war, it is also a way of joining them there.

OVER THE EDGE: EXTREME STATES OF WAR

War brings with it an intensity that, despite the atrocity, horror and heartbreak, is experienced and often looked back upon as a time of a heightened sense of being truly alive. A friend of mine, now 90 something, described, with a glimmer in his eye, that he never felt more alive than when he was a bomber in World War II. 'I felt free.' 'When you set out in that plane, you just didn't know if you would make it back,' he grinned. 'And once back, all you wanted was to set out again.' The feeling of living on the edge of death brought a heightened state of being alive and free. Friends in the Balkans describe a sense of intensity that they miss, despite the horrors of war. 'You felt at the centre of urgent, unfolding historic world events.' In *War is a Force that gives us Meaning*, Chris Hedges describes this intoxication that comes with war. 'The eruption of conflict instantly reduces the headache and trivia of daily life.'[1]

Within the extremes and madness of war, life must also go on. The simplest acts of survival might take on enormous proportions. In the midst of shelling, someone must run from the shelter to fetch water. Vietnam vets describe the bond that develops from covering each other's back from gunfire, while having to pull down your pants. 'It's a closeness you never had before. It's closer than your mother and father . . . than your brother or your sister, or whoever you're closest with in your family. It was . . . y'know, you'd take a shit, and he'd be right there covering you. . . . We needed each other to survive.'[2]

Just as there is an attraction to the intensity of war, a deep connection among those who share in this experience and an alienation from those who know nothing of it, there is also a longing for the ordinary, which now feels out of reach. A friend of mine in Croatia told me a story about how, one day during the war, she and a friend got it in their heads that they had to go shopping for clothes. They took the trip to another town where a shopping centre was open, risking driving across empty highways, where they could see grenades flying overhead.

NO WAY TO RETURN HOME

Returning to the 'ordinary' world may also be impossible. Someone in Croatia described to me how her husband was fighting on the front lines, but it was so close to home he could easily come home for days off. Yet, he could not find his way 'home'. They started to feel deeply estranged from each other. They were living in different worlds, and neither could commute between worlds. He would long to get back to the war, where he felt others understood what he was going through.

After a war, soldiers are asked to return to a world that they cannot always remember. Few are interested in creating a bridge the other way, to understand their war experience. The same is true for war refugees travelling to countries where people know nothing of their experience. I remember the first time I returned from Croatia and, when I would begin to tell people about my experience, I recall seeing how a window would close behind people's eyes, emptiness wash over the face. At first I thought it must be my own excitement and awkwardness in sharing my experience that was creating this reaction in others. I then realized that my experience matched, in some very small way, those who have lived through war and cannot return 'home'. We had touched something awesome in that first seminar in Croatia, and it was not something that I could communicate or share with others when I got back 'home'.

The extreme states of war cannot be understood only within the context of the particular region or time frame of war. Nor can violence be understood only by studying those people who appear violent. A larger systems view is needed. Those of us far from war usually identify with the 'ordinary', while splitting off and projecting extremes, whether glamorous or hideous, on to others. Soldiers can't come 'home' and we close our doors. Journalists, who have spent time in war zones, and others who have worked in hot spots for the UN or other international and human rights organizations also often experience this difficulty coming 'home', dealing with the dynamics of trauma and this sense of being in an 'other world'.

We have seen how the genocide, atrocity and suffering in the Balkans were often summed up as another conflict among those crazy people in the Balkans. Or, in Rwanda, many believed that ancient tribal hatreds had somehow erupted. This helped people at a distance to stay identified with being 'normal' and 'civilized', while those at war were 'crazy' and 'barbarian', and it helped to tie down the position that we could do nothing and were not responsible. The more we split off large chunks of reality in order to identify with 'ordinary' life, the more we co-create violence and then isolate and alienate those who have suffered.

VIGILANCE

Shay records a Vietnam vet: 'I'm so envious of all the normal people who can just go to the mall and hold hands with their wife and walk around. You see, I could never do that, because I'd be looking everywhere. Fuck! I even envy you.' (He is speaking to Shay.) 'I see you walking up the street to the clinic and you're not checking the rooftops for snipers or looking between cars as you pass to make sure there's nobody going to jump you and I'll bet you have no idea who's on the street with you. I can tell you every person two blocks ahead of me and two blocks behind me every second. I see you coming down the street, but you don't see me, because you're in your own world not looking for an ambush. How come you're like that? I envy you.'[3]

War trauma can create an extreme state of hyperalertness and vigilance, along with the inability to return to 'ordinary life'. Shay records a Vietnam vet: 'I haven't really slept for twenty years. I lie down, but I don't sleep. I'm always watching the door, the window, and then back to the door. I get up at least five times to walk my perimeter, sometimes it's ten or fifteen times. There's always something within reach, maybe a baseball bat or a knife, at every door. I used to sleep with a gun under my pillow . . . .'[4]

In Kosovo, after the war, my colleague, Lane, and I sat with groups of people in Mitrovice. They talked about Albanians still on the Serb side of Mitrovice who would call in the night in terrible distress, and how they could not go to that side of Mitrovice to help. They had severe trauma and were barricading themselves in their homes and standing vigilant all night. They did not know the war was over. For them, it was not.

In our forums in Croatia, people often spoke about long periods of no sleep during the war. Ten years later, many could not sleep. One afternoon a man who insisted on coming to the forum, despite serious heart problems, told about how, one night during the war, he awoke in terror with lots of people in his room. He portrayed a vivid description of how shadowy figures were coming for him, from the shapes of floor lamps, lampshades and the refrigerator. He had let out a blood-curdling scream and pounded on the walls until his neighbour ran over. The neighbour checked the apartment everywhere and there had been no sign of anyone breaking in. This neighbour then sat with him the whole night and gave him cognac. That night, that friendship and that cognac were everything to him. The group was touched by his story and later a warm-hearted and lively discussion developed in which, one by one, lots of people began sharing stories and comparing techniques for keeping on the lights, sleeping with the radio on, never turning off the television, and how to sleep with the TV remote control in the hand.

Vigilance is an extreme symptom of combat trauma, yet sleeplessness during and after war is commonplace, often lasting months and years. I remember people from Sarajevo saying, 'No one sleeps in Sarajevo.' It may be useful to consider vigilance not only as a symptom of combat trauma, and not only in relation to the sleeplessness of those suffering trauma and who live in neighbourhoods and regions of violence, but as an attitude of waking up that society needs. We might imagine that, if society picked up this vigilance, more of us would be awake at night, engaged in the issues troubling our communities. In Croatia, we have heard people say several times that, by interacting deeply and thoroughly within a forum setting, they were able to sleep for the first time in years. Shay records a vet: 'I dream of the guys calling to me from the graveyard. They're calling to me, "come on, come on. Time to rest. You paid your dues. Time to rest".'[5]

BERSERKERS

The berserk state is considered a distinctive element of combat trauma and is an extreme altered state of war. In a berserk state, soldiers go into wild and frenzied rage, and sometimes commit outrageous atrocities. The term 'berserk' comes from the Norse word for the frenzied warriors who went into battle naked, or without armour, in a state of possession by gods and/or beasts.[6] Soldiers who have gone berserk and lived through it often have the experience that they cannot remember or recognize the person they became in their berserk state. Berserk states can also persist when the soldier comes home.

Shay says that Vietnam narratives reveal that the events that drove soldiers berserk include betrayal, insult and humiliation caused by a leader, death of a friend-in-arms, being wounded, being overrun, surrounded or trapped, seeing dead comrades who have been mutilated by the enemy and unexpected deliverance from certain death.[7] He sees the berserk state at the heart of the most severe psychological and psycho-physiological injuries of combat trauma.[8]

The berserker is possessed by a mythic rage and urge for revenge, coupled with invincibility. The berserker often feels that he cannot die, because he is already dead. I have heard people describe this feeling that they couldn't die, that it was as if they were already dead. The berserker is finished with life as we know it. The berserker may be seen as a hero to other soldiers, with absolute loss of fear and restraint, wild heroics, and abandonment of any semblance of identity or belonging to the social group. The berserker is full of fire, yet with a cold detachment from life or death. Berserkers often die in battle. If the berserker survives, he may not have a linear memory of his experience and actions. He recalls what people later tell him. The extreme state is outside time and over the edge of what it is possible to comprehend.[9]

SHAPE SHIFTING

The berserker breaks the very boundary of human identity. One way to understand the experience of berserkers is that they reach the outer limits of what it is possible to endure. Their extreme behaviours in turn lie over the boundaries of their known world. Berserkers are untouched by adaptation to a group or moral code. Suffering occurs in retrospect, when berserkers do not recall what happened, but are only told about their wild states, which can include committing unspeakable atrocities. In Norse mythology, it was said that, when berserkers went into battle, their frenzy could transform them into a wolf or bear, howling and foaming at the mouth, and rendered the warrior immune to sword and flame.[10] The experience of the berserker, and those who observe berserkers in battle, is that the berserker has crossed the boundary or limits of being human.

The experience of becoming beast-like or god-like also appears in rituals throughout many cultures. An essential distinction is that the experience is framed, rather than consuming the person. Hunters traditionally practised a kind of shape shifting to become the 'hunted', to get to know its behaviours, and to discover and embody its spirit, as a communion and to help the hunter capture the animal rather than become its victim. Shamanic practice in various cultures involves entering altered and wild states, over the personal and collective boundary of the group.

Shamanic practice can involve shape shifting to embody the spirit of an animal ally, spirit or god. Wearing masks and furs of a wild animal, and making the movements of that animal, allow a dancer to embody certain qualities or in some essential way to become the animal's spirit. An essential distinction is that the Shaman develops an intentional practice to reach the boundaries of his psyche, and to enter altered states and behaviours that go beyond the limits of culture and even 'human' form, to access other worlds, communicate with spirits and bring back important information to the community.

BETWEEN WORLDS

Most of us are attracted to the intensity of experiences over the boundary of our known world, and at the same time we try to protect ourselves by keeping such experiences contained or at a distance. We want to break out of our identity without having to get dashed to bits.

We've been looking at how altered states associated with devotion, longing for community and our capacity to transcend the ordinary world, are roused and exploited to create war. What makes an 'altered state' altered is that it does not fit within our ordinary worldview or ordinary experience. In our fascination with an experience over the boundary of our identity, and in our corresponding urge not to be overwhelmed by it, we sometimes get in a kind of 'trance', caught between worlds.

We now take a short tour into the dynamics of altered states as expressed in rituals, and in relation to experiences of mental disorders. We also look at how conflict itself can be experienced as an altered state at the boundary of our known world, and how whole communities fall into trance.

THE NEWSPAPER

Pick up a newspaper and you might notice two tendencies in you: the urge for intensity and the urge to keep that intensity at a distance. Throughout this book, we've looked at how those of us at a distance to war take part in it, concerning dynamics of justice, terror and trauma. We also take part in the altered states of war, often without realizing it.

It's astounding, even amusing, how we nestle our noses into a newspaper, catching a few minutes of repose in a cafe, or at the breakfast table, catching up on recent violence and devastation in our world. Watch rows of people reading newspapers on the subway, still half asleep, in a foggy dream-like state, as the headlines boldly declare war, tragedy and violence on our streets. We enjoy flipping the channels on TV (or fight about it with our partners), entertained by wild acts of heroism and bloody violence, occasionally wondering if this can't be good for our children.

Many of us find violence in the newspaper and television relaxing and entertaining, because it fulfils two important criteria. It reflects our longing for intensity and the extremes of experience beyond the perimeters of our social adaptation. And it simultaneously fulfils the need to keep it at a distance, outside of the perimeter of our hearts and thoughts. We may have no sense of either a real feeling of participation or an objective awareness – we are either gripped sensationally or coldly detached. Many of the media promote and cater to our need for this altered state created from a combination of sensationalism and distance. Yet there are journalists who risk their lives to enter this territory, who strive to create work that invites us to come right up close without falling into a sensational replay of violence. They invite us to participate and reflect.

When we are unable to reflect, we fall in, while trying to stay out. Our glazed eyes, while sitting on the subway or at the breakfast table reading about today's horrors, reflect a larger social trance and frozenness in our response to violence in our world.

Our awareness of dynamics around altered states is important to understand how violence is stirred and how we respond to it. We need to get to know more about our attraction to breaking out of our ordinary world, our need to dream across the boundary of our everyday existence, along with our urge for familiarity and control.

RITUAL

Altered states are pathways over the edge of our usual patterns of perception and collective identity. Without awareness, these altered states overwhelm us and are sometimes brutal. Even very positive experiences, such as feeling at one with the universe, can be felt as overwhelming and terrifying. Ritual is one way of trying to organize experiences beyond our ordinary world. Rituals value the unknown forces influencing our lives, while providing focus and structure to avoid the chaos and destruction that can occur when such forces are let loose uncontrollably. Rituals might also be understood as an attempt to bring awareness across our usual boundaries of perception.

As an essential and integral part of our lives, ritual can bring renewal and help us contact a sense of the divine. Ritual can provide a container or discipline to hold and cook experiences over the edge of our ordinary identity. Ritual cares for the divine and cares for the community.

Although ritual supports us to connect to these forces over the edge of our ordinary world, it can sometimes have the opposite effect of splitting off these parts of our experience. Having a place for these forces to manifest can act like a release valve. Let a little steam out of the pot and it doesn't boil over. Ritual enactment of the forces over the edge of our collective identity can also therefore serve the purpose of maintaining that identity or status quo.

Carnival

Carnival is a wild and magnificent time – a few days of madness and excess. People play in the streets, drink, dance, go without sleep, make music and dress in costumes, to try on all the wild spirits over the perimeter of everyday routines. For 51 weeks, we uphold our roles and responsibilities, and for a few splendid days we let loose, let out all the pent-up spirits, demons, passions, pleasure and playfulness. After Carnival, we go home. Carnival in this sense does not change culture. It maintains or renews it, providing an outlet and rejuvenating our spirits and capacity to go on.

Theatre and masks

Theatre can be considered a form of ritual and some say it is the earliest of art forms. When the lights go low, we begin to share in the drama on stage. We may be transported to a world outside the ordinary, somewhere awesome and larger than life. A theatre performance creates a frame that allows us to participate in a dramatic experience, without it consuming us or taking us over.

Both ritual and theatre can sometimes be empty – as if we are going through the motions, without ever contacting the creative current over the boundaries of our everyday world. The magic is gone. Yet, when we touch this underlying source, we feel a heightened sense of awareness that comes from stepping beyond our usual identification, and feeling our way into other worlds and worldviews. We are invited to dream and get transported by a human drama that drives and transcends our personal stories. Theatre can access this sort of awareness, which allows us to feel the intensity of our human tales, but with the reflection and heart needed to not just be trapped into replaying them.

Being in two places at once

Joseph Campbell said that, when someone wears a mask of God, the observers of the ritual do not see a person representing or play-acting that God. The observer simply sees God. At the same time, he knows it is his neighbour wearing a mask. These two facts are not contradictory. This is God and it's your neighbour wearing a mask.[11]

Theatre (at its best) is one example of our capacity for this kind of dual awareness, which is needed in order both to have intense experience and not to feel sunk in it. Michael Chekhov described the experience of having his consciousness in the audience, near himself and in each of his partners.[12] The capacity to seat our awareness in more than one place is something vital and intrinsic to whom we are as human beings. If we try to keep distance from the intensity of our experience in order to keep control and remain in the ordinary world, intense experiences flood and overwhelm us. At the same time our search for extremes and intensity is an attempt to knock ourselves out of an attachment to our routines and habits of perception. This means that we are not only longing for intensity, but for a greater awareness that comes from being free from attachment to a lifeless, and limited, singular perspective.

MADNESS OR CREATIVITY?

When we are overwhelmed by perceptions and experiences outside what is considered normal and functional, we may be considered mentally ill. Many have posed questions about how we define mental illness – from whose perspective?

Who's crazy?

In a great film, 'Don Juan de Marco',[13] a young man, played by Johnny Depp, says he is the great lover, Don Juan, and is taken into a mental hospital. The story is really about his psychiatrist, played by Marlon Brando, who has had a crisis of meaning in life. He is helped by his patient to review his previous notions of what is mad and what is sane, and most of all to rediscover the romance of life.

R.D. Laing described psychiatric patients as having a sane response to an insane society. He said: 'The condition of alienation, of being asleep, of being unconscious, of being out of one's mind, is the condition of the normal man.'[14] He was known for being unfazed by the people he worked with, perhaps as a result of his own journeys to the far reaches of his inner world. In one story, some doctors asked Laing for his advice for working with a catatonic patient who was sitting alone, naked, rocking back and forth. Laing stripped off his clothes and sat next to her rocking, and she soon began to talk after having not said a word for months. Laing's comment to the doctors was 'didn't you ever think of doing that?'.

The observer's awareness

In our work, in psychiatric hospitals,[15] using methods of Process-Oriented Psychology with people diagnosed with acute and chronic mental disorders, my husband Jean-Claude and I often see that, when people are considered 'unreachable' and extreme, it cannot be considered only a description of the patient, but must also be looked at in relation to the person who is working with the patient, who may be unable or uninterested to enter the patient's experience and worldview, to make contact and help the person to unfold his or her experience, signals and perception. Conversely, the love, understanding and regard a therapist or doctor has for his or her patient go a long way, particularly if combined with accurate observation of the apparently disturbing experience or behaviour. Describing this dynamic, Arnold Mindell writes: 'Almost all psychiatric textbooks speak of mental diseases in terms of "disintegration of the personality" and "unbalanced and chaotic states" . . . . The concept of chaos and unpredictability is related to the therapist's or observer's awareness and experience.'[16]

As we tend to observe a situation from within unconscious assumptions about what is 'normal', and to see what disturbs us as 'abnormal' and sick, we readily define culturally bound norms without realizing it. Learning about culturally bound experience and behaviour and our tendency to make ethnocentric observations is increasingly important to the field of psychiatry. But entering someone's worldview sufficiently to unfold his or her unique signals, perceptions and emotional states requires awareness training.

The identified patient, keeping the status quo and key to a creative evolution

Understanding perception and altered states requires a systems perspective. Family therapists in the 1960s said that mental illness could not be understood as an individual psychopathology, but had to be studied in the context of the family.[17] The idea was that a family member carried symptoms belonging to the whole family. The 'identified patient' would go over the bounds, for the rest of the family to be able to maintain its status quo. For example, a family in which everyone knows each other's business and no one shuts doors has a catatonic family member. The person who refuses to say a word and sits closed up all day in her room is the 'identified patient' in a family that needs help with its boundaries. Mindell's Process Oriented Psychology adds an important dimension to the study of systems. He consistently emphasizes that the pattern needed for the evolution of a system – whether you view the system at the level of the individual psyche, the family, the community or society – is found within the apparent disturbance and in the interaction of all parts. There is a shift in emphasis from seeing either the individual as 'sick' for being catatonic, or the family as 'dysfunctional' for keeping too many doors open. Rather the family is seen as a potentially creative system, in the interaction between its 'catatonia' and 'open doors'. Creativity arises when awareness is brought into the interaction of all parts of the system. The different parts of the system play out within each family member and between them. Catatonia in this case may be one attempt to express autonomy and introversion and the capacity to drop out of the family's norms to follow one's innermost impulses. The 'open door' policy at first inhibits this capacity to follow oneself closely, but as the family brings awareness to these processes, the 'open door' also reflects the possibility of transparency and closer contact.

Breaking windows

If we perceive or behave outside the perimeter of what is deemed 'normal', it trespasses our own and other's notions of healthy human experience. Such extreme experiences seem to come over us, or our ability just to cope. A woman I know was frequently hospitalized because of her uncontrollable outbursts and episodes of throwing stones through store windows. Her 'rages' and urges to break windows threatened her own capacity to function, and threatened her community.

During a seminar made up of about 60 participants who were mental health professionals, students and people who were hospitalized as a result of acute and chronic mental health difficulties, all learning together, we asked her what it was like throwing rocks through windows.

As she said a few words about what it was like, we noticed her arms swinging and her shyness in relation to us. I experimented with a bit of arm swinging and even flinging my chair and then searched for something safer to throw. Some cushions served the purpose, and soon I invited her to fling her arms and throw pillows together with me. We were tossing them with full energy to the floor, but at one important moment, a pillow was hurled (mistakenly) right at me. She became very shy, and I noticed a 'window' was broken. I tossed one back and encouraged a pillow fight between us, which resulted in playful and warm-hearted contact between us. Behind that toss was an urge for contact. It turned out that what triggered her outbursts on the street was when she felt isolated and thought that people were looking at her like she was strange or ignoring her. Rage was one level of her experience, but underneath it was a longing to break through her own and others' isolation in the community, to break out of the status quo, the limited patterns of relating and make real contact with people. She has regularly stayed in touch with us over the years. Her ongoing personal growth was strongly supported by her close relationship with a very loving psychiatrist.

Extreme states labelled as mental orders carry the impulse and pattern that are needed for a system's evolution. Although, from one view, throwing stones is a destructive and dangerous behaviour that cannot be tolerated in our society, the essence of her behaviour, when discovered and encouraged, was the impulse to break out of isolation and develop deeper contact with people. The extreme state of one individual also carries the information and the patterns that belong to the larger system's evolution.[18] Isolation within modern community is one of the great problems of our time. Her urge to break windows reflects a larger pattern of violence that threatens community and reflects the breakdown of community relationships – and in this case, at its root, brought a call for less isolation and greater contact among us.

Medicine, magic and dipping over the threshold

The history of psychiatry is sadly fraught with the use of brutality to try to suppress or heal the 'altered' or disruptive behaviour of people with mental health disorders. People have been routinely restrained and sedated. The predominant paradigm governing treatment of acute mental health difficulties still involves trying to suppress symptoms to make people more functional. Medications sometimes help to do this. Medications are frequently appreciated by people who are terrified and overrun by experiences out of their control. Yet many people with mental health difficulties refuse to take medication, because of the possible numbing side effects, and the frequent complaint that medications can make people feel even further cut off from their experience of themselves and life.

Frightening experiences over the boundary of our identity can carry meaningful information for the society as well as the individual. Mindell describes, in *City Shadows*, how individuals carry processes belonging to the society. It is not only the person who suffers the symptom who can pick up the process and bring awareness to it. It is information belonging to the whole system so any of us might do that. In some cultures, we've seen how a particular individual with extreme experiences may develop a shamanic capacity to enter altered states and other worlds, communicate with spirits from the other side, and travel back again to heal others or help in community. Our capacity to bring awareness along into the territory over the boundary or our collective identity is paramount to our relationships and to enhance and expand culture. Artists dip across the threshold; researchers test the limits of our knowledge; psychologists and spiritual leaders deal with forces of the unconscious and unknown. Each is involved with the awesome and sometimes brutal experience of going over the perimeter of what is familiar. Their task is to go between worlds, to bring back their discovery or guide us across to a new worldview, or to discover a creative interaction between worlds.

Across cultures, there is also a strong tendency to want to eradicate what lies outside the boundaries of what we consider normal, whether we do this through medicine, therapy or magic. In some cultures, people who have perceptual or behavioural experience outside the status quo are seen as troubled or possessed.

We tend to be afraid of the unknown and naturally want to eliminate experiences that appear to threaten our certainty, safety and survival. This tendency to disassociate from chunks of our experience and try to eradicate disturbances to our identity is not only a pervasive psychological attitude, but also a major social and political issue.

CONFLICT AS AN ALTERED STATE

We've looked at how our longing for experience outside the ordinary world can be aroused and exploited to make war. We've looked at altered and extreme states during war and after. We've looked at altered states in our reactions to violence. We've looked at how we express altered states over the boundary of our collective identity in ritual. We've looked at how altered states serve to maintain the status quo as well as holding patterns and possibilities for the system's evolution. And we've touched on altered and extreme states in respect to mental health and notions of 'madness'.

One way to understand conflict is that it is an encounter with the edge of our identity and what lies over this edge. As we are up against the boundary of what we define as normal, we tend to lose awareness in this territory. We therefore often experience conflict as an altered state, a frightening meeting with the unknown and, until now, we have had few patterns for staying aware within conflict.

When we meet conflict, we may feel taken up in the intensity of charged emotion, or we cut off from it. We freeze as if caught in headlights. We may feel caught between worlds, fuzzy and confused. Our frozenness and lack of fluidity in dealing with conflict in turn lead to an escalation of conflict.

CAUGHT IN A PARALLEL WORLD

In the atmosphere preceding war, as violence stirs, whole communities get immersed in brewing forces beyond their control that they are unable to escape and feel unable to meet. In a kind of trance, people find themselves playing out parts in a growing nightmare from which they can't awaken. It becomes a living hell, as if pulled into a parallel world. It is like a dream in which you thought you were just walking out the door, when you found yourself in a strange and terrible place, unable to find your way back. You meet phantoms, going about life as best they can, with frozen eyes, terrified or too certain, lacking reflection. There is no-one to turn to. You are in a closed system and everyone is in it. Events stretch out, one after the other. There is no beginning – you don't remember how it started – and there is no end – it's impossible to return home.

↓ **Figure 20.1** Gaki-zoshi, Scroll of the Hungry Ghosts, late twelfth century. (By courtesy of the National Kyoto Museum.)

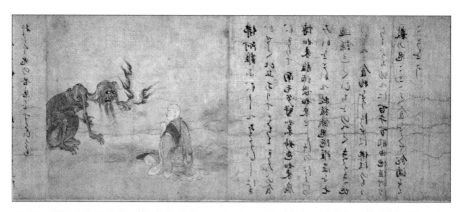

This parallel world is inhabited by hungry ghosts,[19] tormented spirits that cannot rest. In Buddhism, hungry ghosts are associated with people who were killed without proper burial, rendering their spirits homeless. This occurs for example when people are killed away from home or in mass executions.[20] Buddhist thought notes the realm of the hungry ghosts as a realm of insatiable hunger.[21] As conflict brews, whether in our own hearts, or within our communities and nations, we are in a sense these hungry ghosts, suffering, insatiable, often trapped between worlds, stranded in history and longing to satisfy ourselves.

Chapter 21
Cutting through

Witnessing the fall into the nightmare

One afternoon in a forum in Croatia, the group moved into a spontaneous re-enactment of the period before the war in which they had been pulled into the nightmare of the former Yugoslavia.

Earlier that day, the group had been in an intense interaction around current conflicts between Croats and Serbs in post-war Croatia. In facing the terrible difficulties of reconciliation after the atrocities that they lived through together, the conflict cycled. At one point, several forum participants faced each other, Serbs and Croats, in an escalating debate, in which each side sounded increasingly righteous, with facts to prove their 'side'. Many felt locked into the conflict. Many were in great pain as the trauma and tragedy of the war were reawakened. Others were simply fed up with the endless conflict and wanted no part of it. We took a break.

Lane and I huddled together to sort our thoughts, and then gave a brief presentation of 'roles' that are often present in situations of intractable conflict. There were the roles of the two parties in conflict. There was a 'ghost role' standing nearby, who whispered repeatedly in each side's ears, 'You are right and I'll give you the facts to prove it' – fanning the escalation of arguments. Another role suffered the conflict and felt helpless. The role of 'helper' tried to offer solutions. The role of the one who walks away took distance. And yet another essential ghost role profited from the whole affair at every turn. We drew these roles as a map, and then decided to experiment, making a visual/kinaesthetic map in the centre of the large circle of 80 participants.

We asked for people to volunteer to step into these roles, just as a 'visual'/kinaesthetic way to map the background dynamics of intractable conflicts. They needed only to stand in the role and make a simple gesture to represent it. Two people came forward to represent the two roles in conflict, standing face-to-face, and mirroring each other with fists in the air. One person now came in to represent the ghost role, standing between them, righteous and pleased, rooting them (both) on. Someone came in and stood near by in a collapsed position, head in hand, to represent the suffering. The 'helper' came in and made a gesture of trying to bring them together; a 'vacationer' took his distance, turned his back and with arms clasped behind his head, relaxed; and the profiteer lurked, rubbing his hands together in excitement.

After this brief presentation, people said they recognized all these roles in their communities and even inside themselves. We opened up the afternoon forum, for the group to decide how to go forward. Whereas the group interactions usually involved dialogue and people entering the middle of the room to present the different positions and roles in a given interaction, the quality of interaction now transformed. Perhaps inspired by the attempt to physically present the structure of intractable conflict, the group spontaneously entered a ritualized re-enactment of the period before the war. One participant said he wanted to represent the forces that pulled the region into war. He wanted to pull on someone's arm to represent this, so I offered mine. He began to pull. I resisted. He pulled harder. The group fell silent and the moment seemed to prolong. I felt my own heart racing, viscerally taken into this 'role' momentarily and I tasted a drop of this terrifying experience that had seized the region. The group was transfixed. He gripped and pulled harder, I resisted strongly. Very suddenly, without warning, one participant ran into the middle of the room and pulled us apart in one absolute and congruent move. The whole room burst into spontaneous applause. Someone said: 'Only that is what never happened in the period before and during the war. No one broke this pull.' Another participant jumped up and came into the middle of the room. She said there was another essential difference, too. While I had enacted someone resisting the pull, she said: 'What really happened was this.' She then asked the man to pull again, and she and another participant, who jumped in to join her, enacted sleep-walkers, in a trance, arms in front of them, eyes closed, following the guy without resistance wherever he went.

Others came in, and a kind of ritualized re-enactment continued to unfold. Every person in the room was riveted. The focus on re-enacting the trance and the fall into hell gave a sense of 'witness' to their communal involvement in the tragedy. This spontaneous enactment broke a spell, creating a narrative, telling the story together, as Croats, Serbs and Muslims.

GUILT VERSUS RESPONSIBILITY

After an interaction about issues of accountability in another forum, a very thoughtful man who had come for the first time to a forum spoke eloquently about how he had always felt a victim of the terrible events in his region. He said that he realized for the first time that he had been not only a victim of this vicious war, but also a part of its creation – a part of the collective movements that had unfolded so atrociously. He said he had never considered this before. He differentiated his new sense of awareness and responsibility from guilt. He said maybe he had been unable to feel any responsibility until now, out of fear of guilt. He discovered that he did not feel guilty, but rather engaged with the possibility of making a difference to the future, and hopeful for the first time since the war.

The capacity to witness and bring awareness along into our part in unfolding collective events can contribute to conflict prevention. That won't necessarily be possible in the middle of an extreme tactic of terror. Nonetheless, the early mobilizing of nationalist forces requires our naivety and compliance. Our awareness of the emotional dynamics that influence us as individuals and in community can be nourished, as easily as these dynamics can be exploited, through grassroots movements, forums and democracy building. Time and again, after these forums, people have told us that they can't help but wonder, if only they had had such experiences before the war, things might have gone differently.

THE WARRIOR'S CALL – CUTTING THROUGH

To break free from violent cycles of conflict may feel impossible, or not even possible to consider. The 'warrior' in us is called, however, to the task – not to kill the enemy, but to cut through the closed system, to awaken from the nightmare. A sword is needed that can cut through the trance, to contact a realm of creative possibility that underlies the locked conflict. The group's spontaneous enactment of the period before the war that I described above, and its bold moves to break free from the trance, gave them the opportunity to bear witness to their story together and to step out of it. People looked around at each other with new eyes.

If the 'sword' is motivated by power, it won't achieve the task of breaking free from a cycle of violence. It will recreate it. To cut through the spell of a nightmare calls for sitting up straight in bed and opening the eyes.

In large groups dealing with strong conflict, I have repeatedly seen this capacity of an individual or a whole group to step right off the wheel. It does not come from a pretence of 'goodness' or of letting go of their feelings or viewpoints. It doesn't come from a prescription of forgiveness or tolerance. It comes from the heart and willingness to engage in conflict, to go all the way, to enter and participate in the polarized mythic roles driving the conflict, while having the readiness or willingness at a certain moment not only to consider that you are on one side, but also to discover yourself in the other. At this moment, we know we are all of those roles and none of them. Someone

↑ **Figure 21.1** Kali. (By courtesy of Dan and Kristen Ciprari.)

suddenly shifts point of view, and is able not only to hear and listen to what the other has said, but also to feel with the person, to take his or her side, to care for the experience and story. At this point, roles may recede, in a sense of compassion for the whole problem, the whole story. 'An angel passes.'

We take part in the battle, but with freedom from its grip. We are not so easily sucked in. There's a sense of choice – often for the first time – not to just sleepwalk in the ruts of history. When our viewpoint and the role we usually inhabit are fully expressed and heard, we are free to hear and to enter the other viewpoints. We contact something truer than one position of one group or another, and deeper than the underlying roles. We realize we are the players, connected to one another in this story, to the pain, to its impossibility and hopelessness, but also to something awesome and hopeful that brings a fresh start.

DEMONS, DRAGONS AND INDIVIDUATION

To develop the capacity to 'stop the world', in our own personal history or the history of our community, nation or world, we need to participate in the forces that move and drive us, while not falling prey to them. Awareness comes from recognition of the 'edge' of our identity, which defines and limits our perspective, moment to moment. Awareness comes from leaving a chronic point of reference, to face the unknown, in our own psyche and in those whom we most fear and thought were our enemies.

The journey of the 'hero', as Joseph Campbell described,[1] is a story we tell again and again, perhaps in every culture. We are called to leave home and set out on an adventure.[2] At first, we refuse the call, attached to our 'ordinary world' and old worldview. With help from mentors, we eventually cross the threshold and meet a series of tests. In a final ordeal, we face our 'enemy'. We struggle and are transformed in an essential way, before returning home, changed, bringing a contribution to others.

In Tibetan Buddhist thought, after death we enter a realm or 'bardo' where we have to face and struggle with the terrifying demons of the 'other side'. Jung's concept of individuation involves the process of grappling with the mythic forces shaping our lives, as we become conscious and creative participants in our own stories. Jung often spoke of the importance of not just being open to or possessed by forces of the unconscious, but able to answer them, grapple with them, struggle fully and thoroughly, in an act of being humbled, cooked and differentiated. Jung said that, one way or the other, we will be shaped by these mythic forces – our choice is whether we want to be 'dragged by the collar' or 'walk upright and notice the signposts' along the way.

PULLED BY THE COLLECTIVE COLLAR

We've been on a constant search in our religions, arts and sciences to understand and express our creative and destructive struggles. Yet, we have hardly begun to consider how mythic forces drive our social, political and economic interactions and violent conflicts. The less we are aware of what pulls and propels us, both as individuals and collectively, the more open we are to those who play a deadly game with these dramatic forces. Just as Jung described individuation as a choice we each make (again and again) to be dragged by the collar or to meet the psychological forces shaping our lives, we have similar choices to make at a collective level, to take part in the creative potential of our neighbourhoods and world.

PART 5

AWARENESS AT THE HOT SPOT

CHAPTER 22
WAKE UP

THE URGE TO AWAKEN

We've seen how our unconscious longing for justice and accountability serves as an arsenal for another round. We have seen how psychological dynamics are used to create terror tactics. We've seen how historical collective trauma runs like a vein of fuel that is intentionally ignited in repeating nightmares. We've seen how our high ideals and longing for community, our devotion, sense of unity and wish to transcend the limitations of our ordinary lives, when unconscious, provide a torch for violence. And we've seen how the less we are aware of the psychological and mythic forces shaping us, the more they are exploited. But, we also have an urge to be conscious, to wake up.

THE 'WAKE-UP' CALL

Even our innate urge to awaken, when undeveloped, is exploited to promote violent conflict. White supremacists use the 'wake-up' call, urging us to not be entranced by liberal politics. In a speech, Hitler said, 'Once you heard the voice of a man, and it spoke to your hearts, it awakened you, and you followed that voice . . .'[1] Milosevic called out to Serbs to awaken. Hutu extremists used the wake-up call to motivate the murder of Tutsis.

WAKING UP TO AWARENESS

The idea running through this book is in essence also a kind of wake-up call – that awareness is the needed ingredient to move from replaying conflict, to the capacity to embrace the forces that shape us, rather than be run over by them.

Chapters in Part 5

Through Part 5, I take a look at some wide questions about consciousness. I suggest a long-term outlook that awareness is on the rise, although I recognize that the ideas presented here in broad strokes might sometimes feel distant, when considering the difficulties of their practical application in complex and intractable political, economic and social problems, or if feeling trapped within a violent region or neighbourhood.

This chapter takes a brief look at what people mean by 'awareness' in different fields and within different cultures. I glance at the notion that awareness arises from going beyond a one-sided attachment or identification, as it appears in Jungian psychology, Buddhist thought, Mindell's Process Oriented Psychology, and in the traditional concept of the 'elder' who looks after the whole community, its ancestors and its future, as well as how we make it through ethical crises and intractable conflict. I also look at basic concepts in systems theory, chaos and complexity theory, considering the idea of non-linear change, such that even with intractable and complex problems, a small input could make a difference. Chapter 23 takes a look at how chaos and complexity theory are being considered in warfare and in conflict resolution. Chapter 24 goes on to consider how evolving worldviews influence how we perceive, including our approach to conflict. Chapter 25 looks at how we behave at the hot spots of our interactions, focusing on Mindell's concept of 'hot spots' as points of potential escalation and potential transformation. I include an example of working with a hot spot at a forum. I particularly look at dynamics of decentralization and crackdown at hot spots, and how awareness can emerge on the 'battlefield' and as individuals, we can make a difference.

CONSCIOUSNESS ARISES AS A CREATIVE PROCESS

One way to understand consciousness is that it does not come from one part dominating the other parts of our nature. We could say that consciousness arises out of a creative process – the interaction and relatedness between different parts of us, including our inner and outer conflicts, and from contact to an underlying creative current.

Jung's concept of individuation involves a shift of focus from the 'ego' as centre of the personality to the 'Self', which guides us in a process of discovering our wholeness. According to Buddhist thought, the cause of suffering is that we make our ego the centre of existence. This is caused not by evil, but by unconsciousness. As we recognize projections and dissolve attachment to our identity, we begin to awaken. Chogyam Trungpa points out that Buddhism is more related to some schools of western psychology than to western religion.[2] Buddha means 'the awakened one'.

Arnold Mindell describes a fluid awareness, accompanying the interaction between all parts of our experience – what is closer to our identity and what we first experience as disturbing or unknown – while closely following the underlying creative impulse. We have seen how the notion of 'deep democracy'[3] means an interest in the whole, rather than one part winning over another, whether our focus is on an individual or a group.

ELDERS, LEADERSHIP AND INNER LIFE

Just as we could say consciousness for an individual involves an experience of wholeness, and not only being one-sided, on a collective level elders hold the interests of the whole community at heart, and not just one position or the other.

In some communities, elders hash over the problems of community and, while their interactions might include fights about power, their purpose is usually not to do with one side dominating the other, but rather to support a community's sustainability and discern its direction. Wise people, who have lived long and/or have big enough hearts to no longer be attached to a given position or polarity, can sometimes facilitate an encounter between all parts of community.

While one notion of leadership is to congruently express a particular viewpoint with which we identify, usually in opposition to another view, an alternative concept of leadership is to facilitate an interaction of all points of view within oneself and others, knowing that it is the whole process that actually leads us.[4] In ancient China, a leader was sometimes described as a sage-king (or -queen), able to sustain an inner and outer focus and the wisdom to take action in support of the whole community.[5]

When we are in favour of only one side of ourselves or we think that only one part of us leads, other parts stage a kind of revolution. 'I' try to enforce decisions, and other parts of me who were not consulted act out. 'I' make a decision to get out of bed, but the one who likes to stay under the duvet makes me sluggish all morning, if her viewpoint isn't considered too.

In our personal lives, we may feel compelled by archetypal forces that take us over – we fall in love, we get the urge for an adventure, or long for a sense of meaning, we struggle with oppression, meet our thirst for power, struggle as mothers, fathers, children or partners, and with our sorrows and anxiety as we encounter inner demons, moods or illness. We can never dominate or control these wild forces, but we can discover the creative impulse underlying our experience and facilitate inner meetings, outer ones and their expression.

ETHICAL CRISES, ZEN KOANS AND INTRACTABLE CONFLICT

When we find ourselves in an ethical crisis, we meet the limits of a worldview, based in domination, right and wrong, or one side winning over the other. Ethical crises revolve around the problem of when there is no apparent 'right' answer. Ethical problems put us in a bind, not only because we are not clear about what choice or path to take, but also because our internal system of power and morality, in which one side is right and the other is wrong, no longer seems to be adequate. Jung described a kind of 'cooking' that occurs inside us when we meet ethical crises. He said: 'All the greatest and most important problems of life are fundamentally insoluble. This must be so, for they express the necessary polarity inherent in every self-regulating system. They can never be solved, but only outgrown.'[6] He saw 'individuation', the process of psychological maturation and becoming a whole personality, as a process of grappling with the polarities of our psyche, such that we embrace the opposites and our wholeness and touch into a creative function that underlies these polarities and directs the psyche's evolution.[7] Similarly, a Zen Koan is an unanswerable question, such as: 'What is the sound of one hand clapping?' Meditating on a Koan brings a kind of 'enlightenment', transcending our limited dualist perspective. Or when we are in an intractable and locked conflict, our heart and awareness can dip under the opposing positions and find a way to embrace all points of view.

WHAT IS AWARENESS?

I've been using the word 'awareness' in relation to the dynamics behind violent conflict, to mean not only being informed about what is going on, but getting to know ourselves, how we respond and react and take part in the various dynamics occurring within us and between us, in relationship, community and society. Awareness brings up the possibility of facilitating conflict, rather than just having conflict, and the possibility of not being seized into large-scale polarizations and war.[8]

Let's stop to look at some different perspectives about what 'awareness' means. Depending on one's field of interest, one's culture and unique personality, everyone has a different take, a different experience of what awareness is. Some may see awareness as an activity that involves pulling together different strands of information to form a hypothesis, or the interpretation or analysis of events. Many people assume that awareness originates in the mind. Some cultures see awareness as occurring in the heart. A mountain climber may experience awareness as a sense of acute attention and connection to his or her body, in relationship to and in synch with the mountain. In Native American culture, awareness involves recognizing the interrelationships of all elements of nature. In Aboriginal culture in Australia, awareness is recognizing how individual events and qualities arise from the 'dreaming'. A musician may consider awareness as the interplay of attention to the momentary tone or rhythm and the unfolding and underlying music moving him or her. For a psychologist, awareness may be fluidity to discover one's wholeness in relation to many aspects of the personality. A spiritual leader may consider awareness the understanding of his or her actions in the world in relation to God. A cook's awareness is both on the individual ingredients and the whole dish or meal, and on how his or her own attitude in handling the food is an essential ingredient.

A common essence of these different descriptions of awareness is our interest in the relationship of the parts to the whole, within a particular realm or question. Reductionism and analytic thinking study the relationship between the whole and its parts, by breaking the whole down into its parts. Synthetic thinking involves seeing, intuiting and guessing how things interconnect, putting together a puzzle or forming a hypothesis that includes and makes sense of the parts. Awareness seated in the heart may be experienced as the ability to experience how a single perspective or feeling is relative to other positions and perspectives, and the ability to feel into different angles, and others' experience, as if you were inside their shoes or heart.

AWARENESS, SYSTEMS AND COMPLEXITY THEORY

Developments in systems thinking reflect our underlying interest in the relation of the part to the whole that crosses cultures and fields. Learning about our interconnectedness and the interaction of all parts of a system is increasingly important in various fields, whether we are interested from a spiritual, social or scientific vantage point. The study of systems interactions currently pervades the fields of ecology, economy, politics and sociology, and in the sciences across fields of mathematics, biology to physics and astronomy. There's a buzz and excitement about the newest discoveries referred to as complexity theory and the study of non-linear systems.

For our purposes here in mentioning complexity theory, in relation to conflict and awareness, it will be useful just to touch on the basics of systems theory and chaos theory. Systems theory has been described as a science of 'wholeness'.[9] It suggests that a system is more than the sum of its parts. We cannot understand a system by reducing it or dissecting it into parts. Systems theory includes the importance of looking both at what emerges from inside the system and at what influences it from outside the system, and this entails determining at what level we choose to view a system. Systems theory also focuses on communication and feedback between interacting elements within a system and with the environment outside the system being viewed.

Chaos theory arose from the discovery that systems display at times an extreme sensitivity, which has been termed famously 'the butterfly effect'. The term refers to how weather patterns or systems exhibit extreme non-linear tendencies, such that the movement of a butterfly's wings in China will affect the weather on some other continent in the world.[10]

Chaos theory demonstrates how, at a certain moment when a system is far from equilibrium, it displays chaotic behaviour, such that the previous state of the system breaks down, but then, with a small input, the system can transform or evolve into a higher level of organization. Linear relationships no longer apply. Apparently small inputs do not yield small results.

Ilya Prigogine and Isabelle Stengers describe how 'each individual action or each local interaction has a collective aspect that can result in quite unanticipated global changes'.[11] In a model of how chaos theory could be applied to economic activity, they show how the respective growth of urban populations and manufacturing or service activities are linked by strong feedback and non-linearities, such that a chance factor such as the place and time where a single new business starts could trigger a major shift in the economy of a region.[12]

As chaos theory developed in various fields and scientists began to try to map this non-linear behaviour in general terms, complexity theory emerged.[13] Complexity theory focuses on feedback within a system, highlighting the interdependencies throughout any given system, and observing the non-linear evolution of systems. Complexity theory studies evolution as it 'unfolds over a stunningly wide range of temporal and spatial scales – from seconds and nanometers at the molecular level to geologic epochs and continents at the macro-evolutionary level. The mathematical theory of evolutionary dynamics attempts to articulate a consistent conceptual description of these processes – what is similar and what is different across these scales.'[14]

The impact of the 'new science' of complexity is noted by its interdisciplinary relevance. Researchers describe 'archetypal aspects of non-linear phenomena, independent of the conventional discipline in which they are observed'. For example, similar patterns, 'coherent structures', can be observed in the turbulent atmosphere of Jupiter, in giant earth ocean waves (tsunamis), in the spatial spread of certain epidemics and, on a microscopic scale, in the behaviour of certain unusual solid materials.[15]

When we consider the systemic and global issues that we face – social, political, economic, ecological and psychological – and when interventions seem all but hopeless, it is important, even heartening, to begin to consider the non-linear dynamics of systemic change.

CHAPTER 23
CHAOS, WARFARE AND CONFLICT RESOLUTION

THE APPLICATION OF COMPLEXITY THEORY TO WARFARE AND CONFLICT RESOLUTION

The study of non-linear systems invites the question of how these ideas might be applied to understanding conflict and conflict resolution. Certainly violence and war reflect systems that are in a far-from-equilibrium state that have non-linear tendencies – the political or social system may be in crisis and small events can have giant repercussions. While writing this work, I went online to find out who was looking into this exciting area. My first discovery within moments of typing the words 'conflict' and 'chaos' into my search engine surprised me. I found an article written by someone in the US Air Force about how complexity theory can be applied to warfare. I should not have been surprised, as it is actually the premise of this book, that tactics of war are designed, making use of knowledge of how we interact in systems – concerning dynamics of justice, power, trauma and altered states. Non-linear dynamics of systems are also considered in creating tactics of warfare.

The author cites the 'butterfly effect' as it might be applied to warfare, looking at the 'sensitivity to initial conditions' (the term used to describe the extreme sensitivity in far-from-equilibrium systems), which he noted were the 'state of the international economy, the state of the enemy's and our own political landscape, culture, as well as the state of many individual minds'.[1]

Anyone who still thinks words like 'butterfly effect' have to do only with mad scientists or 'new age' philosophers up at night concocting wild theories, should glance over this article. It is sobering to realize that this butterfly is being observed in its effect not only on weather patterns, but also on warfare.

To describe the interdependency of elements in any system, the author used the example that, during the Vietnam war, the North Vietnamese influenced the attitudes of Americans at home.[2]

The article by Major Weeks discussed how complexity theory helps us to understand the interrelationship of political, social, economic and emotional factors of world conflict. But nowhere in the article does it mention that complexity theory may help us in the long term to understand the interrelationship of societies and nations and the development of conflict, in order to help us find ways of dealing better with conflict without resorting to bombs. I understand that the article is about the application of complexity theory in the author's area of expertise, just as another author might have stuck to the application of complexity theory to ecology, or a particular question in biology. Still, I naively held out hope that the author might have included in his article even three words in the direction of a longer-term goal of finding alternative ways of dealing with conflict.

In his conclusions, Major Weeks recommends that Blitzkrieg (bombing strongly and quickly) is warranted, so that there isn't time for the feedback in the system to adjust. He highlights the importance of 'intelligence', given the extreme 'sensitivity to initial conditions' inherent in complex adaptive systems.[3] He suggests that, had we been able to use complexity theory for predictive purposes, we would have been able to predict the influence of the tactics of the North Vietnamese military on the civilian population of the USA, which was difficult to analyse with traditional tools.[4] I couldn't help but wonder what he imagined exactly would be done with a prediction concerning this 'interdependency'. Might we have interned those Americans in the anti-war movement, as we did Japanese Americans in World War II?

PERENNIAL QUESTIONS

As we consider the application of complexity theory to understanding warfare or conflict resolution, we touch on broad questions about how we use our awareness, and a perennial question about the nature of awareness itself. How can we be a part of an evolving system and be aware of it? How does our awareness and action within a system influence it?

THE 'FITTEST'

In Weeks' article about complexity theory and warfare, he clarifies his reason for applying complexity theory to warfare. He writes:

> Warfare ensures the survival of the fittest. Of course, the reason for the CAS (complex adaptive systems) approach is to ensure that our organization is the 'fittest' as opposed to the enemy.[5]

While complexity theory is based in a paradigm of understanding the evolution of systems, and certainly studies the process of selection in evolving systems, the author in his use of the phrase 'survival of the fittest' refers to Darwin's theory of evolution as a statement of domination. His use of the notion of 'survival of the fittest' is an example of how an idea that comes from one framework can be misused or abused in another. The phrase 'survival of the fittest' has a history of misuse with the development of 'Social Darwinism',[6] which contributed to racist thinking and notions of racial superiority.

Here, the implication is that the USA dominates the world because it is the 'fittest'. Complexity theory, which focuses on the interaction and feedback within systems, arising out of the study of the evolution of systems, is being applied within a framework of power and military dominance.

This is a bit like studying ecology in order to figure out how to use up non-renewable resources as fast as possible, or studying the complex human organism in order to try to find ways to kill it. Although the countries that we would bomb are seen as part of a complex evolving system in relation to us, there is no interest or thought about the well-being of that whole system.

THE MYTH OF POWER

It is not just the military, however, that is immersed in the notion of one part dominating another. Regardless of our political views, most of us are deeply embedded in a worldview of power and barely notice it. Based on this notion of being the 'fittest', many people in the USA could think that, if other nations are upset at US behaviour, it must be because they are jealous. In countless ways, we look for our advantage over others. When we dominate with one part of ourselves, in favour of another part, as individuals, communities and between communities, we perpetuate this worldview. We try to gratify one part of ourselves, losing awareness or concern for its impact on other parts, or its long-term effects.

This occurs in our community relationships, politics, in business and economics, in our handling of ecology and the environment. The environmental movement, the anti-globalization movement and various social movements actively address these dynamics.

Social activism is in turn often tied to a worldview oriented towards power, trying to right the power imbalance. Yet some of the greatest social activists have inspired us to step beyond a worldview of oppression and reaction to build new possibilities. A worldview oriented towards 'power' focuses on forcing one part over another and resistance. A worldview oriented towards the interaction of all parts of the system observes its capacity to evolve.

EDGE OF CHAOS AND TRANSFORMING CONFLICT

Ideas from complexity theory arise not only in the military, but also in the fields of organization development and conflict resolution.[7] The term 'edge of chaos' (or chaotic edges) is used among people studying complexity theory, and refers to the dynamics of a system far from equilibrium, to describe the region or moments that are ripe for evolution, just before the system has gone over the border into chaos. The field of organizational development works with organizational conflicts and change. It has begun to look at the application of chaos and complexity theory to understand and intervene in organizations. When an organization is closer to equilibrium, there's a tendency for more rigidity and difficulty in dealing with disturbances or change. Organizations at 'the edge of chaos' – which we can intuitively imagine are organizations in a time of great flux, or with changing rules and a more fluid structure – are more ready for innovation and transformation.[8]

Arnold Mindell has used the term 'edge'[9] for many years to describe the value systems that structure and limit how an individual or group identifies, influencing behaviour, communication and perception. The 'edge' also refers to the border of what is unknown, to our dreams and emerging attitudes, beyond our usual identity. Mindell and colleagues' 'worldwork'[10] with large groups in conflict includes a focus on 'hot spots' (see Chapter 25) at the 'edge' of a community or organization's identity, with a comprehensive theory and methods for observing and working with these dynamics that are potentially volatile and potentially transformative. The emerging pattern for change becomes increasingly disturbing and more accessible as the system reaches the 'edge'. In practical terms, working with these methods in business and social organizations, and as described in community forums, in times of turmoil, with facilitation, people experience interactions that transform their relationships and conflicts, and put them in touch with their creative direction. Mindell developed the concepts and methods of Process Work out of the evolutionary orientation of Jungian psychology and his training in theoretical physics, following a task to link psychology and physics[11] and to study and follow the mysterious ways of nature.

THE HEAT AND FRICTION OF CONFLICT AS FEEDBACK

In our personal relationships and in community, it's not easy, but certainly possible to feel strongly on one side of a conflict, while still being interested to discover more about the other side of the conflict and to facilitate the encounter.

As long as you are identified with only one side of the interaction, either you will feel dominated or you will try to dominate, whether intentionally or unintentionally. We perpetuate the conflict, while trying to assert ourselves, explain, justify, defend, attack or even mediate. If we stay identified with only one position, conflicts will cycle and escalate in the system's search for feedback and contact with itself.

The heat and friction in conflict are a kind of feedback between us, drawing us in, reminding us of the systemic dynamics that we are part of, that we cannot escape, even as we try to identify only with our separate identities and positions. With awareness of feedback, we can shift consciously between all points of view within the system. Now the interaction can transform or evolve.

But, how are we able to develop this fluidity of perspective? One starting point is to notice what side we are on. If we bring awareness to our view, at a certain moment, we may discover the opposite position in us, too. We can find all parts of the interaction inside us as individuals, as well as between ourselves and others. A system interaction occurs simultaneously at all levels – inside the individual, in relationship, in community and in the world. We gain fluidity in our inner world as we meet, grapple and grow beyond the edges of our identity, and discover that the locus of our awareness is no longer tied to a particular point of view, but rather moves between different vantage points, and, into the field between us that holds the whole interaction.

Being aware of different positions inside us is not about being wishy-washy or unable to take a stand. Difficulty in taking a clear stand happens in part because an opposite or complementary position is inside us too, although we remain largely unaware of it. While trying to take a stand on a particular issue, we battle internally, and come off defensive, aggressive or confused.

Getting to know the different sides of ourselves, we can differentiate things, take a position, go to our 'opponent's' side and support the whole interaction focusing on how communications can begin, rather than break down at the hot spots of our interaction.[12] Relationships, teams, organizations and community forums can actively do this together, discover the polarized roles around a particular issue and, rather than stay locked inside them, facilitate a creative encounter.

THE BATH – OUR PART AND THE WHOLE

If you are interested in facilitating conflict towards its resolution or transformation, it helps to be aware that any polarized situation that you encounter will activate your own relationship to issues involved. Trying to be neutral or objective by considering yourself outside the dynamics involved is inadequate to the job of facilitating. It is useful to strive to be aware of how your own personal and collective history and your own limits of perception involve you in the system, so that you can facilitate the interaction of all parts, including the one you may be inhabiting. Naturally, there will always be limits to your awareness and areas where you are stuck within a particular perspective, rather than able to facilitate it.

Carl Jung described the process of analysis or therapy as being in a bath together, therapist and client. You share the same water and splash each other. The process touches and changes you both. Yet, the therapist's or analyst's role is to accompany the client in bringing awareness and differentiation into his or her life experiences, dreams and individuation process.

As a facilitator in conflict zones, it's vital to be aware of how you play a part – due to your personal history, even your subtlest feelings, as well as how you are perceived. For example, when Lane and I facilitated post-war forums in the Balkans, we needed to be aware that being US citizens influenced our attitudes and the way we were perceived. We needed to be alert to the limits of our own perception of what people were facing in their communities. We also needed to be aware that the 'roles' we inhabited were not only our own, but also belonged to the field we were facilitating. Examples of just some of the roles that belonged to the field, but that we might have inhabited at any moment, are: the role of the person or nation who tries to come in from the outside to enforce his or her good ideas; the role of the person or nation who looked on and did nothing; the one who can facilitate; the one who believes and has hope in the group; the guest; the one who feels deeply; or the outsider.

CHAPTER 24

GETTING BACK IN BED TOGETHER – AN AWARENESS REVOLUTION

SEPARATE BEDS

It can be a brutal experience to be stuck in an intractable conflict. When each side accuses the other, each side feels locked in. It feels next to impossible to shift.

In the post-war conflicts between Serbs and Croats, Croats sometimes confided in us privately that they wanted to talk about and acknowledge the atrocities that were carried out by Croats, but they felt that they could not do so until Serbs spoke first, acknowledging Serb responsibility for the war, and the ethnic cleansing and atrocities that occurred in the Serb-occupied areas of Croatia and in Bosnia.

I remember talking to a Croat participant 'woman to woman'. I said it's like in a personal relationship. No-one wants to be the first to acknowledge their part in a long-standing conflict, particularly if you feel you were treated unjustly, and that right was more on your side. I told her that, over the years, in my own relationships and in my work with couples, I'd come to realize that there was no fun in the belief system that it was hurting me or downing me to make the first move. Rather I've come to feel excited by the prospect of what I might learn, if I step over the 'edge' of my position, and of the whole system, rather than insist that the other person does it first. From the viewpoint of the system, it doesn't matter who does it first. This woman who always took an active part in these forums bloomed. Rather than staying tied to her previously one-sided perspective, she found joy in stepping out of her usual position, into other positions and roles.

In this way, each of us is a reflection of the community body, with different positions and roles that need to be appreciated, inhabited and stretched. In this way, shifting to the 'other' side doesn't feel like giving up something, but like growing. In one forum, someone referred to the problems of Serbs and Croats trying to begin dialogue around reconciliation issues in Croatia as similar to the problem of a couple who have had a fight and are sleeping in separate beds. The question of who will be the first to go to the other's bed became a joke among us for the rest of the forum.

Conflict and awareness

In facilitating conflict and change within an organization, we may ask people first to represent the different viewpoints and also to discover the underlying roles moving them, such as the role of initiating change and the role of resisting change, or the roles of authority and rebel. This brings people an experience of being more than an individual within an organization. People may feel connected to the underlying purpose or creative drive of the organization and how it emerges through their tensions and conflicts. Similarly, in community, social and political forums, the issues become differentiated and communication deepens as each position and 'role' is filled, and people begin to identify with the heat and potential creativity of working with a problem that is greater than their individual differences. This is a shift of awareness from feeling a 'part', and often a 'victim' of a system, to identifying with the whole story and its potential evolution. Time and again, in the forums in Croatia, people have said to us that, if anyone had told them they would be feeling so connected to each other in a mixed group of Serbs, Croats, Muslims, as well as other ethicities, they would plainly and simply not have believed it. They felt a sense of unity and direction that included their differences, conflicts, tragedies and unanswered questions.

The meal awakens the taster

Our interactions in this way awaken awareness. Awareness is not added into the interaction from the outside like salt to a meal. Rather the taste of a good meal awakens the taster. Yet, when we feel pushed and pulled within a field of interactions, awareness is certainly not a characteristic of our behaviour that we can take for granted.

In Chinese philosophy, the term 'Wuwei' (or 'effortless action') refers to action that is not based in power, but rather awareness, and connection to the 'chi' or underlying field moving us. Yoga teaches that experiencing the body in the distinct yoga postures allows us to contact an underlying life force, as it manifests in the separate archetypal poses.[1] In conflict, we can become aware of our reactions and responses, while at the same time we are in contact with an underlying field from which our responses are arising. We relate to the broader issues underlying our different positions, and to a dynamic field under-lying the archetypal roles and moving us through our encounter.

MAP MAKING AND THE TERRITORY

In the midst of pressing conflicts, it is natural not to be able to move from your positions. Stuck within our singular vantage points, we look out. Map making is a simple and interesting example of how we think we are objective, without recognizing our vantage point. In recent years, there has been increasing aware-ness about the importance of questioning assumptions about the 'objective' or 'neutral' nature of maps, with the realization that maps are naturally dependent on social, cultural, economic and political contexts.[2] What's on a map and what's not is determined not simply by what's in the environment, but by the person who produced it.[3]

Maps are created from a particular position and, until this position is explic-it, the apparent 'objectivity' simply marginalizes what's not on the map, without necessarily making any reference to this fact. 'Try to find the location of bicy-cle trails on your automobile road map, or the closest toxic waste dump location on your tourist map.'[4] Maps affect us much like a governing paradigm, in their influence on our worldview, what questions we are able to ask and what questions we do not ask.

Many maps represent networks of roads leading between towns, or the boundaries of nation states and their territories, emphasizing these aspects rather than other ways we might relate to a region, such as respect for the peo-ple and cultures who are indigenous to the region, or the plight of refugees entering a region, the plant and animal life, the ecosystems, the colours and tex-tures, or the spiritual aspects of the land.

Maps have also been used as a weapon of power. In Brian Harley's descrip-tion of how the map relates to issues of power and knowledge in his article 'Maps, knowledge and power', he writes:

> As much as guns and warships, maps have been the weapons of imperialism. Insofar as maps were used in colonial promotion, and lands claimed on paper before they were effectively occupied, maps anticipated empire. Surveyors marched alongside soldiers, initially mapping for reconnaissance, then for general information and eventually as a tool for pacification, civilization and exploitation in the defined colonies.[5]

And

> . . . the state guards its knowledge carefully: maps have been universally censored, kept secret and falsified.[6]

Maps have been essential to the notion of a nation state. A primary concern for nation states is the territory they occupy, which must be defended at all costs. If the 'nation state' is the main way we relate to land, it can arouse a sense of the sacred.[7] We call it our motherland or fatherland. The nation state may replace a spiritual relationship to one's land, and the nation state is now worth dying and killing for.

Maps also reflect our tendency to revise history, to erase the beauty, the stories and the trauma of what happened on that hillside. We get used to the notion that a particular region belongs to someone. Maps also symbolize our tendency to define a region or political problem 'objectively', without getting inside it.

WHAT WE NOTICE – EVOLVING WORLD VIEWS

Shaped by different fields of thought, culture, place and evolving over time, our worldviews, as individuals and collectively, influence our notion of awareness, and our attitudes toward dealing with conflict.

Scientific method

In our attempt to understand nature, scientific research has sometimes been criticized as an attempt to 'dominate', subdue or control nature. A main goal of scientific method, however, is to increase our awareness, knowing that it is easy to be unconscious of the various factors influencing a particular situation and our assumptions and perception. Scientific method is based in an understanding that the observer easily impacts on and interprets the observed. With scientific method, we can formulate a hypothesis about how various phenomena hang together and then test our hypothesis by reducing our uncertainty concerning the correlation between various events. If we make a hypothesis that caffeine speeds people up in the morning, we will need not only to monitor coffee drinking and measure speed, but also to determine if it is indeed the caffeine that is responsible, and not other variables in the morning routine, such as oats, yoga or chance.

Scientific method used to objectively determine the causal correlation of events has been crucial for countless developments in all fields of science. The disadvantage of this approach is that it becomes increasingly difficult to study a situation when your interest or goal is not to break things down and isolate a particular factor, but to look at the interaction of various factors.

Evolving systems

A teleological orientation asks questions about the inherent direction of an evolving system. Rather than looking to the cause of something, it asks where it is heading. Inherent in an oak seed is the development of an oak tree. The notion of 'final causes' in biology suggested that vital forces directed the evolution of the living system, whereas the development of the mechanistic paradigm involved looking for psychochemical causal phenomena which could explain life processes as a sequence of causes and effects.[8] The notion of 'teleology' often presupposed a purpose, a 'final' goal or even consciousness. Henri Atlan points out that this way of thinking can ignore the importance and possibility of the unexpected.[9] Complexity theory observes that systems are not only 'causal' (cause and effect) or 'final' (the inherent purpose unfolds), but rather evolutionary and creative, in a way that includes the unexpected, and such that previously unsuspected properties emerge.

In describing evolving and self-organizing structures, Ilya Prigogine, who received a Nobel Prize for his pioneering work, said: 'This is something completely new, something that yields a new scientific intuition about the nature of our universe. . . . It is, if you will, something profoundly optimistic.'[10]

Teleology and dreaming in psychology

Jung's work was based on a teleological premise and is its hallmark. Whereas Freud asked questions and looked for answers about where the dream or neurosis came from and what caused it, Jung was interested in where the dream and so-called neurosis were unfolding, where they were evolving, leading the individual in a process of development towards increased wholeness, differentiation and his or her unique creative expression.[11]

Arny Mindell works with the creative direction found within the deepest, sentient level of experience, in our subtlest body sensations that precede signals, communication or symptoms.[12] Mindell observed that what disturbs our identity as individuals, couples, groups or organizations reflects the emerging 'dreaming' process. Dreaming can be discovered not only in night-time dreams, but in our body experience and symptoms, unintended communication signals, our extreme states and conflicts. At first, we view the new pattern as a disturbance to our identity or something unexpected. If we shift our locus of awareness and discover the relationships and feedback between all parts, we discover that what, at first, seems disturbing or meaningless, suggests a potential and evolving direction.[13]

THE INDUSTRIAL, INFORMATION AND AWARENESS REVOLUTIONS

Industrial Revolution

The Industrial Revolution is often considered as to how it impacted our worldview and the course of history. The Industrial Revolution refers to giant technological, economic and social changes in the 18th and 19th centuries in Great Britain, Western Europe and North America, which went on to impact the rest of the world. Machinery took over much of the work on farms and people flocked to cities to find work in industry – deeply affecting migration patterns, culture, community, family, economics and our perception and relationship to the world in a 'mechanistic' orientation.

The industrial age also impacted our approach to conflict through transportation, flight, communication and weapons. Later, technological advances culminated in the atomic bomb, along with a collective reckoning that 'civilization' had achieved such technological advancement that we could obliterate ourselves, and that we lagged ominously behind in our capacity to find alternate solutions to world conflict.

Information revolution

The IT or Information Technologies Revolution has shifted our focus to communications and access to networks of information and feedback among us. The internet has given us an extraordinary access to a vast source of information in each other and for the first time in human history people are flooded with too much information.

With a world view based on communicating in autonomous and interconnected networks, the information age also brought new forms of warfare, involving 'information warfare teams', 'infiltrating enemy information networks' and computer driven precision strikes.[14] Intelligence analysts say that their job is like drinking from a fire hose. The quantity of information creates massive problems to sort and interpret it. Monitoring of information that forgoes civil and human rights, particularly in the post-9/11 climate is extremely troubling. Yet, it is both heartening and frightening to realize that the sheer amount of information collected in the information age cannot be controlled and dominated. Something else is needed.

Awareness and imagination

Information, no matter the massive amount, without awareness, wisdom and imagination, doesn't add up to much. William Irwin-Thompson wrote,

"Imagination is needed to shape a theory or a hypothesis, and Whitehead argued a long time ago that ... a heap of facts was useless, and neither a Homeric epic nor a scientific theory of evolution could ever be produced from mere facts."[15] Yet the beauty of the information revolution is that exchanges and feedback are going in all directions, such that we live within a bubbling chaos and creativity that no one controls.

Creativity arises within the great net of interactions with surprising twists and turns. As an example, go to research something on the internet and just as you find yourself down a depraved alley, you suddenly alight on just the link you need, that triggers shifts in your direction. Insight, a new impulse, a new connection or thought arises through the interplay of information, outside of our intended search. It reminds me of musicians improvising. At certain moments, the music seems to momentarily fall apart, becoming a bit disconnected and chaotic. Just as an audience loses their attention, the musicians are smiling, present, at ease in this chaos, knowing this is the place the music might just spring to life, as they follow the unexpected turn, into a great sound.

Various fields, once separate, increasingly overlap, stimulating interdisciplinary research and applications. Where the 'edges' of our fields of activity meet, it's a chance to question assumptions and worldviews. Along with a breakdown of old boundaries, there's potential for both further differentiation within and between fields and the discovery of new and underlying worldviews that cross disciplines. We might even say that creativity and awareness can arise where we bump into each other.

We have an uncanny access to one another in the information age. Still, our ability to deal with community relationships and world conflict has barely begun. Networks of information aren't enough. We need tools to facilitate relationship in this vast exchange, towards the possibility of finding a deeper access, creativity and contact to one another.

CHAPTER 25

HOT SPOTS AND THE DIFFERENCE THAT MAKES A DIFFERENCE[1]

NETWORKS AND DECENTRALIZATION

The growing networks within and between communities and organizations are decentralized, made up of self-reliant individuals and groups, linking ideas and resources.[2] With the information age, we said 'think globally and act locally' and began to think of life as a great network with many 'heads'[3] or nodes, in a world with increasing social, political and ecological awareness. Our individuality, autonomy, leadership, contribution and sense of responsibility are valued in this worldview, along with our intricate interdependence. Communication and transportation connect us more and more easily, so that geographical distance cannot separate us. In the early 1980s, John Naisbitt cited the shift from hierarchy to networks as one of the 'megatrends' shaping the future.[4] Unlike a centralized bureaucracy, the parts of a network are independent and interlinked. Rather than filling only one 'role' or function within an organization or family, we needed fluidity and the capacity to assume some responsibility not just for our part, but also for the whole.

DECENTRALIZATION, THE BACKLASH OF POWER AND MODERN WARFARE

Decentralization and networking opened up whole new worlds and ways of communicating, locally and globally.[5] Yet, if we look around at the political landscape these days, and the conglomerate multinational companies, decentralization may appear like a pipe dream. The trend towards decentralization, autonomy, networking and democracy (which countered a trend of centralization of power and hierarchies) appears to be countered by an opposite trend, even a backlash, of stepped-up centralization of power and dominance of immense proportion.

These two trends appear in modern war. Terrorist cells are decentralized structures. The structure develops as a way for terrorist activities to thrive, because there is no centre to aim for. The inability to 'control' the decentralized structure of terrorist activity has in turn led to an escalation of attitudes and actions supporting crackdown, centralization of power and unilateral military dominance of the USA on the world stage.

DECENTRALIZATION AND POWER IN THE FORMER YUGOSLAVIA

There was an important interplay of decentralization and centralized power in the tragedy of the former Yugoslavia. Before Marshal Tito died, he attempted to ensure that Yugoslavia had a strong confederation, with representation from all the different, semi-autonomous regions. After Tito died, there was a confederation in place, but a 'hole' left in the role he had filled. Although he ruled the country with much greater freedom than other communist countries, Tito was a dictator and clearly inhabited the role of 'centralized power'. Of particular controversy in what led to the breakdown of Yugoslavia and the horrendous war, Vojvodina and Kosovo, provinces of Serbia, had been given partial autonomy, with representation and voting rights in the confederation. This was meant as a form of protection and to include their voices in the confederation.

But, around this issue, Serbia disagreed and, when Tito died, Serbia made moves to pick up the vacated role of centralized power, putting the confederation into turmoil. Serbia's actions led to Slovenia's decision to leave the confederation, seeking autonomy as an independent nation, followed by Croatia and Bosnia, and the atrocities that followed. Trends towards both centralized power and decentralization appear within the dynamics of nationalism – in Serbia's move for a Greater Serbia and in the response of separation. Also, Croatia's drive to separate from the former Yugoslavia and become its own nation state was out of both the urge for self-representation, protection and autonomy and its own surge of nationalist and centralized power.

HOW WE BEHAVE AT HOT SPOTS

When a system is in flux and appears chaotic, there is a hole for someone to step in and try to seize power. This dynamic of chaos and crackdown occurs at a 'hot spot'. Arnold Mindell describes 'hot spots'[6] as those points in a system where something vital has been touched, and the status quo is disrupted. In a group meeting or forum, for example, hot spots are moments of tension, sudden flare-ups and zings. You can recognize a 'hot spot' in a meeting when someone says something followed by sudden laughter in the group or a tense silence and the tendency to move on, for the group to act like it didn't happen. A hot spot is like a little tear in the fabric of the status quo, through which a disturbance pops up. If we ignore a hot spot repeatedly, it will come back and conflict will flare or escalate. In a region of severe conflict, touch a hot spot and you will touch a well of pain and outrage, and trigger symptoms of trauma. Trying to avoid hot spots, however, will only exacerbate the pain and volatility of conflict. If we address the 'hot spot' carefully, this is the spot of potential transformation. In our work in Croatia, we sometimes described 'hot spots' as doorways from past to future. Conflicts cycle at hot spots, repeating history. Hot spots, if we enter them carefully and with awareness, are doorways to a different future.

In an interaction, if a hot spot has been missed a few times, there may be a sense of confusion or commotion, or a loss of interest or hopelessness. At the next return of the hot spot, someone may become agitated, upset or slam a door. At this point, someone will usually try to take control of the situation with power. In a group someone might raise a voice to try to bring order, to gather everyone back or make explanations to bring clarity. In a heated situation in which violence threatens, the police may be called, or the military.

At hot spots, there are erratic signals and the sense that something 'out of the ordinary' or 'out of control' might happen. At the hot spot, people may become frightened and yet are eager and relieved to explore the hot spot, when the interaction is facilitated. People also readily understand that, when the hot spot is only repressed, it will come back, more dangerously and out of control. Once a group has experienced working through a hot spot with facilitation, they are usually eager to stay with such a spot when it arises. Hot spots occur at all levels of a system's interaction. You can find hot spots within your community, your relationship interactions and inside your own heart, and war zones might be considered hot spots of the globe.

HOT SPOTS: NON-LINEARITY, DECENTRALIZATION AND SENSITIVITY

As mentioned before, hot spots appear at the boundaries or 'edge' of a system.[7] It's interesting to look at how we behave at hot spots, in view of the study of non-linear systems. We saw that linearity refers to the idea that a small input will yield a small incremental result. Non-linearity describes a system that is highly sensitive and a small input can set the system off towards chaos or towards a transformation.

At hot spots we behave in all sorts of non-linear ways. A fairly linear conversation around a 'central' theme at a meeting or around the dinner table will become non-linear at a hot spot. Let's say someone makes an indirect attack or raises a charged issue. The first tendency will be for the group to move on, to return to its homeostasis (steady state) and its current direction, acting as if it didn't happen. A trained eye notices these spots as they occur, and everyone can intuitively recognize the experience of a hot spot.

When a hot spot returns for a second or third time, interactions become increasingly non-linear. There is an increased rapidity of interactions. Several people may talk at the same time, or there are different levels of conversation at the same time, creating misunderstanding. Separate but overlapping themes are introduced. There may be increased movement and changes in voice tone, or there may be a change of mood in the atmosphere. Although there are cultural variations in regard to style and how much non-linear or simultaneous communication occurs anyway, and in the specific behaviours, the basic pattern seems to be cross-cultural.

At hot spots a spontaneous decentralization also occurs. In a group, people will turn and whisper to someone near them to express their reaction or point of view. The group may dissipate, or people may stand and gather in small groups. At a hot spot within an organization, subgroups or break-off groups spontaneously form. This decentralization process can be understood as a pathway to an apparent breakdown of the old system, and towards a change in the self-organization and creative evolution of the system, if it is picked up with awareness. In a group interaction or forum, we may frame the hot theme and ask people to break into small groups and talk together about it. We may suggest taking a coffee break in which people gossip about the process and then bring back their gossip to the group. Or an exercise could be offered that supports people to reflect upon and differentiate their perspectives in small groups and individually.

Sometimes, when a group begins to have such 'non-linear' interactions, people feel nervous or afraid that everything is going to fall apart. There will be various attempts to make order out of the apparent chaos.

We can return to the hot spot and carefully and thoroughly look at the whole interaction there. This will be just over the 'edge'[8] of the system's usual communication patterns. In one organization, people were talking about their communication difficulties and wondering about the future. A hot spot came up in a sarcastic comment that passed very fast, putting the newer members of the organization in their place. It became clear that there was an 'edge' to talk about rank, authority and decision-making in this organization. The hot spot was a signal for us to talk directly about issues of authority, with all the feelings involved. Hot spots also lead to non-linear and surprising twists and turns, as new dimensions are brought to the problem at hand.

A HOT SPOT BETWEEN TWO PEOPLE IN A FORUM

The multiple, non-linear and decentralized interactions that pop up at the hot spot often represent different dimensions and subthemes of the issue being discussed in the first place. In a forum in Croatia, one afternoon, we were talking about issues of accountability and reconciliation that people face in their regions. One man began to whisper and make jokes with his friends. A woman, sitting near them, turned and asked the man to please be quiet. He said 'no way' and used a term that referred to her as a 'girl'. The atmosphere sort of sizzled between them. This was a hot spot, a point that people often attempt to ignore, repress or control in a meeting. We soon discovered that this hot spot was both volatile and a doorway for a group transformation. One possibility would be to return to the hot spot that must have been touched just before the whispering started. Another possibility is to address the momentary hot spot between the two participants. We moved our focus in this case to their interaction. A process of 'decentralization' had occurred, first in the whispering and joking, then in the interaction between the two participants and now in the multiplicity of issues that promptly poured forth.

Lane and I supported the two of them to complete their interaction together. First his whispering and joking upset her and then she was furious at what she felt was a sexist, ageist and dismissive comment and attitude towards her. On his side, he was upset at the way she had talked to him, as her elder – he felt she did not respect him. They interacted about issues of gender and age. She felt put down and was outraged by his attitude, stemming from his social rank as a middle-aged man in relation to her as a young woman. He remained cool and she became increasingly upset, as a result of the rank dynamics around gender and age. The more he seemed 'cool', the more emotional and upset she became.

As we facilitated their interaction, a new dimension arose in their awareness of each other, and a striking transformation for their relationship and for the whole group. He was trembling slightly. As we asked about his trembling, his 'cool' attitude shifted and he said to her, with genuine feeling, that he had not meant to hurt her with his jokes. His voice cracked: 'If I don't laugh, I will cry.' In this moment, she changed in her identification from feeling oppressed by him, to realizing that his joking and his 'cool' arose not only out of his social rank. It arose out of a well of pain around the issues of war that we were discussing. At first glance it looked like all the 'rank' was on his side, including being middle-aged, male, acting 'cool' and dismissive of her, and refusing any accountability for his behaviour, whereas she was terribly upset. Suddenly she realized her privilege of having not experienced a personal trauma during the war where he had severe trauma, and that, although she felt relatively free to express her emotion, he did not. As they continued to speak together, weaving the different threads that had frayed at the hot spot, the group entered a deeper level of understanding and grappling with the meaning of accountability and its complexity, also in relation to the issues facing Serbs, Croats and Muslims in the region.

HOT SPOTS AS BIFURCATION POINTS – THE EMERGENCE OF AWARENESS

Hot spots may be considered the 'bifurcation points' of a system. Prigogine[9] described how a system in a far-from-equilibrium state reaches a point of bifurcation, leading either to disintegration or to a radical change in a process of self-organization.[10]

We have seen that the hot spot represents the point that a conflict may escalate and communication appears to break down and at this point the system can also transform to a new level of organization. This can bring a differentiation and deepening of community. We've seen that, around the 'chaos' at a hot spot, our search to dominate and take control makes us easy to manipulate. Chaos becomes an excuse for a crackdown and for the use of power to dominate. The non-linear tendency of systems can also lead to what complexity theory refers to as 'emergence' – a new pattern emerges, a more differentiated level of self-organization.

At hot spots of conflict, the potential emergence is awareness or consciousness. We know that hot spots in our interactions in community, society and globally, all too often escalate into brutal violence and tragedy. Yet, hot spots of conflict may actually represent an attempt to evolve in our capacity to relate and interact with awareness.

BUTTERFLIES AND INDIVIDUALS – THE DIFFERENCE THAT MAKES A DIFFERENCE

The non-linear tendencies at hot spots make for extra sensitivity to the feedback and relationships between elements and subsystems. This increased sensitivity means that we get more easily and rapidly pulled and pushed into the shifting subsystems of the field. This sensitivity is readily tapped and exploited to tip an unstable region into war. When trying to facilitate within such a field, extra sensitivity is required to bring awareness into the movement of the field, its feedback and communication.

Just as the sensitivity of a system that is 'far from equilibrium' can lead us into the drastic movements of war, this sensitivity also allows apparently small interventions to yield large-scale shifts. When you find yourself thinking it's impossible to intervene in the entrenched and intractable problems of our world, think of that famous 'butterfly'. Listen for and remember the awesome stories of how one individual's actions transformed systems around them. My favourite is the story of Rosa Parks. Rosa Parks was asked to get up and move to the back of the bus one day, like every other day. Only on that great day in 1955, in Montgomery, Alabama, USA, Rosa Parks later explained, 'I was tired'. 'I didn't feel like getting up one more time.' She was tired, fed up with having to get up to move to the back of that bus because she was black. That day, for her, that pattern was over. She didn't stand up and move to the back and, even after the driver insisted, she refused, until she was forcibly removed. That event, that day, triggered the bus strike in Montgomery. Black people stopped taking the bus. They walked. They walked everywhere. And this movement evolved into the civil rights movement that has had an inspiring and massive influence not only on American society, but also throughout the world and for all movements of oppressed peoples.

BOUNDARIES, COLOURS AND COOKIES

We need boundaries to know who we are and to be able to engage and interact with each other, within and between various subcommunities. We need boundaries to become conscious. We need to be aware of ourselves as individuals to be able to disagree and to be intimate with someone else or to engage in community. If we do not feel welcomed, invited in our cultural identity within community, we feel isolated. If we are part of a dominant or majority group, we may have a missing sense of cultural identity, and feel disconnected to community, despite every privilege.

But, why is the other guy in my gang, religion, ethnic group or nation someone I'll die for and kill for? Although our identification with a group can bring up our deepest feelings of love, devotion and loyalty, the way we identify with one group and consider the other group our enemy is in some respects a lot less personal than we realize. As a field is polarized, we are mobilized. Kids in gangs might as easily have ended up with the other gang if they lived down the street. Family members in mixed marriages and partnerships were frequently driven apart during the war in the former Yugoslavia, as were friends and neighbours.

In the former Yugoslavia, the spoken language used to be called Serbo-Croatian in Serbia and Croato-Serbian in Croatia, in order to emphasize some differences in grammar and vocabulary. Friends have told me that kids had to learn these distinctions in school. During the 1990s, these differences in language, which had not mattered much to most people, now took on gigantic proportions. I heard of conferences where participants insisted on having two translators, one for Serbian and one for Croatian. Apparently small cultural differences could also be loaded. I quickly learned that Croats kiss on the cheeks two times when greeting and Serbs three times. Hedges writes: 'In the Balkans, there were heated debates over the origin of gingerbread hearts – cookies in the shape of hearts. The Croats insisted the cookies were Croatian. The Serbs angrily countered that the cookies were Serbian. The suggestion to one ethnic group that gingerbread hearts were invented by the other ethnic group could start a fight.'[11]

The sensitivity to conditions at a hot spot means that most anything can fuel and amplify the situation. Violent conflict and war are stirred through exploiting this tendency in us. Kids in gangs refer to colours, tattooed words and street boundaries as a serious matter of life and death. The colour boundary – red, yellow, black, brown and white – has structured our traumatic world history. Historians have shown how the notion of race was developed and/or used to promote notions of racial superiority and inferiority for political purpose, economic exploitation and colonization.[12]

THE SPHERE OF FEELING

Awareness requires differentiating things in our feelings and thoughts, but it also requires a kind of resonance or compassion. Most of us tend not to learn about or get involved with issues unless we feel personally involved. Only then can we step into the other's shoes. Have you ever noticed how you are more interested in the news of a particular region if you have visited there and walked on those streets? If I see something in the news about Kosovo, I want to know: 'was it Pristina or Mitrovice?' I remember eyes, and the stories we heard, the music, the translations of dramatic songs of freedom, songs that had been banned for many years. I remember the young UN soldiers protecting Serb enclaves, the sand bags, barbed wire, burned-out buildings, the upside-down car, the garbage on a hillside, the beauty of the green hills when you make it through the delays at the border from Macedonia. If I'd never been there, I know that, when I read the news, it would be harder to follow what is going on, or to have the same level of interest and feeling.

We all have limits to what we learn about, amid the endless issues facing us as a world. We all have some issues that are of more concern to us than others. We've seen how privilege on one side, and oppression and pain on the other, can often limit our capacity to feel into the lives of others and even our own lives.

HOT SPOTS AND CONSCIOUSNESS, BATTLES AND BUTTERFLIES

At hot spots, we get excited and terrified. We've seen how violence is stirred at hot spots, at the edges of our identity defined by culture, ethnicity, religion, politics, economics and land. We easily lose our orientation at hot spots and do whatever it takes to be safe. At hot spots, we get terrorized and have an urge to control and to dominate. We rally into opposing positions. The sensitivity and non-linear tendencies at hot spots make for dramatic and destructive movements of the field. We may feel swallowed into a living hell. We may feel cut off and distant. Throughout this book, we've seen how hot spots touch the wounds of history, and can trigger a replay of traumatic experience and brutal injustice, along with altered states of consciousness that act as fuel, easily set alight to exacerbate these dynamics.

Yet, hot spots also tap our deepest feelings and contact with each other in relationships, and a creative, potential underlying conflict. It is exciting to consider that a hot spot is where consciousness can arise and heart for one another. It is a point of irritation and stimulation that can wake us, and make us have a dialogue. Over the last few years, people interested in complexity theory have sometimes said that consciousness is the most surprising and puzzling 'emergent phenomenon' of all.[13]

It is in our deepest nature to reflect. It is in our nature not only to get swallowed up in polarizations and battles, but also to get to know the conflicts in us, and our wholeness. In Creation myths sometimes the gods try to get to know themselves through us, their creation.[14]

A colleague from India[15] said to me that, in the *Bhagavad Gita*, Arjuna's dialogue with Krishna on the battlefield was like having a facilitator with you in the midst of conflict. He pointed to the centre of the room, in a 'worldwork' conference where 300 people from 30 countries were going deeply into conflicts among us, while learning to facilitate these intense interactions.[16]

This is also the task of individuation, not only to feel pushed and pulled by inner and outer forces, but also to engage and facilitate an interaction on this 'battlefield' of our personal lives and struggles.

Although we all share in the underlying forces and patterns of nature, at the same time we each have an utterly personal path. You could say we are those butterflies in the 'butterfly effect', capable not only of being swallowed up in currents and storms, but also of following our subtlest feelings and, at any moment from the furthest corners of the world, to influence the weather of history. When it all seems too much, on both a political and personal scale, I like what Gandhi said: 'Whatever you do will be insignificant, but it is very important that you do it.'[17]

Appendix

Chart of symptoms of post-traumatic stress disorder in individuals and signs of communal and collective trauma

The following is a list of post-traumatic stress disorder (PTSD) symptoms from the *Diagnostic and Statistical Manual of Mental Disorders*, 4th edn (DSM-IV)[1] (left column) as well as a corresponding list I have developed to show the symptoms of group or community trauma (middle column) and collective dynamics of trauma within the wider society (in the right-hand column).

PTSD symptoms in the individual	Group or community signs of trauma	Collective dynamics of trauma in the wider society
A *The person has been exposed to a traumatic event in which both of the following were present:*	A *The group or community has experienced an event or series of events that were shocking and that:*	A *Events have occurred that lie outside fundamental values concerning human rights:*
1 The person experienced, witnessed or was confronted with an event or events that involved actual or threatened death or serious injury, or a threat to the physical integrity of others	1 Upset and threatened fundamental social values and caused serious threat to the welfare and survival of the group or community	1 This may involve atrocities that crossed boundaries of international humanitarian law and conventions of war
2 The person's response involved intense fear, helplessness or horror. Note that, in children, this may be expressed instead by disorganized or agitated behaviour	2 Caused terror, helplessness and horror in a group or community	2 Events may have caused widespread terror, uprooting of large populations and genocide

PTSD symptoms in the individual	Group or community signs of trauma	Collective dynamics of trauma in the wider society
B *The traumatic event is persistently re-experienced in one (or more) of the following ways:*	B *The community trauma may be re-experienced in some or all of the following ways:*	B *Trauma replays and persists, and history repeats in some or all of the following ways:*
1 Recurrent and distressing recollections of the event, including images, thoughts or perceptions. Note that, in young children, repetitive play may occur in which themes or aspects of the trauma are expressed	1 Recurrent distressing recollections of past events	1 Historical traumatic events and memory are manipulated and experienced as an intrusion, without sense of control or choice
2 Recurrent distressing dreams of the event. Note that, in children, there may be frightening dreams without recognizable content	2 Group and community 'dreaming', often in the replay of polarizations and conflict	2 Traumatic experiences replay in repeating oppression and cycles of revenge. Archetypal roles of oppressor and oppressed are mythic in nature and proportion
3 Acting or feeling as if the traumatic event were recurring (includes a sense of reliving the experience, illusions, hallucinations and dissociative flashback episodes, including those that occur on awakening or when intoxicated). Note that, in young children, trauma-specific re-enactment may occur	3 While talking about or debating an issue, a hot spot is touched and the traumatic event is actualized and reoccurs, through strong affects, flashbacks and visceral responses. This may occur when a group is in an altered state of consciousness	3 The past is not only revived in memory but reoccurs (e.g. while killing Muslims, Serb paramilitaries thought they were defending against the Turks from several centuries past)
4 Intense psychological distress at exposure to internal or external cues that symbolize or resemble an aspect of the traumatic event (The DSM-III-R version of PTSD, mentions anniversaries as triggers in individual trauma)	4 A group, subgroup or community may experience outrage, distress and tension when a new event symbolizes or resembles an aspect of an earlier community trauma, e.g. when the police who beat Rodney King were acquitted	4 Anniversaries of traumatic events are used to awaken outrage and urge for redemption, e.g. Slobodan Milosevic used the 600-year anniversary of the battle of Kosovo to launch the nationalist movement in Serbia.
5 Physiological reactivity on exposure to internal or external cues that symbolize or resemble an aspect of the traumatic event	5 Reactivity to any issue that relates to the original conflict. When a new event reminds the group or community of a past trauma, the community experiences the atmosphere and tension of the original traumatic event and outbreaks of violence may occur or violence can be readily mobilized	5 Reactivity and mobilization in nationalist movements. Tendency for people to be easily pulled and pushed into polarized reactions, swayed by leadership and disinformation in the media

PTSD symptoms in the individual	Group or community signs of trauma	Collective dynamics of trauma in the wider society
C Persistent avoidance of stimuli associated with the trauma or numbing of general responsiveness (not present before the trauma), as indicated by at least three of the following:	*C A group or community attempts to avoid the issues associated with the community trauma. There is a lack of responsiveness, or a sense of cutting off from the issues and the pain and outrage involved:*	*C Persistent avoidance of the issues surrounding atrocity and trauma, as a result of privilege on one side and pain and suffering on the other. A general numbing of responsiveness regarding the suffering and trauma in our world:*
1 Efforts to avoid thoughts, feelings or conversations associated with the trauma	1 Group or community attempts to avoid the topics that touch upon its trauma	1 Society avoids facing past atrocities, carried out by some groups against other groups
2 Efforts to avoid activities, places or people that arouse recollections of the trauma	2 Group or community activities are avoided that could re-trigger trauma or open up troublesome issues	2 Society avoids controversial subjects that could touch upon the reality of atrocity that occurred, e.g. the issue of land rights of Native Americans is avoided
3 Inability to recall an important aspect of the trauma (the term 'psychogenic amnesia', used in DSM-III-R)	3 Group or community suffers from amnesia, claiming that the event never happened or it is irrelevant now, and refuses to deal with problems of accountability	3 Collective amnesia sets in: 'It was so long ago.' Or history is revised and the events counted out of our collective story. Accountability is sidestepped or refused
4 Markedly diminished interest or participation in significant activities (in young children, loss of recently acquired developmental skills such as toilet training or language skills)	4 Hopelessness and disinterest in group and community activities and community growth. Burn-out is widespread	4 Pervasive hopelessness about politics, low voter turnout and people feel its pointless to get involved with social action
5 Feeling of detachment or estrangement from others	5 Widespread feeling of isolation within group or community, lack of community spirit	5 Disinterest towards oppressed groups, desensitization to atrocities and dehumanization
6 Restricted range of affect, e.g. unable to have loving feelings	6 Restricted ability to recognize the painful issues facing the community. Lack of expression of reactions of outrage and grief	6 Limited feeling about the tragedy of history in social discourse. TV watching. The reaction of society does not match the magnitude of the events
7 Sense of a foreshortened future, e.g. does not expect to have a career, marriage, children or a normal life span	7 A lack of belief in prospects for the future of the group or community. People leave the group or young people emigrate from the region or country	7 Decision-making occurs with no long-term perspective, with no sense of future and sustainability. Failing and missing leadership

PTSD symptoms in the individual	Group or community signs of trauma	Collective dynamics of trauma in the wider society
D Persistent symptoms of increased arousal (not present before the trauma), as indicated by two or more of the following:	D Group or community agitation as indicated by some or all of the following:	D Collective agitation including some or all of the following:
1 Difficulty falling or staying asleep	1 Persistence in a dominant pattern of communication and interaction and inability to stop and reflect as a group or community	1 Fear of introspection as a society. Society focuses on productivity, trying to avoid past ghosts. But the ghosts will not rest
2 Irritability or outbursts of anger	2 Irritability and outbursts of violence in community	2 Repression, terror tactics and acts of terrorism
3 Difficulty concentrating	3 Difficulty establishing focus and clarifying the group or community's issues	3 Lack of focus and commitment to global themes and long-term issues
4 Hypervigilance	4 Group or community is guarded and poised for conflict. Vigilance rises in oppressed communities, guarding against discrimination or attack. Vigilance rises among groups with social rank, out of fear of feeling guilty or losing privileges. Vigilance in standing for oppressed groups may be referred to as 'political correctness'	4 Sensitivity and vigilance between nations. Nations are poised for war. Vigilance and reactivity in political discourse and preparation for violent conflict
5 Exaggerated startle response	5 If a person or subgroup says something that touches on a hot spot, the community may be quick to jump, scapegoat and suppress the issue, or strongly react against it	5 Large sections of society are easily startled after a traumatic event. As an example, after the shocking events of 9/11, many Americans were easily startled, reacting to events that could be symbolically or otherwise linked to events of 9/11 (e.g. jumping someone on the airplane who stood up). Political and military responses are reactive and retaliatory
E Duration of disturbance (symptoms in B, C and D) of at least one month	E Duration of the above disturbances in B, C and D, over time: months, years or decades	E Duration of the above disturbances in B, C and D over months, years, decades or generations
F The disturbance causes clinically significant distress or impairment in social, occupational or other important areas of functioning	F The disturbances cause disruption or impairment of group or community functions	F The disturbances impair the wider society's infrastructure, around economic, political and legal functions. International bodies disrupted (e.g. the UN faced disruptions when the USA refused to consider international opinion and international law)

ENDNOTES

PREFACE

1. Behan H (1995) Jean-Luc Godard. Press Conference at 1995 Montréal Film Festival www.filmscouts.com/scripts/interview.cfm?articleCode=2800 (accessed May 2004).
2. Mindell A (1986) Rivers Way. London and Boston: Viking-Penguin Arkana; Mindell A (1988) City Shadows: Psychological Interventions in Psychiatry. London: Routledge; Mindell A (1995) Sitting in the Fire: Large group transformation using conflict and diversity. Portland OR: Lao Tse Press; Mindell A (2000) Quantum Mind. Portland OR: Lao Tse Press; Mindell A (2002) The Deep Democracy of Open Forums. Charlottesville VA: Hampton Roads.
3. Desmond Tutu discusses South Africa with Charlie Rose, New York, 16 March 2004. Seen 17 March 2004, KCTS, Seattle.

INTRODUCTION: WELCOME TO 'THE WAR HOTEL'

1. Altered states, described in Part IV, refer to experience and perception beyond the boundaries of what we consider our normal state of mind.
2. Gutman R, Rieff D (eds) (1999) *Crimes of War: What the public should know.* New York: W.W. Norton; see also Crimes of War Project 1999–2003: www.crimesofwar.org/resources/resources.html (2002–2004).
3. Paulo Freire used the term 'conscientization'.
4. Heany T. Issues in Freirian pedagogy: http://nlu.nl.edu/ace/Resources/Documents/FreireIssues.html (accessed 2003); Freire P (1973) Education for Critical Consciousness. New York: Seabury. For a short biography of Paulo Freire: A Homage by Moacir Gadotti, General Director, Paulo Freire Institute, Professor, Universidade de Sao Paulo and Carlos Alberto Torres Director, Paulo Freire Institute and Director, Latin American Center, UCLA: http://nlu.nl.edu/ace/Homage.html (accessed 2003).
5. Zinn H (2003) *Passionate Declarations: Essays on war and justice.* New York: Perennial, Harper Collins.

6. Parekh B (1989) *Gandhi's Political Philosophy*. London: Macmillan Academic and Professional Ltd, pp. 94, 95.

7. Parekh (1989, pp. 90, 104).

8. Chan W (ed. and trans.) (1963) *A Sourcebook in Chinese Philosophy*. Princeton, NJ: Princeton University Press, p. 208; Perry JW (1987) The Heart of History: Individuality in evolution. New York: State University of New York Press, p. 77.

9. Mindell A (1995) *Sitting in the Fire: Large group transformation using conflict and diversity*. Portland, OR: Lao Tse Press.

CHAPTER 1: IN THE NAME OF JUSTICE

1. Press release, The Hague, 14 February 2003: www.un.org/icty/pressreal/22003/p.278-e.htm Full text on www.un.org.icty (accessed January 2004).

2. Dahl F (2003) Hardline nationalists win Serbian general election: Radical party led by war crimes suspect. Reuters News Agency. *Toronto Star*, 29 December; Robinson M (2003) Serbs back party led by war crimes suspect. *The Scotsman*, 29 December.

3. The Forest People's Program, 31 October 2000. *People of Clay: The Twa of Rwanda*. Television Trust for the Environment: www.tve.org/news, www.forestpeoples.org (accessed January 2004).

4. Longman T (2001) Christian churches and genocide in Rwanda. In: Bartov O, Mack, P (eds), *In God's Name: Genocide and religion in the 20th century*. New York: Bergahn Books, pp. 139–159.

5. See Zinn H (2002) *A People's History of the United States*. New York: Longman Publishers.

6. Rieff D (1996) *Slaughterhouse: Bosnia and the failure of the West*. London: Vintage, Random House, p. 103.

7. Sucic, Daria Sito reports on comment of Biljana Plavsic, Prague, Czech Republic, Open Media Research Institute, Special Report: Pursuing Balkan Peace, No. 36, 10 September 1996.

8. Arnold Mindell describes history as present and structuring our momentary interactions in his theory and methods of Process Oriented Psychology and worldwork. See Mindell A (1995) *Sitting in the Fire*. Portland, OR: Lao Tse Press.

9. Glover J (2001) *Humanity: A moral history of the twentieth century*. London: Random House, p. 411. Glover writes: 'This book would not have been written without the belief that the past is alive in the present.' He quotes R.G. Collingwood, from his autobiography (p. 411): 'So long as the past and the present are outside one another, knowledge of the past is not of much use in the present. But suppose the past lives on in the present; suppose, though encapsulated in it, and at first sight hidden beneath the present's contradictory and more prominent features, it is still alive and active; then the historian may very well be related to the non-historian as the trained woodsman is to the ignorant traveler.'

10. Daniel Chandler refers to the term hegemony as used by Gramsci, an Italian Marxist thinker (1891–1937), in a course on Marxist Media Theory, at Aberystwyth, the

University of Wales: www.aber.ac.uk/media/Documents/marxism/marxism10.html (accessed November 2003).

11. Pfaff W (2002) Geopolitics have changed for the worse: The temptation of hegemony. *International Herald Tribune*, 11 September.

12. Pfaff W (2002).

13. Bielefeldt in dialogue between Heiner Bielefeldt and Mohammad Saeed Bahmanpour (2002) in The politics of social justice: religion vs. human rights? From the debate, What about faith? At London's Goethe Institute, Open Democracy website, www.opendemocracy.net (accessed 2003).

14. Robinson G (2001) The peace of the powerful. In: Carey R (ed.), *The New Intifada*. London: Verso, p. 112.

15. Robinson G (2001, p. 112).

16. Robinson G (2001, p. 112).

17. Robinson G (2001, pp. 112–115).

18. Robinson G (2001, pp. 112–115).

19. This idea that ethnic conflict erupted was often the flavour of the news and the error has been commented on by several authors. See Gutman R, Rieff D (eds) (1999) *Crimes of War: What the public should know*. New York: W.W. Norton; Crimes of War Project 1999–2003: www.crimesofwar.org.

20. Little A, Silber, L (1995) *The Death of Yugoslavia*. London: Penguin Books; also personal discussions and experience in the former Yugoslavia.

21. In a search regarding the percentage of mixed marriages, I found quite a discrepancy in figures. Glover writes that about 40 per cent of all families were ethnically mixed. Glover A (2001, p. 132).

22. Little A (2001) Viewpoint: The west did not do enough. In: World: From our Correspondents. In: BBC News Online, 29 June.

23. Gutman R, Rieff D (eds) (1999, p. 52).

24. YES Project (1993) Los Angeles, facilitated within YES together with Jean-Claude Audergon and David Crittendon.

25. See Mindell A (1995).

26. Havel V (1991) Protest. In: *Antaeus Plays in One Act*. London: Tangier.

27. Bresan V (director) (1996) How the War started on my Island. Production Company HRT Zagreb.

28. The terms and theory of 'high' and 'low' dreams developed by Arnold Mindell.

29. See endnote 28.

CHAPTER 2: SUFFERING, PRIVILEGE AND BEING RIGHT

1. Morris B (2001) *Righteous Victims*. New York: Vintage, Random House, p. 161.

2. Dershowitz A (2003) *The Case for Israel*. Hoboken, NJ: John Wiley & Sons, pp. 15, 30. During these periods, approximately a million Jews immigrated to the USA.

3. Morris B (2001, p. 73); Isaacs A, Alexander F, Law J, Martin E (eds) (2000) *A Dictionary of World History*. Oxford: Oxford University Press, p. 317.

4. Dershowitz A (2003, p. 51).

5. Benny Morris places the figure at 700 000. The official Israel count was 520 000 and the Palestinian figure is as high as 900 000 (Morris B, 2001, p. 260; see also Dershowitz A, 2003, p. 85). Various interpretations of events emphasize whether Palestinians left in response to requests from surrounding Arab countries to clear the area for an invasion, were expelled or fled in terror. Morris B (2001, p. 257) describes four specific stages. The first, between December 1947 and 1948, when some 75 000 upper and middle class Arabs fled into neighbouring regions, expecting to return once the hostilities had ended. A second stage of mass flight from urban neighbourhoods and rural areas in the spring of 1948, caused by Jewish military attack or fears of attack, and terror created by atrocities, including Deir Yassin. The third and fourth stages, in July and October 1948, in which 300 000 more Arabs became refugees. During this last period, there was less 'spontaneous' flight and more direct expulsion or harassment.

6. Articles in the *International Herald Tribune*, 11–12 August 2001.

CHAPTER 3: TRIBUNALS, TRUTH COMMISSIONS, LUSTRATION AND COMMUNITY FORUMS

1. www.icc.now.org/html/pressqandaicc.pdf (accessed 2003), www.un.org/law/icc/statute/iccq&a.htm, copyright 1999 and www.un.org/news/facts/iccfact (accessed 2003).

2. United Nations: www.un.org/icty/index.html (accessed 2003). On 25 May 1993, the UN Security Council created the 'International Tribunal for the Prosecution of Persons Responsible for Serious Violations of International Humanitarian Law Committed in the Territory of the Former Yugoslavia since 1991', in the belief that accountability would 'contribute to the restoration and maintenance of peace'.

3. US Institute for Peace: 'Rwanda: Accountability, War and Crimes of Genocide', Release date 1995, Project on International Courts and Tribunals: www.pict-pcti.rg/courts (accessed 2003).

4. The ICTY and the Truth and Reconciliation Commission in Bosnia and Herzegovina, press release, from ICTY website 2002. Full text of President Claude Jordan's speech made on 12 May 2001 in Sarajevo in an address to those working on a Bosnian Truth and Reconciliation Commission.

5. US Institute for Peace, Rwanda: Accountability for War Crimes and Genocide: usip.org/pubs/specialreports/early/rwanda1.html (accessed 2003).

6. Questions and answers regarding the International Criminal Court: www.icc.nw.org/html/pressqandaicc.pdf (accessed 2003).

7. Human Rights Watch Report 2000: www.hrw.org (accessed 2001, 2003).

8. Personal discussion in Croatia.

9. These are: Argentina, Bolivia, Chad, Chile, East Timor, Ecuador, El Salvador, Germany, Guatemala, Haiti, Malawi, Nepal, Nigeria, Panama, Peru, Philippines, Sierra Leone, South Africa, South Korea, Sri Lanka, Uganda, Uruguay, Federal Republic of Yugoslavia and Zimbabwe. Groups in Bosnia-Herzegovina, Cambodia, Indonesia, Jamaica, Mexico and Morocco have also called for the establishment of Truth Commissions in their countries. Truth Commissions – US Institute of Peace Library: www.usip.org/library/truth.html (accessed 2002).

   A Truth Commission has also been called for in America, in relation to Native Americans, African Americans and also American involvement in supporting state terror and genocide in Guatemala, Nicaragua, Honduras, El Salvador. A Truth and Reconciliation Commission has been suggested to examine past racist practices and propose methods to redress.

   54th and 55th UN conference, summer 1999, Ciapas: UN Commission for Human Rights, proposal to create a special investigation of human rights abuses against indigenous people.

10. Ignatieff M (2001) Introduction. In: Edelstein J, *Truth and Lies*. London: Granta Books.

11. From an account I heard of proceedings in the Truth Commission, South Africa.

12. Edelstein J (2001) *Truth and Lies*. London: Granta Books, p. 130.

13. Response by Archbishop Tutu on his appointment as Chairperson on the Truth and Reconciliation Commission, November 1995.

14. Edelstein J (2001, p. 92).

15. Roht-Arriaza N (ed.) (1995) *Impunity and Human Rights in International Law and Practice*. New York: Oxford University Press.

16. See our website for discussion and examples of such community forums, CFOR, Community Forums or Community Force for Change (www.cfor.info). See also www.worldwork.org.

17. President Claude Jordan's Speech in Sarajevo, 12 May 2001, to people working on a Bosnian Truth and Reconciliation Commission. Press release and full text of Jordan's speech, International Criminal Tribunal for the Former Yugoslavia, ICTY website (accessed 2002).

18. Mindell A (2002) *The Deep Democracy of Open Forums*. Charlottesville, VA: Hampton Roads.

19. Mindell A (1995) *Sitting in the Fire*. Portland, OR: Lao Tse Press, pp. 27, 81. See also Audergon A (2004) Trauma and the nightmare of history. In: Totton N (ed.), *Psychotherapy and Politics International*. London: Whurr Publishers. See also Part 3 of this book for information on community trauma and Part 5 for a discussion of the dynamics of conflict at 'hot spots'.

20. Michnick A, Havel V (1993) Justice or revenge. *Journal of Democracy* 4: 20–27.

21. Personal discussion.

22. Home C, Levi M (2002) Prepared for Trust and Honesty Project, Budapest, Collegium, October.

23. Michnick A, Havel V (1993).

24. Weschler L (1992) The velvet purge: the trials of Jan Kavan. *The New Yorker*, 19 October: p. 92.

25. Michnick A, Havel V (1993, p. 21).

CHAPTER 4: ACCOUNTABILITY AND RETURN TO THE GANGES

1. The involvement of the US government over the years in supporting regimes committing grave human rights violations and murder is well known, yet many Americans know nothing of it. It is not reported much in mainstream news. See Campbell D (2003) Kissinger approved Argentinean dirty war. *The Guardian*, 6 December. Declassified US files expose the backing of the junta during the 1970s, in which some 30 000 people were arrested, tortured and killed.

2. Chomsky N (2000) *Rogue States*. London: Pluto Press, p. 4.

3. Amnesty International Library USA, Indecent and internationally illegal, the death penalty against child offenders. AMR51/143/2002 and Executions worldwide since 1990, ACT 50/010/2000: www.amesty.org, (accessed 14 December 2000).

4. Saeed Bahmanpour M, Bielefeldt H (2002) The politics of social justice: religion vs. human rights? Dialogue on Open Democracy website: www.opendemocracy.net (accessed 2003).

5. News search. See also www.socialjusticecenterofmarin.org/issues/US.truth.commission.html (2003).

6. Neill AS (1995) *Summerhill*. London: St Martin Press (originally published in 1960).

7. Summerhill, Suffolk, UK.

8. Gilbert GM (1995) *Nuremberg Diary*. London: De Capo Press.

CHAPTER 5: TERROR

1. See definitions: Council of Foreign Relations: www.cfr.org (2003).

2. Whitaker B (2001) The definition of terrorism. Guardian Unlimited, 7 May. He writes that a book discussing attempts by the UN and international bodies to define terrorism runs to 1866 pages without any firm conclusion. See also International Policy Institute for Counter Terrorism, www.ict.org.il (accessed 2003) and Council on Foreign Relations: Terrorism: Questions and Answers: www.terrorismanswers.com/terrorism/introduction.html (accessed 2003).

3. Attacks on property, such as a pipeline in Columbia owned by multinational oil companies, are sometimes considered terrorism. Military strikes, which killed Palestinian women and children in a market place, are not typically considered terror, because the strikes were carried out by the army, and the civilian deaths were claimed as a mistake. Strikes by Palestinian terrorist groups on military targets are, on the other hand, considered acts of terror. Whitaker B (2001).

4. Whitaker B (2001). A British anti-terrorism law got round the problem of fuzzy definitions by listing 21 international terrorist organizations by name. The list included Hizbullah, which, though armed, was a legal political party in Lebanon, with elected members of parliament. The Iranian 'Mujahedeen' was banned, but not its Iraqi equivalent, the INC, which was financed by the USA.

5. Simpson JA, Weiner ESC (eds) (1989) *Oxford English Dictionary*, 2nd edn. New York: Oxford University Press.

6. The official definition of terrorism contained in Title 22 of the US Code, Section 2656f(d).

7. Ganor B, ICT Director, International Policy Institute for Counter Terrorism, September 1998: www.ict.org.il (accessed 2001).

8. Federal Bureau of Investigation. The Terrorism Research Center: www.terrorism.com (accessed 2002)

9. GA Res. 51/210 Measures to eliminate international terrorism, UN Office of Drugs and Crime: www.unodc.org/unodc/terrorism.defintions.html (2001–2003).

10. Mandela N (1995) *Long Walk to Freedom: The autobiography of Nelson Mandela*. London: Little Brown & Co., pp. 320, 321.

11. Sorrig K (1997) Torture consolidates power. In a paper published by the Rehabilitation and Research Centre for Torture Victims, International Rehabilitation Council for Torture Victims.

CHAPTER 6: TERROR TACTIC: CHAOS AND CRACKDOWN

1. Silber L, Little A (1995) *Death of Yugoslavia*. London: Penguin Books, p. 110 .

2. *Encyclopedia Columbia*, 6th edn (2001). New York: Columbia University Press: Bartleby.com (accessed 2001–2004).

3. Hamburg D (2002) *No More Killing Fields: Preventing deadly conflict*. Carnegie Commission on Preventing Deadly Conflict. Lanham, MD: Rowman & Littlefield, pp. 24–26.

4. Zivkovic M (1994) The wish to be a Jew: the power of the Jewish trope in the Yugoslav conflict. Article presented at the 9th International Conference of Europeanists, March 31–April 2 1994, Chicago: www.unice.fr/urmis-soliis/Docs/Cahiers_6/cahiers_n6_zivkovic.pdf (accessed 2003). Zivkovic quotes Serbian writer, Vuk Draskovic, in 1985 'Serbs are the 13th, lost and the most ill-fated tribe of Israel'. This story was resurrected, among others, and put to the service of political agendas in the mid-1980s.

5. Quoted in *The Workers Power* (1999) The break up of Yugoslavia: www.workerspower.com/wpglobal/balkanpamphletch4.html (accessed 2003).

6. Silber, Little (1995, p. 147).

7. International Work Group for Indigenous Affairs (2001) *The Indigenous World 2000–2001*. Copenhagen: IWGIA, pp. 167–174.

8. International Work Group for Indigenous Affairs (2001, p. 173).

9. International Work Group for Indigenous Affairs (2001, pp. 173–174).

10. International Work Group for Indigenous Affairs (2001, pp. 173–174).

11. Search and review of all articles in the *Washington Post* and *New York Times*, on violence in Genoa surrounding the WTO demonstrations in 2001.

12. See www.redpepper.org.uk/intarch/x-genoa-3.html (accessed 2003) and italy.indymedia.org/news/2001/08/5448.php, www.davidgrenier.weblogger.com/2001/07/20 and www.indymedia.org/front/php3?article_id54288&group+webcast (accessed 2003). See also Guardian Unlimited (2001) Torture in police cells was horrific. *The Observer*, 29 July: awww.indymedia.org/front.php3?article_id=56127 (accessed 2003).

13. Guardian Unlimited (2001).

14. BBC report (2001) G8 Britons tell of police 'brutality', July 26: www.bbc.co.uk/1/hi/uk/1457920.stm. Press release by Jakobi S (2001) London, Director of Fair Trials Abroad: www.statewatch.org/news/2001/jul/genoat.htm (accessed 2003).

15. BBC report (2001).

16. See www.indymedia.org.

17. Personal discussion.

18. Paul Wolff has gathered these declassified documents onto a website: www.cointel.org (accessed May 2003).

19. US Senate (1976) Intelligence Activities and the rights of Americans: final report of the Select Committee to study government operations with respect to Intelligence activities, 26 April: www.cointelpro.org (accessed January and May 2004).

20. Churchill W, Vander Wall J (1988) *Agents of Repression: The FBI's secret wars against the Black Panther Party and the American Indian Movement.* Cambridge, MA: South End Press.

21. Churchill W, Vander Wall J (1990) The advent of terrorism. In: *The COINTELPRO Papers: Documents from the FBI's secret wars against dissent in the United States.* Cambridge, MA: South End Press, p. 4. See later edition with the COINTELPRO documents: Churchill, Vander Wall (2002, p. 306).

22. Churchill W, Vander Wall J (1990, p. 306).

23. This was so ludicrous as to provoke COINTELPRO veteran John Ryan to refuse to participate. Ryan, who had two commendations to his credit during a 21-year career, and who was less than 2 years short of retirement at the time, was fired as a result of his stand. See Churchill (1990) *The COINTELPRO Papers*, chapter 8 or Churchill, Vander Wall (2002, p. 307).

24. Meanwhile, Plowshares 'terrorists' such as Katya Komisaruk, Jerry Ebner, Helen Woodson, Lin Romano, Joe Gump, Ann and Jim Albertini, George Ostensen, Richard Miller and Father Carl Kabat were being ushered into long prison sentences for such things as 'conspiring' to trespass at US nuclear facilities. See Endnote 23.

25. The CISPES operation included time-honoured COINTELPRO tactics such as the use of infiltrators/provocateurs, disinformation, black bag jobs, telephone intercepts, conspicuous surveillance (to make targets believe 'there's an agent behind every mail box'). See Endnote 23.

26. Chomsky N (2001) The world after September 11, AFSC Conference, 8 December 2001. *ZMagazine*: www.zmag.org/chomskyafter911.htm (accessed 2001–2004).

27. Carter J (2002) The troubling new face of America. Editorial by former President Jimmy Carter in the *International Herald Tribune*, 6 September.

28. Nullis C (2002) UN rights chief blasts terror war. *International Herald Tribune*, 6 September.

29. Carter J (2002).

CHAPTER 7: TERROR TACTIC: THE BOGEYMAN AND DEMONIZING

1. Warner M (2000) *No Go the Bogeyman*. London: Vintage p. 381. I was also inspired by Warner's use of the images of the 'Bogeyman' seen in Figures 7.2 and 7.3.

2. Weber L (2001) *The Holocaust Chronicle*. Lincolnwood, IL: Publications International Ltd.

3. Al-Jalahma UA, of King Faysal University in Al-Damman (2002) The Jewish holiday of Purim. Saudi government daily *Al-Riyadh*, two-part article, 10 and 12 March. Following US condemnation, the editor of Al-Riyadh apologized for printing this article and retracted these lies.

   worldnet.com – posted 13 March 2003: 'Saudi news: Jews use teen blood in pastries. Columnist in daily paper claims "fact" of "Jewish vampires".'

   The Jewish Bulletin archives, 29 March 2002: A myth that never dies, an Editorial: www.jewishbulletin.ca/archives/Mar02/archives02mar29-07.html (accessed 2004).

4. Weber L (2001, p.103).

5. Winant H (2000) Race and race theory. *Annual Review of Sociology* **26**: 169–85.

6. Herek G (1992) Stigma, prejudice and violence against lesbians and gay men. In: Gonsiorek J, Weinrich J (eds) (1992) *Homosexuality: Research implications for public policy*. London: Sage Publications, pp. 60–80; Newton D (1978) Homosexual behavior and child molestation. A review of the evidence. *Adolescence* 13: 29; Groth AN, Birnbaum HJ (1978) Adult sexual orientation and attraction to underage persons. *Archives of Sexual Behavior* 7: 175–181.

7. Facts about homosexuality: http//psychology.ucdavis.edu/rainbow/html/facts_molestation.html (accessed 2003).

8. Leys S, Appleyard C (trans.), Goode P (trans.) (1972) *The Chairman's New Clothes: Mao and the Cultural Revolution*. London: Allison & Busby; Lifton RJ (1970) *Revolutionary Immortality: Mao Tse Tung and the Cultural Revolution*. London: Pelican.

9. Williams S (writer, director) (1994) The Mao Years. Ambrica Productions, WGBH Boston and Channel 4 television, UK (seen on Channel 4 television, London, 25 May 2003).

10. Enterprise, OR, USA.

11. *American Heritage Dictionary of the English Language* (2000) Boston, MA: Houghton Mifflin.

CHAPTER 8: TERROR TACTIC: DEHUMANIZATION

1. Gutman R, Rieff D (eds) (1999) Incitement to genocide. In: *Crimes of War: What the public should know*. New York: W.W. Norton.

2. The Holocaust History Project, Still Images from *Der Ewige Jude*, by Stig Hornshøj-Møller: www.holocaust-history.org/der-ewige-jude/stills.shtml.

3. Metropolitan Police, UK: www.met.police.uk/drugs/campaigns/ratonarat.htm.

4. Stannard D (1992) *The American Holocaust: The conquest of the New World*. New York: Oxford University Press, pp. 261–268.

5. Churchill W (1997) *A Little Matter of Genocide*. San Francisco, CA: City Lights Books, p. 1, and Stannard (1992), p. 268.

6. Stannard D (1992, p. 240–241).

7. Stannard D (1992, p. 240–241).

8. The ethnic cleansing of the Native Americans, particularly the driving of Indians westward, was used as a model for Hitler's policy of 'lebensraum' or 'living space' (Churchill W, 1997, p. 52).

9. Churchill W (1997) Holocaust and denial in the Americas 1492 to present. In: *A Little Matter of Genocide*. San Francisco, CA: City Lights Books, p. 182.

10. Stannard D (1992, p. 121).

11. Stannard D (1992, p. 121).

12. Stannard D (1992, p. 240).

13. Stannard D (1992, p. 240). Stannard refers to Takaki R (1979) *Iron Cages: Race and culture in 19th century America*. New York: Alfred A. Knopf.

14. Stannard D (1992, p. 122).

15. Stannard D (1992, p. 245).

16. Vietnam War Crimes Hearings, 1971: http://members.aol.com/warlibrary/vwchle.htm (accessed 2003)

17. Venables R (1990) Senior Lecturer, American Indian Program, Cornell University, Northeast Indian Quarterly, Spring 1990.

18. Venables R (1990).

19. Venables R (1990).

20. de Birchgrave A (2004) Daily dehumanization. *Washington Times*, 6 January.

21. Levvy G (2004) Daily dehumanization. *Ha'aretz* (newspaper), 12 April.

22. Elon A (2001) The deadlocked city. *New York Review of Books*, 48(16): 18. This is a review of Wasserstein B (2001) *Divided Jerusalem: The struggle for the Holy City*. Boston, MA: Yale University Press.

23. Lerner M (2001) Threats dehumanize Jews who question Israel. Los Angeles, CA, *LA Times*, 18 May. Rabbi Michael Lerner is editor of the journal *Tikkun* and author of *Jewish Renewal: A path to healing and transformation* (1995). New York: Harper Collins.

24. Glick C (2002) No tolerance for genocide. *Jerusalem Post*, 2 August.

25. Moore M, Anderson JW (2001) Suicide bombers give an edge to Palestinians. *Washington Post*, 19 August.

26. Images were seen in countless newspapers worldwide. April and May 2004.

CHAPTER 9: TERROR TACTIC: DESENSITIZATION AND NORMALIZATION

1. Zinn H (2003) *A People's History of the United States*. New York: Pearson Longman, p. 30.
2. Douglas F (1995) *Narrative of the Life of Frederick Douglass*. New York: Questia.com, p. 46.
3. Douglas F (1995, p. 46).
4. Zinn H (2003, p. 29).
5. Zinn H (2003, pp. 30–38).
6. Zinn H (2003, p. 34).
7. Zinn H (2003, p. 34).
8. Zinn H (2003, p. 35).
9. Afro-American Almanac – African American History: www.toptags.com, Historical Documents (accessed 2003).
10. www.Toptags.com (accessed 2003).
11. Zinn H (2003, p. 31).
12. Zinn H (2003, p. 36).
13. Zinn H (2003, p. 36).
14. Zinn H (2003, p. 367.
15. See Endnote 9.
16. US Senate (1976) Intelligence Activities and rights of Americans: final report of Select Committee to study government operations with respect to Intelligence activities, 26 April.
17. Sales W Jr (1994) *From Civil Rights to Black Liberation: Malcolm X and the Organization of Afro-American Unity*. Cambridge MA, South End Press; Churchill W, Vander Wall J (1988) *Agents of Repression: The FBI's secret wars against the Black Panther Party and the American Indian Movement*. Cambridge MA: South End Press.
18. Browning CR (2004) *The Origins of the Final Solution: The evolution of Nazi Jewish policy September 1939–1942*. Lincoln, NE: University of Nebraska Press.
19. Browning CR (2004, p. 424).
20. The Danish Center for Holocaust and Genocide Studies: www.holocaust-education.dk/tidslinjer.asp.
21. The Florida Center for Instructional Technology, The Holocaust Time Line 1933–1945, compiled from a variety of sources including the US Holocaust Memorial Museum in Washington DC; South Carolina Voices: Lessons from the Holocaust, and others: http://fcit.coedu.usf.edu/holocaust/timeline/TEXTLINE.HTM.
22. Weber L (2001) *The Holocaust Chronicle*. Lincolnwood, IL: Louis Weber Publications International Ltd, pp. 85–86.
23. Weber L (2001).
24. Long B (1940) Memo from Assistant Secretary of State, Breckenridge Long to State Department officials, Public Broadcasting Station, America and the Holocaust, 26 June: www.pbs.org/wgbn/amex/holocaust/filmmore/reference/primary/#bar (accessed April 2004).

25. Amnesty International. It's in our hands: stop violence against women. London, Amnesty International Publications: www.amnesty.org (accessed 2004)

26. Hawkins D, Humes M (2002) Human rights and domestic violence. *Political Science Quarterly* **117**: 231–57.

CHAPTER 10: TERROR TACTIC: TARGETING LEADERS

1. Danner M (1997) *The New York Review of Books*, 4 December.

2. Sarafian A (2002) Armenian Forum. Report on Kurdish and Armenian Genocides, Focus of London Seminar; Sarafian and Fernandes, keynote speakers.

3. Fernandes D (2002) Armenian Forum, Report on Kurdish and Armenian Genocides Focus of London Seminar; Sarafian and Fernandes, keynote speakers. Fernandes D (1998) The Kurdish genocide in Turkey 1924–1998. *Armenian Forum* **1**: 57–107.

4. Cowan J (1992) *The Aborigine Tradition*. Boston: Elements Books, p. 83.

5. Conflict archive on the internet: http://cain.ulst.ac.uk/hmso/spa1922.htm (accessed April 2004).

6. Ewing KD, Gearty CA (2000) *The Struggle for Civil Liberties: Political freedom and the rule of law in Britain 1914–1945.* London: Open University Press.

7. De Baroid, C. (2000) *Ballymurphy and the Irish War.* London: Pluto Press, p. 96.

8. Wilson G. *Eight Centuries of England in Ireland: A synopsis of Irish history*: www.tripod.com (accessed 2002); De Baroid C (1989, 2000, p. 199).
   Keogh D (2002) Preface. In: Moody TW, Martin FX (eds), *The Course of Irish History*, 4th edn. Boulder, CO: Roberts Rinehart Publishers.

9. Cummings M, IAUC National Secretary, and Fox T, IAUC Human Rights Director, 3 May 1998, 'Human rights violations in Northern Ireland', Excerpts from Human rights reports: www.iauc.org/hrexcerpts.htm (accessed 2004) and De Baroid C (1989, 2000) *Ballymurphy and the Irish War.* London: Pluto Press, p. 199.

10. De Baroid C (1989, 2000, p. 200).

11. Mandela N (1995) *Long Walk to Freedom: The autobiography of Nelson Mandela,* London: Little Brown & Co, p. 233.

12. Marcy S (1967) The stakes in China's struggle: revolution vs restoration: www.workers.org/marcy/cd/index.htm (accessed 2003).

13. ChinaWN.com (2003).

14. ChinaWN.com (2003).

15. Valentine D (2000) *The Phoenix Program*. Lincoln, NE: iUniverse.com; New York: Harper Collins – William Morrow Company (1990); Avon books (1992); also Moyar M (1997) *Phoenix and the Birds of Prey: CIA's secret campaign to destroy the Viet Cong.* London: Airlife Publishing; Cook J (1997) *The Advisor: Phoenix Program in Vietnam.* London: Schiffer Publishing Ltd.

16. Prados J (March 2003) *Lost Crusader: The secret wars of CIA Director William Colby.* New York: Oxford University Press.

17. Elliston J (dossier ed.), McGehee R (former CIA officer and critic of agency) (1971)

Vietnam's Phoenix Program. *New York Times*, 3 August, p. 10. From www.backspace.com/notes/2003/02/06/x.html, www.vwip.org/articles/m/ McGeheeRalph_VietnamsPhoenixProgram.htm, and Documents from the Phoenix programme, on the website, 'The Memory Hole', www.thememoryhole.org/phoenix, supplied and introduced by Doug Valentine. See also Valentine D (2000).

18. Ralph McGehee, see Endnote 17.

19. Ralph McGehee, see Endnote 17.

20. Social Design Notes, Psy Ops Comics IV: Vietnam (2002–2003): www.backspace.com/notes/2003/02/06/x.html. See also Valentine D (2000).

21. Farnsworth E on 30 April 1996 interviews Hersh B about William Colby, The Warrior Priest, Online News Hour, Public Broadcasting Station, www.pbs.org; Press Reports about William Colby from Arlington National Cemetery at time of his death: www.arlingtoncemetery.net.

22. Falk R (2001) The Vietnam syndrome. *Nation Magazine*, 9 July. Richard Falk teaches international law at Princeton University.)

23. Falk R (2001).

24. Chomsky N (1991) *Media Control*. New York: Seven Stories Press.

25. Hanley, C., Choe, S.H. and Mendoza, M. (2001) *The Bridge at No Gun Ri: A hidden nightmare from the Korean war*. New York, Henry Holt & Co., pp. ix, x.

26. Abdul-Quader S (2004) Associated Press writer. Over 600 killed in Fallujah, April: News24.com; also reported in Houston Chronical, Denver Post, and elsewhere.

27. Kraehenbuehl P (2004) Statement of Director of operations for the International Committee of the Red Cross, in Red Cross describes systematic abuse in Iraq. *International Herald Tribune*, 8–9 May.

28. *Herald Tribune*, 10 May 2004; Okabe M (2004) Briefing – Associated Spokeswoman for the Secretary-General of the United Nations, UN Headquarters, New York, 14 April (www.un.org/News/ossg/hilites/hilites_arch_view.asp?HighID=20 – accessed May 2004); Associated Press, 8 January 2004, Amnesty confusion angers relatives in Iraq. The Guardian Unlimited; Associated Press, 6 October 2003, US Military closes makeshift prison Camp Cropper; Charleston.net: www.charleston.net (accessed June 2004); Marqusee M, June 2004, 'The lessons of Abu Ghraib', *Red Pepper* (raising the political temperature), London: www.redpepper.org.

29. US Senate (23 April 1976) Supplementary detailed Staff Reports on Intelligence Activities and the Rights of Americans, Book III, Final Report of the Select Committee to Study Governmental Operations with Respect to Intelligence Activities, see Michigan State University Libraries Electronic Resources or Public Broadcasting, pbs.org/now/politics/cointelpro.html (accessed April 2004). Full report and documents on www.cointelpro.org.

30. See Endnote 29.

31. Churchill W, Vander Wall J (2002) *The COINTELPRO Papers: Documents from the FBI's secret wars against dissent in the United States*. Cambridge, MA: South End Press, pp. 95–99.

32. Churchill W, Vander Wall J (2002, pp. 95–99).

33. Churchill W, Vander Wall J (1988) *Agents of Repression: The FBI's secret wars against the Black Panther Party and the American Indian Movement*. Cambridge, MA: South End Press.

34. Churchill W (1999) Wages of COINTELPRO still evident in Omaha Black Panther Case. In: *Zcommentary*, *ZMagazine*, March.

35. Churchill W (1999).

36. International Secretariat of Amnesty International (July 1998) News Release Subject: 'Crucial information 27 years too late for Black Panther'. AI INDEX: AMR 51/41/98 1.

37. Churchill W, Vander Wall J (2002) – see Endnote 29.

38. Over 50 000 pages of the Senate Committee Hearing, Church Committee records became declassified and available to the public from 1992. These can be accessed on www.cointel.org (accessed 2003, 2004).

39. US Senate GPO (23 April 1976) Intelligence Activities and the Rights of Americans, Book II, Final Report of the Select Committee to Study Governmental Operations with Respect to Intelligence Activities, 94th Congress, 2nd session. In Introduction and Summary, C. Summary of Main Problems 1. The number of people affected by Domestic Intelligence Activity. Declassified documents arranged by Paul Wolf, accessed on www.cointel.org or by the Michigan State University Libraries, Electronic Resources (http://er./lib.msu.edu – accessed 2003, 2004).

40. Bear A (2002) Encounter, interview with Robert Manning, Boston. *Boston Globe Magazine*: www.boston.com/globe/magazine/2002/1006/encounter.htm (accessed 2003).

41. Rogovin ZV (1996) 1937: Stalin's Year of Terror. Lecture by Rogovin ZV, University of Melbourne, Australia, 28 May.

42. Courtois S, Werth N, Panné JL, Paczkowski A, Bartosek K, Margolin JL (1999) In: Kramer M (ed.), Murphy J (trans.), *The Black Book of Communism: Crimes, terror, repression*. Boston, MA: Harvard University Press.

43. McShea B (2000) *Opening the Book, Remembering Communism and Counting the Victims*. Boston, MA: McShea Publisher, The Harvard Salient, Commencement Issue.

44. Judt T (2003) In book review for Courtois et al., *Black Book of Communism*, Harvard University Press, www.hup.harvard.edu/reviews/COUBLA_R.html (accessed April 2004).

45. Ryan A (2003) *New York Times Book Review* – see endnote 42 above.

46. See discussion about leadership in Mindell A (1993) *The Leader as Martial Artist*. San Francisco, CA: Harper Collins; Mindell A (1995) *Sitting in the Fire*. Portland, OR: Lao Tse Press.

47. Mindell A (1993, pp. 148–160).

48. Mindell A (1993, p. 50).

49. Mindell (1993) also looks at leadership as a role belonging to the community.

50. Sheehan SM (2003) *Anarchism*. London: Reaktion Books, p. 25.

51. Hirsch E (1992) *Urban Revolt: Ethnic politics in the nineteenth-century Chicago Labor Movement*. Berkley, CA: University of California Press, Chapter 2.

52. Sheehan (2003, p. 7).

53. Sheehan (2003, p. 10).

CHAPTER 11: TERROR TACTIC: TORTURE, BREAKING BODY AND SPIRIT

1. References for torture: United Nations High Commission for Refugees UNHCR www.unhchr.ch/html/menu3/b/h_cat39.htm (accessed 2002) and Office of Human Rights OHR UN http://dcc2.bumc.bu.edu/refugees/definitions.htm (accessed 2002).

2. Sorrig K (1997) Brutal torture is practiced systematically all over the world. A series of articles on torture and activities of Research Center for Torture, RCT and International Rehabilitation Council for Torture Victims, IRCT, Copenhagen newspaper, *Berlingske Tidende*.

3. Genefke I (1997) medical director of RCT, Copenhagen. Torture as a global problem – creating awareness of torture. Report of International Rehabilitation Council for Torture Victims, IRCT activities.

4. Sorrig K (1997) Torture consolidates power, Copenhagen. Paper of Rehabilitation and Research Center for Torture Victims. International Rehabilitation Council for Torture Victims.

5. Reegali DM (2002) Presentation at conference: Working with Trauma and Transcultural Approaches to Treating Torture Survivors, coordinated by David Jones, Lutheran Family Services Refugee Center, Portland, OR, USA. See also Blum W (2002) *Rogue State*. London: Zed Books, pp. 49–57.

6. Reegali DM (2002). See also Waller D (1998) Weapons of torture: a TIME investigation turns up evidence of loose controls and US companies shipping stun guns to countries that practice torture, 6 April: www.cnn.com/ALLPOLITICS/ 1998/03/31/time/weapons.html (accessed 2003, 2004).

7. The Medical Foundation for the Care of Victims of Torture (www.torturecare.org.uk link to 'Surviving torture', wbur.org/documentaries/torture – accessed 2004).

8. Reegali DM (1998) Presentation at conference: Working with Trauma and Transcultural Approaches to Treating Torture Survivors, coordinated by David Jones, Lutheran Family Services Refugee Center, Portland, OR, USA.

9. IRCT (1997) *Torture as a Global Problem*. Copenhagen: IRCT Report.

10. Reegali DM (1998) Presentation at conference: Working with Trauma and Transcultural Approaches to Treating Torture Survivors, coordinated by David Jones, Lutheran Family Services Refugee Center, Portland, OR, USA.

11. Cassese A (1996) *Inhuman States: Imprisonment, detention and torture in Europe today*. London: Polity Press.

CHAPTER 12: TERROR TACTIC: TARGETING THE SOUL OF COMMUNITY

1. Allen B (1996) *Rape Warfare: The hidden genocide in Bosnia Herzegovina and Croatia*. Minneapolis, MN, University of Minnesota Press

2. Ramet SP (1996) *Balkan Babel: The disintegration of Yugoslavia from the death of Tito to ethnic war*, 2nd edn. Boulder, CO: Westview Press, p. 287.

3. Gutman C (September 2000) Kosovo: Burned books and blasted shrines, an interview with Riedlmayer A. *Courier News*. NJ: UNESCO: www.unesco.org/courier/2000_09/uk/signe.htm.

4. US Tibet Committee; see www.ustibet.org.

5. Heine H (1821) *Almansor.* The now famous quote is inscribed in a memorial at the Dachau concentration camp.

6. American Library Association: www.ala.org (accessed 2003).

7. Asian Art and Architecture: Art and Design: 382/582 Template.cfm?Section=Intellectual_Freedom_Issues&Template=ContentManagement/ContentDisplay.cfm@ContentID=28402 (accessed 2003).

8. Religious Tolerance Organization: www.religioustolerance.org/wic_burn1.htm (accessed 2003).

9. Miesel S (2001) Who burned the witches? In: *Crisis: Politics, Culture and the Church magazine, The Morley Institute.* Washington DC: Trinity Communications, pp. 21–6 (posted on www.catholicculture.org).

10. Stephens W (2000) *Demon Lovers: Witchcraft, sex and belief.* Chicago IL: University of Chicago.

11. Stephens W (2000).

12. Gover K (2000) Bureau of Indian Affairs, A formal acknowledgement was made of the US role in the abuse of Native American children, 8 September: www.hermanlaw.com/boardschool.htm and http://mytwobeadsworth.com/brdschoollawsuit/81403.html (accessed 2003).

    Davis J (2001) American Indian boarding school experiences: recent studies from Native perspectives. *Magazine of History,* Winter: 15. Organization of American Historians, Bloomington, IN.

    Archuleta M, Child B, Lomaswaima T (eds) (1999) *Away from Home: American Indian boarding school experiences.* Phoenix, AZ: Heard Museum.

13. Smith A (2003) *Soul Wound: The legacy of Native American schools.* Amnesty Now 29(2). amestyusa.org/amnestynow/soulwound.html (accessed 2003).

CHAPTER 13: TERROR TACTIC: DISINFORMATION

1. *Oxford English Dictionary*, 2nd edn, 1989. Oxford: Oxford University Press.

2. Chomsky N (2000) *Rogue States*. London: Pluto Press.

3. Bagdikian B (1997) *Media Monopoly*. Boston, MA: Beacon Press.

4. Solomon N (2002) Journalists doing somersaults: self censorship and the rise of the corporate media state. In: Kick R (ed.), *You are Being Lied To*. New York: The Disinformation Company Ltd, p. 26,

5. Smith H (2003) Blix: I was smeared by the Pentagon. *The Guardian*, 11 June.

6. Chomsky N (2002) *Media Control*. New York: Seven Stories Press, p. 12; Chomsky N (1982) Intellectuals and the state. In: *Towards a New Cold War: Essays on the current crisis and how we got there*. New York: Random House; Ewen S (1998) *PR! A social history of spin*. New York: Basic Books.

7. Chomsky N (2002, p. 15).

8. Gutman R, Rieff D (eds) (1999) *Crimes of War: What the public should know*. New York: W.W. Norton, pp. 193–194.

9. Silber L, Little A (1995) *The Death of Yugoslavia*. London: Penguin, p. 147.

10. Silber L, Little A (1995, p. 147).

11. Pervanic K (1999) *The Killing Days*. London: Blake Publishing, pp. 3–27.

12. Gutman R, Rieff D (1999, p. 56).

13. Churchill W, VanderWall J (2002) *The COINTELPRO Papers*. Cambridge, MA: South End Press, p. 132.

14. Churchill W, VanderWall J (2002, p.12).

15. Churchill W, VanderWall J (2002, pp. 136–137).

16. Churchill W, VanderWall J (2002, pp. 216, 217); COINTELPRO, The Sabotage of Legitimate Dissent, The Jean Seberg Smear: www.whatreallyhappened.com/RANCHO/POLITICS/COINTELPRO/SEB.seb.html (accessed 2002).

17. Lee MA, Solomon N (1990) *Unreliable Sources: A guide to detecting bias in news media*. New York: A Lyle Stuart Book, Carol Publishing Group, p. 127.

18. The concept of the 'edge' is central to the theory and practice of Process Oriented Psychology (A Mindell), and refers to the perimeter of how we identify, the belief systems governing our awareness, and the gateway into the unknown.

19. David Hamburg stated that one of the things blocking violence prevention is idealistic thinking. Hamburg D (2002) *No More Killing Fields: Preventing deadly conflict*. Carnegie Commission on Preventing Deadly Conflict. Lanham, MD: Rowman & Littlefield.

Chapter 14: Beyond terror

1. Younge G, Black I (2003) War crime vote fuels US anger at Europe. *The Guardian*, 11 June

2. Staff and agencies (2003) US detains children at Guantanamo Bay. *The Guardian*, 23 April.

3. BBC evening news, 12 June 2003.

4. Weir P (director) (1998) 'The Truman Show'. Paramount Pictures with Jim Carrey as Truman.

5. Mindell A (1993) *The Shaman's Body*. San Francisco, CA: Harper, p. 199. The term 'death walk' refers to an attitude that 'every step could be your last'. According to Don Genaro (from Carlos Castaneda's works on the teachings of Don Juan), a band of male warriors lived in the mountains. When one member disobeyed the group's

rules, he had to face the others. If he was found guilty, they lined up to shoot him. If he walked in such a special way that no one could pull the trigger, or if he survived his wounds, he was free. Some survived, because of their personal power, freedom and detachment.

6. Mindell developed the term 'ghost roles': Mindell A (2000) *Quantum Mind*. Portland, OR: Lao Tse Press, p. 550.

7. Mindell A (2000, p. 549).

8. Mindell A (2000, pp. 550–551).

9. Mindell A (1993) *The Leader as Martial Artist*. San Francisco, CA: Harper Collins, p. 25. Mindell describes roles as Time Spirits or Zeitgeister, emphasizing the archetypal, temporal and transitory nature of roles in a personal or group field.

10. In his important contributions to the field of linguistics, Noam Chomsky described how language has a 'deep structure' and 'surface structure'. As a result of 'transformational rules' a single deep structure can transform into various possible utterances at the surface structure level. Conversely, two very different deep structures can result in the same surface structure utterance, a sentence with two possible meanings. See Chomsky N (1965) *Aspects of the Theory of Syntax*. Boston, MA: MIT Press. I am interested in how this concept is useful metaphorically to describe the interaction of roles as a kind of 'deep structure' to personal and collective interaction and conflict. The interaction of the roles of the oppressed and oppressor can result in different outer versions of the conflict. Conflicts also transform, when people are not frozen in one role or the other, but can interact with awareness within the two roles.

11. Mindell A (2000, p. 549).

12. The ability to communicate about trauma in a collective/group setting is vital for reconciliation and building sustainable community, but it takes great care. If individual stories are not heard in community, the individual never feels that she or he can truly return. If the collective stories are not heard, the society cannot move forward. Yet, telling the story can evoke or re-trigger trauma for both the person telling the story and those listening. The isolation surrounding the experience will be compounded, if the community cannot hear the story. The reasons the community cannot hear the trauma also deserve care, understanding and attention. (Trauma is the subject of Part 3 of this work.)

13. Mindell A (1995) *Sitting in the Fire*. Portland, OR: Lao Tse Press; Mindell (1993).

14. Parekh B (1989) *Gandhi's Political Philosophy: A critical examination*. London: Macmillan, p. 103; reference to Iyer R (1986) *Moral and Political Writings of Mahatma Gandhi*, Vol II. Oxford: Clarendon Press, pp. 67ff.

15. Parekh B (1989, p. 89).

16. Mandela N (1995) *Long Walk to Freedom: The autobiography of Nelson Mandela*. London: Little Brown & Co, p. 751.

CHAPTER 15: OUR STORY – THE DYNAMICS OF TRAUMA

1. American Psychiatric Association (1994) Posttraumatic stress disorder 309.81. *Diagnostic and Statistical Manual of Mental Disorders*, 4th edn. Washington DC: APA, pp. 424–42.

2. See the appendix for a list of symptoms of post-traumatic stress disorder in individuals, as well as a corresponding chart that I have created for community trauma and collective dynamics of trauma in the wider society.
    Audergon A (2004) Collective trauma: the nightmare of history. Psychotherapy and Politics International 2(1).

3. Rieff D (1996) *Slaughterhouse: Bosnia and the failure of the West*. New York: Touchstone Books, p. 103.

4. Hermann J (1997) *Trauma and Recovery: The aftermath of violence – from domestic abuse to political terror*. New York: Basic Books, p. 1.

5. Hermann J (1997).

6. Mindell defines metacommunication as communicating about our communication, the ability to comment on a message, its sender or its effect. Mindell A (1998) *City Shadows*. London: Routledge, p. 40.

7. Shay J (1994) *Achilles in Vietnam: Combat trauma and the undoing of character*. New York: Touchstone Books, p. 188.

8. Shay J (1994, p. 188) and personal experiences.

9. Shay J (1994, p. 189).

10. Shay J (1994, p. 188).

11. Bracken P (2002) *Trauma: Culture, meaning and philosophy*. London: Whurr Publishers Ltd.

12. Robben ACGM, Suarez-Orozco, MM (eds) (2002) *Cultures under Siege: Collective violence and trauma*. Cambridge: Cambridge University Press.

13. Renouf V (2000) *To Life, LeChaim*. London: Minerva Press, p. 69.

14. Renouf V (2000, p.70).

15. Churchill W (2002) I am indigenist: Notes on the ideology of the Fourth World. In: *Acts of Rebellion: A Ward Churchill Reader*. London: Routledge.

16. Sells M (2001) Kosovo mythology and the Bosnian genocide. In: Bartov O, Mack P (eds), *In God's Name*. New York: Berghan Books, pp. 183–184.

17. Sells M (2001, p. 190).

18. Holocaust revision theories.

19. Suny RG (2001) Religion, ethnicity and nationalism. In: Bartov O, Mack P (eds), *In God's Name*. New York: Berghan Books, pp. 25–26.

20. Suny RG (2001, pp. 25–26).

21. Sells M (2001, p. 194).

22. Longman T (2001) Christian churches and genocide in Rwanda. In: Bartov O, Mack P (eds), *In God's Name*. New York: Berghan Books, pp. 152–153.

CHAPTER 16: TRAUMA AND REFUGE

1. Shay J (1994) *Achilles in Vietnam: Combat trauma and the undoing of character*. New York: Touchstone Books, p. 17.
2. Shay J (1994, p. 20).
3. United Nations High Commission for Refugees (2003) *Global Refugee Trends*. Geneva: UNHCR, p. 2.
4. United Nations High Commission for Refugees (2004) *Basic Facts: Refugees by Numbers*. www.unhcr.ch.
5. www.refugeecare.org.uk.

CHAPTER 17: REPLAYS OF VIOLENT CONFLICT AND BREAKING THE CYCLE

1. In personal relationships, there is a useful way of dealing with this phenomenon to interrupt cycles of mutual blaming. You can stand accountable for what you are accused of – even if it's only 1 per cent. You can almost always find that 1 per cent. This can break the cycle of mutual accusations and revenge, but you have to accept that 1 per cent fully, without 'buts', defensiveness or a returned accusation at the end of your sentence! After assuming accountability, the process can go on to make sure all sides are supported to express themselves as fully as possible and interact. See Mindell A (1995) *The Dreambody in Relationship*. London: Routledge.
2. Shay J (1994) *Achilles in Vietnam: Combat trauma and the undoing of character*. New York: Touchstone Books, p. 96.
3. Mollon P (2002) *Remembering Trauma, A Psychotherapists's Guide to Memory and Illusion*. London: Whurr Publishers, p. 2. Mollon refers to Alford CP (1997) *What Evil Means to us*. New York: Cornell University Press and Mollon P (2000) Is human nature intrinsically abusive? Reflections on the psychodynamics of evil. In: McCluskey U, C-A Cooper (eds), *Psychodynamic Perspectives on Abuse. The cost of fear*. London: Jessica Kingsley.
4. Morris B (2001) *Righteous Victims: A history of the Arab-Israeli conflict 1881–1999*. New York: Vintage Books, p. 311. (Morris cites Segev T (1994) *The Seventh Million*. Tel Aviv: Keter/Domino, p. 368 (in Hebrew).)
5. Shay J (1994, p. 89).
6. Selden K, Selden M (eds) (1990) *The Atomic Bomb: Voices from Hiroshima and Nagasaki*. Armonk, ME: Sharpe Publisher.
7. Iccho I, Mayor of Nagasaki (2003) Nagasaki peace declaration, ZNET, Japan and Ogle G (1997) The story of the Hibakusha: survivors of Hiroshima and Nagasaki, Australia, *Greenleft weekly*, 10 August, greenleft.org.au (accessed April 2004).
8. See Mindell A (2002) *The Deep Democracy of Open Forums*. Charlottesville, VA: Hampton Roads. See also CFOR (Community Forums or Community Force for Change): www.cfor.info.
9. The term 'hot spots' as used by Arnold Mindell is mentioned throughout this book and discussed in detail in Chapter 25.

10. Moreno JL (1985) *Psychodrama*, 7th edn. New York: Beacon House.

11. Boal A (1985) *Theatre of the Oppressed* (C McBride, trans.). Theatre Communications Group; Boal A, Jackson A (1999) *Legislative Theatre: Using performance to make politics*. London: Routledge.

12. See our projects combining theatre, Process Work and community forums (www.processwork-audergon.com, www.cfor.info), and see Improbable Theatre (www.improbable.co.uk).

13. Odyssey 8: 78ff, quoted in Shay J (1994, p. 188).

14. Although different from war trauma, personal and family trauma from abuse carries the same pattern. The trauma is both personal and political. We have worked with many patients with trauma from abuse in psychiatric hospitals and worked with these dynamics in community forums on mental health.

CHAPTER 18: BEYOND THE ORDINARY

1. Bartov O, Mack P (eds) (2001) *In God's Name*. New York: Berghahn Books. This collection of essays addresses the active involvement of religion, in tandem with the state in organized murder in the cases of the Armenian, Jewish, Rwanda and Bosnian genocides.

2. Term 'high' and 'low' dream used in Arnold Mindell's Process Oriented Psychology.

3. The Columbine shootings, April 1999, in Colorado, USA.

4. Gellner E (1998) *Nationalism*. London: Phoenix, p. 3.

5. Bae JH (text), Shamar I (artwork) (2001) *In the World of Gods and Goddesses: The mythic art of Indra Shamar*. Novato, CA: Mandala Publishing, p. 10 (or www.mandala.org).

6. Bae, Shamar (2001, p. 57).

7. Trungpa C (2002) In: Sakyong M, Baker J, Casper M (eds), Eddy G (illustrator), *Spiritual Materialism*. Boston, MA: Shambhala Publications.

8. Shay J (1994) *Achilles in Vietnam*. New York: Touchstone Books, p. 49.

9. Shay J (1994, p. 39).

CHAPTER 19: WITH THE FIELD

1. The *Bhagavad Gita* is a central religious text in India. It is a relatively brief episode of the Mahabharata. Thomas P (1957, 1989) *Epics, Myths and Legends of India*. Bombay: D.B Taraporevala Sons & Co. Private Ltd, pp. 49–56; Waterstone R (1995) *India*. London: Duncan Baird Publishers, pp. 60–61.

2. Frazer (1964) *The New Golden Bough*. Edited and with notes and Foreword by Gaster, Theodor. New York: a Mentor Book from New American Library.

3. Sinha I (1993) *Tantra: Search for ecstasy*. London: Hamlyn, p. 52.

4. Atran S (2004) Understanding suicide terrorism. *Interdisciplines* (Interdisciplines.org). McCaurley C (2002) Psychological issues in understanding terrorism and the

response to terrorism. In: Stout CE (ed) *The Psychology of Terrorism: Theoretical understandings and perspectives*, Volume III, pp. 3–29. Westport, CT: Praeger.

5. Personal conversations with Anty Heretik and Stanya Studentova.

    Radio Prague ENews, report on 10-year anniversary of the Velvet Revolution, and Rob Cameron, 22 January 1999: http://archiv.radio.cz/news/EN/1999/22.11.htm (accessed 2004); information about Marta Kubisova on www.raffem.com/martaKubisovany.htm.

6. Several studies have shown that combat veterans with war trauma use alcohol and drugs to try to control the symptoms of insomnia, nightmares, irritability and outbursts of rage. Drug abuse ultimately compounds their difficulty and sense of alienation. See Hermann J (1997) *Trauma and Recovery*. New York: Basic Books, p. 44.

    In Croatia, people spoke about how it was not only the most severely traumatized who used alcohol; rather abuse of alcohol is a widespread problem throughout society in the aftermath of the war.

CHAPTER 20: OVER THE EDGE

1. Hedges C (2002) *War is a Force that Gives us Meaning*. Oxford: Public Affairs.

2. Shay J (1994) *Achilles in Vietnam*. New York: Touchstone Books, p. 40.

3. Shay J (1994, p. xviii).

4. Shay J (1994, p. xiv).

5. Shay J (1994, p. xvi).

6. Shay J (1994, p. 77) and see his notes.

7. Shay J (1994, p. 80).

8. Shay J (1994, p. 98).

9. Shay J (1994) describes how the berserker state is debilitating psychologically for the survivor, and a leading cause of death in war.

10. *Probert Encyclopedia of Norse Mythology*: www.probertencylopaedia.com/D4.HTM (accessed 2003).

11. Campbell J (1976) *The Masks of God: Creative mythology*. New York: Viking, Penguin.

12. Chekhov M (1991) *To the Actor*. New York: Harper Collins, p. xxiii.

13. Levin J (director) (1995) Don Juan de Marco, film.

14. Laing RD (1990) *The Politics of Experience and the Bird of Paradise*. London: Penguin Books, p. 24.

15. Audergon A (1992) Gates of society: Investigating life on a psychiatric ward, manuscript adapted from PhD dissertation; Audergon A, Audergon JC (1994) Looking for unicorns. *Journal for Process Oriented Psychology* 6(1). Together with Jean-Claude Audergon, I have been applying process work to work with people in mental hospitals, over many years. 'Gates of society' is about a project in an inner city in the USA, and 'Looking for unicorns' describes the first few years of a project in the UK. We conducted many seminars over a period of 10 years in a project in the UK, with psychiatric professionals and people using these services and studying together.

We have also facilitated several forums on community mental health in the UK, with psychiatric professionals, patients, carers and family members, and other people involved in community service, such as housing, law and policing.

16. Mindell A (1988) *City Shadows*. London: Routledge, pp. 11, 12.

17. Family therapists, such as M Bowen (systems) and S Minuchin (structural family therapy).

18. Mindell A (1988).

19. Harrel S (1974) When a ghost becomes a God. In: Wolf AP (ed), *Religion and Ritual in Chinese Society*. San Diego, CA: Stanford University Press, pp. 146–148.

20. Bryant D (2004) *Ancestors and Ghosts: The Philosophic and Religious Origins of the Hungry Ghost Festival*. http://homepagespics.edu.hk/faculty/bryantd/asian_studies/hungry_ghosts.htm#intro (accessed August 2004)

21. Trungpa comments on the realm of the hungry ghosts. Fremantle F, Trungpa C (1975/1992) *The Tibetan Book of the Dead*. Shambhala Pocket Classics. Boston, MA: Shambhala, pp. 15–16.

CHAPTER 21: CUTTING THROUGH

1. Campbell J (1972) *The Hero with a Thousand Faces*. Princeton, NJ: Princeton University Press.

2. The 'Hero's Journey' has also been used not only to understand the individuation process, but also to understand the roots of story structure and support writers in creating stories. See Vogler C (1998) *The Writer's Journey: Mythic structure for writers*. Seattle WA: Michael Wiese Productions.

CHAPTER 22: WAKE UP

1. Glover J (2001) *Humanity: A moral history of the twentieth century*. London: Pimlico, p. 329.

2. Trungpa C (1992) In: Fremantle F (trans.), Trungpa C (commentary), *The Tibetan Book of the Dead*. Boston, MA: Shambhala, p. xviii.

3. Mindell A (1995) *Sitting in the Fire: Large group transformation using conflict and diversity*. Portland, OR: Lao Tse Press.

4. See Mindell A (1993) *The Leader as Martial Artist: Techniques and strategies for resolving conflict and creating community*. San Francisco, CA: Harper Collins.

5. Chan, Wing-Tsit (1969) *A Source Book on Chinese Philosophy*. Princeton, NJ: Princeton University Press; Perry JW (1987) *The Heart of History: Individuality in evolution*. New York: State University of New York Press, p. 76.

6. Jung C (1968) *Collected Works*, Vol. 13. Princeton: Princeton University Press, p. 16.

7. Jung CG (1978) *The Collected Works*, particularly Vol. 8, *Structure and Dynamics of the Psyche*. London: Routledge & Kegan Paul.

8. Mindell A (1995).

9. von Bertalanffy L (1968) *General Systems Theory: Foundations, development, and applications*. New York: George Braziller, p. 37.

10. Gleik J (1987) *Chaos: Making a new science*. New York: Penguin Books.

11. Progogine I, Stengers I (1984) *Order out of Chaos*. New York: Bantam Books, p. 203.

12. Ibid, pp. 197–203.

13. Santa Fe Institute: www.santafe.edu/sfi/organization/vision.html (accessed 2002).

14. Crutchfield JP, Schuster P (eds) (2002) Preface. In: *Evolutionary Dynamics: Exploring the interplay of selection, accident, neutrality, and function*. Santa Fe: Santa Fe Institute.

15. *About Chaos*, a quarterly online interdisciplinary journal of non-linear science, published by the American Institute of Physics, Boston, MA. In 'About us', 'Paradigms of nonlinear science': http://chaos.aip.org/staff.jsp#motive (accessed 2002, 2004).

CHAPTER 23: CHAOS, WARFARE AND CONFLICT RESOLUTION

1. Weeks, Major MR (2001) US Air Force, Chaos, complexity and conflict. In: *Air and Space Power Chronicles, Air and Space Power Journal*, 16 July, Maxwell Al.: www.airpower.maxwell.af.mil/airchronicles/cc/Weeks.html (accessed 2002, 2004).

2. Weeks MR (2001).

3. Weeks MR (2001), p. 9.

4. Weeks MR (2001), p. 5.

5. Weeks MR (2001), p. 6.

6. For a range of references on Social Darwinism, see: http://en.wikipedia.org/wiki/social_Darwinism (accessed August 2004).

7. Olson E, Eoyang G, Beckhad R and Vaill P (2001) *Facilitating Organizational Change: Lessons from Complexity Science*. San Francisco, CA: Jossey-Bass/Pfeiffer.

   Lucas C, Milov Y (1997) *Conflicts as Emergent Phenomena of Complexity*. CalresCo Group. Paper presented in Russian at the Ukrainian Conflict Resolution Association Seminar, November 1997.

8. Dent EB, University of Maryland (2003) The complexity science OD practitioner. *Organization Development Journal* 21(2).

9. Mindell A (1986) *Rivers Way*. London: Penguin.

10. Mindell A (1995) *Sitting in the Fire*. For an excellent synopsis of 'worldwork', see Totton N (2000) *Psychotherapy and Politics*. London: Sage Publications, pp. 45–48.

11. Mindell A (2000) *Quantum Mind*. Portland, OR: Lao Tse Press.

12. Hot spots are discussed in detail in Chapter 25. See Mindell A (1995) Sitting in the Fire: Large group transformation using conflict and diversity. Portland, OR: Lao Tse Press.

CHAPTER 24: GETTING BACK IN BED TOGETHER – AN AWARENESS REVOLUTION

1. Micheelle Edwards, Mana Yoga Center, Hanalei, Kauai, Hawaii.

2. Cogswell C, Schiotz U (1996) Navigation in the information age: potential uses of GIS for sustainability and self-determination in Hawaii. MA Thesis in social and cultural anthropology, California Institute of Integral Studies, section 2.1.1 maps and culture (www.hawaii-nation.org/gis/2-theory.html#2.1.1 – accessed 2002, 2004).

3. Cogswell C, Schiotz U (1996, 2.1.1); refer to Turnbull D, Watson H (1993) *Maps are Territories, Science is an Atlas*. Chicago IL: University of Chicago Press, p. 5.

4. Cogswell C, Schiotz U (1996, 2.1.1).

5. Cogswell C, Schiotz U (1996); refer to Harley JB (1988) Maps, knowledge and power. In: Cosgrove D, Daniels S (eds), *The Iconography of Landscape*. Cambridge, MA: Cambridge University Press, p. 282.

6. Cogswell C, Schiotz U (1996); refer to Harley JB (1989) Deconstructing the map. *Cartographica* (2): 1–20.

7. Cogswell C, Schiotz U (1996); refer to Berry T, Swimme B (1992) *The Universe Story*. New York: Harper, p. 213.

8. Atlan H (1991) Uncommon finalities. In: Thompson WI (ed.), *Gaia: A Way of Knowing*. West Stockbridge, MA: Lindisfarne Press, p. 120.

9. Atlan H (1991, p. 110.

10. Quoted in Campbell J (1982) *Grammatical Man*. New York: Touchstone Books.

11. Jung CG (1970) *Collected Works of CG Jung*, Vol. 8: *Structure and Dynamics of the Psyche*, Bollingen Series. Princeton, NJ: Princeton University Press.

12. Mindell A (2000) *Quantum Mind*. Portland, OR: Lao Tse Press.

13. Mindell A (1986) *River's Way*. London: Penguin; Mindell (2000).

14. Mahnken TG (1996) War in the information age. Joint Force Quarterly, Winter 1995–96, pp. 39–43.

15. Thompson WI (ed.) (1991) Preface. In: *Gaia: A Way of Knowing: political implications of the new biology*. West Stockbridge, MA: Lindisfarne Press, p. 8.

CHAPTER 25: HOT SPOTS AND THE DIFFERENCE THAT MAKES A DIFFERENCE

1. Gregory Bateson, an influential system's thinker defined information as 'the difference that makes a difference'. Bateson G (2000) Foreword by Bateson MC. In: *Steps to an Ecology of Mind: Collected essays in anthropology, psychiatry, evolution and epistemology*. Chicago IL: University of Chicago Press.

2. Lipnack J, Stamps J (1986) *The Networking Book*. London: Routledge, p. 7.

3. Virginia Hine, who died in 1982, introduced the acronym, SPIN, describing sociocultural trends with the words 'Segmented, Polycephalous (many headed), Ideological, Network', in Lipnack, Stamps (1986, p. 5).

4. Lipnack J, Stamps J (1986, p. 2).

5. Lipnack J, Stamps J (1986, p. 3).

6. Mindell A (1995) *Sitting in the Fire: Large group transformation using conflict and diversity*. Portland, OR: Lao Tse Press.

7. Mindell A (1995).

8. Mindell A (1993) *The leader as martial artist*. San Francisco, CA: Harper Collins, pp. 39, 44, 90–91.

9. Prigogine I, Stengers I (1984) *Order out of Chaos*. New York: Bantam Books.

10. Combs AR, Robertson RR (1995) *Chaos Theory in Psychology and the Life Sciences*. Englewood Cliffs, NJ: Lawrence Erlbaum Associates, p. 44.

11. Hedges C (2002) *War is a Force that gives us Meaning*. London: Public Affairs, p. 32.

12. Graham P (1990) *The Idea of Race in Latin America, 1870–1941*. Austin, TX: University of Texas Press.

    Young R (1994) *Colonial Desire: Hybridity in Theory, Culture and Race*. London: Routledge.

13. For example, neuroscientists such as Francis Crick and Chris Koch in Goodwin B, Solae R (2000) *Signs of Life: How complexity pervades biology*. New York: Basic Books, p. 145.

14. Mindell A (2000, p. 582); Von Franz ML (1995) *Creation Myths*. Boston, MA: Shambhala.

15. Conversation with Sharad Sakorkar in Newport, OR, March 2004.

16. Global Process Institute (GPI), Portland, OR, USA, sponsors World Work seminars, internationally, teaching and applying a process work approach to conflict resolution and working deeply with a broad spectrum of political and community issues (www.processwork.org).

17. Quote: Princeton.edu/~atrangsr/quotes0.html (accessed April 2004).

APPENDIX: CHART OF SYMPTOMS OF PTSD IN INDIVIDUALS AND SIGNS OF COMMUNAL AND COLLECTIVE TRAUMA

1. American Psychiatric Association (1994) 309.81 Posttraumatic stress disorder. In: *Diagnostic and Statistical Manual of Mental Disorders*, 4th edn. Washington DC: APA, pp. 424–442.

INDEX